GREAT ARTISTS STEAL

Quarto

First published in 2026 by Frances Lincoln,
an imprint of The Quarto Group.
One Triptych Place, London, SE1 9SH,
United Kingdom
T (0)20 7700 9000
www.Quarto.com

EEA Representation, WTS Tax d.o.o., Žanova ulica 3, 4000 Kranj, Slovenia
www.wts-tax.si

A catalogue record for this book is available from the British Library.

ISBN 978-1-83600-258-1
Ebook ISBN 978-1-83600-259-8

10 9 8 7 6 5 4 3 2 1

Design by Nicki Davis

Publisher Philip Cooper
Editorial Director John Parton
Managing Editor Laura Bulbeck
Editorial Support Róisín Duffy
Senior Designer Isabel Eeles
Senior Production Controller Rohana Yusof

Printed in Guangdong, China TT052026

MIX
Paper | Supporting responsible forestry
FSC® C016973

GREAT ARTISTS STEAL

HOW ARTISTS REALLY GET THEIR IDEAS

DEBRA N. MANCOFF

FRANCES LINCOLN

CONTENTS

HOW ARTISTS REALLY GET THEIR IDEAS

'Good artists borrow, great artists steal.'
Attributed to Pablo Picasso

Picture the scene: thirteen figures crowd together on one side of an oblong table. The tabletop is littered with the remains of a communal meal. Yet the figures ignore the modest repast; they turn to one another, some rising from their seats as if they have just received shocking news. Each is individualized, portrayed with distinct facial features, striking expressions and distinguished by age. Each gestures with significance, pointing to themselves, to the sky or to another at the table. Some lean towards one another, others lean away. In contrast, two figures sit motionless: one among those on the left and the figure in the middle. This description evokes an iconic work of art: Leonardo da Vinci's *Last Supper* (1495–98). However, the same words can summon up another work: Tavares Strachan's life-size, sculpture ensemble of 2023, *The First Supper (Galaxy Black)*. The reference is deliberate, confirmed by the title as well as the composition. Strachan intended that the viewer see his ensemble through the lens of Leonardo's painting, raising questions about his motives. Why did he tie his work so closely to that of Leonardo? Was it to honour the work of an esteemed painter of the past or a desire to disrupt a venerable perception? Did he intend his work to be compared to the earlier rendition, to be regarded as a contemporary counterpart, a response or even a correction? Was the reference an essential part of his creative process or an act of intellectual theft? Behind each consideration lurks another, blunter question: can a work of art be regarded as great if it is based on a steal?

Pablo Picasso reportedly said, 'Good artists borrow, great artists steal.' Although he meant it as a provocation, his differentiation between 'borrow' and 'steal' defines the role of authenticity in the arts. To borrow implies a temporary state, taking something with the intention of returning it. There is no such implication in stealing; what one takes, one keeps. Legitimate or not, theft implies new ownership. Throughout the history of the arts – across time, medium, place and culture – past work provides a rich resource for present expression and future innovation. Artists learn how to handle materials, construct a composition or convey meaning by emulating what has been previously done. This is true for all artists in all the arts, from the ancient bards who retold the tales of their ancestors to the musicians who incorporate known motifs to engage their listeners, to the poets, novelists and filmmakers who offer fresh accounts of familiar tales. Critic A.O. Scott

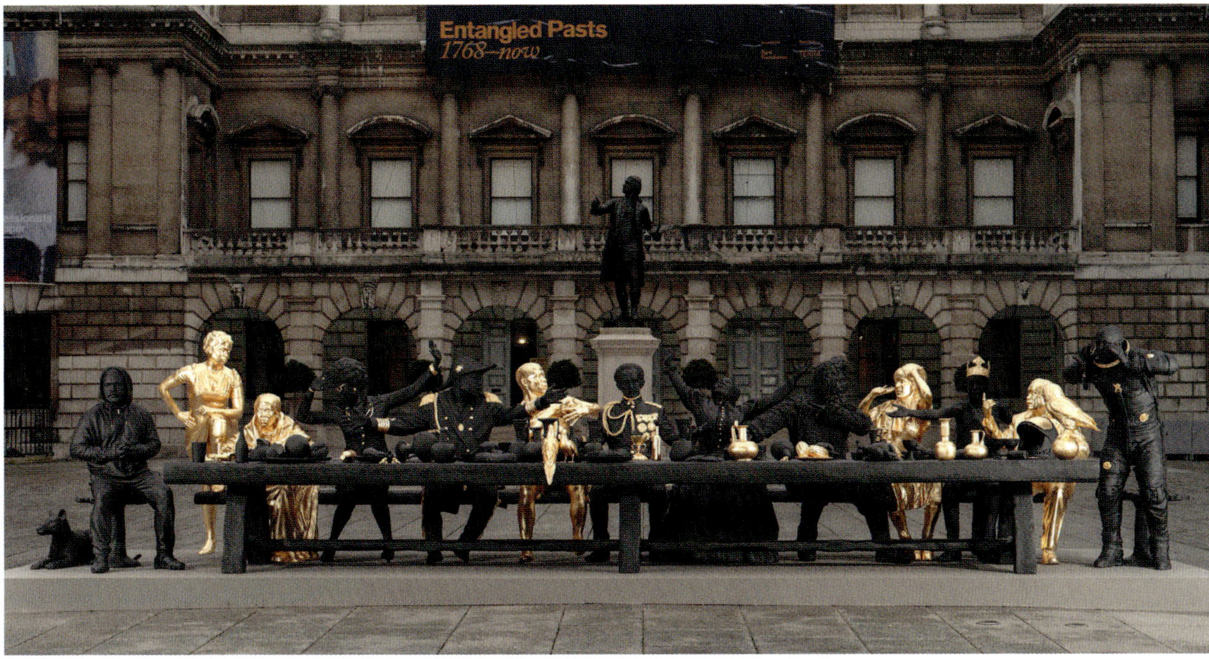

▲ Tavares Strachan (b. 1979), T*he First Supper (Galaxy Black)*, 2021–23, bronze, black patina, gold leaf, 217 x 929 x 268 cm (86 x 366 x 106 in). Installation view, 'Entangled Pasts, 1768-now: Art, Colonialism and Change', Royal Academy of Arts, London, 2024.

▼ Leonardo da Vinci (1452–1519), *Last Supper*, 1495–98, tempera and oil on plaster, 460 x 880 cm (181 x 346 in)

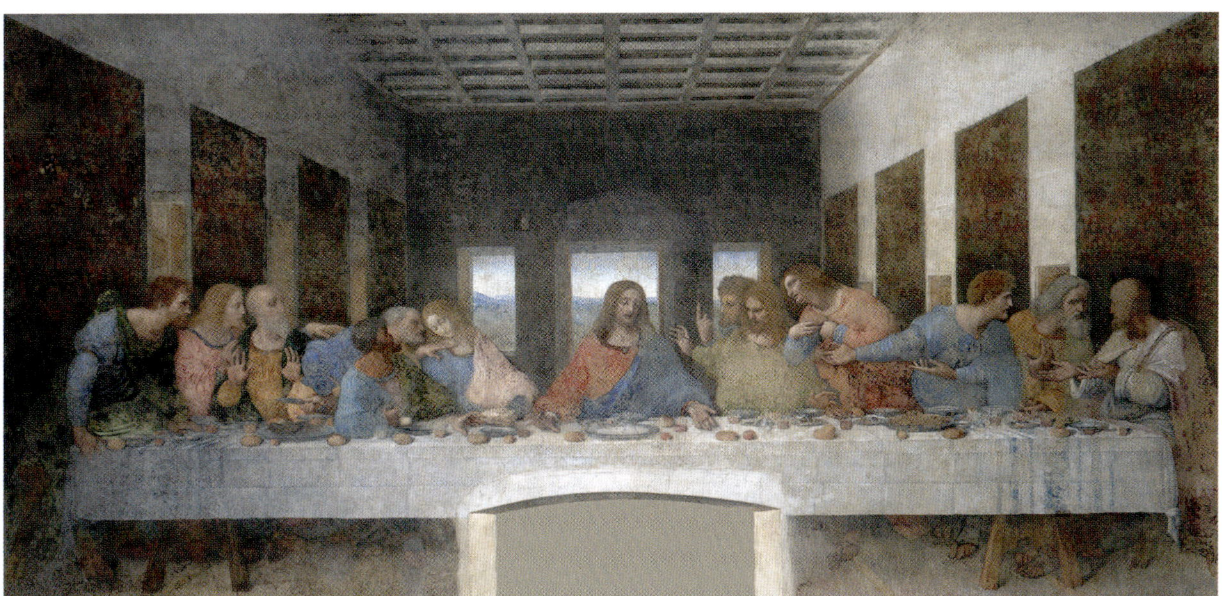

has observed that 'without imitation, our literature would be threadbare'.[1] However, mere imitation is not the means to compelling creation. In an address at the University for Creative Arts in London, fashion designer Jonathan Anderson noted that 'Originality is non-existent'. Inspiration could be found everywhere – in other media, in history books, even in their dreams. However, he cautioned them to 'Only steal from things that speak directly to you. If you do this, your work will be authentic.'[2] The art of theft is nowhere more valuable – or more clearly seen – than in the visual arts, where it may take the form of craft or medium, colour, figure or composition, or in the content expressed through symbol and narrative, all made new through individual interpretation. It is less the act of stealing that matters than what artists do with what they steal. The creative act is in the motive and the means for the theft, and the greatness derives from how each artist makes what they steal their own.

The word 'steal' carries uncomfortable connotations. To describe what an artist does as stealing sounds like an accusation or an insult. According to the *Oxford English Dictionary*, 'to steal' is transgressive, an act of stealth fuelled by subterfuge. Yet, over the ages, artists have used the word to describe various aspects of their development, whether copying a work to learn technique, experimenting with another artist's style, or replicating an element as a means to acknowledge influence or add meaning to their own artistic expression. The notion that absolute originality is essential to artistic achievement is relatively new. Prior to the rise of western Modernism in the early twentieth century, artists regularly employed references to other works to situate themselves within established traditions. The incorporation of a visual reference was not seen as a compromise of originality; creativity resided in the way an artist transformed that reference.

There are various nuanced ways that artists have appropriated the works of others. By replicating a form, taking up an old technique or conforming to a convention, an artist embraces – and extends – traditions that have endured over time. Throughout history and across cultures, artists have learned style and technique by copying previous work, whether in the studio of their instructor as part of their training or in a museum as part of their own search for understanding. Artists work together – side by side or in collaboration – to exchange ideas and share influences. They adopt, adapt and assimilate materials, narratives and imagery to build from influence to innovation. Many artists employ an overt connection to a prior work to pay tribute to an artist or an idea they admire, or they do so as a direct challenge to authority. Ultimately, the act of appropriation is at its best transformative, changing the perception of established works while creating something authentic and new.

Art is never made in a vacuum, and to fully appreciate Strachan's *First Supper* we must put Leonardo's *Last Supper* – and its conventions – in context. Leonardo did not choose his subject; the last meal shared by Jesus and his apostles was a customary decoration for dining halls in religious orders. Leonardo depicted the most traditional moment in the narrative, when Jesus startles his disciples by saying, 'One of you shall betray me' (Matthew 26:2). The earliest known depictions downplay the drama, as seen in a sixth-century mosaic in the church of Sant'Apollinare Nuovo in Ravenna. Jesus, in a regal purple robe, gestures in conversation while his companions respond with open mouths and wide eyes. Only Judas – on the right – has no reaction. All the figures recline as they would have at a Roman banquet; a common motif at the time used to indicate a communal dinner. This basic scheme, with some changes, endured for nearly a millennium. By Leonardo's time, figures sat rather than reclined, Jesus moved to the middle of the group and Judas was singled out, usually on the front side of the table, as seen in the fresco painted by Domenico Ghirlandaio for the Church of San Salvatore in Ognissanti. Admittedly, Leonardo does not stray far from precedent; his innovation is in the emotional power of the scene, conveyed by the individual apostles' reactions and by the contrasting stillness of Jesus and Judas, who is now seated with the others, leaning on the table gazing dispassionately back at his companions. And while we view Leonardo's interpretation as the reigning standard, in subsequent centuries old conventions persisted – Plautilla Nelli portrayed Judas on the front side of the table in her *The Last Supper* (1550s) – while others were revived, as seen in the reclining figures portrayed by James Tissot in *The Last Supper: Judas Dipping his Hand in the Dish* (1886–94).

A childhood memory prompted Strachan to take up the subject. He recalled that a print of Leonardo's *Last Supper* hung above a collection of family photographs in his grandmother's dining room in the Bahamas. The presence of 'all these Europeans hanging over a family of people from West Africa in the Caribbean' struck him as curious.[3] He had devoted his work to recovering history's neglected figures – particularly those with roots in the African diaspora[4] – recording their names in his *Encyclopedia of Invisibility*, a book he compiled and bound for display. He realized that by appropriating an enduring subject and an iconic composition, he could give those who had been overlooked or forgotten a rightful place in the canon of art history, as well as the prominence they deserved. *First Supper* is a monumental ensemble consisting of thirteen, life-size, cast bronze figures, some coated in gold and others in a metallic paint called Galaxy Black. His figures represent diversity over time, identity and national origin, each connected in their own way to the African diaspora. Robert Henry Lawrence, Jr, the first African American astronaut, stands on the far right; Shirley Chisholm, the fourth figure from the left, was the first Black woman elected to the House of Representatives in the United States. Next to her is Marcus Garvey, the Jamaican-born political activist; also from Jamaica, centre right and raising her arms to the sky, is Mary Seacole, a battlefield nurse who cared for British soldiers during the Crimean war. Haile Selassie, former Emperor of Ethiopia, takes the position held by Jesus, and he is as still and composed as the figure in Leonardo's composition. As in the print, there is food on the table, but Strachan offers catfish, rice, chicken and breadfruit – all foods eaten across the Caribbean with origins in Africa. Strachan includes himself as well. Seated slightly apart to the left, he is seen, dressed in a hoodie with a dog at his side, in the position reserved for Judas. He takes on the transgressive role, explaining, 'All of us make mistakes. Who is not Judas?'[5]

Strachan had many motives for making *First Supper*: personal, historical, activist, restorative. However, he was also motivated by his desire to create a work of art that projected power, presence and beauty. Through his reference to Leonardo's work he reached back to make a connection with more than a thousand years of history, but he also challenged his contemporary viewers to revisit their assumptions about who is granted a place in the history of art.

We will continue that journey of discovery in the pages that follow, looking at works by artists across time and culture to understand how they, too, seized upon conventional ideas, and through reinterpretation and innovation made them their own. Whether copying the work of a master, using a subtle reference or a direct quotation from a known work, revising a subject or using symbolic imagery for clarity or critique, this journey will take us from tradition to transformation, revealing that great things happen when great artists steal.

Tradition as a foundation

The opening section of the book, *Traditions*, demonstrates that artists inherit both subjects and visual languages. From subjects and themes, to materials and techniques, to symbolic gestures and compositional methods, traditions shape what can be recognized and understood. A multi-armed figure signals Shiva; a woman holding a child evokes centuries of Madonna and Child imagery. Conventions have always allowed artists to communicate across time and geography.

The Madonna and Child, a seemingly simple motif, carries immense theological and emotional weight. When Filippo Lippi painted his Madonna lifted by two angels, he was entering a lineage nearly a millennium old. The faint halo, delicate wings and intimate exchange between mother and child rely on viewers' familiarity with established imagery. Yet Lippi's interpretation was immediate and human. The sacred and the secular existed in delicate balance. Tradition for this work was not a constraint, but a scaffold that allowed individuality to emerge.

Elsewhere, other artists draw strength from past masters. Courbet looked to Rembrandt; contemporary artists revisit ancient sculptural ideals; architectural forms reappear in altered guises. By daring to compare themselves with revered predecessors, artists assert their own place within a continuum.

Tradition also travels across cultures and media. James McNeill Whistler's 'Nocturnes', informed in part by Japanese Edo-period aesthetics, reveal how compositional restraint and tonal subtlety can cross continents. What might begin as admiration becomes assimilation; what is assimilated becomes personal style. Under the mirrored domes of the Shah Cheragh mosque in Shiraz, Monir Shahroudy Farmanfarmaian encountered a synthesis of geometry, reflection and spiritual architecture that shaped her mature work. Uniting the mathematical precision of Islamic ornament with contemporary abstraction, her practice demonstrates that inheritance need not be nostalgic. Ancient aesthetics can emerge in contemporary expression, proving that tradition remains fertile when reimagined rather than merely preserved. Such encounters have not erased existing traditions, but enriched them.

Learning curve

If tradition provides a framework, learning provides a method. *Learning Curve* examines apprenticeship, imitation, observation and experimentation.

In Renaissance workshops, apprentices prepared pigments, stretched canvases and copied their masters' compositions. By repeating forms and gestures, they internalized proportion, anatomy and design. Even established artists continued to study others' achievements. Copying was not viewed as plagiarism but practice: a way of understanding how images are constructed and how effects are achieved.

In 1874, Claude Monet hastily titled his depiction of the sun rising over the harbour of Le Havre as *Impression: Sunrise*, remarking that it 'couldn't really pass for a view of Le Havre.' The label, intended casually, defined an entire movement: Impressionism. Monet had studied paintings by J.M.W. Turner in London, but transformed atmospheric observation into his own personal language of light and colour. Technical knowledge and perceptual experimentation combined to generate something new.

Artists watch, compete with and build upon one another's discoveries. Blanche Hoschedé's proximity to Monet illustrates how creative development unfolds within circles of influence. Observation leads to emulation; emulation to experimentation; experimentation to distinction. Even artists who resist formal teaching inevitably teach by example.

Van Gogh's engagement with Millet's *The Sower* offers a vivid example of how imitation can become a transformative act. Millet's striding labourer embodied rural endurance and moral gravity. When Van Gogh revisited the motif in 1888, he retained the recognizable gesture but altered its meaning through his individual marks and colours. The earthy naturalism of Millet's palette was replaced with lemon yellows, violet fields and complementary contrasts. The figure no longer dominates the land as a heroic worker, but moves within a landscape animated by a blazing sun and an ancient tree trunk that anchors the composition. By shifting emphasis from social realism to cosmic rhythm, Van Gogh made the image his own. Artists take what they need – a solution to composition, a treatment of light, a handling of paint – and adapt it. Every breakthrough rests upon accumulated knowledge.

Creative exchange

Creative Exchange focuses on dialogue across time and space. Some exchanges are collaborative; others are competitive. Raphael's realization of Bramante's grand design for St Peter's Basilica demonstrates how vision can be shared, adapted and extended. Caravaggio's dramatic chiaroscuro inspired generations of painters such as Artemisia Gentileschi and Georges de la Tour, who absorbed his lessons while moving in new directions. Cross-cultural exchange has repeatedly expanded what artists consider possible. In the late nineteenth century, Japanese *ukiyo-e* prints entered European collections and studios, offering radically different approaches to cropping, flattened viewpoints and composition. Mary Cassatt and Berthe Morisot studied them while experimenting with colour lithography. What began as fascination became assimilation. The impact of Japanese *ukiyo-e* art on many other European artists and designers reshaped western approaches to composition, colour, perspective and surface pattern. Later, photography, cinema and mass media blurred the boundaries between high art and popular culture, influencing framing and the portrayal of movement. Ideas migrated, mutated and recombined. In such contexts, theft becomes an engine of possibility: to take from another discipline or tradition is to test its potential elsewhere.

Each encounter with previous art expands the available visual vocabulary: fragments gathered from disparate sources are recomposed into something unexpectedly cohesive. In the twentieth century Robert Rauschenberg combined found objects with painted surfaces, collapsing distinctions between art and everyday life. By integrating what already existed into new configurations, he questioned authorship as he expanded it. Such strategies make influence visible rather than concealed. Borrowing becomes part of the subject, conveying that images are nearly always cumulative. Creative exchange ensures art remains shared and dynamic rather than isolated and static.

Influence & innovation

Influence & Innovation examines moments when artists honour tradition precisely by breaking its rules. Classical ideals are explored and destabilized; hierarchies are inverted; authority is both acknowledged and challenged. Michelangelo's Adam drew upon ancient sculptural ideals, embodying the classical conception of perfected form. Yet he reinterpreted the gesture and the charged space between figures with an unprecedented sense of dynamism.

Later artists have revisited similarly canonical images, sometimes respectfully, sometimes irreverently. Reference can become revision. Through adaptation, artists may contradict symbols of oppression or revive neglected histories. An icon may be dethroned; a marginal figure moved to centre stage. Influence can sometimes become a tool of revision, while innovation grows from deep engagement with what already exists. By studying, absorbing and reshaping earlier achievements, artists arrive at new solutions. The chain of influence lengthens, each link altering the shape of the next.

Pablo Picasso's engagement with Cézanne, for instance, propelled modern painting into radical territory. Following Cézanne's focus on structure, Picasso dissected and reassembled form, pushing the focus beyond his predecessor and altering the trajectory of twentieth-century art. He took, and he transformed.

Connections and transformations

In *Meaningful Connections*, influence becomes personal and, at times, political. Artists engage in dialogue with images that carry authority, reinterpreting them for new contexts. A martyr's stance may acquire contemporary resonance; a compositional strategy once used to glorify power may be repurposed to question it. A borrowed and reshaped motif carries layered meanings. Ancestry is acknowledged, while it is changed. The past becomes a tool for reflection, critique or reclamation. Exchange can also be intimate and symbolic. Motifs evoke memory, identity and heritage. Borrowing becomes a way of articulating personal identity within a broader lineage. At times, influence bridges both geography and centuries.

The final section, *Transformations*, brings the argument to its fullest expression. Borrowing is overt and unapologetic. Swagger is stolen; a goddess becomes mortal; a schoolboy's prank is repurposed; a procession is reimagined for contemporary streets. By altering recognizable motifs, artists invite their viewers to reconsider both past and present. When transformation succeeds, the source material acquires fresh resonance.So through theft, an artist may reclaim heritage, correct a wrong or undermine an assumption. A pose once associated with aristocratic privilege can be adopted by a bohemian; a sacred image can be humanized, and a symbol of suffering can be redirected towards hope.

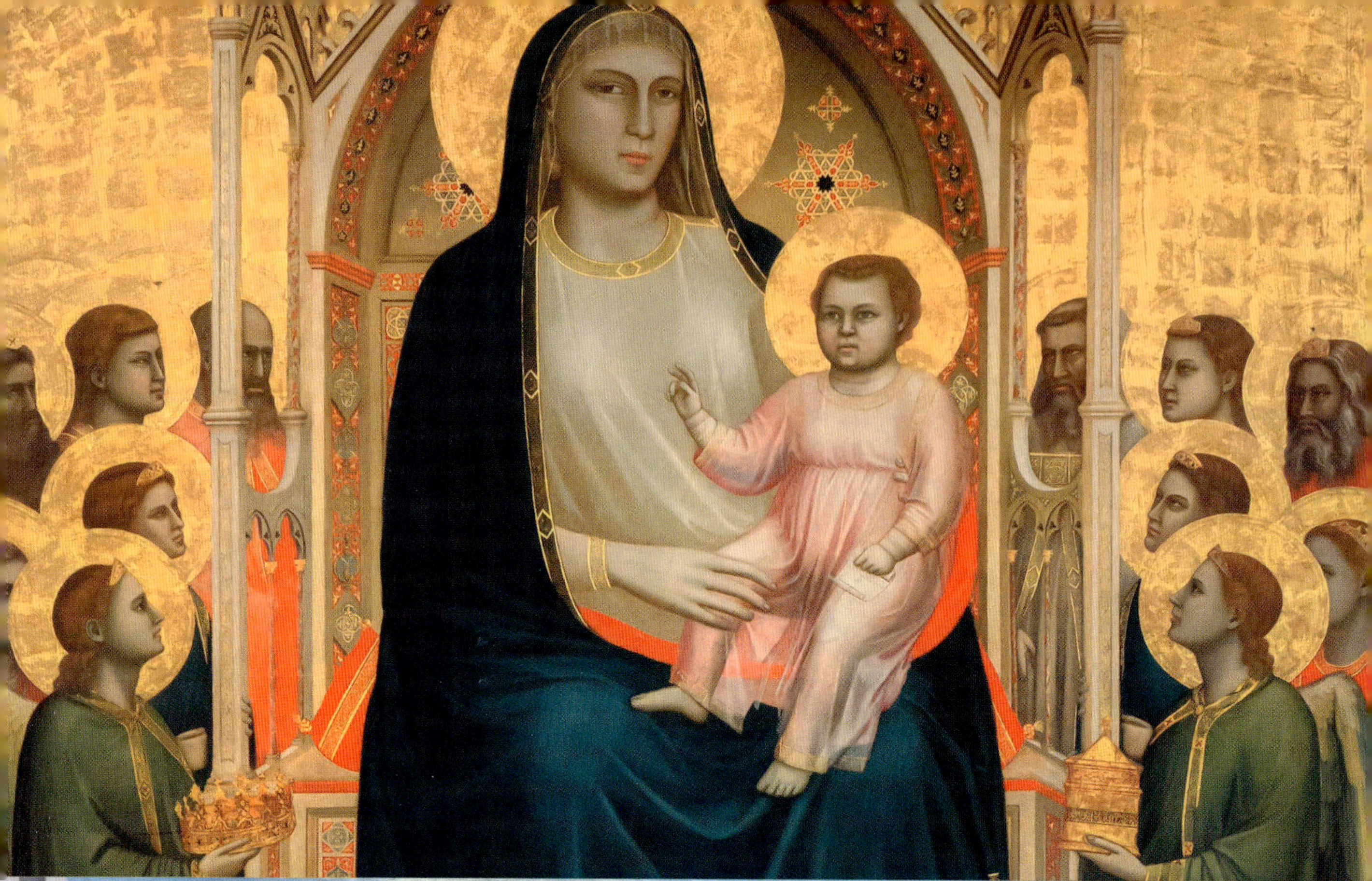

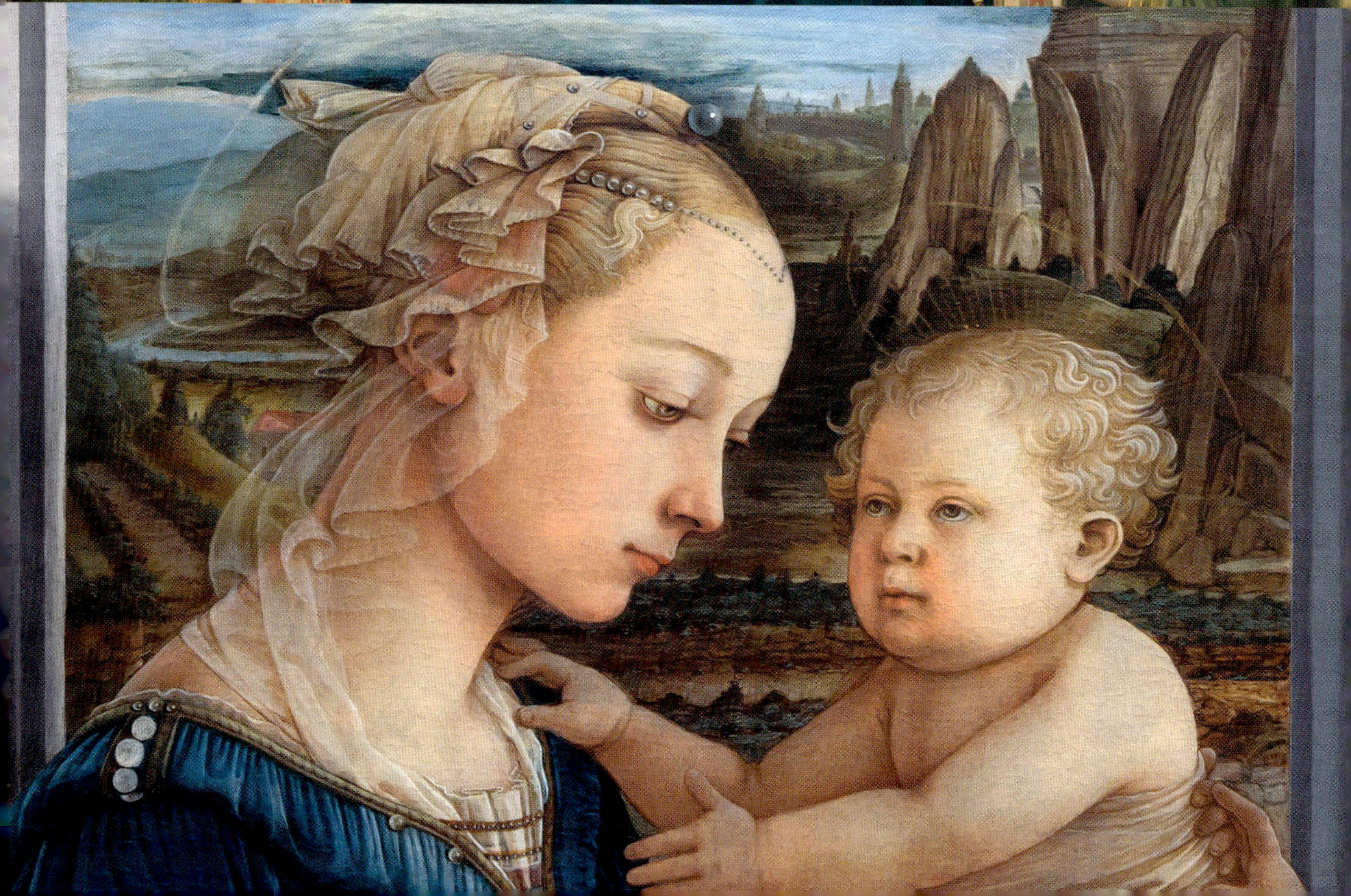

TRADITIONS

From handling materials to symbolic meaning, traditions shape the visual arts. Traditions carry content, continuity and culture. Through established postures and gestures we recognize a multi-armed deity as Shiva or a loving mother as the mother of Christ. Artists craft their own lineage – and dare comparison – by taking on the subject of a past master. They give new life to a time-honoured technique from their own heritage or expand their vision by adapting ideas from other cultures, nations or media. The possibilities are endless when artists steal to make a tradition their own.

SHIVA'S ETERNAL DANCE

How centuries of Hindu history have informed the Shiva Nataraja

Encircled in flames, Shiva, the divine cosmic dancer, performs the *tandava*. Each movement embodies energy and grace. He nimbly balances on one foot as he twists his lithe torso, and his four sinuous arms – each representing a cardinal direction – sway in a mesmerizing rhythm. His long, unruly locks fly around his head, but his demeanour is serene, reassuring his worshippers that this wild dance that begins in destruction will culminate in renewal. In Hindu belief, Shiva is part of the *Trimurti*, the three divinities that empower the universe. Brahma, the creator, is the source of all life; Vishnu, the preserver, maintains life's order. However, Shiva is the destroyer; with his ecstatic dance he burns up the world to make way for regeneration, infinitely fuelling the cycle of time.

Multiplicity is a defining force in Hindu cosmology. In a universe charged with boundless potential, layers of meaning co-exist. In such a syncretic construct, individual beings – whether divine or legendary – have many aspects, and Shiva exemplifies this concept. He can appear as an extreme ascetic, his skin ashen from ritual fires and hair matted in neglect. As a fearless warrior he wears a garland of skulls, and snakes writhe on his wrists in place of bracelets. When he marries his hair is brushed smooth and glossy, and he wears silk garments and gold ornaments to enhance his sensual allure. However, he attains his highest beauty as the *Nataraja* (Lord of the Dance), and as he gyrates within a halo of flames, a set of gestures and attributes, repeated over the ages, give meaning to his movements.

The origin of this iconography is obscure; Shiva's oldest known image is as the generative power symbol, the lingam (phallus), linked to the Indus Valley prior to the emergence of the sacred Vedic texts that form the foundation of Brahminic belief (*c.* 1,500–900 BC). The multi-armed dancing god is first described in literature around AD 500, with stone carvings appearing a century later.

▶

Shiva as Lord of the Dance (Nataraja)
c. eleventh century, Chola Period (India, Tamil Nadu, 880–1279), copper alloy, H 63 cm (27 in), D 57 cm (22 in)

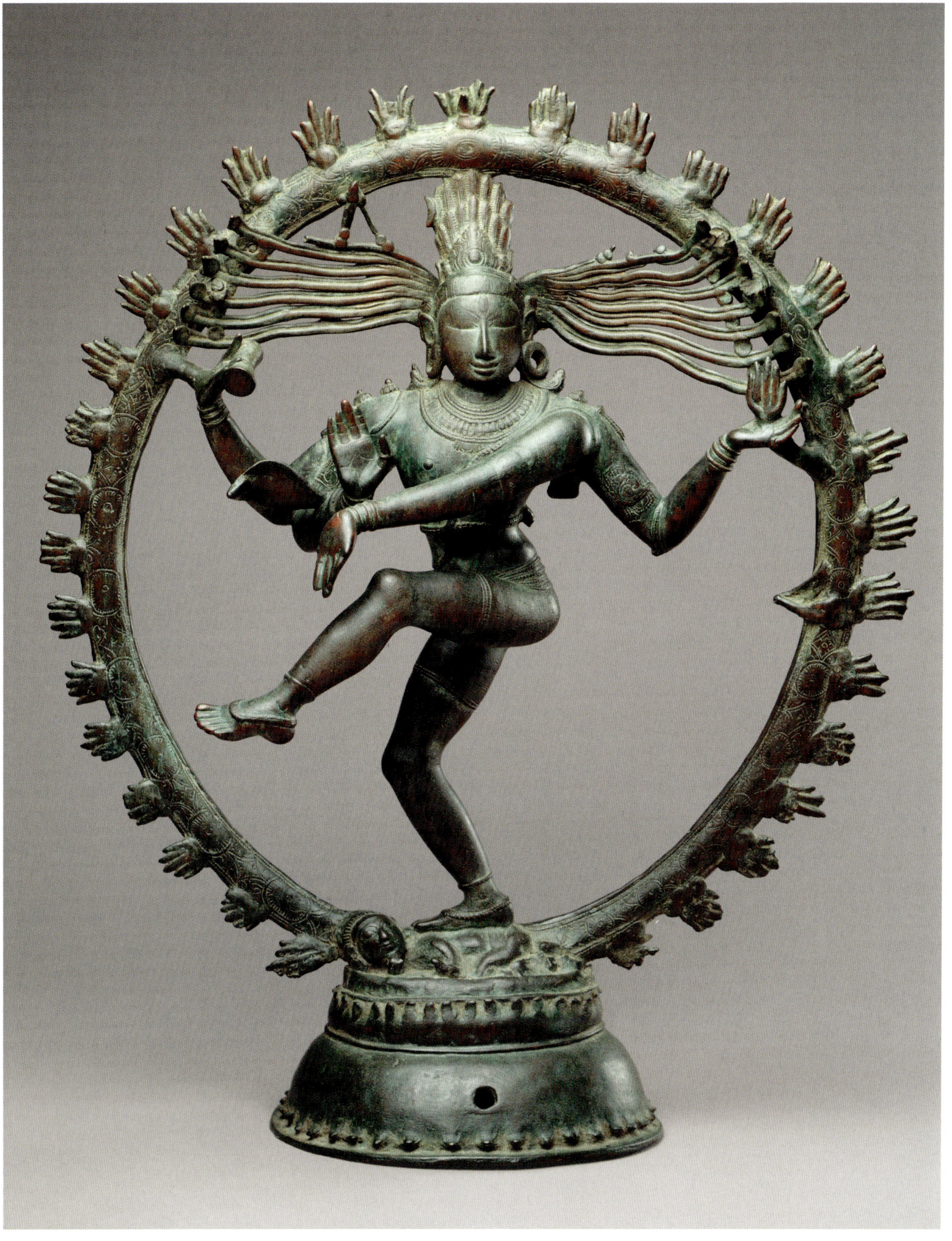

The enduring depiction of the *Nataraja* – with four arms and nimbly balanced on a single foot – emerged as a set of refined conventions during the imperial era of the Chola Dynasty (ninth to thirteenth centuries), a time of political expansion outwards from the Tamil region of southern India distinguished by a sophisticated culture and superb craftsmanship, notably in cast metals. Naturalistic in form and dynamic in composition, this eleventh-century *Nataraja* represents the height of the tradition, not only in its beauty but also in the ensemble of gestures and objects that explain the sacred dance.

In his upper left hand, Shiva holds the *agni*, the flame of destruction; in his right is the *damaru*, an hour-glass-shaped drum that beats the pulse of creation. He extends his lower right hand, palm out, fingers extended, in the *abhaya mudra*, the gesture that proclaims 'fear not', as he points his lower left hand toward his raised foot. In this way, Shiva directs the worshipper's attention to the agile movement that demands mastery and embodies control. His right foot roots him to the ground, where he tramples the Apasmara Purusha, a demonic incarnation of spiritual ignorance. With this message of reassurance, Shiva demonstrates how he protects the cycle of life throughout time. And the message is carried down through the generations by the repetition of gestures and attributes of the *Nataraja*, every rendition linked to the last, renewed by the act of creation. ●

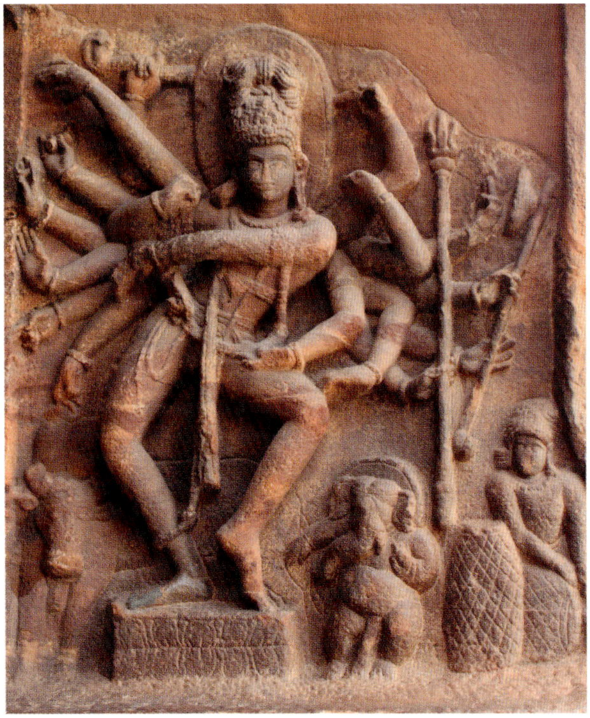

Nataraja, Dancing Shiva
Chalukya Dynasty (India, sixth to seventh centuries), sandstone

This wall relief from the Badami Cave Temples, depicts Shiva with eighteen arms, each clasping a symbol of his divine power or performing a *mudra* (significant hand gesture). Along with the objects associated with his most fearsome aspect – the axe, the trident and a serpent – are a drum and a flaming torch. These will endure as standard attributes of the *Nataraja*. Flanked by his elephant-headed son, Ganesha, and his bull, Nandi, Shiva's swaying arms and supple steps forecast the dynamic movements of the *tandava*.

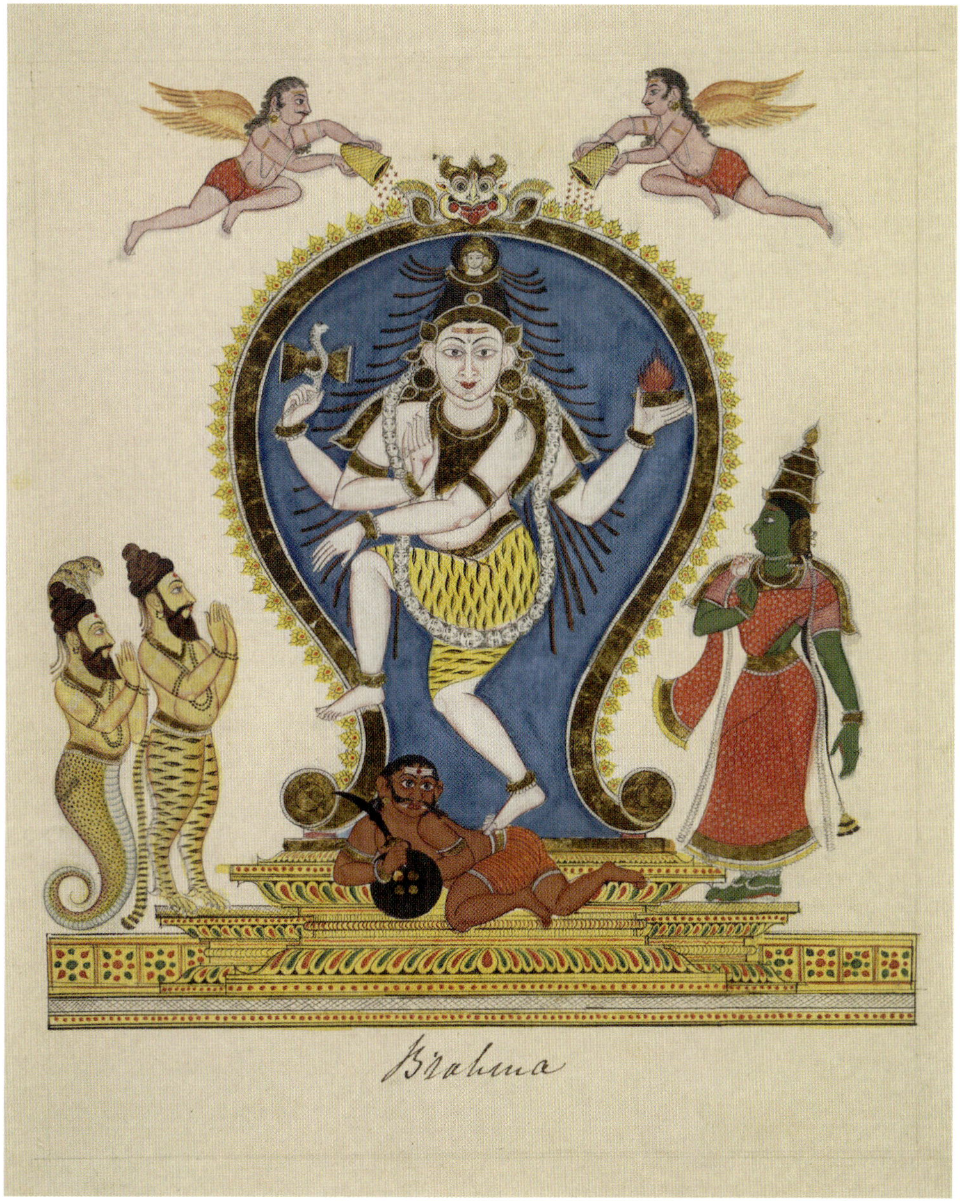

▲

Nataraja, Dancing Shiva
c. 1820, paper and gold paint

In this painting, Shiva (misidentified on the inscription as Brahma)[1] dances within a fire-rimmed, ornamental arch. He holds the *agni* and *damaru*, performs the appropriate gestures and tramples the Apasmara Purusha beneath his foot. His attributes also include a tiger skin, a garland of skulls and a personification of the Ganges, peeking out of his matted hair. These conventions are key to recognition of both the deity and the dance, so that the faithful – like the two pious worshippers on the left – comprehend his essential role in the cycle of existence.

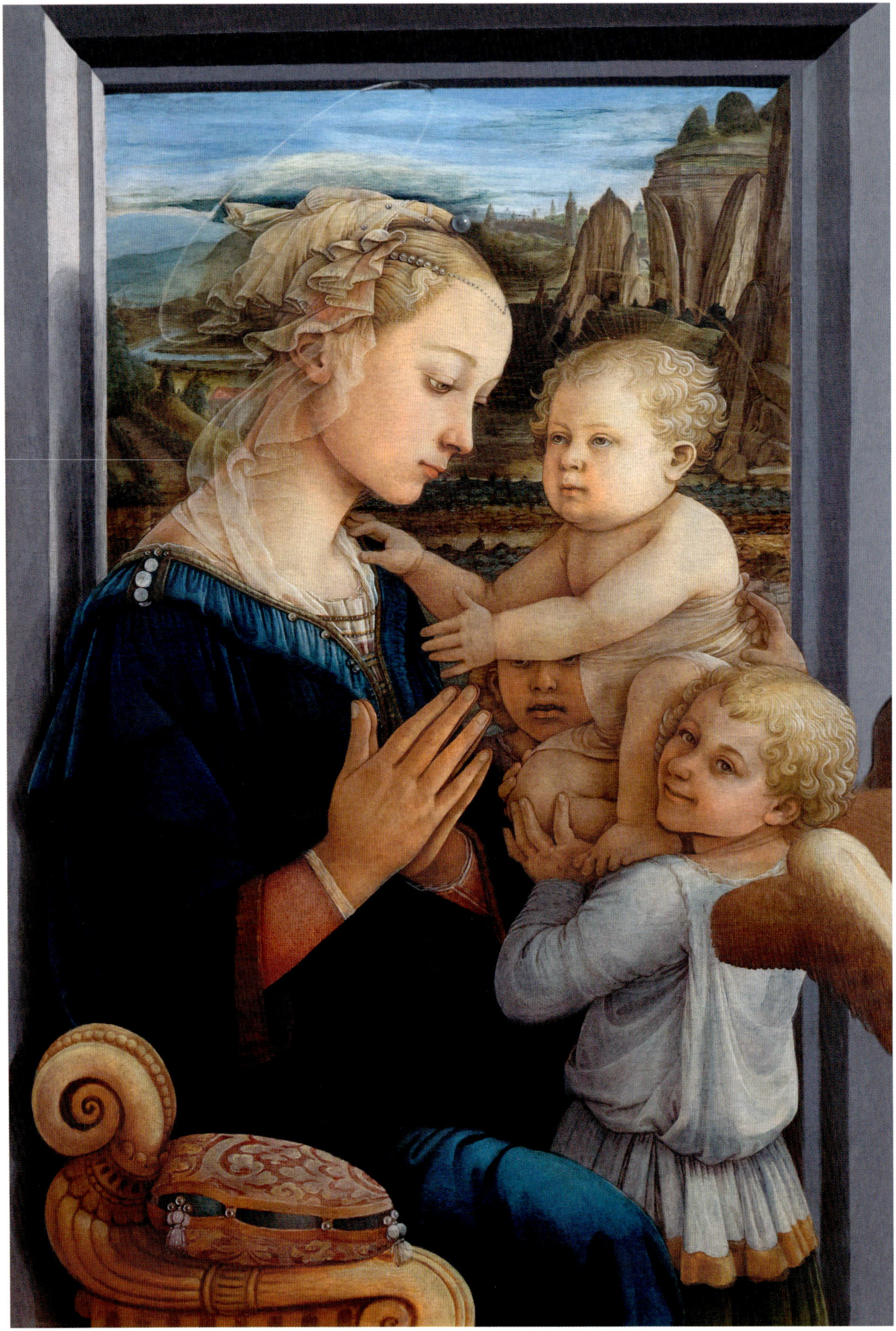

THE HUMAN IN THE DIVINE

How Lippi drew upon 1,000 years of depicting the Madonna and Child

The image of a young woman with an infant portrays an essential bond shared across culture, history and chronology. As a subject in the arts, a mother and child is instinctively understood, with a universal – and deeply emotional – appeal. The Christian iconography of the Madonna and Child combines both the human and the divine in an evolving balance of the sacred and the secular, as seen in Fra Filippo Lippi's depiction of *Madonna and Child with Two Angels*. With her elegantly cut garments and intricately braided hair, this mother could be any fashionable, fifteenth-century Florentine woman; lifted by two boys, her golden-haired child reaches out to be embraced. Only the faint halo encircling her head, and the wings sprouting out of the back of the boy who turns to the viewer with a cheeky smile, identifies her as Mary in the holy Christian dyad of the Virgin Mother and her child.

Lippi's interpretation draws upon nearly one thousand years of tradition. The earliest known depictions of the Madonna and Child have been found on the walls of Roman catacombs (in approximately the second century AD), but the written revelation that the Holy Spirit fathered Mary's child is a century older. In the Gospel of Matthew 1:18–25 (written in about the late first century AD), an angel informs Joseph of the child's divinity in a dream. Mary's role as the human conduit for the divine evolved into the concept of *Theotokos* (God-bearer), defined at the Council of Ephesus in 431, which allowed her to be understood both as the mortal mother to God's child and as the metaphor of God's earthly throne and, eventually, the church itself. By the thirteenth century the hierarchical Mary of the *Theotokos* was eclipsed by the more maternal *Maestà* (Virgin in Majesty), still regal and often surrounded by angels but demonstrating tender devotion and even smiling with pleasure as she holds her son securely in her lap. By the time Lippi took up the subject, the idea of a Humanist Madonna was well-established. As well as the mother of God, she represented a superior model of human maternity, caring for her divine child with compassion, goodness and unwavering devotion.

◄

Fra Filippo Lippi (*c.* 1406–69)
Madonna and Child with Two Angels
c. 1460–65, tempera on wood, 95 x 62 cm (37 x 24 in)

In style and material display, Lippi's interpretation is fully secular. Although Mary's gown is in her signature shade of blue, it is of a contemporary cut; the latest Florentine fashion. And, like blue textile dye, the ultramarine pigment Lippi used to paint the robe was exorbitantly expensive. The gold thread trimming her gown, the diaphanous veiling of her headdress and the delicate pearl *ferronnière* that encircles her brow are also symbols of affluence. Her serene blonde beauty represents a contemporary preference; it is believed that Lippi's model was his young wife, Lucrezia Bruni.[1] The child seems eager to be held, his right hand on his mother's shoulder and his yearning gaze fixed on her face. However, Mary's eyes are respectfully directed downwards, and she presses her hands together in a devotional gesture. Carefully balancing a striking secularity with traditional iconography, Lippi has depicted Mary as a woman who her viewers would readily recognize. Chosen by God – and embodying Humanist ideals – she accepts her role as the human caregiver to the divine child. It is a fully credible scene of presentation, linking Mary to her mission, and the foreground angel welcomes the viewer to contemplate this message, bridging a thousand years of tradition with a bright smile and a knowing glance. ●

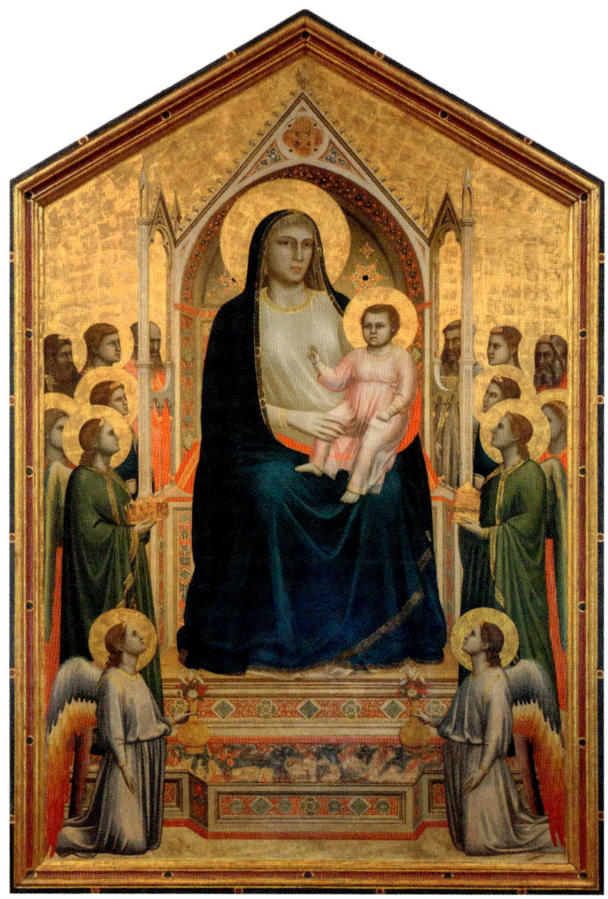

▶

Giotto di Bondone (*c.* 1267–1337)
Ognissanti Madonna
c. 1310, tempera on panel, 325 x 204 cm (128 x 80 in)

This early Renaissance altar painting illustrates the transition from the medieval *Maestà* to the fully Humanist Madonna of the fifteenth century. Seated on a throne and surrounded by saints and angels, Mary is both a mother and the Queen of Heaven. She, in turn, is the throne for her son, a dignified toddler who sits fully upright and gestures in blessing. Mary's composure is regal, but her firm hand on her child's leg and her subtle smile are remarkably natural. In Giotto's work Lippi discovered how to draw the human out of the divine.

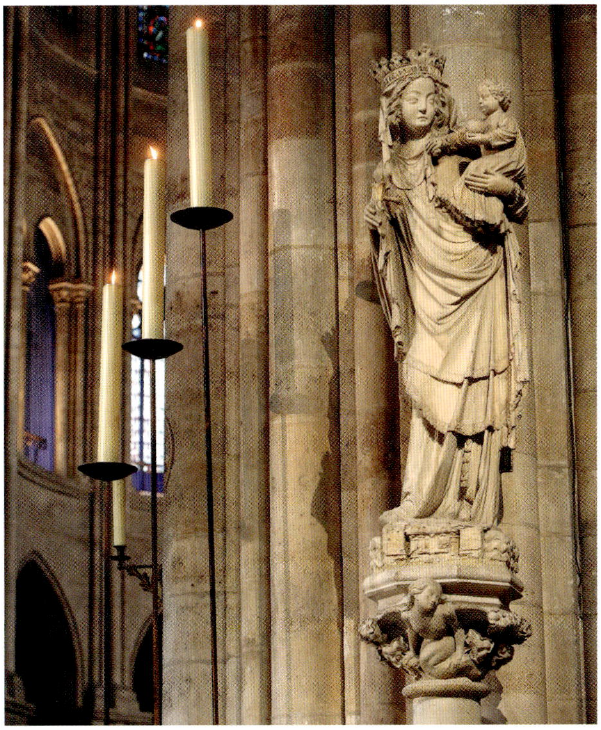

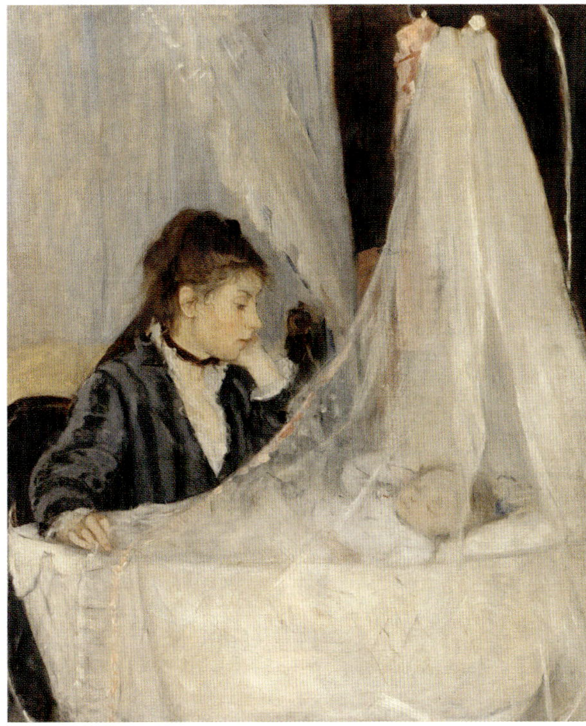

▲

Unknown artist
Virgin of Paris (*Notre-Dame de Paris*)
early fourteenth century, stone, H 180 cm (71 in)

Nearly contemporary with Giotto's painting, this elegant French sculpture offers a different understanding of the Queen of Heaven. Robed and crowned, Mary is portrayed as an earthly queen, holding a lily as an attribute of her purity. Her lithe proportions and reserved expression conform to contemporary standards of refined beauty. This, too, was a form of naturalism, reflecting the sophisticated tastes of the French court during the Gothic era. Her glance is affectionate, and her grasp on her child is firm; he perches on her arm, holding an orb that symbolizes his worldly reign.

▲

Berthe Morisot (1841–95)
The Cradle
1872, oil on canvas, 56 x 47 cm (22 x 18 in)

Four hundred years after Lippi, the artists associated with Impressionism based their subjects on the life around them rather than mythological or biblical literature. As a middle-class woman, Morisot's daily life was domestic, surrounded by her family. Here, she portrays her sister Edma watching her new-born daughter, Blanche, secure in a curtained cradle. Edma embodies the complexity of new motherhood: attentive and devoted, vigilant, yet slightly in awe of the child before her. Although fully secular, the long tradition of the Madonna is present in this – and every – iteration of the subject in western art.

CLOSE-UP COPY

How Courbet mirrored Rembrandt's self-portraits

Courbet moved to Paris from his native Ornans in eastern France in 1839 to pursue a career as a painter. In the galleries of the Musée du Louvre, where he copied the works of renowned European masters, he discovered an affinity for the work of Rembrandt van Rijn, whose warm-toned palette and expressive brushstrokes presented a striking contrast to the chilly hues and meticulously smoothed surface of conventional contemporary art. Above all, he admired the Dutch painter's ability to endow every subject with the depth of human experience; whether an image of Christ, a likeness of a known sitter or an unnamed mother caring for her child, Rembrandt's interpretation resonated with real life. More than anything else, Courbet aspired for authenticity in his art, so to develop his mastery of emotion and character he turned to one of Rembrandt's signature subjects. From 1842 to 1854 Courbet painted roughly twenty self-portraits, including this wide-eyed, flushed and frantic image known as *The Desperate Man*.

No one will ever know who painted the first self-portrait; a reflected image was no doubt the original inspiration. They were rare – or remain unrecognized – until the fifteenth century, when a rising sense of professional worth prompted artists to literally paint themselves into the picture. One approach was to include themselves as a minor figure in a crowd, as Raphael did in *The School of Athens* of *c*. 1509–11 (see p.65). His presence is modest, but he faces outwards to look at the viewer as if to claim credit for his work. Autobiographical self-portraits, depicting an artist with the tools of the trade or dressed in fine attire as proof of success, soon followed. Others recorded their appearance at specific times in their lives as a youth, a bridegroom, in maturity and old age. This became Rembrandt's route, and in more than one hundred self-portraits – in every medium – he charted his appearance from fresh-faced youth to humbling old age. Courbet's own exploration of the subject, however, had less to do with his likeness at specific times in his life; using historic examples, his own image and a mirror he embarked on a masterclass in human expression.

As *The Desperate Man*, Courbet lunges forward, nearly bursting out of the surface plane. Plunging his strong-fingered hands through his thick, dark hair, he seems overtaken by his emotions: eyes wild with fear, mouth open in astonishment. Scholars have puzzled over the source of his 'desperation', but seen in the context of his early self-portraits *The Desperate Man* is rightly read as part of his exploratory practice to expand the expressive capacity of his expertise. Over a little more than a decade, Courbet painted himself with a black spaniel (1842), as a wounded man (1844), holding

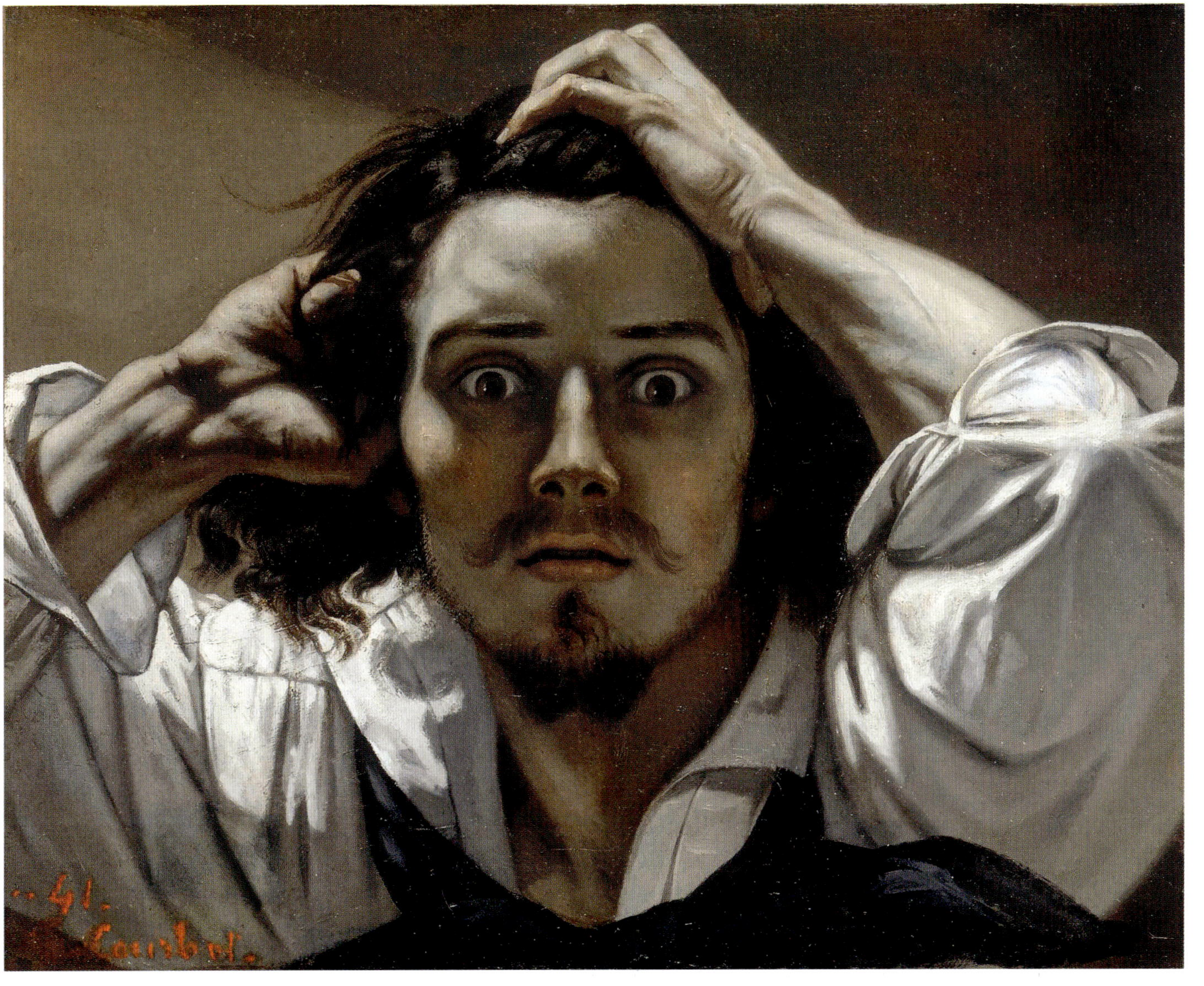

a cello (1847) and smoking a pipe (1849), and while his dark, good looks are unmistakable, in contrast to those artists he most admired these portraits are not autobiographical. At this stage of development, he was turning to the model who was ever-ready and always knew exactly how to pose. Although he would describe these portraits as '*ma vie*', he admitted to Alfred Bruyas, his foremost patron, that he took up the subject to pose in character as 'a man in his death throes' or a man of 'ideals and abundant love', as the means to better comprehend and render an 'authentic pose'.[1] As compelling as they are, Courbet's self-portraits were less a portrait of his life than a training exercise, a record of his desire to master the depth and breadth of human expression by studying the man in the mirror. ●

▲

Gustave Courbet (1819–77)
The Desperate Man
1843–45, oil on canvas, 45 x 55 cm (18 x 21 in)

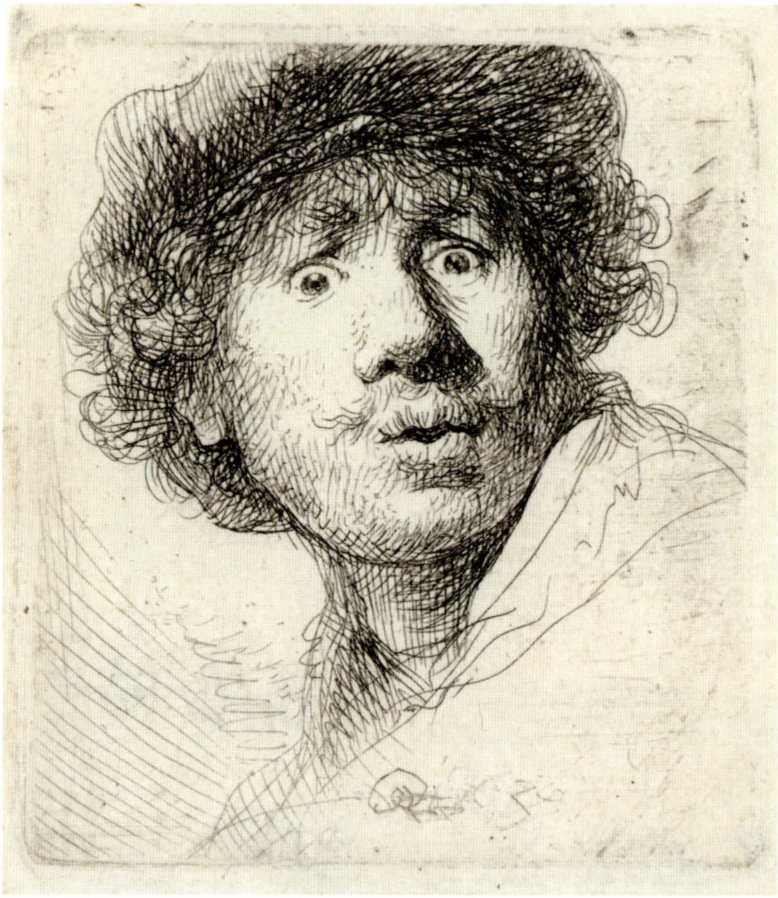

▲

Rembrandt van Rijn (1606–69)
Self-Portrait in a Cap
1630, etching and drypoint, printed from a dirty plate, 5 x 5 cm (2 x 2 in)

With rounded eyes and pursed lips, Rembrandt embodies a state of astonishment. This etching is one of four expressive studies; the others featuring laughter, a frown and open-mouthed alarm. Few artists have created as many self-portraits as Rembrandt, and while many of the roughly one hundred examples feature his changing likeness as he aged, this set – with dishevelled hair and distorted features – was made to study facial expression. It is easy to imagine him making faces into the mirror, exaggerating his features for emphasis.

▶

Gustave Courbet
Man with Leather Belt
1845–46, oil on canvas, 100 x 82 cm (39 x 32 in)

In this moody portrait, Courbet depicts himself as a handsome, young romantic. His deeply shadowed eyes veer away from the viewer and his expression is pensive, as if lost in poignant thought. Resting his jaw on his right hand, he leans on a thick, leather-bound sketchbook. A stick of chalk in a holder is ready for use when the mood strikes him. More than in any other of his early self-portraits, Courbet draws upon an older tradition than his expressive studies; here he presents himself as an artist with the tools of his trade.

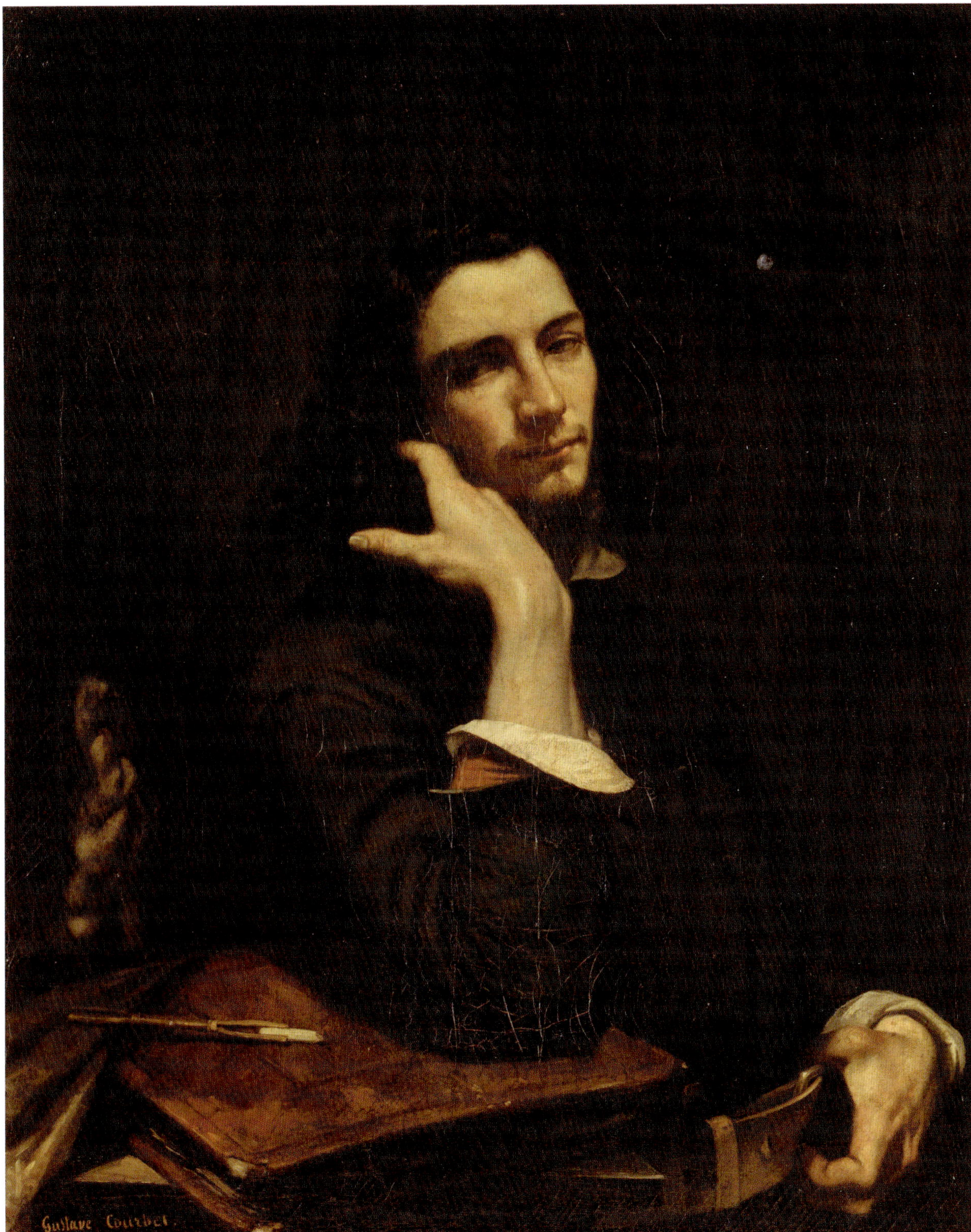
Gustave Courbet.

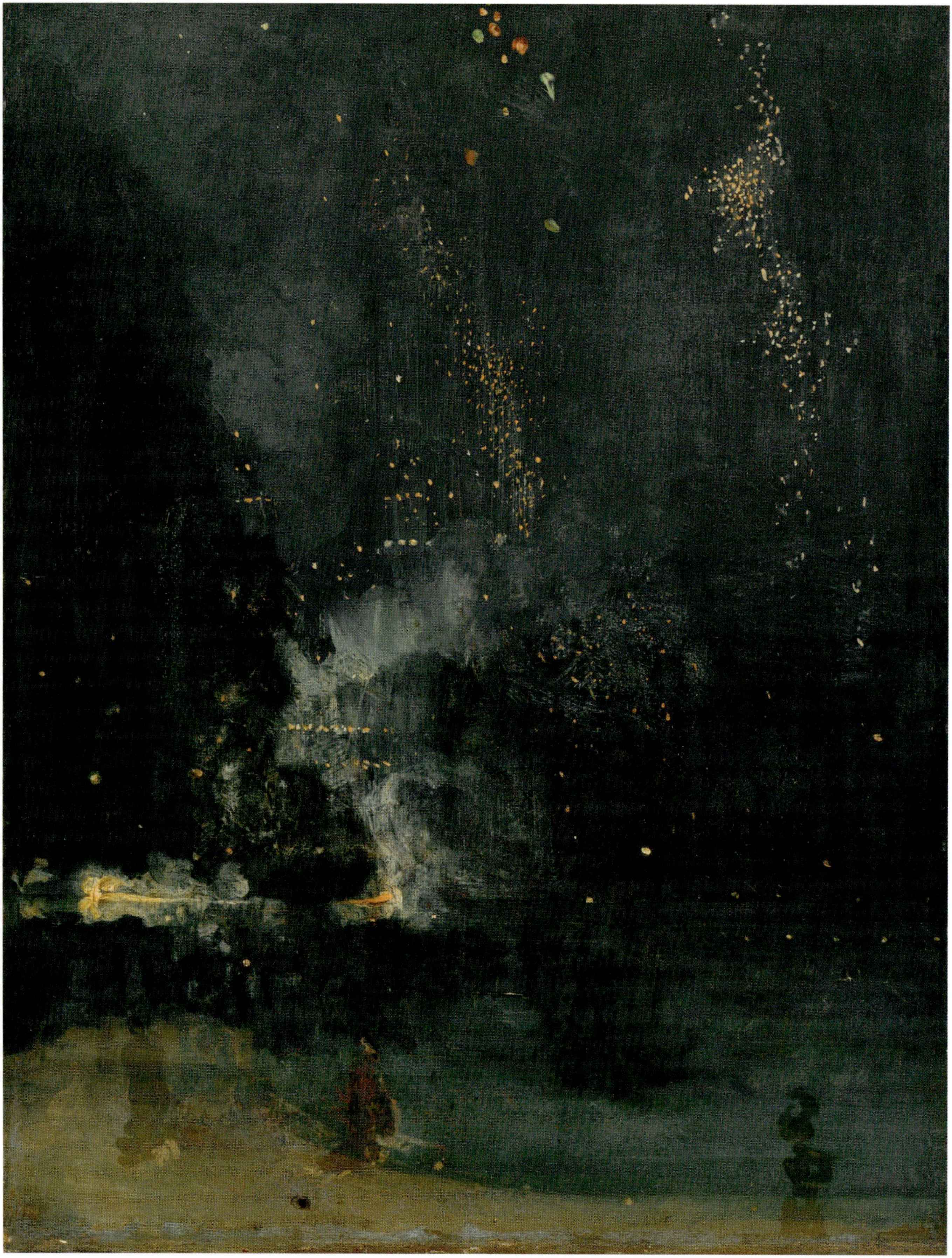

LIGHT EFFECTS

How Whistler looked to the Edo era to light his nocturnal scenes

James McNeill Whistler sought to purge his painting of any content other than visual in pursuit of an expression that existed solely as art for art's sake. To this end, he replaced descriptive titles with musical references – symphony, caprice, arrangement – to emphasize colour harmonies. When painting landscapes, he blurred the familiar features of known locations with evocative, and often ambiguous, atmospheric effects. Nowhere is this more evident than in his 'Nocturnes', in which he depicted sites along the River Thames near Chelsea, London, at night. He called them his 'moonlight pictures', using swathes of colour to render the pure sensation of nocturnal luminescence over the water without topographical specificity or romantic reference. Perhaps his greatest challenge – with the most sensational consequence – was a fireworks display over Cremorne Gardens (a popular pleasure gardens in the Victorian era), presented as a purely visual effect without delineating the transfixed crowd or works that ignited the spectacle.

Whistler was a notorious magpie, looking at and borrowing ideas from the works of his peers to solve pictorial problems. He based his confining interior arrangements on those of Edgar Degas. The vast seascapes painted by Gustave Courbet shaped his own coastal views, whether he painted from the shore of an ocean or a riverbank. However, when it came to a fiery display – from an erupting volcano to the fleeting flare of fireworks – Whistler found western tradition wanting. The longstanding, descriptive practice of focusing on the source of the explosion rendered the dynamic spectacle static, a result of an action rather than the essence of its experience. Whistler turned instead to examples he knew from *ukiyo-e*, the colourful, Edo-era wood-relief prints that captured scenes of contemporary highlife pleasures created to appeal to discerning Japanese collectors. Since the late 1850s, when Japan opened to trade with western nations, European aficionados bought them too, and, by the mid-1860s Whistler had amassed an impressive collection. It is widely believed that he owned a print of Utagawa Hiroshige's *Fireworks at Ryogoku Bridge*, from the series 'One Hundred Famous Views of Edo'.[1]

◀

James McNeill Whistler (1834–1903)
Nocturne in Black and Gold, the Falling Rocket
1875, oil on panel, 60 x 47 cm (24 x 18 in)

In Hiroshige's print, the rocket traces a fiery trail while glittering stars spangle the night sky. The ephemerality of the spectacle is implied through lightness of touch; the explosive light fades from view. Whistler pushed the evanescence further, transforming the track of his rocket into a dazzling, yet dwindling, cascade of sparkling light. Both the print and the painting convey a fleeting sensation, but Whistler's medium of oil on panel gave him greater range to modulate his tone from the blazing orange of the fire boats on the river to the palest flicker of light disappearing into the dark, fog-laden black atmosphere. The painting debuted in 1877 to the puzzlement of viewers and critics alike, with the anonymous critic for *Punch* pondering, 'Above, all fog; below, all inky flood; For subject – it had none.'[2] When John Ruskin, one of the most esteemed cultural writers of the day, accused the painter of 'flinging a pot of paint in the public's face', Whistler sued him for libel.[3] At the trial, questioned about how he set prices on his paintings, Whistler declared that value was not based on hours of labour but the knowledge he had accrued in a lifetime. And at the core of that knowledge was how to steal: when to imitate, when to assimilate and how to transform appropriation into innovation. ●

▶

Utagawa Hiroshige (1797–1858)
Fireworks at Ryogoku Bridge,
from 'One Hundred Famous Views of Edo'
1858, woodblock print, ink and colour on paper,
34 x 22 cm (13 x 9 in)

Hiroshige's 'One Hundred Famous Views of Edo' (in fact, 119 views) features the sites and activities that made nineteenth-century Edo (now Tokyo) the centre for sophisticated culture in Japan. The bridge over the Sumida River was the site for evening entertainments that often culminated with a fireworks show. As seen here, the spectacle drew large crowds gathering on the bridge and on boats in the water, but Hiroshige's high point of view diminishes the role of the spectators, concentrating the viewer's attention on the dazzling display.

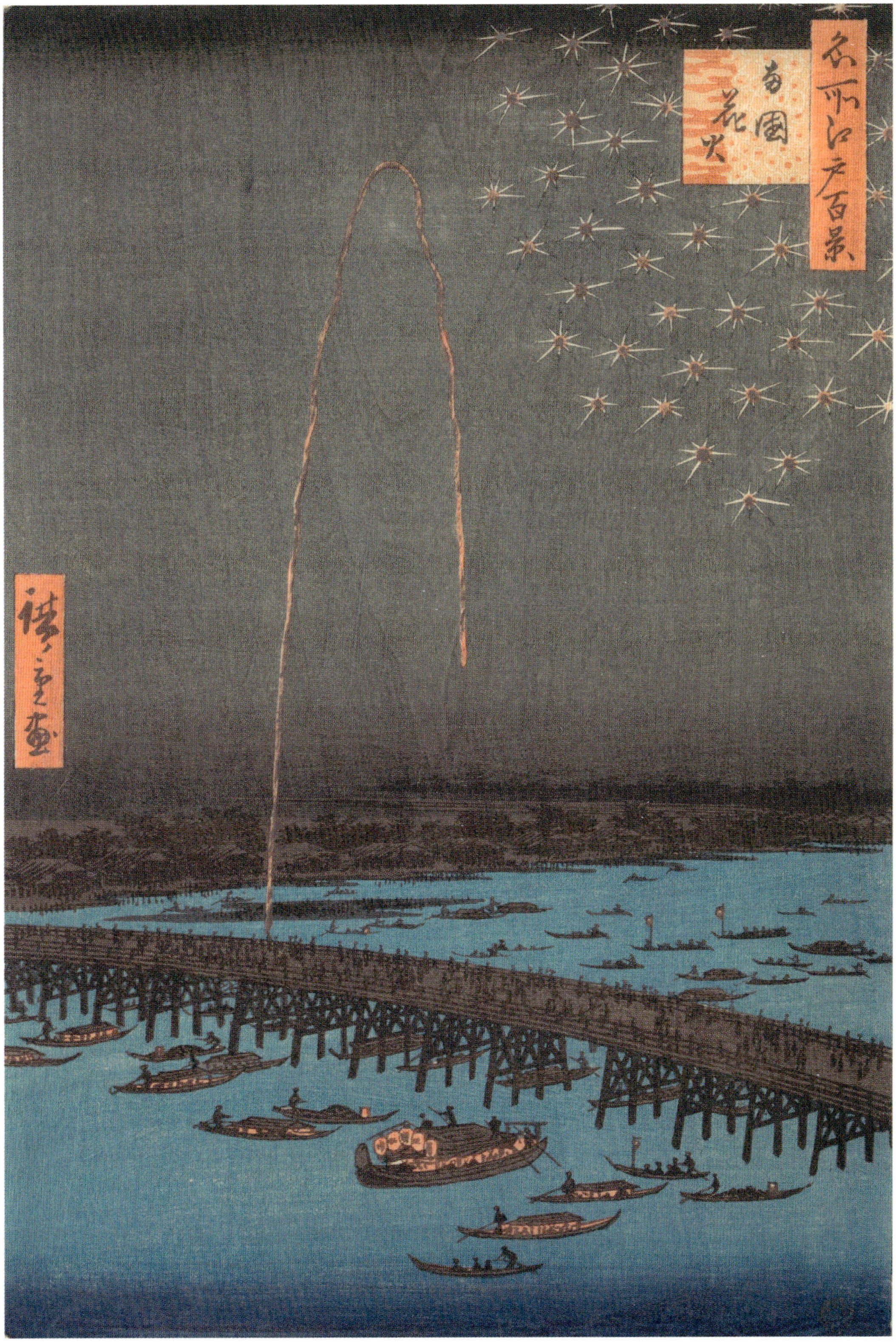

Unknown artist
First Performance of Handel's Music for the Royal Fireworks, 27 April 1749
1749, hand-coloured print, 27 x 20 cm (11 x 8 in)

Commissioned by King George II to celebrate the end of the War of the Austrian Succession, George Frideric Handel's *Music for the Royal Fireworks* debuted in London with a celebratory display. This print documents the spectacle on the River Thames in schematic detail. Striving for accuracy has dulled the excitement, stressing the source of the pyrotechnics over the effect. An example of the Western tradition Whistler sought to move away from. Despite the buoyant spirit of this illustration, the actual event fell far short of expectations. Rain muted the fireworks and a riverside pavilion caught fire.

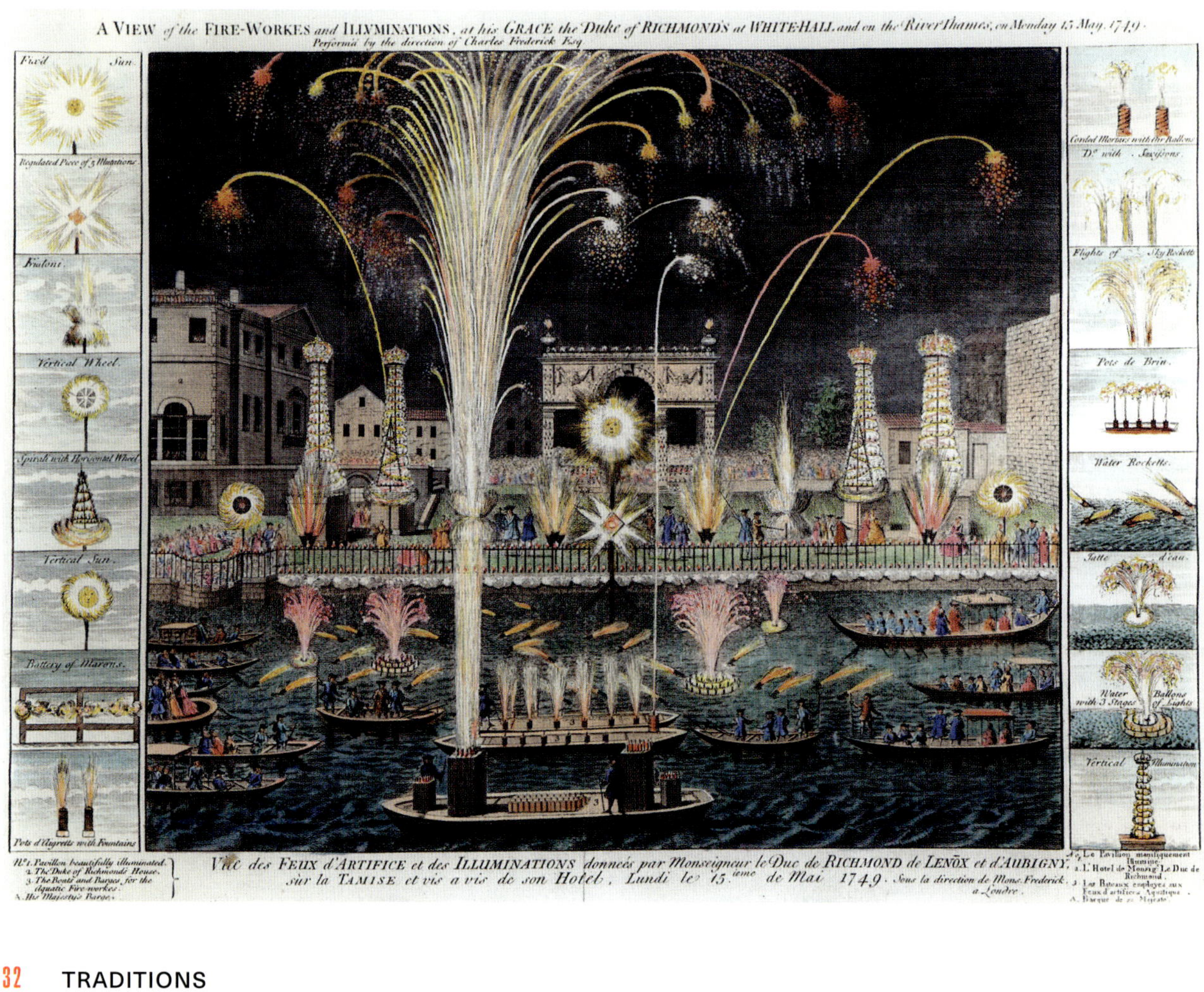

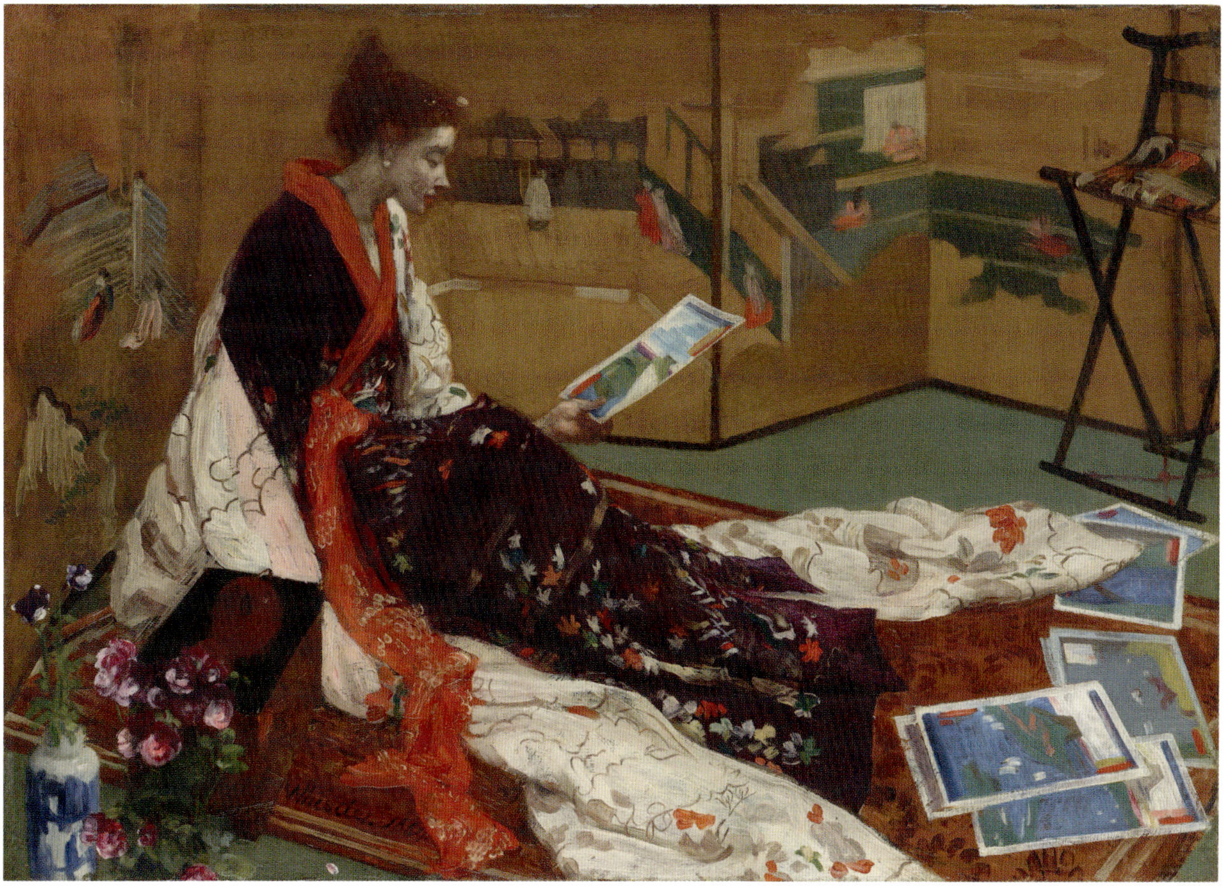

▲

James McNeill Whistler
Caprice in Purple and Gold: The Golden Screen
1864, oil on panel, 50 x 69 cm (20 x 27 in)

When Japan opened its markets in 1858, Whistler became an avid collector, buying painted furniture, lacquered boxes, porcelain, prints and garments. He displayed them in his home, but also used them as picturesque props. Whistler was particularly proud of his collection of *ukiyo-e*, paying top price for full suites of prints by such masters as Utamaro and Hiroshige. Here, his kimono-clad model holds an impression from Hiroshige's series 'Famous Views of the Sixty-odd Provinces', featuring famous sites across Japan. Whistler's interest soon shifted from novelty to aesthetics, seeking new ideas for his own work.

MIRRORING TRADITION

How Monir merged ancient aesthetics with contemporary expression

Under the glittering mirrored domes of the Shah Cheragh mosque in Shiraz, Monir Shahroudy Farmanfarmaian discovered a new path in her art. With a wide-ranging education, a successful career as a commercial artist in New York and rising acclaim in the international art world, Monir was admired for her cosmopolitan perspective, combining contemporary abstraction with references to Persian aesthetics. She had returned to Iran as a newly-wed in 1957 after living in the United States for more than a decade, and soon found herself drawn to traditional arts and crafts. Monir travelled the country, seeking out regional weavings, ceramics and jewellery. Through her collection, her knowledge and appreciation for the arts of her homeland deepened, but this particular visit in 1966 to the monument known as the 'King of Light' sparked a new sense of possibility for her own practice. Surrounded by reflected light heightened by the illumination of 'lamps blazing', the 'very space seemed on fire'. She felt transported: 'I imagined myself standing inside a many-faceted diamond and looking out at the sun.'[1] Here was the inspiration she needed to bind up the disparate threads of her art and life – twining the traditional with the contemporary, the culturally specific with the cosmopolitan, the abstract with the symbolic – as seen in the geometric, mirrored sculptures that became the hallmark expression of her six-decade career.

There are several legends attached to the origin story of the technique known as *ayeneh-kari* (mirror-work). The use of mirrors as mosaic tesserae is sometimes attributed to Queen Tash Khatun's commission of renovations in the Shah Cheragh complex (*c.* 1344–49) as used to intensify the interior light.[2] Another tale asserts that the kings of the Safavid Era (1501–1722) imported Venetian mirrors for the palace women's quarters; if they arrived shattered, the pieces were used for decoration so that the expensive glass would not be wasted.[3] The technique flourished through the nineteenth century, covering the walls, doorways, window frames and ceilings of public and domestic spaces alike with precisely cut pieces of glass that were embedded in plaster to create meticulous geometric patterns. When Monir resolved to employ this technique, she embraced every aspect of its

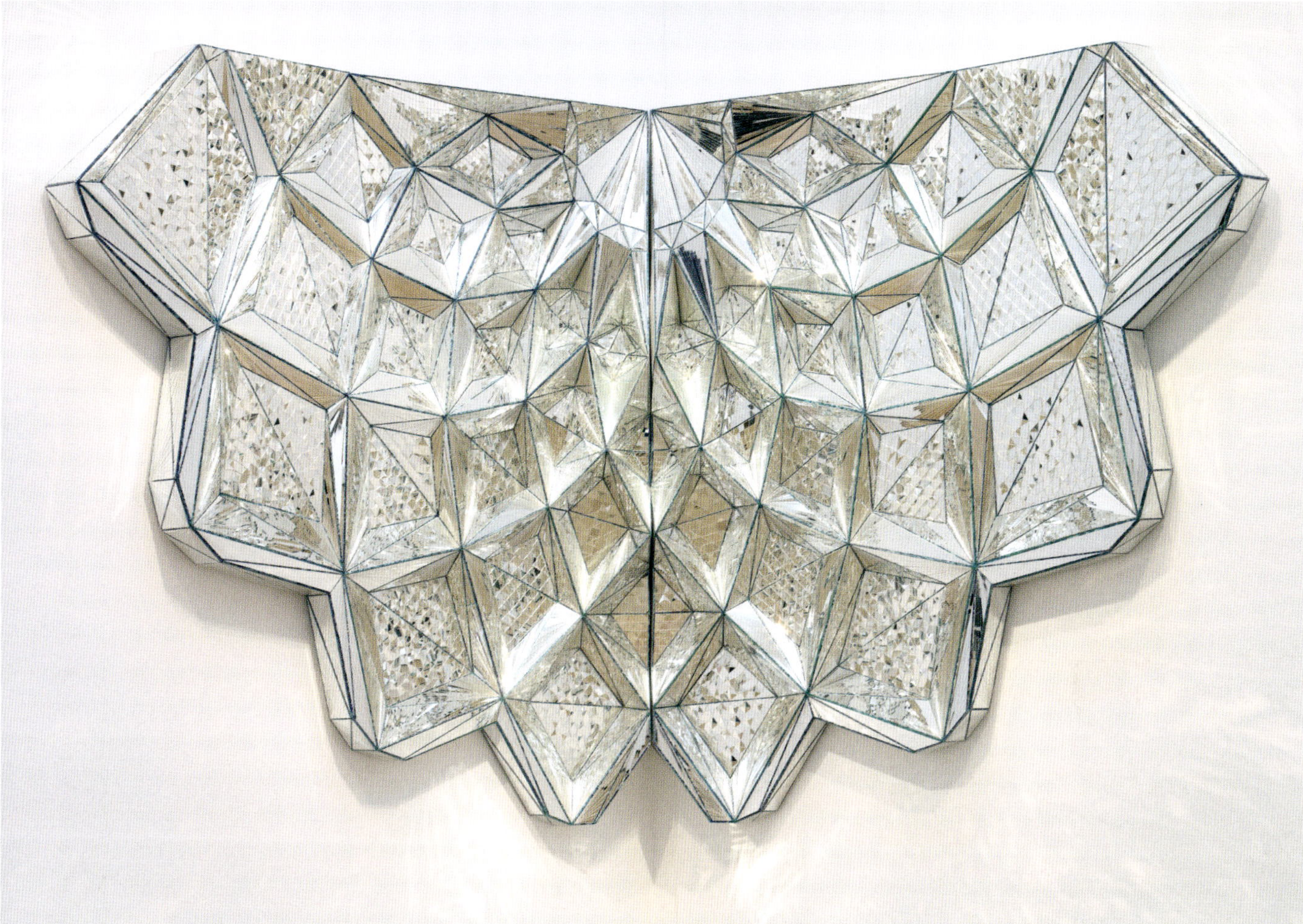

authenticity, enlisting the aid of master craftsmen who cut and assembled the glass according to her designs. She also studied the principles of sacred geometry, Sufi architecture and cosmology, and the symbolic language of forms: triangles, squares and hexagons. Building knowledge and confidence, she began to experiment, mixing the mirrors with tesserae crafted from reverse-painted glass and conventional stone. And she freed the shining veneers from their supporting walls, creating self-contained sculptures to be displayed both as single entities and in ensembles.

The subtitle of this work, *Muqarnas*, links Monir's sculpture to the structural element that connects the circular base of a dome with the squared set of the arches that support it. Similar to a pendentive, a muqarnas resembles a concave triangle that features an intricate surface pattern of three-dimensional tiers or cells. Monir plays on the expected shape, bending the sides of the two-part, wing-like structure and blunting the upper corners to turn three sides into four.

▲

Monir Shahroudy Farmanfarmaian (1922–2019)
Untitled (*Muqarnas*)
2012, mirrors, reverse-glass painting and plaster on wood, 150 x 218 x 30 cm (59 x 86 x 12 in)

Within the form is a pattern of mirrored glass cells – squares and lozenges – which are, themselves, devised of smaller glass tesserae. Selected elements are painted on the reverse, adding colour but also blocking the reflection. This compelling complexity is not solely decorative. As an architectural element, the muqarnas balanced structural soundness, symbolic geometry and beauty, and it was this convergence of form and meaning that Monir sought in her art. *Untitled (Muqarnas)* is a late-life work – the artist was ninety when she designed it – revealing that although she continued to experiment with other forms and mediums, she found unlimited potential in her ongoing engagement with tradition, ignited by a revelatory visit to the 'King of Light'. ●

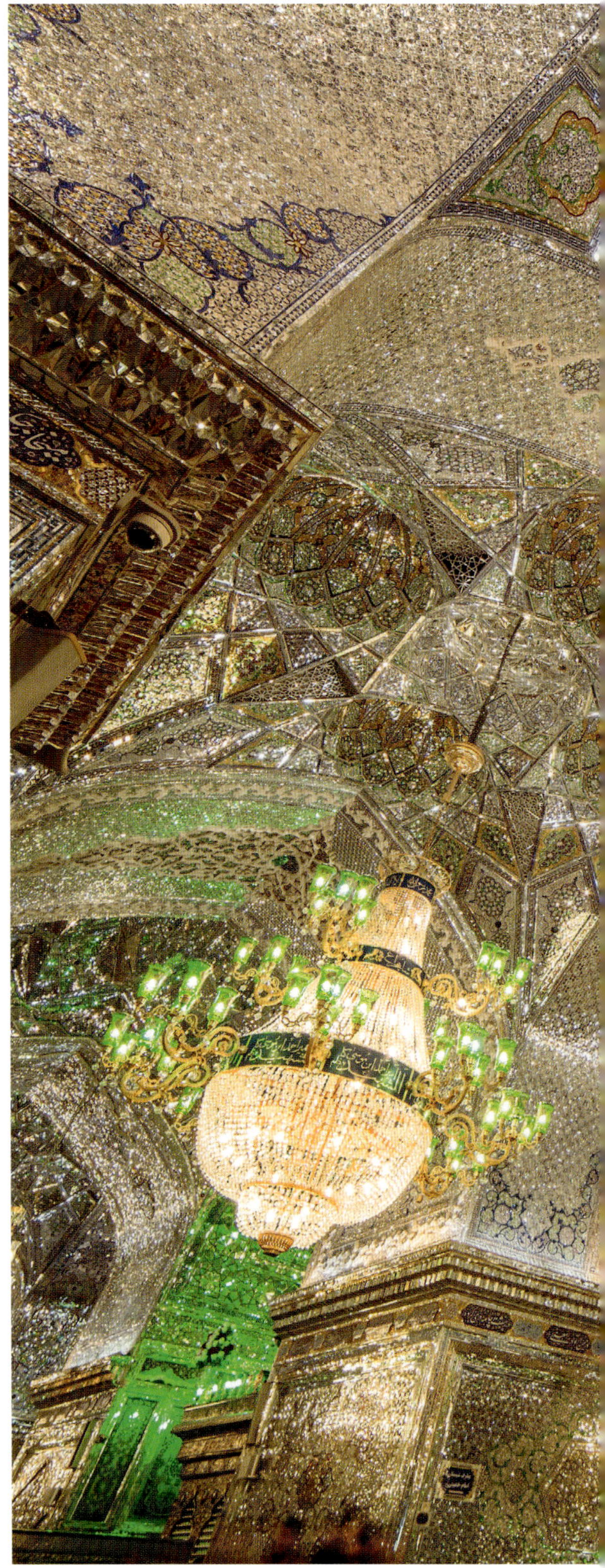

▶

Unknown artist
Interior of Shah Cheragh shrine, Shiraz, Iran
fourteenth century, mirrored glass

Founded in the thirteen century as a funerary monument, the religious complex derives its popular name, the 'King of Light', from the mirror mosaics applied to the walls and ceiling of the mosque a century later. Initially torchlight illumination created a dazzle of light; the golden chandeliers were a later addition. When Monir visited in 1966, she sat in the interior for hours, watching as the architecture dissolved into glittering patterns. The experience prompted her to study the craft, as well as the philosophy and science of mirror mosaics, with an enduring dedication that fuelled her career.

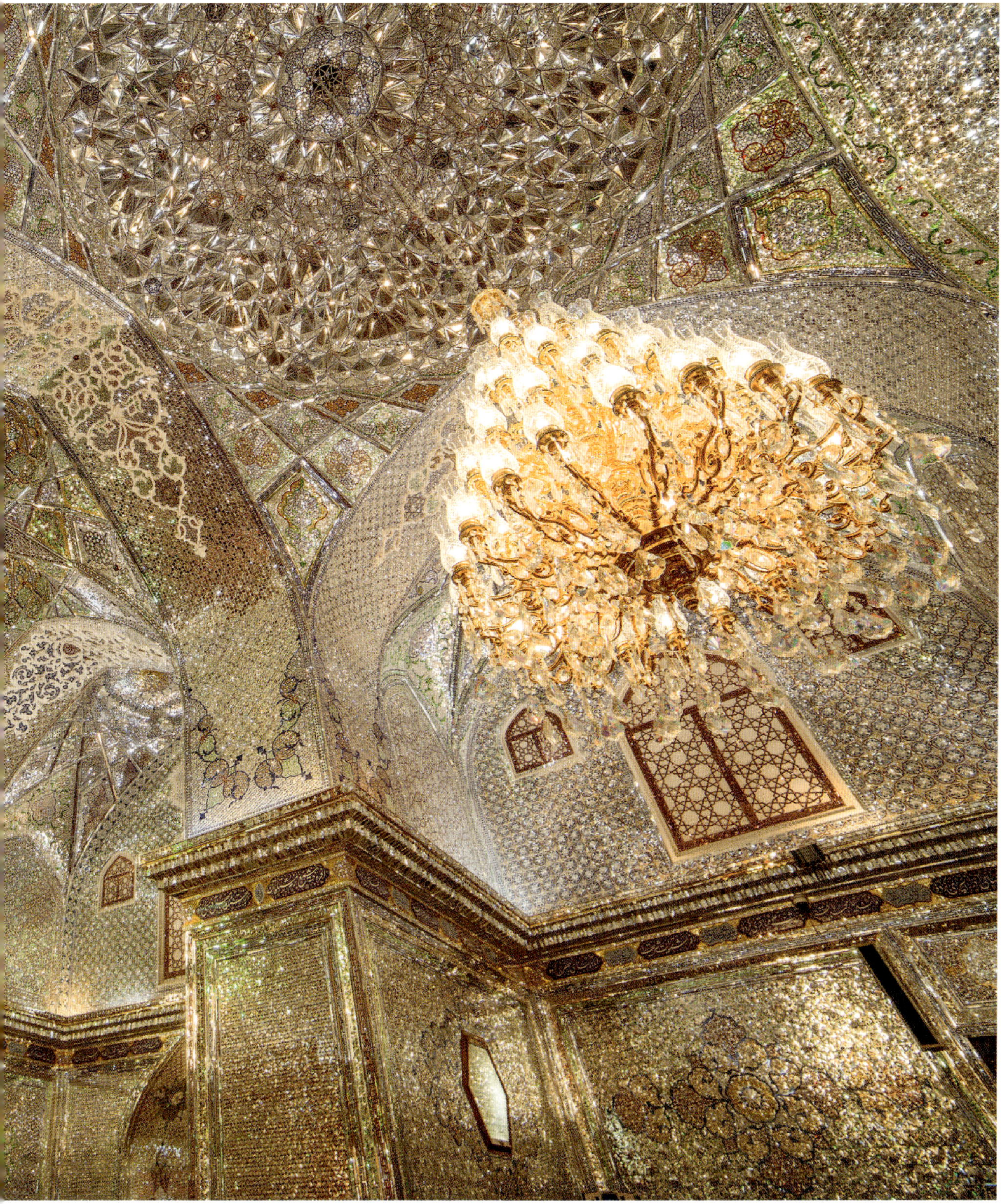

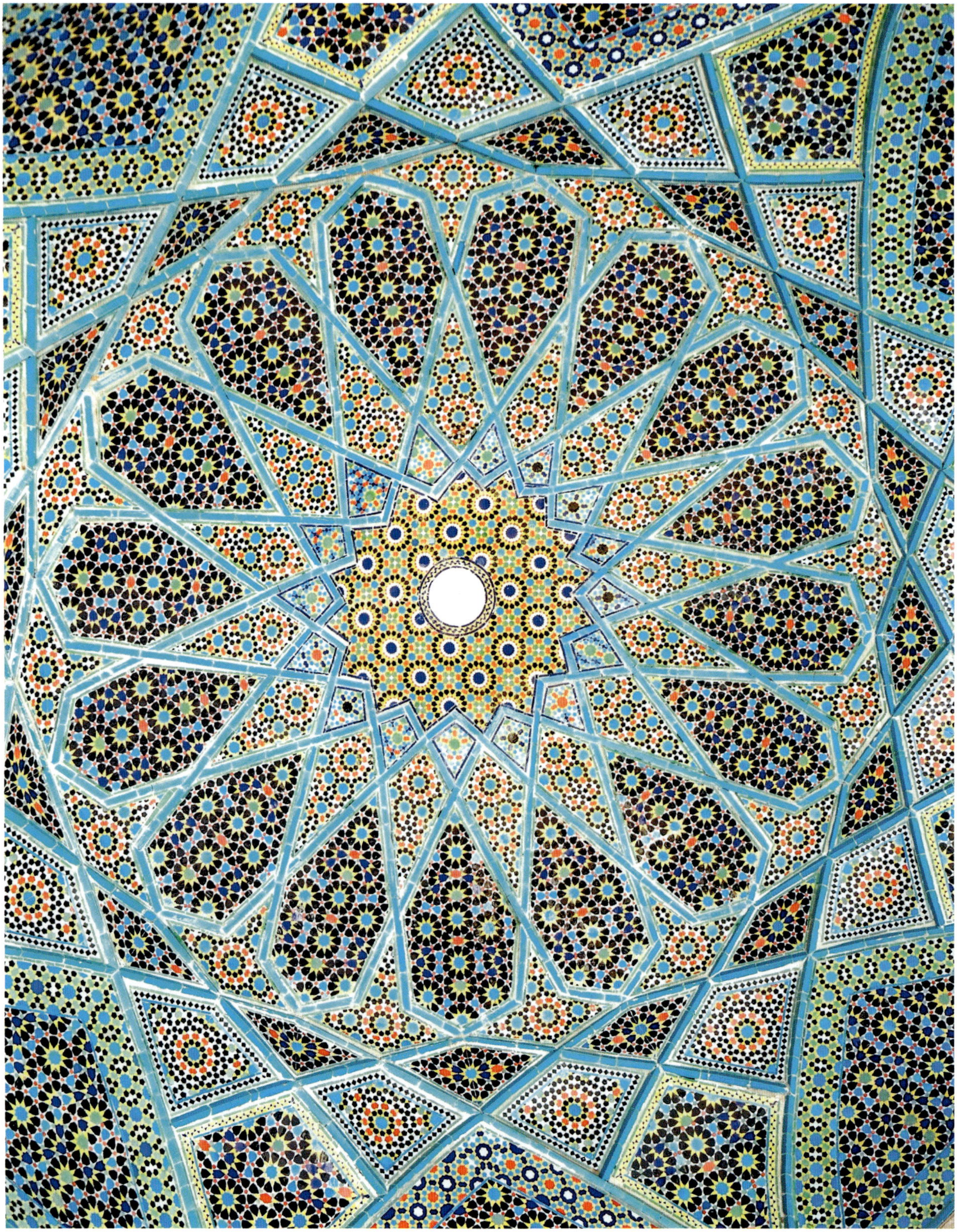

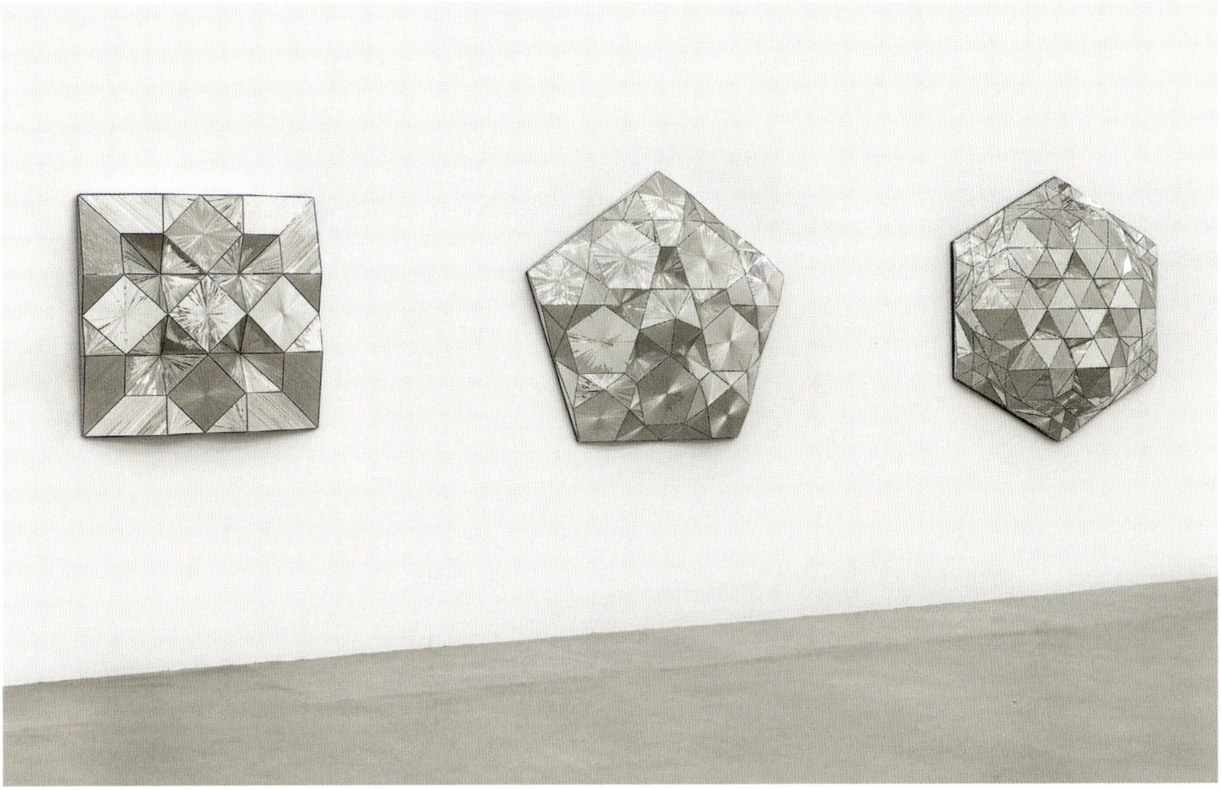

Monir Shahroudy Farmanfarmaian
Detail of 'Third Family' (series of eight sculptures)
2011, reverse-painted glass, mirrored glass, plaster, dimensions variable

Monir's 'families' are composed of eight mirrored panels in the essential forms of Sufi geometry: the triangle, square, pentagon, hexagon, heptagon, octagon, nonagon and decagon. Taken together they represent the essential principle of unity through multiplicity. Each individual shape also carries meaning. Here, the square may be read as the four cardinal directions and the pentagon as the five senses. The hexagon has many meanings, including the six virtues: generosity, self-discipline, patience, determination, insight and compassion. Each sculpture has its own pattern of faceted mirrors derived from the panel's geometric form.

Unknown artist
Ceiling mosaic, Tomb of Hafez,
Musalla Gardens, Shiraz, Iran
c. 1773, enamelled tile mosaic

The exquisite mosaic patterns in Persian tilework are more than just decorative. A circular floriate pattern like this one that embellishes the pavilion of the tomb of the court poet Hafez (*c.* 1325–90) evokes the Garden of Paradise, as well as the unity and infinity of divine power. Here, in contrast to the mirror mosaics in the Shah Cheragh, the tesserae are small, precisely cut shards of glazed ceramics, assembled in a traditional geometric pattern. Rather than the play of reflected light, this technique provides rich colour and a lustrous surface.

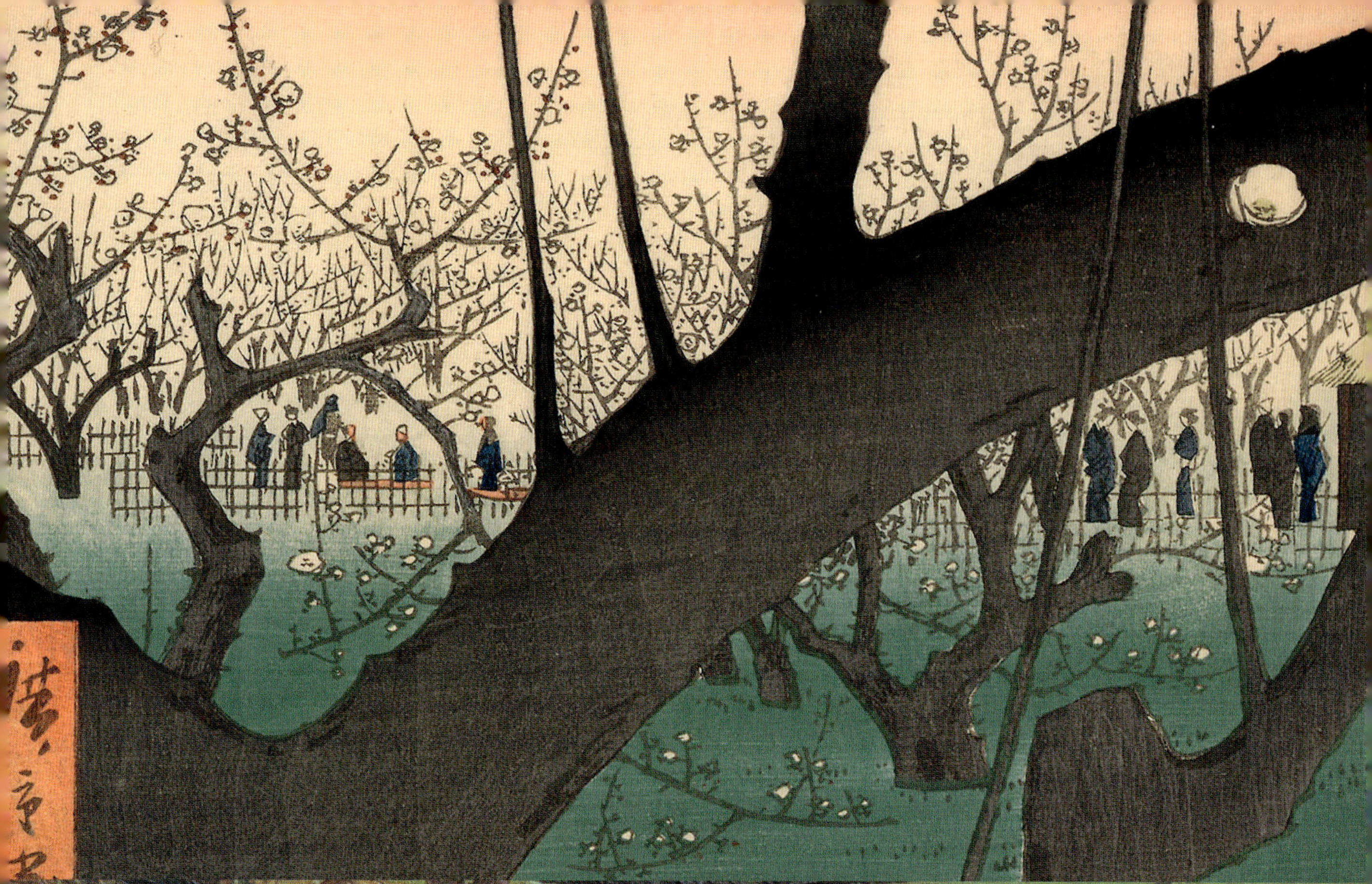

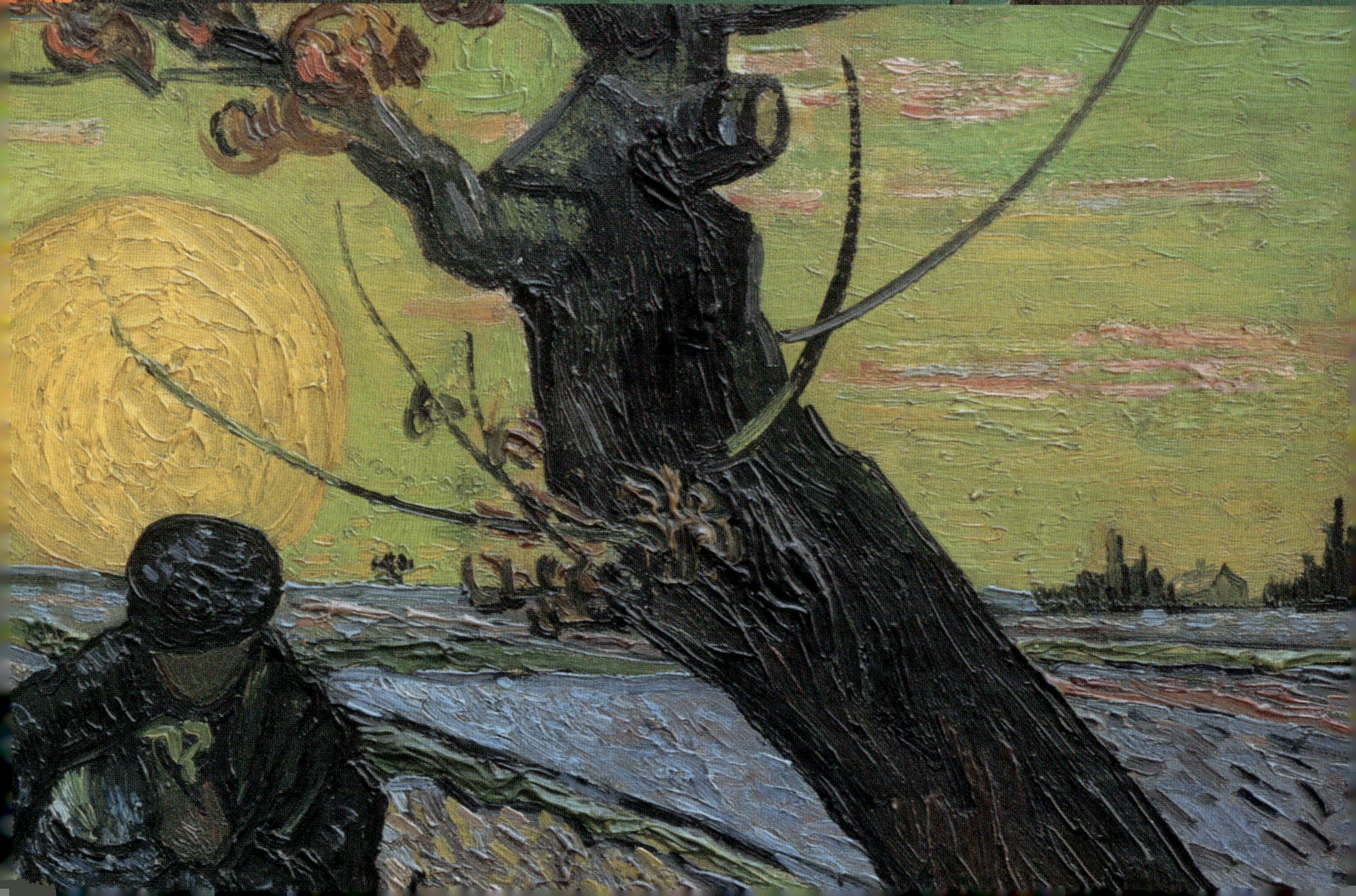

LEARNING CURVE

Throughout time, aspiring artists have turned to others to learn their craft. Imitation has always been part of an artist's education. An apprentice prepares materials and watches the master, and then copies their work. Solitary students replicate works displayed in museums or reproduced in books. An accomplished practitioner continues to learn from the work of others; even an artist who claims not to teach, does so by example. Any artist who wants to learn, steals through observation, emulation and experimentation. Stealing those skills is key to conquering the learning curve.

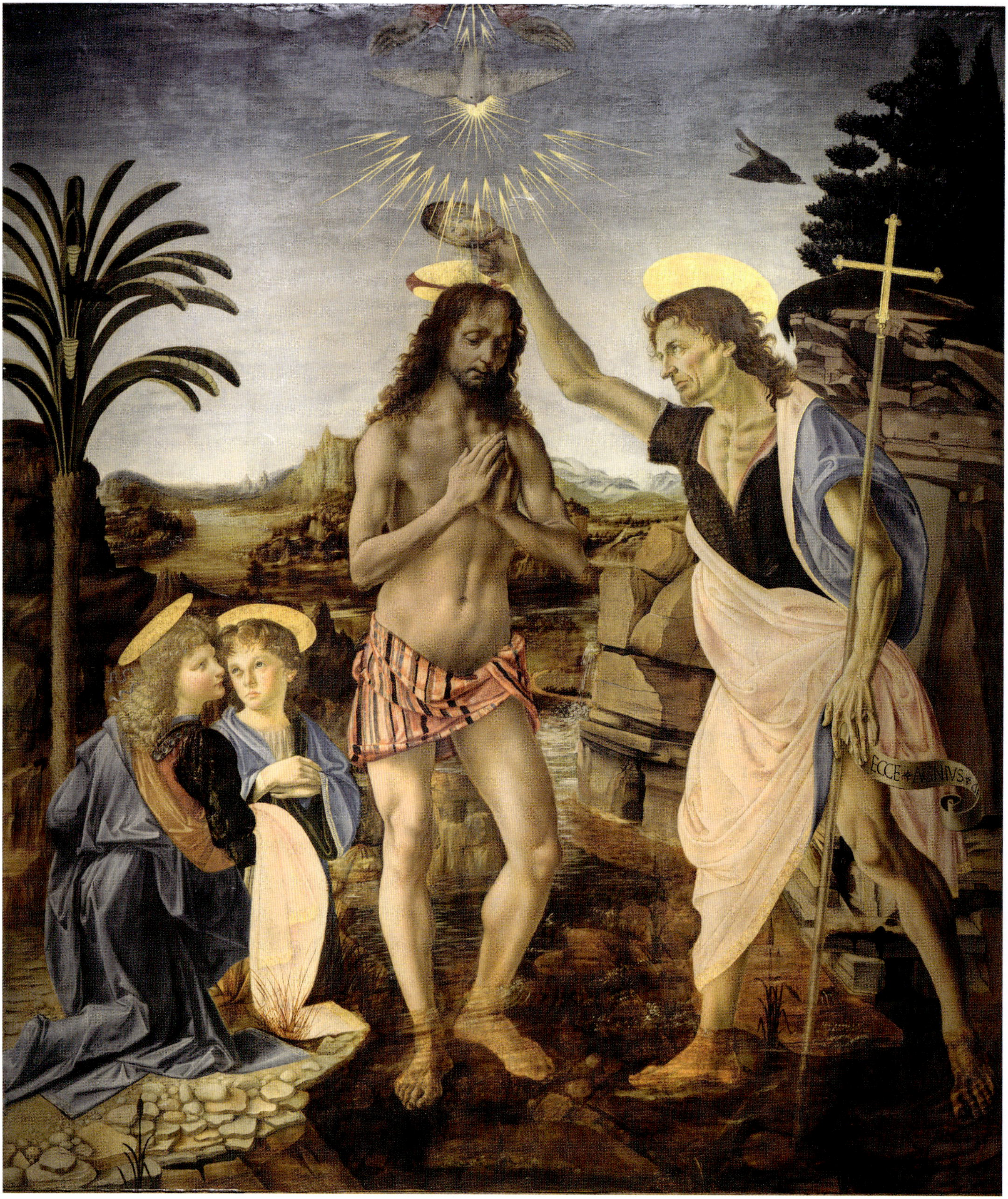
ECCE AGNIVS

HANDS-ON TRAINING

How Verrocchio's *Baptism of Christ* had a helping hand from Da Vinci

The workshop of Andrea del Verrocchio was one of the most productive in Quattrocento Florence.[1] Although trained as a goldsmith, Verrocchio accepted commissions in every medium, from painted altarpieces and bronze sculpture to luxury decorative arts. He enjoyed prestige patronage from the church, as well as from the Medici family and other prominent citizens. At the height of its success in Florence (*c.* 1465–75), Verrocchio's workshop was a hive of activity; in *Lives of the Artists* (1550), Giorgio Vasari claimed that the 'ever labouring' master was 'never at rest'.[2] This unceasing productivity depended upon the traditional organization of the workshop itself. As much a training ground as a studio, Verrocchio relied upon the support of an assembly of apprentices, resident assistants and auxiliary assistants, many of whom contributed directly on works attributed solely to the master.

In Verrocchio's day, the artist's workshop retained the organizational structure and the hierarchy of the medieval trade guilds. Boys – the rare female apprentice was likely the master's daughter – were apprenticed to a workshop between the ages of eleven and fourteen, receiving food, lodging and, occasionally, a small wage in exchange for rudimentary tasks: making brushes and preparing such basic materials as plaster, clay and glue. Servants took care of the most menial chores, but an apprentice could also not refuse to do whatever was asked of them. Older apprentices taught the younger ones, and over the course of three to five years a successful apprentice's responsibilities increased to include grinding pigment and preparing panels. During free time, the apprentice would practise drawing, copying whatever was in the workshop. Instruction was informal, and the master rarely taught or even commented, but the apprentice was exposed to all the activity in the shop and a sharp apprentice learned by observation. After this initial period was completed, an apprentice could rise to an assistant, earning a salary, taking on minor commissions and, if deemed sufficiently talented, working directly with the master. To accommodate a high volume of work, a master hired younger artists with proven skills as journeymen or temporary assistants.

◀

Andrea del Verrocchio (*c.* 1435–88)
The Baptism of Christ
c. 1470–75, oil on wood, 177 x 151 cm (70 x 59 in)

An impressive roster of assistants passed through Verrocchio's shop in a full-time or temporary capacity, including Sandro Botticelli, Lorenzo di Credi, Pietro Perugino, Domenico Ghirlandaio, Filippino Lippi and Leonardo da Vinci. Many went on to have illustrious careers, prompting the poet Ugolino Verino (also known as Ugolino di Vieri) to write: 'Whatever painters have that is good they drank of Verrocchio's stream.'[3]

Leonardo entered Verrocchio's shop around the age of fourteen and by seventeen he had become an assistant. Around that time, Verrocchio had taken on the commission of an altarpiece for the monastic church of San Salvi in Florence, featuring the Baptism of Christ. The lean, rugged figure of the Baptist typifies Verrocchio's mature figure style. Hard lines define body contours and describe the meticulously rendered anatomy. With its delicate features, pliable grace and feathery brushstrokes, the golden-haired angel on the left appears to have been painted by a completely different hand. Since the sixteen century, the figure has been attributed to Leonardo. Vasari asserted that although Leonardo was 'then quite young', his work was 'much better than the other parts' of the painting, going as far to suggest that after seeing the angel, Verrocchio 'resolved never again to touch a brush'.[4] While this is hardly true – Verrocchio had a decided preference for sculptural commissions – Leonardo's hand has been detected in a few subsequent works from the shop. In fact, other passages in the painting, including the second angel, the hands of God and the dove suggest the work of other assistants, and it is speculated that Leonardo created the softer passages in the distant landscape. This practice of an assistant's uncredited contribution continued through the nineteenth century. No acknowledgment was given, nor was it expected, for this was the way of the workshop. ●

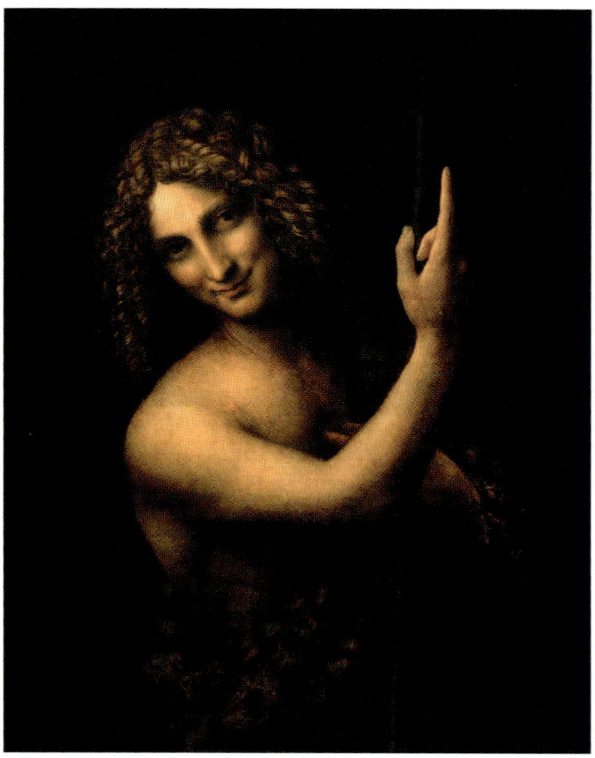

◀

Leonardo da Vinci (1452–1519)
Saint John the Baptist
c. 1511–16, oil on panel, 69 x 57 cm (27 x 22 in)

Painted late in life and unfinished at the time of his death, *Saint John the Baptist* represents Leonardo's distinctive – and revolutionary – mastery of chiaroscuro. By modelling form through the modulation of tone – rather than delineating form with line and colour – Leonardo created the illusion of an actual figure in space. This, along with the saint's enigmatic expression, seemingly lit from within, are characteristics of Leonardo's renowned works, such as *Mona Lisa* and *Salvator Mundi*; a nascent presence in the figure of the golden-haired angel.

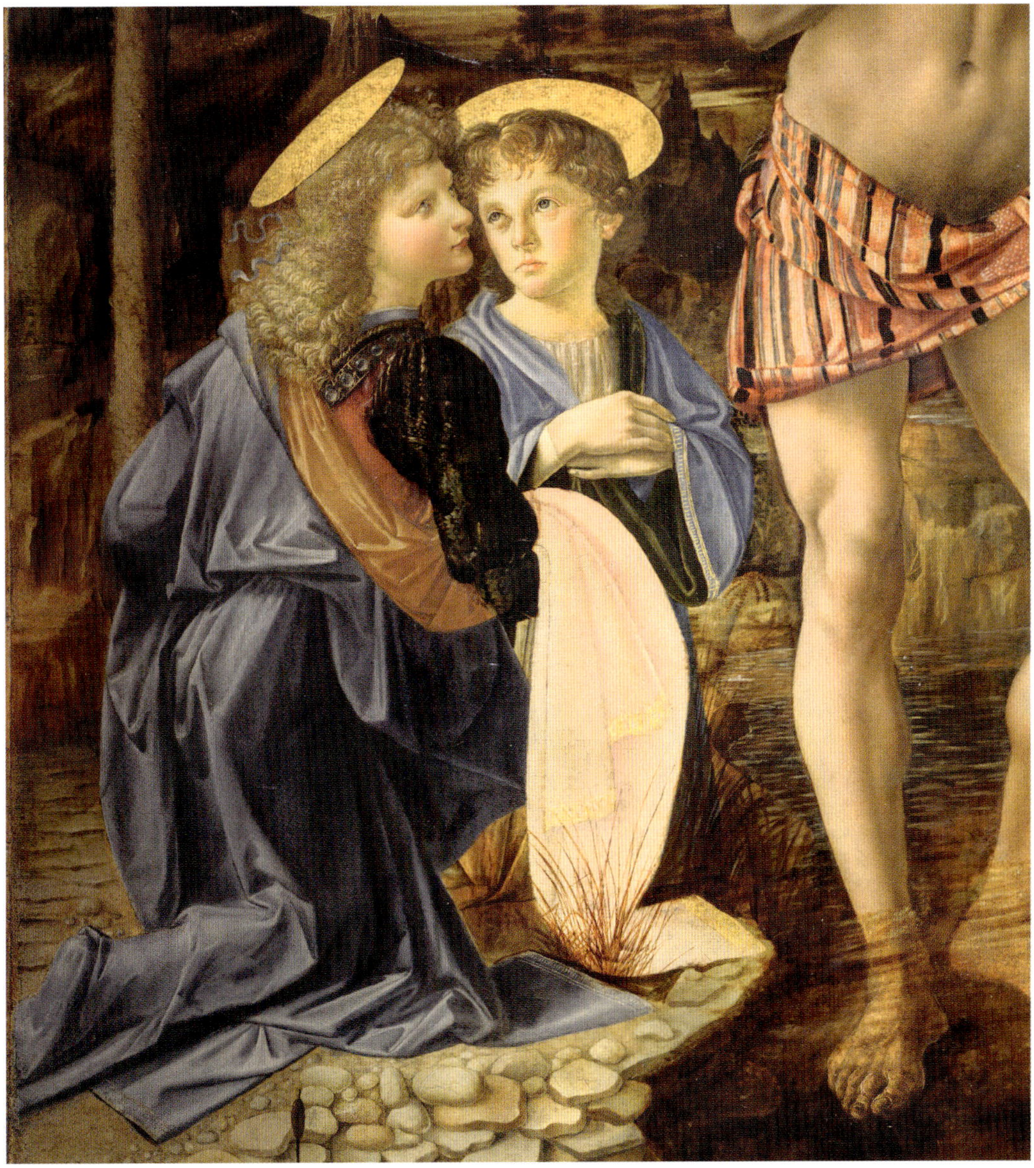

Andrea del Verrocchio
The Baptism of Christ, detail of the left angel

Although the chiselled features, serene expression and supple pose of the angel on the left presents a striking contrast to the weathered, sinewy main figures, it is the handling of form and paint that really sets them apart. Verrocchio typically delineated the contours of the body with precise lines, whereas the painter of the angel modulated tone to shape volume, as clearly seen in the transition between the angel's jaw and neck. That, and the deft rendering of the angel's wheat-blond curls, connect the figure to the hand of Leonardo.

ATMOSPHERIC IMPRESSIONS

How Monet learned to paint the air from Turner

In an interview with journalist Maurice Guillemot, Claude Monet admitted that he had chosen the title for a groundbreaking painting in haste. In 1874, he and several of his friends were organizing an independent art exhibition – open to all – as an alternative to the official, juried Salon. When asked to title his depiction of the sun rising through the mist over a harbour, he suggested 'Impression', explaining that it 'couldn't really pass for a view of Le Havre.'[1] In Monet's day, the term referred to a fleeting thought rather than a finished work, but Monet clearly regarded his painting as finished. When the exhibition opened late in April, many conservative critics pounced on the title as provocative, flaunting the sketch-like state of the work, and the artists associated with the exhibition quickly became known as the Impressionists. The art critic Jules Castagnary, however, understood Monet's unorthodox approach, writing that the artist's insight was to 'render not the landscape, but the sensation provided by the landscape.'[2] Although Castagnary deemed this a true innovation, Monet had drawn upon a chain of influence that allowed him to advance the scope of *plein-air* painting to capture the effect of atmosphere as well as the play of colour and light.

Monet was around sixteen when he met the landscape painter Eugène Boudin, who in his own youth had met Jean-François Millet and Constant Troyon, among the first French painters to adopt *plein-air* practice. Boudin gained a reputation for seaside scenes at fashionable resorts, working on a small scale and finishing quickly with little need for touching up in the studio. He often sold them on the spot. Through Boudin's informal instruction during painting expeditions, Monet learned the value of an immediate response, recording what he saw intuitively, in pure tones and expressive strokes. Throughout the 1860s, Monet continued to work outdoors, painting in urban parks, suburban picnics, and along the northern coast, but his turning point came in the fall of 1870, when he fled Paris for London to avoid the mass mobilization of troops for the Franco-Prussian War. Visiting the National Gallery, Monet discovered the boldly atmospheric seascapes of J.M.W. Turner, but he found an even stronger influence beyond the walls of the gallery. Monet was captivated by the fog cloaking the River Thames in the early hours of the day. Painting the buildings along the river, as they emerged from the morning mist, Monet expanded his understanding of his subject from the effects of light and reflection to include the quality of the air itself.

Monet returned to France late in 1871; a year later he settled his family in suburban Argenteuil. He then visited Le Havre, his boyhood home, in

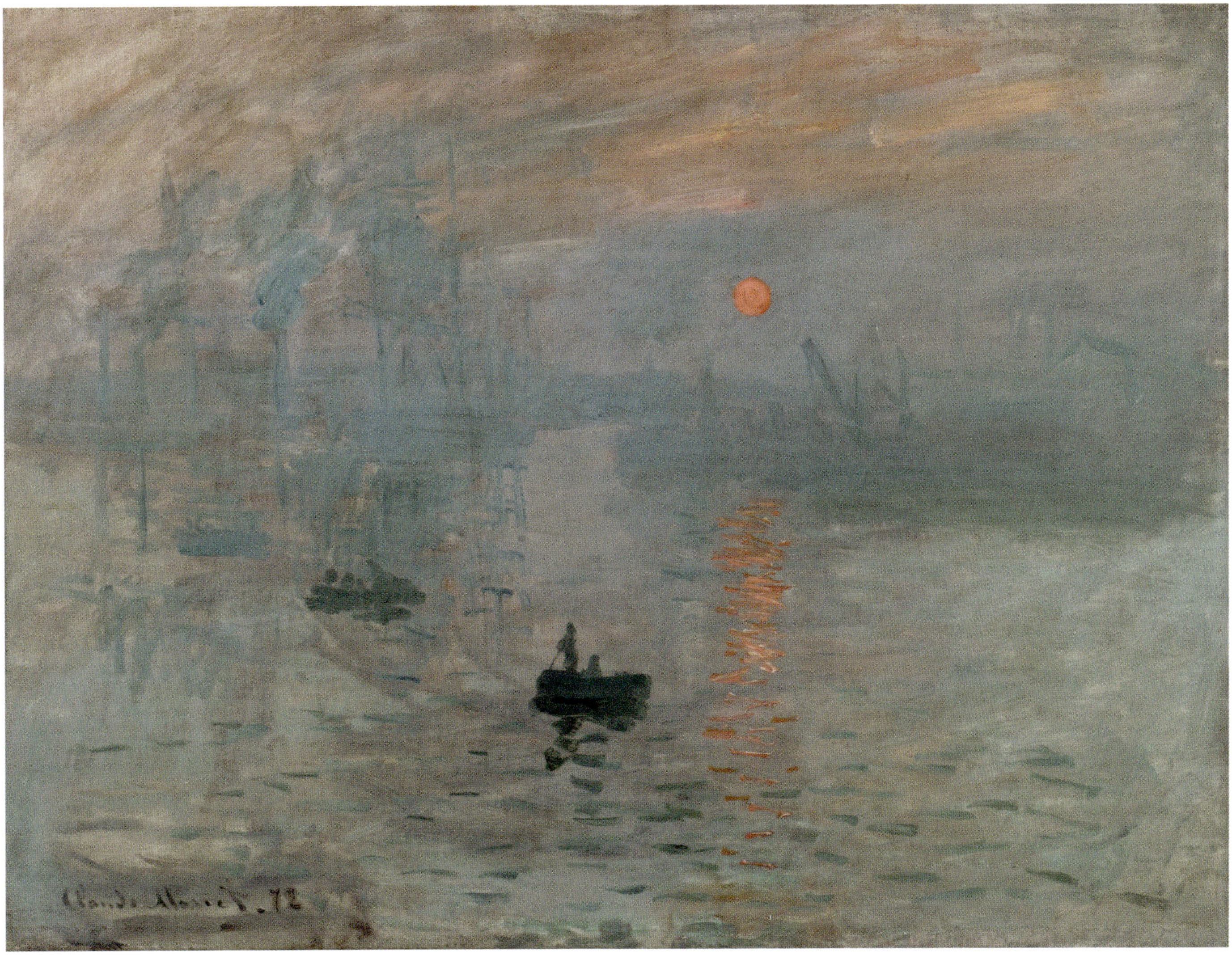

the following year, staying at a harbourside hotel. Perhaps the transforming effects of the mist over the water reminded him of those mornings in London, and he set up his easel at the window to capture the harbour coming to life. Monet dissolved the anecdotal elements and local markers into a blue haze of ambiguity. All the telling details – the bobbing boats, the docked ships, the factory smokestacks in the distance – are engulfed in mist. Everything is seen through the cool, damp air, with the rising sun casting a dazzling reflection on the water. More than a sketch or a view, *Impression: Sunrise* is a sensory experience. Through observation and experiment – and London's fog – Monet discovered how to convey the physical sense, as well as the visual qualities, of a place through colour on canvas. ●

▲

Claude Monet (1840–1926)
Impression: Sunrise
1872, oil on canvas, 48 x 63 cm (19 x 25 in)

J.M.W. Turner (1775–1851)
The Fighting Temeraire
1839, oil on canvas, 91 x 122 cm (36 x 48 in)

Monet left no record of the paintings that he saw in the National Gallery. Turner's spectacular tribute to the now derelict battleship that triumphed in the Battle of Trafalgar (1805) had been acquired by the Gallery in 1856; it was likely on view. The setting heightens the contrast between history and progress as the towering warship is hauled by a squat, utilitarian tugboat to be dissembled for parts. Atmospheric effects – the mist over the water, the shifting clouds, the setting sun casting reflections on the water – have the power of first-hand observation, even though Turner did not witness the event.

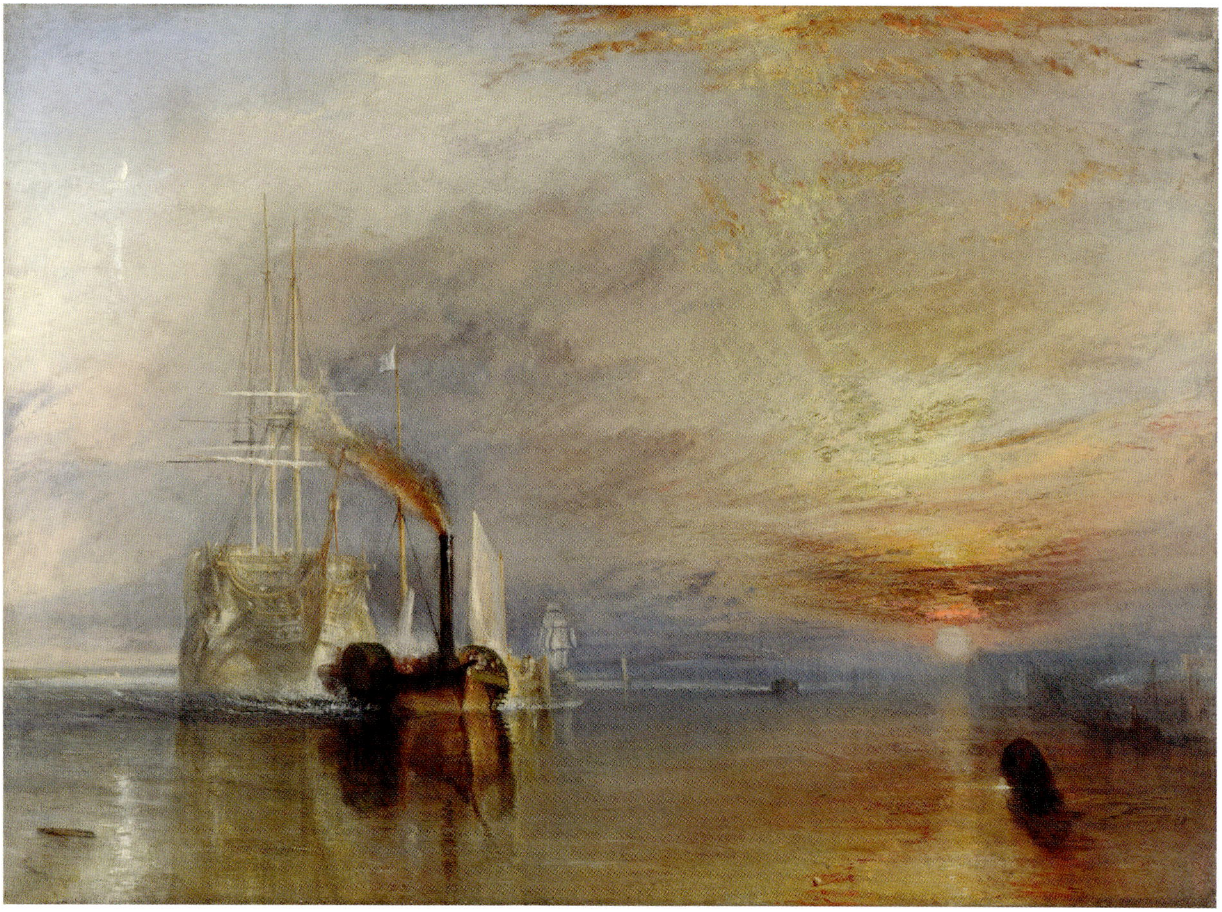

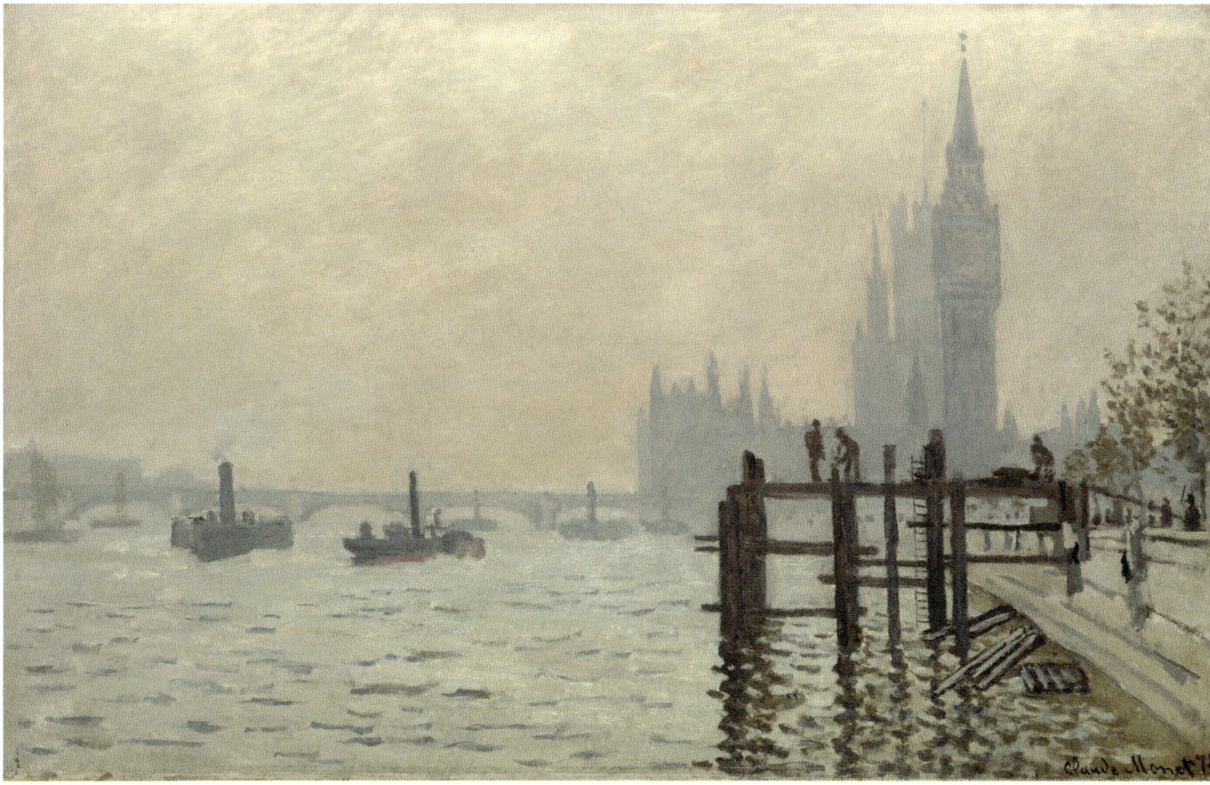

Claude Monet
The Thames Below Westminster
1871, oil on canvas, 47 x 73 cm (19 x 29 in)

Monet's stay in London was brief, but his fascination with the fog, which he regarded as the city's sole source of beauty, shifted his focus from colour to atmosphere. He applied *plein-air* practice – immediate response, expressive brushstroke, colour capturing the fleeting effects of light – to simulate the chill and damp of dawn. The distinctive forms of the newly built Houses of Parliament and Westminster Bridge, as well as the boats on the water and figures on the wharf, are firmly rendered yet softly muted by haze.

THE HEROIC LABOURER

How Van Gogh made Millet's *The Sower* his own

After more than a decade of trying different professions – art dealer, teacher, bookseller, cleric – Vincent van Gogh believed that he could best realize his potential as an artist, and rejecting formal training he embarked on an intense course of self-study. He consulted drawing manuals, including Karl Robert's *Fusain sans maître* (*Charcoal Drawing without a Master*) and Charles Bargue's *Exercises au fusain* (*Charcoal Exercises*), and adopted the widely recommended practice of copying works of art. Rather than turning to the conventional canon of Renaissance painting or antique sculpture, Van Gogh chose reproductions after the works of Jean-François Millet, who was widely regarded as the master of rural realism. In 1880 he asked his brother Theo to post a copy of Millet's print suite 'Labours of the Fields'. He had already made a sketch after a print of Millet's painting, *The Sower* (1850) to improve his figure drawing. The image itself soon took on greater significance, and by the time he wrote to Theo a few weeks later to report on his progress, he had copied *The Sower* five times. However, he felt compelled to 'go back to it again', explaining 'the figure haunts me so'.[1]

While Van Gogh was hardly alone in his admiration for Millet, his interpretation of agricultural labour transformed the figure of the farm worker from an anecdotal stereotype into an expressive embodiment of the strength, skill and the endless effort needed to cultivate the land. Millet's heroic labourers resonated with Van Gogh's growing belief in the nobility of farm labour; for the rest of his career, he repeatedly sought out rural locations and drew parallels between his often exhausting exertion while painting in the fields with that of those who worked them. Van Gogh saw a special significance in the subject, linking Millet's painting with the biblical parable of the sower who must choose the right soil to insure the health and bounty of his harvest (Matthew 13:1–23; Mark 4:1–20; Luke 8:4–15). In his desire to reach others in need of compassion and consolation, Van Gogh adopted the passage as a personal parable. Art could serve the soul as well as a sermon; he only needed to find the skill and a sympathetic audience.

Over the years, Van Gogh drove himself relentlessly, trying different styles and new locations in pursuit of his artistic vision. He experimented with *plein-air* painting and Pointillism, studied the flower paintings of Claude Monet, and collected and copied Japanese prints. In the summer of 1888, having settled in Arles, he returned to the theme of the striding sower, replacing Millet's earthy, naturalistic palette and sturdy technique with glowing hues and a loose, expressive stroke. By late

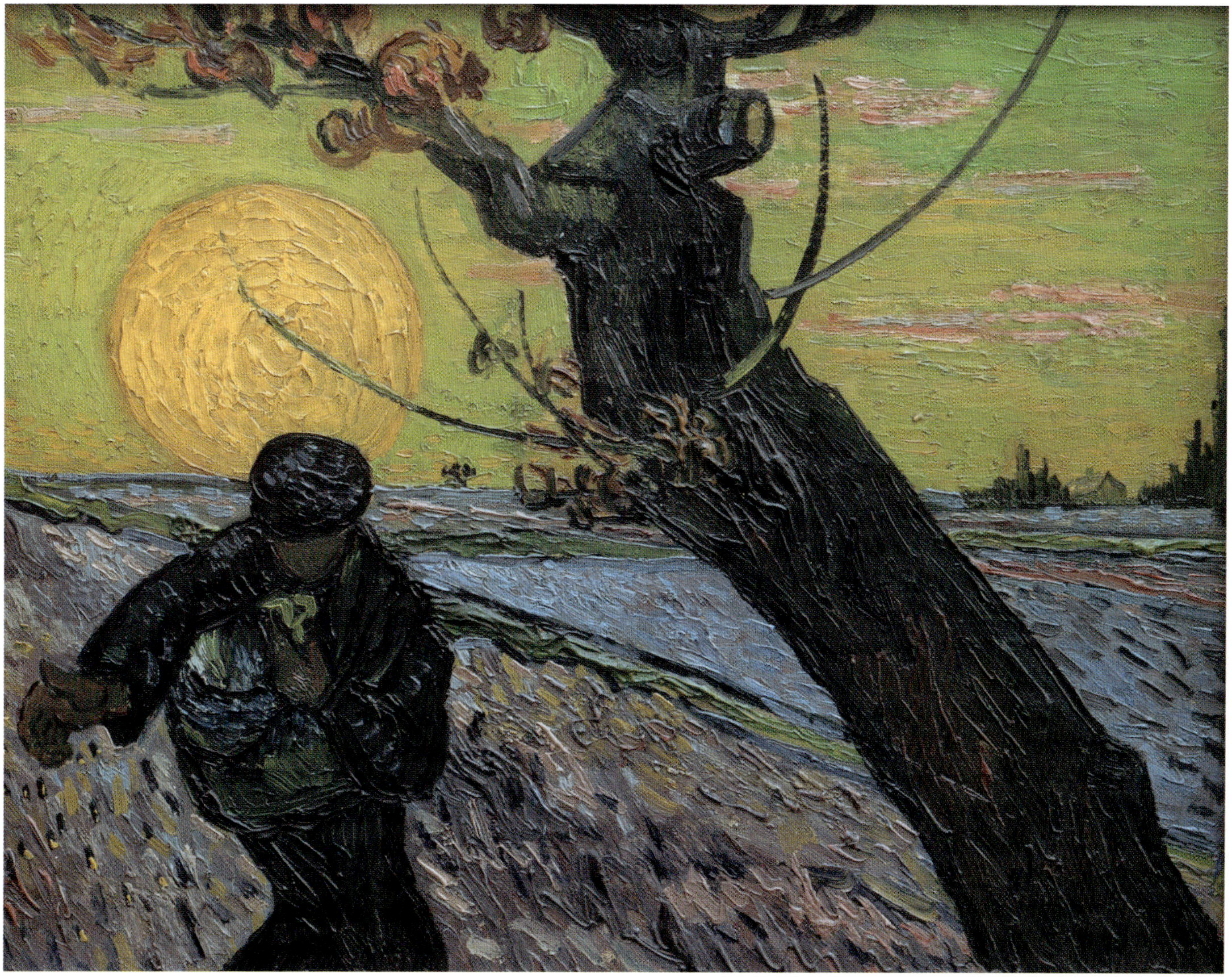

autumn, he tried a different arrangement, moving the figure to the foreground; rather than dominating the field, the sower seems to simply be passing through it. Although the figure has force, it is no longer the heroic worker portrayed by Millet. Van Gogh situates the true, enduring power in nature, represented in the old tree trunk that slices through the right side of the composition and the massive disc of the setting sun. He included a sketch of his new composition in a letter to Theo that November, describing his vivid palette: 'lemon yellow' for the sun, 'green-yellow' for a sky studded with pink clouds, a violet field and his sower in 'Prussian blue'.[2] Although his reverence for Millet never diminished – he would return to the 'Labours of the Field' for a small set of colourful paintings in 1889 – he had at last made the haunting figure his own. ●

▲

Vincent van Gogh (1853–90)
The Sower
1888, oil on canvas, 33 x 40 cm (13 x 16 in)

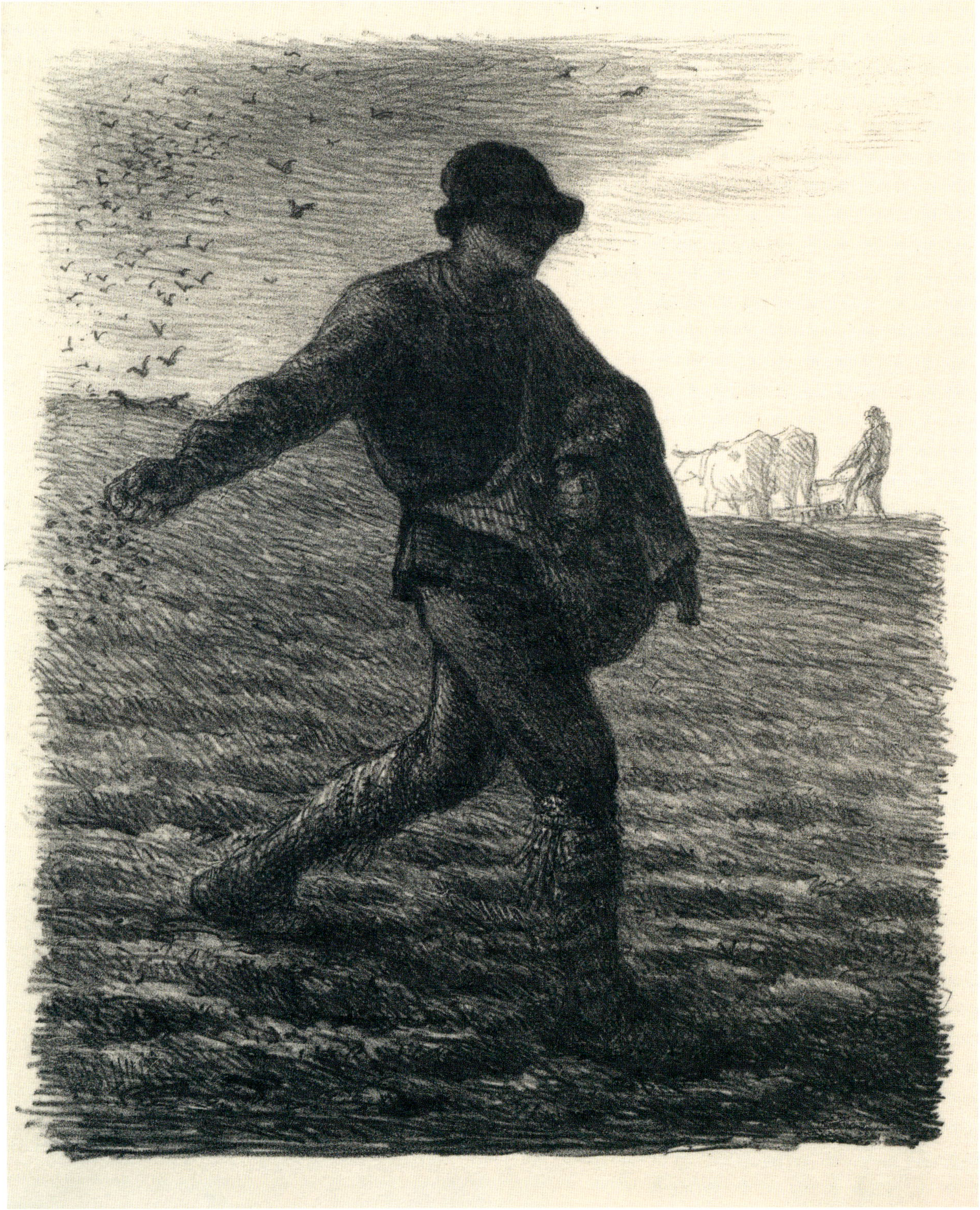

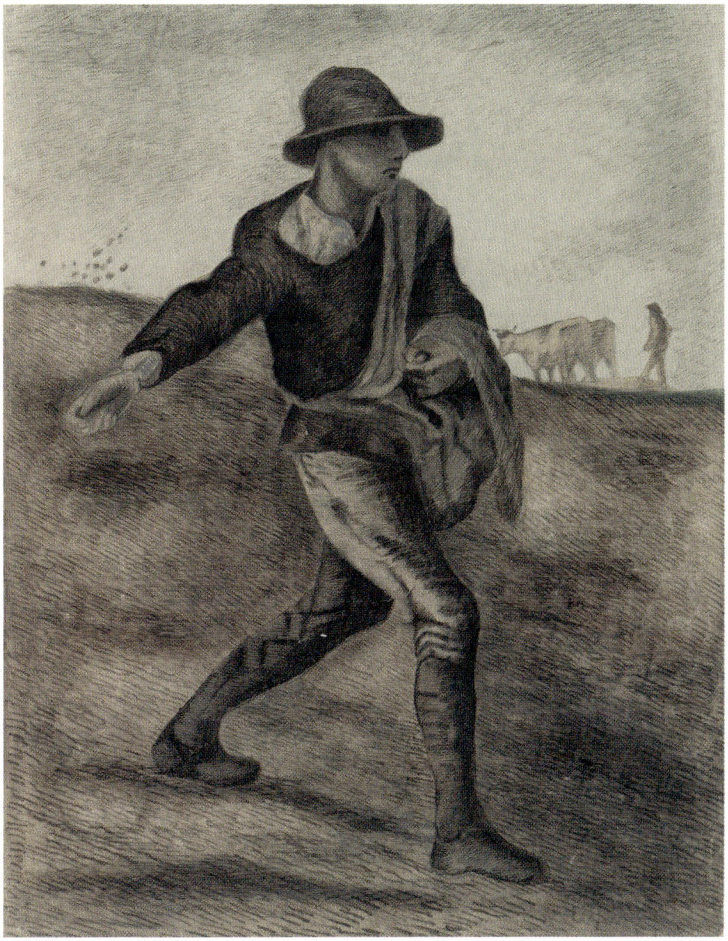

◀

Jean-François Millet (1814–75)
The Sower
1850, lithograph on thin laid paper; second (final) state 1879, 30 x 20 cm (12 x 8 in)

A lithograph of *The Sower* was released within a year of the painting's debut at the official Salon, where it was praised for its energetic movement. In contrast to the traditionally humble depiction of agricultural workers, Millet conceived the sower as a heroic figure, as confident and grandly proportioned as a classical athlete. Van Gogh never saw the painting, and it is uncertain whether he had a copy of the lithograph or worked from an etching made after the lithograph in 1873.

▲

Vincent van Gogh
The Sower (*after Millet*)
1881, pencil, pen, brush and ink, watercolour on paper, 48 x 37 cm (19 x 15 in)

Van Gogh's copy of *The Sower* presents a less heroic figure with slighter proportions. The swinging motion of the arm lacks the grace and power of the original; the stride is shorter, less confident. Van Gogh's point of view is higher, reducing the dominance of the figure's position. The sower's defined facial features and the differentiation between his undershirt and smock humanizes but diminishes the figure, making it appear more of a man than an icon. This is one of many copies that Van Gogh made.

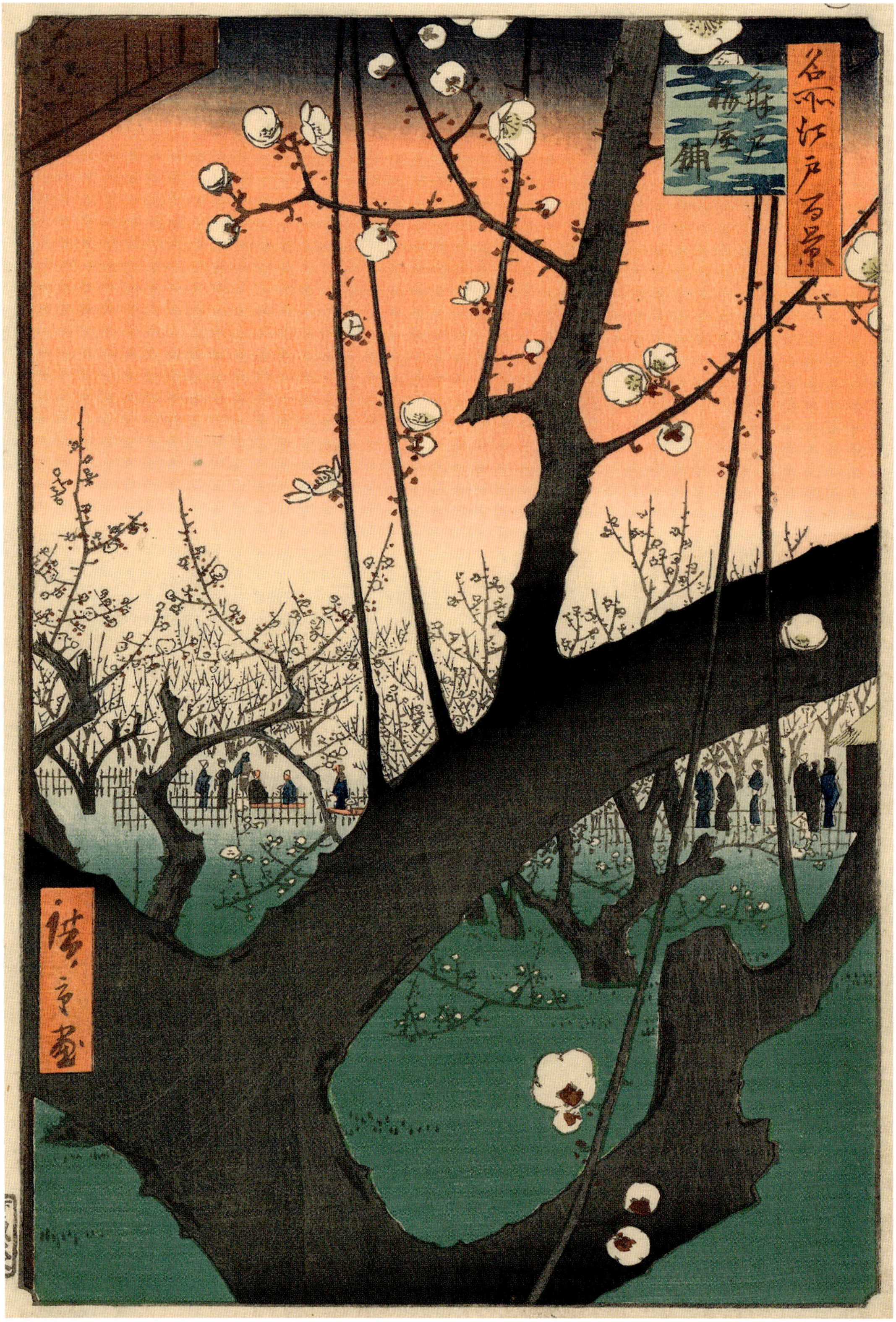
名所江戸百景

◀ ▼

Utagawa Hiroshige (1797–1858)
The Plum Garden at Kameido
from 'One Hundred Famous Views of Edo'
1857, colour woodblock print, 35 x 23 cm (14 x 9 in)

Vincent van Gogh
Flowering Plum Orchard (*after Hiroshige*)
1887, oil on canvas, 56 x 47 cm (22 x 19 in)

Van Gogh began to collect Japanese prints while living in Antwerp in 1885. He was particularly intrigued by the foreground placement of bold diagonals, which offered an dynamic alternative to balanced western composition. In 1887 he copied three prints, including the *Plum Garden*. He meticulously rendered the forms and matched the saturation of the colourful inks in oil. The lessons in form and colour stayed with him, and when he painted *The Sower* a year later, he transplanted the thrusting form of Hiroshige's tree from the garden in Japan to a field in southern France.

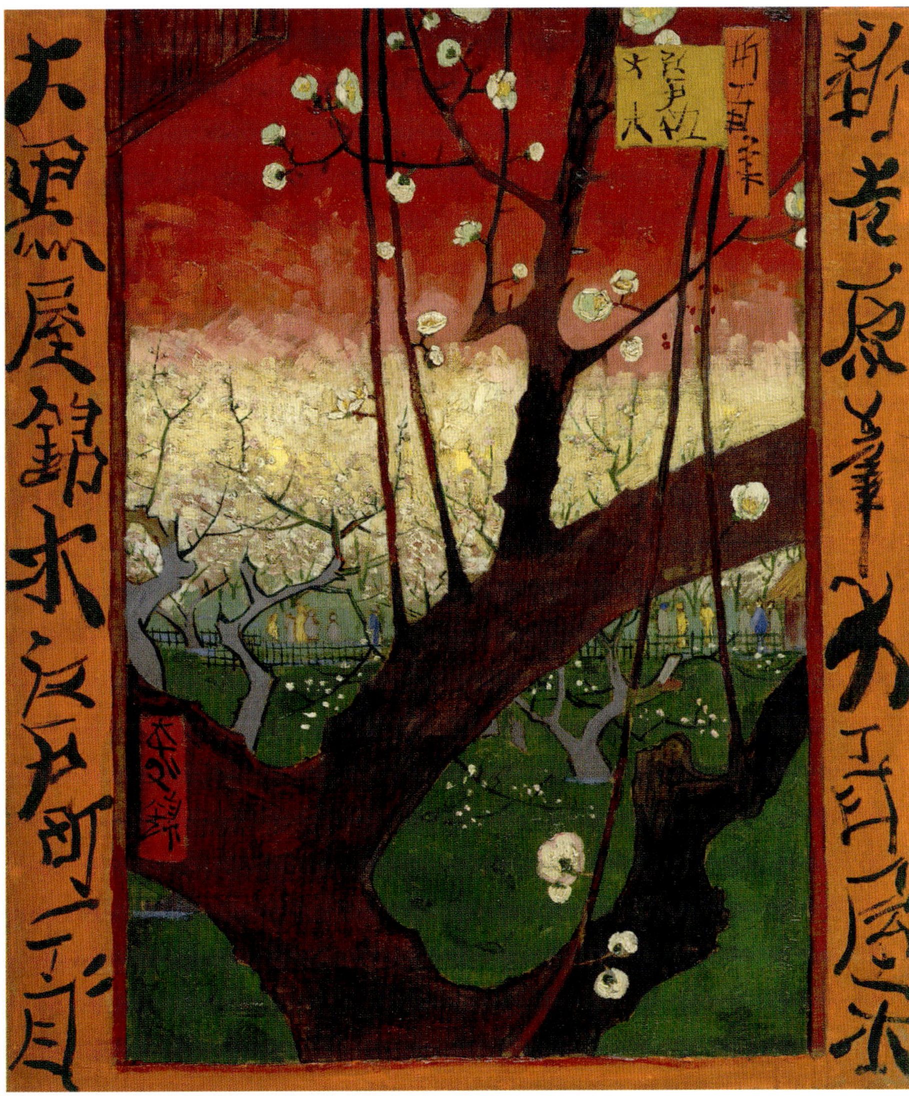

WATCH & LEARN

How Hoschedé-Monet adapted Monet's *en plein air* painting to her own style

Blanche Hoschedé met Claude Monet in 1876 when, as a rising artist, he was hired by her father, Ernest, to paint decorative panels in the dining room in their château in Montgeron. Within a year, the elder Hoschedé declared bankruptcy, and Blanche, along with her mother, Alice, and her five siblings, moved into Monet's household.[1] Monet's wife Camille died two years later, after which Monet and Alice became life companions, and he embraced her children as his own. Monet welcomed Blanche's keen interest and evident talent in the arts, and by the time he moved the family to Giverny in 1883, she was involved in his daily routine of preparing paints and canvases, loading the wheelbarrow to haul painting equipment into the local fields, and fetching supplies as he needed them.[2] He treated her as his apprentice, encouraging her to set up her own easel to try her hand at the subject of the day.

As a young painter, Monet approached his work in a spirit of camaraderie, urging his friends to come along on *plein-air* expeditions and inviting them to his home to paint in his garden. However, by the time he settled in Giverny, he preferred a solitary practice; only a rare guest was invited to join him at work. Increasingly taciturn, he turned away young artists who sought his advice, but with Blanche it was different. It is not clear when she took on the role of assistant, but by the mid-1880s they had forged a relationship that was mutually beneficial, resembling a traditional apprenticeship in that she learned while helping the master, observing his practice and absorbing any instruction he wished to share. He, in turn, respected her identity as an artist, giving her career advice and showing her work to patrons, as well as painting several portraits of her working at her easel. Also, at this time, Monet began to paint the distinctive grain stacks that appeared cyclically in the local farmer's fields and, working alongside him, Blanche painted them too.

This depiction of grain stacks under an autumn sun reveals that while Blanche fully absorbed her stepfather's example of capturing the visual sensations of light and atmosphere in dazzling colour, she did not simply mimic his style and subject. In this case, she has painted not the traditional, conical stacks featured in Monet's famed series, but a group of stooks (*moyettes*) – upright, pyramidal forms, secured at the top.

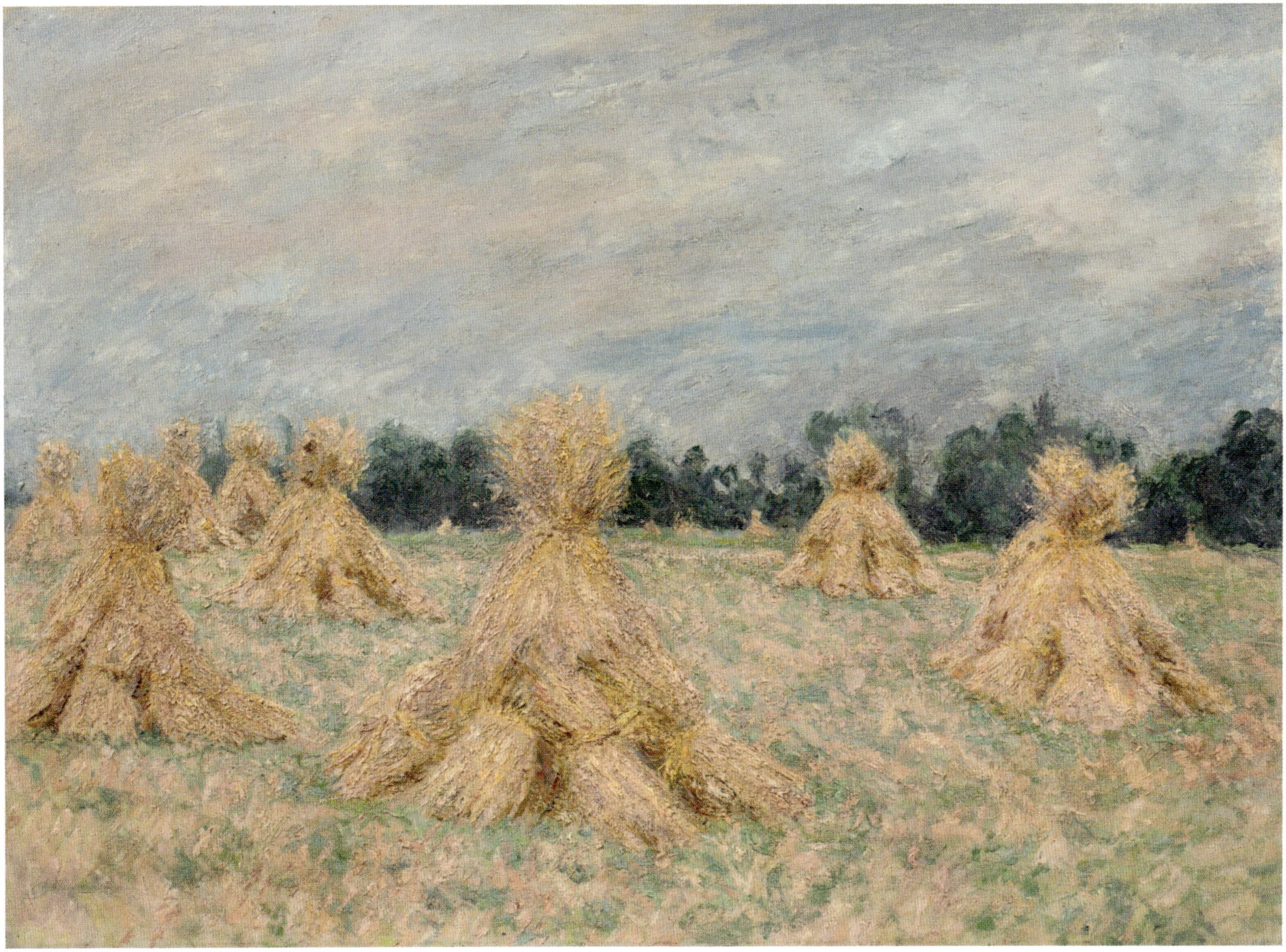

The more angular shapes are emphasized with a linear stroke that she carries throughout the depiction, to create a more cohesive view of the landscape that Monet achieved with his deft yet jabbing brush marks. Her palette, seen here in the gold-russet tones of the field, the rich blue-greens of the distant forest, and the volatile, rose-pink clouds is warm and suffused with light. Blanche remained in Giverny until 1897, when she married Monet's eldest son, Jean, and they moved to Rouen. However, she often visited, continuing to paint with her father-in-law and reprising his iconic subjects with a fresh point of view. ●

▲

Blanche Hoschedé-Monet (1865–1947)
La Moisson (Les Moyettes)
c. 1894, oil on canvas, 54 x 73 cm (21 x 29 in)

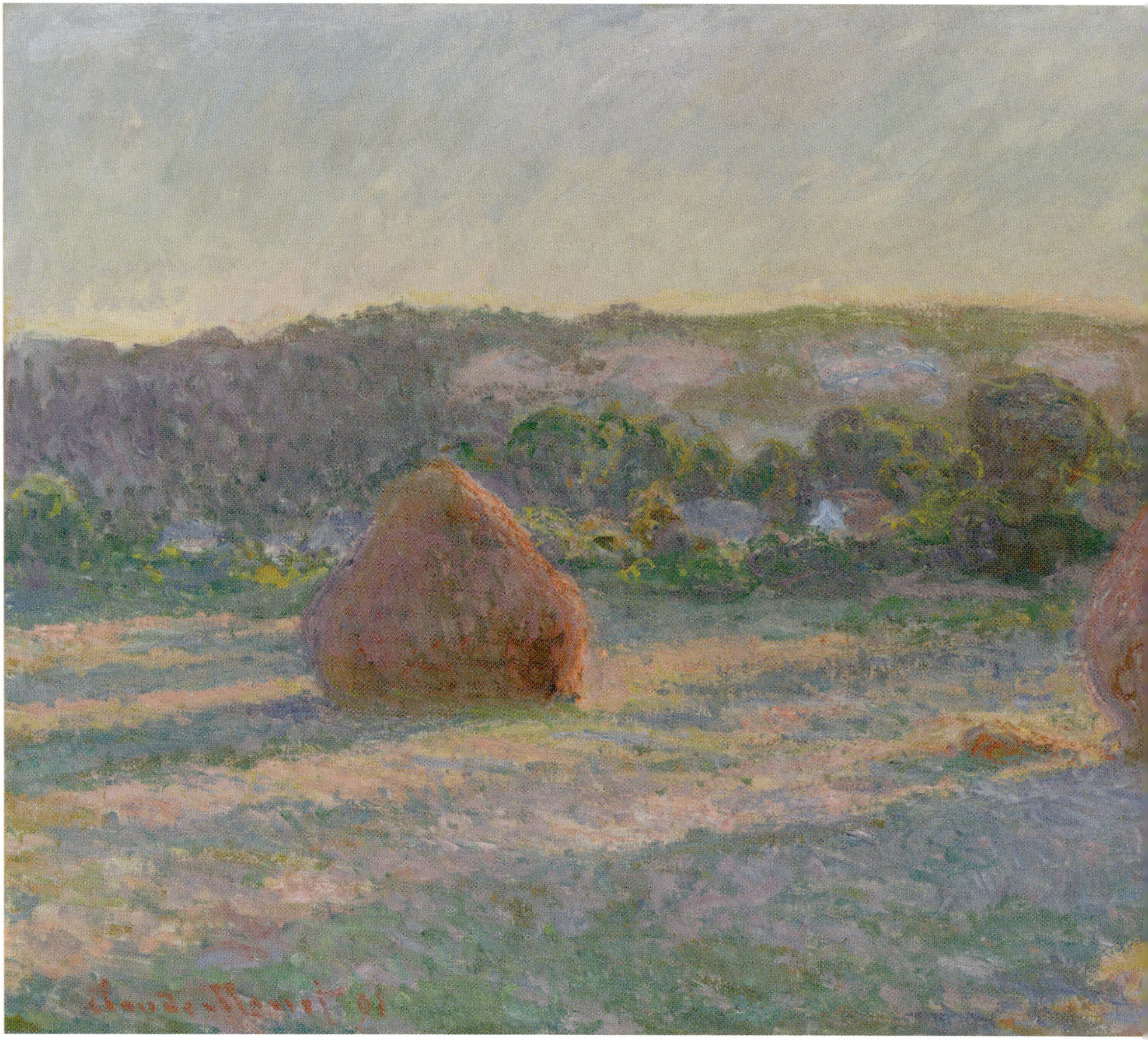

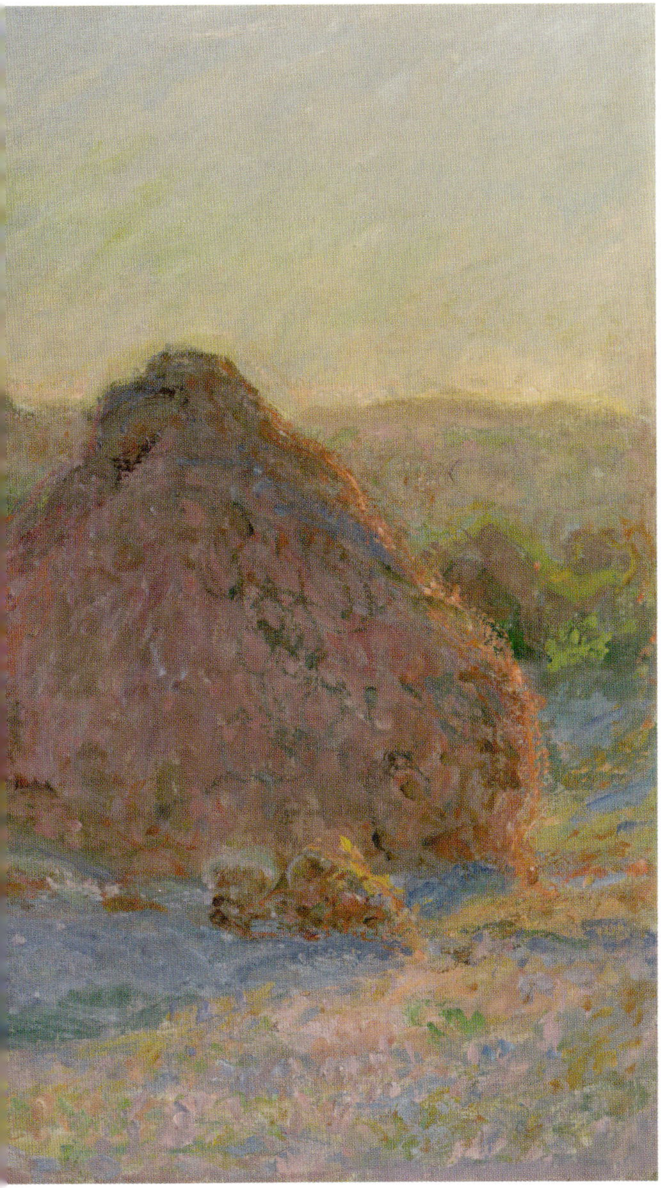

Claude Monet (1840–1926)
Haystacks, End of Summer
1890/91, oil on canvas, 60 x 100 cm (24 x 39 in)

The haystacks gave Monet a solid, stable surface on which he could observe the ephemeral effects of light. Blanche's assistance was essential in what he called his 'campaign'. As the day wore on she handed him different canvases and a fresh palette so he could capture the fleeting effects without interruption. His portrayal of late summer sun features a slightly muted tonality, evoking the dusk of dying light. Blanche also painted these haystacks, in warmer, richer hues, but her approach was the same, focusing upon light and atmosphere rather than the landscape.

Berthe Morisot (1841–95)
Hanging the Laundry out to Dry
1875, oil on canvas, 33 x 40 cm (13 x 16 in)

Morisot took up *plein-air* painting early in her career, well before she struck up a friendship with Monet. Rather than hauling her supplies out to a rural field, Morisot set up her easel in elegant Parisian parks. She painted the countryside when on holiday, often from a balcony or window of the family's summer house. Here she demonstrates her ability to translate the sensation of seasonal warmth and sunlight into pure, luminous colour.

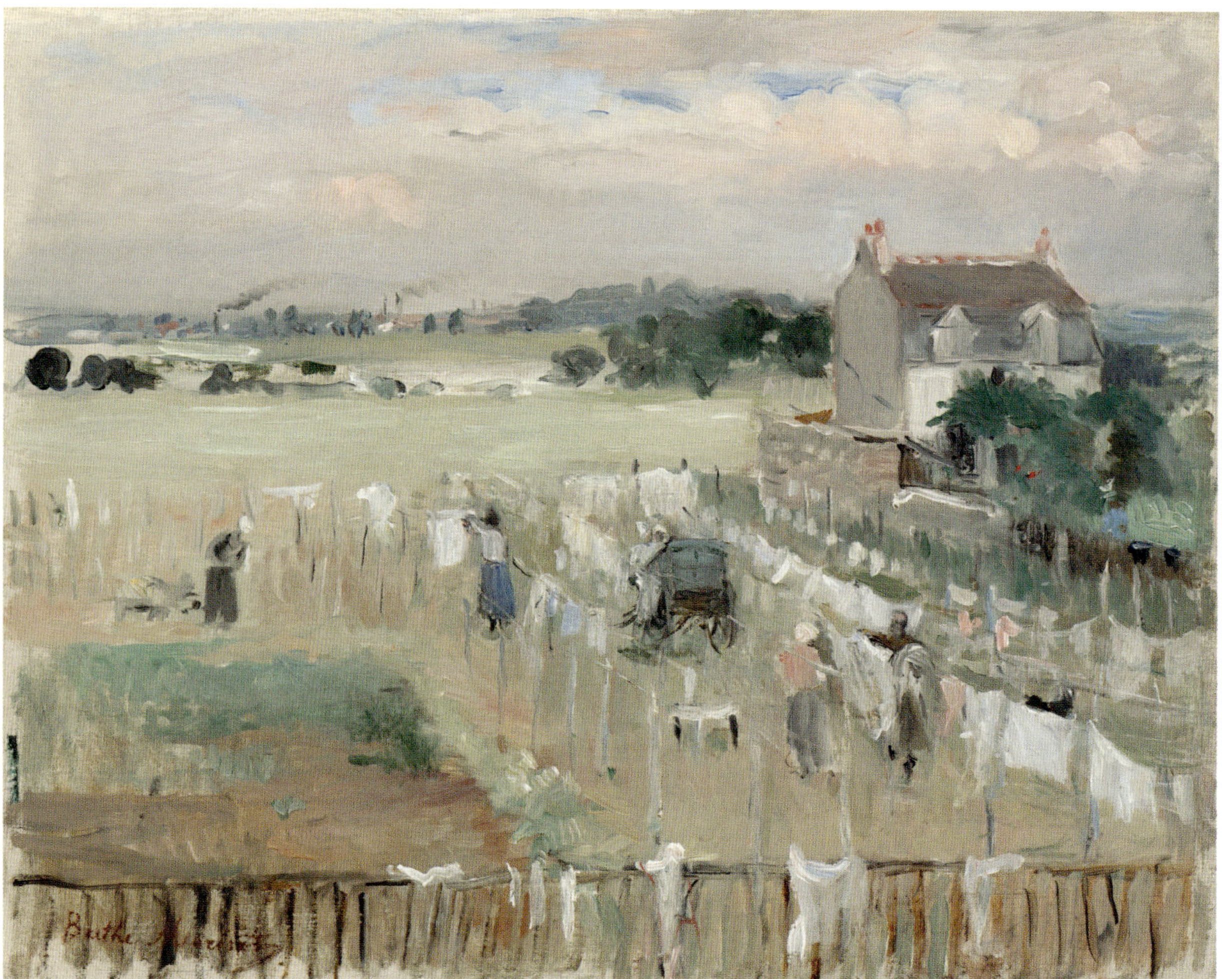

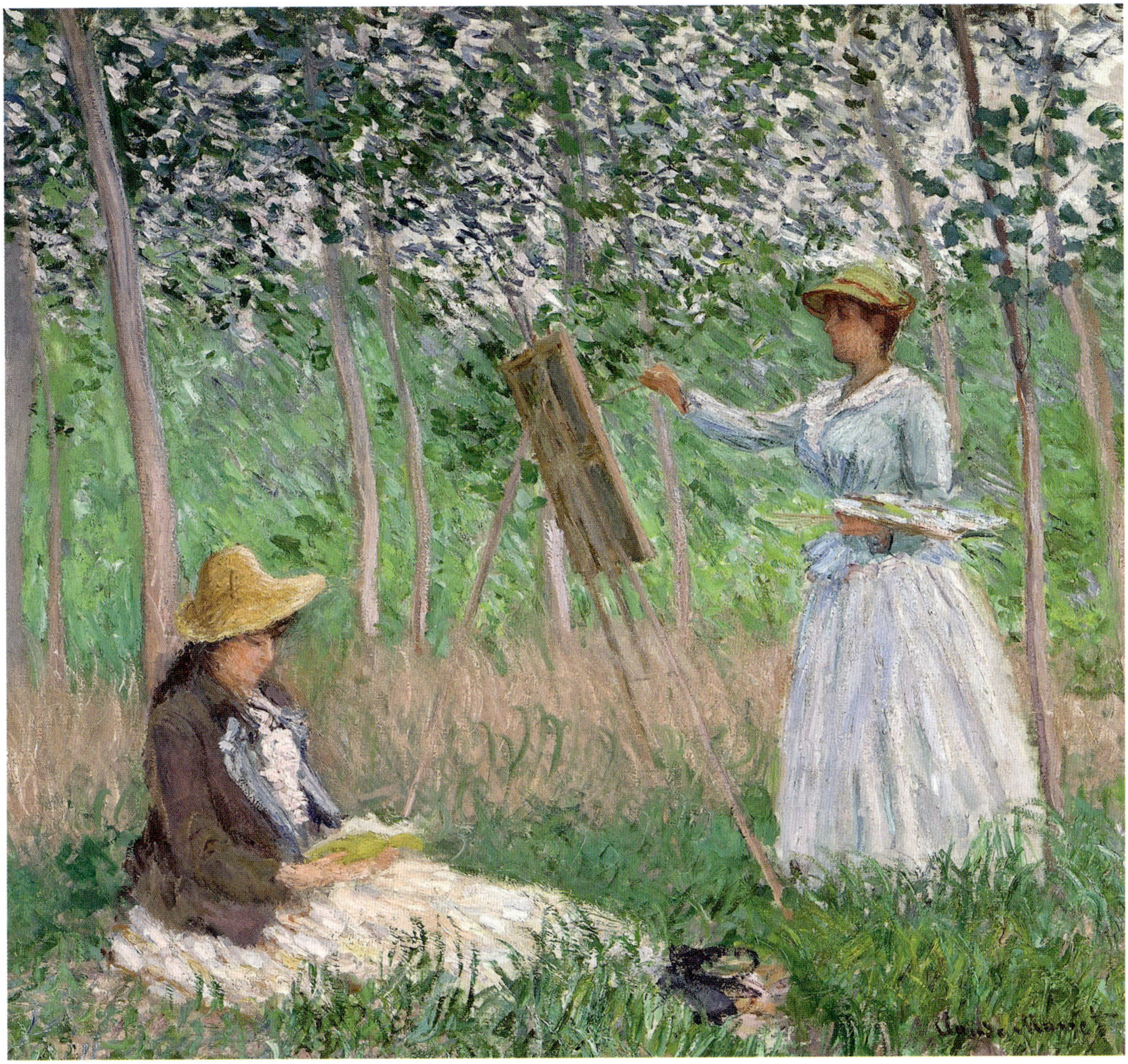

▲

Claude Monet
In the Woods at Giverny, Blanche Hoschedé at Her Easel with Suzanne Hoschedé Reading
1887, oil on canvas, 91 x 97 cm (36 x 38 in)

In his portraits of Blanche at her easel, Monet conveys her sense of purpose. Here, in a cool grove of trees with the sunlight sparkling through the branches, she stands roughly an arm's length from her canvas, giving her a simultaneous view of her subject and her painting. She appears to paint with her whole body: riveted gaze, upright posture, applying her mark with control that runs from shoulder to hand. Unlike her sister, Suzanne, who whiles away her time reading, Blanche is at work, painting in the open air.

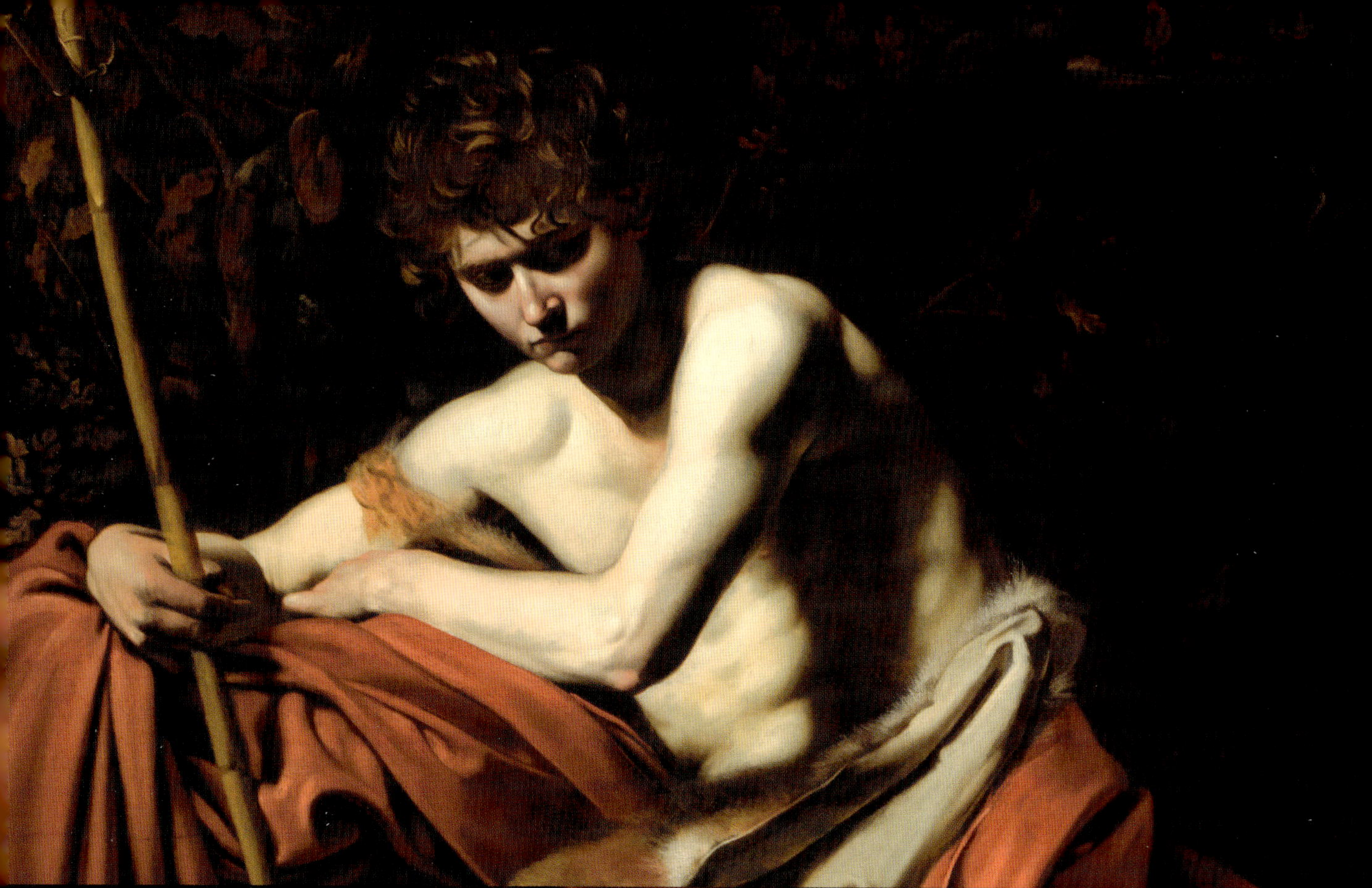
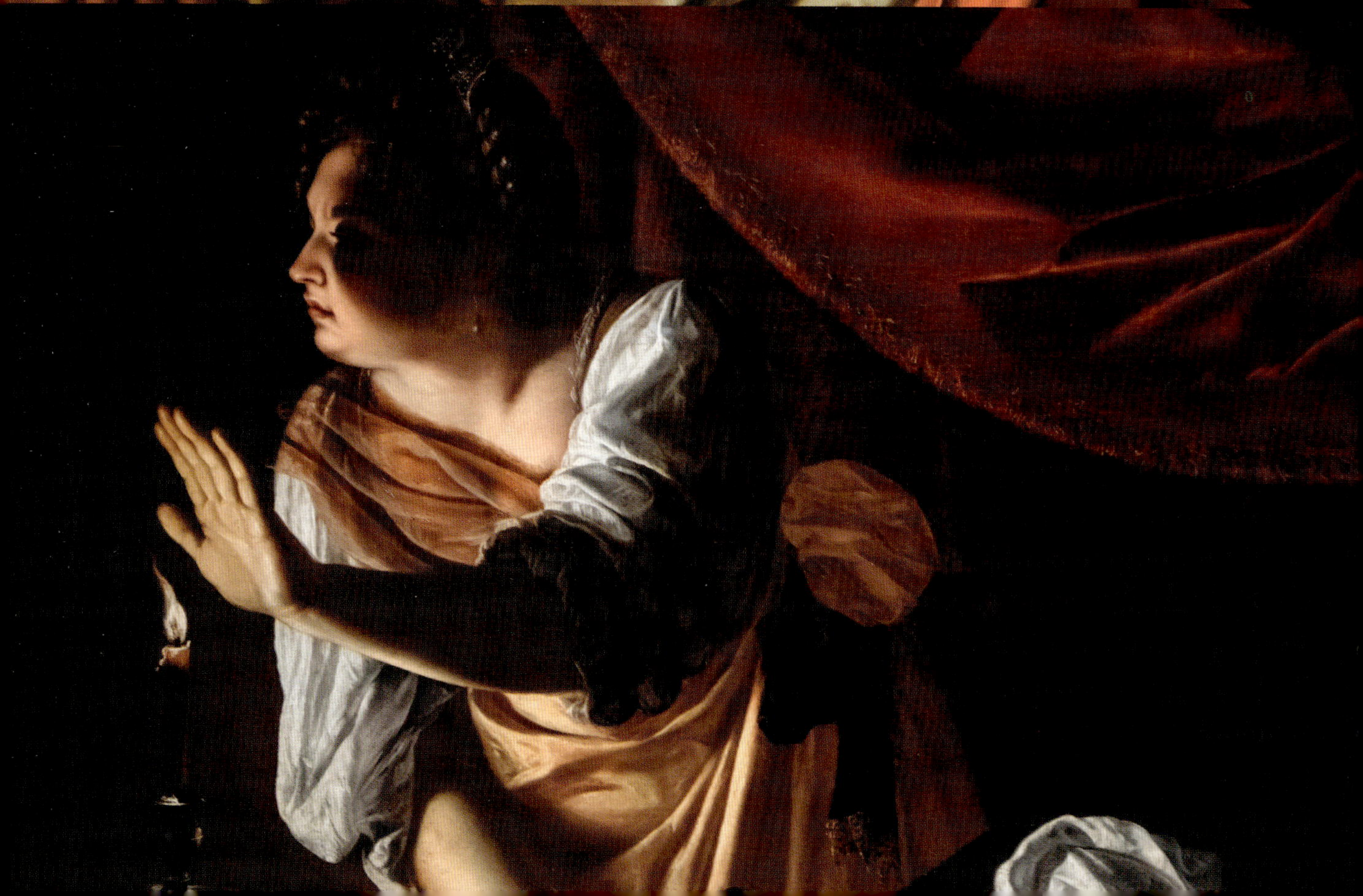

CREATIVE EXCHANGE

Artists steal from one another, taking, trading or transposing ideas to expand their own repertoire. They may be prompted by outright admiration, realizing their own potential through the lens of another's vision. One artist's innovation can be passed from generation to generation, transforming an experiment into the fuel for a movement or into a standard practice. The exchange can be mutual, collaborative or openly competitive. It does not matter whether the exchange involves a subject or style, a technique or a medium – or even permission – artists find creative inspiration in their colleagues' work.

WHAT MIGHT HAVE BEEN BUILT

How Raphael realized Bramante's grand design for St Peter's Basilica

When called to Rome by Pope Julius II to design and execute a cycle of frescos in the papal apartments in 1508, the young Raphael appeared to be an unlikely choice. Born in Urbino, he received early training from his father, the moderately talented Giovanni Santi, who died before Raphael reached adolescence. His subsequent training has not been fully traced, but by the time he sought work in Florence in 1504, his ability to express beauty and serenity, notably in his depiction of the Madonna in tranquil outdoor settings, won wide acclaim. This new – and supremely prestigious – commission demanded a monumental approach beyond his previous work. The chamber where the Pope signed the most significant documents – the Stanza della Segnatura – was to be decorated with allegorical representations of theology, philosophy, law and poetry. Although Raphael had little experience in this type of challenge, he had learned to glean ideas from older, more accomplished, artists. And he applied this skill in his design for *Philosophy* (later to be known as *The School of Athens*), a gathering of the great thinkers of the classical and contemporary world.[1] The steal is in the setting, which Raphael based on a building currently under construction: Donato Bramante's Basilica of St Peter, designed to signal a new era of power for the Roman Catholic church.

The original basilica was founded by Constantine I – the Roman emperor who adopted Christianity as the state religion – in the mid-fourth century. Believed to be the site of St Peter's burial, it was the church where the Pope celebrated mass. Over the centuries, St Peter's drew vast numbers of pilgrims, and the immediate surroundings were filled with makeshift markets and hostels. By the time Julius II ascended to the papacy in 1503, the building had fallen into disrepair. The Pope viewed it as a symbol of decay, and despite nearly a thousand years of history, he had the building demolished and the site cleared for a glorious new basilica. Julius chose Bramante as his architect, who quickly produced a daring and grandiose plan to please the Pope. His design featured Roman elements enlarged to an unprecedented scale, linking the classical past with the Christian present, as well as proclaiming Julius'

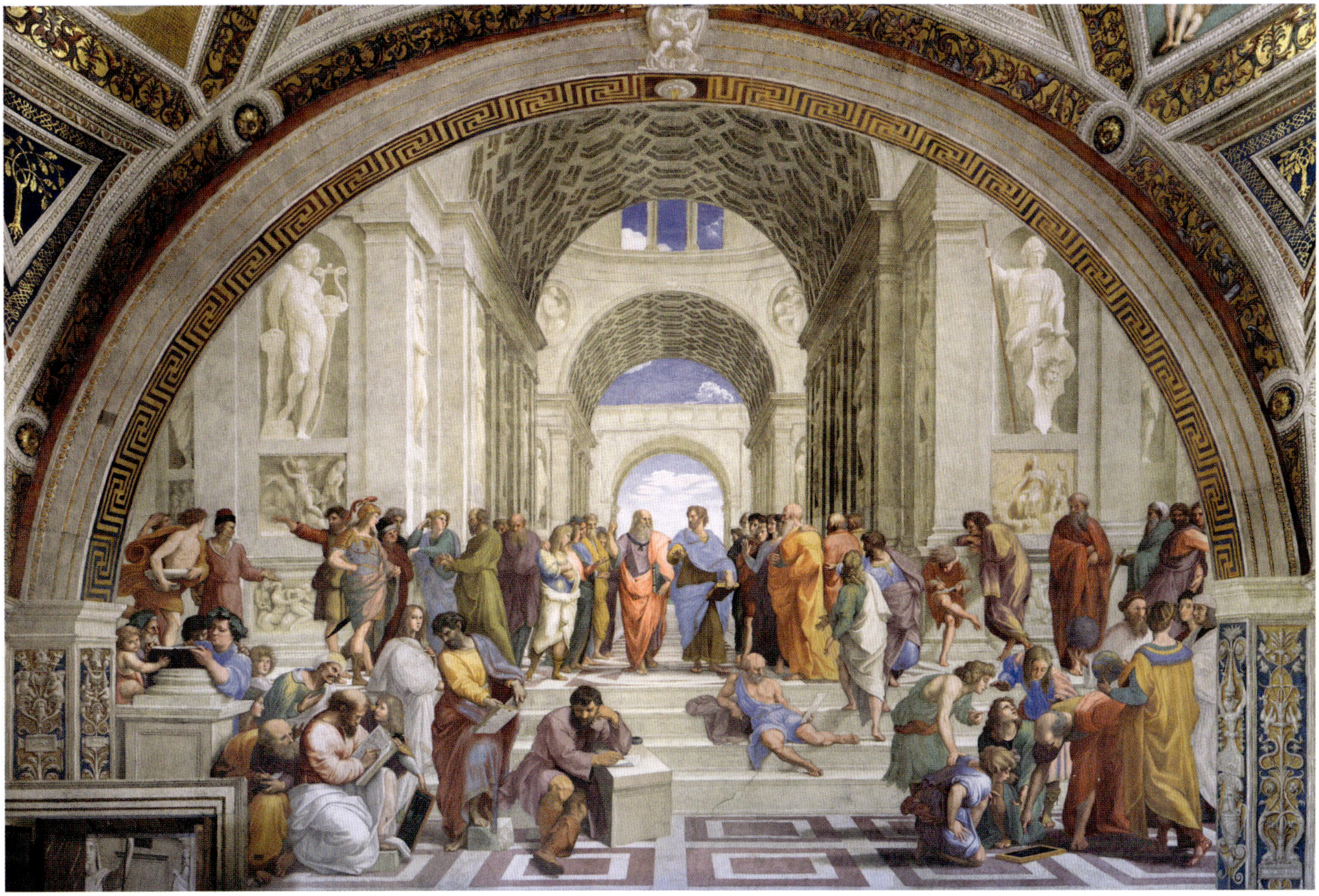

imperial vision for the papal state. However, when Julius died in 1513, with Bramante dying just a year later, only the central supporting walls stood on the site and the exterior plan was known solely through a medal struck for the ground breaking in 1506.[2]

In *The School of Athens*, Raphael personified philosophic thought as a lively debate over the Ideal (represented by Plato pointing skywards) and the Real (signified by Aristotle gesturing to the earth). They are surrounded by founders of ancient philosophy and science, including Socrates, Pythagoras, Euclid and Ptolemy. Raphael portrayed a number of these figures in the guise of his contemporaries. Plato's leonine beard and craggy visage resembles that of Leonardo da Vinci. Seated alone in the front foreground, Heraclitus, wearing a sculptor's dusty tunic and boots, has Michelangelo's broken nose and sulking demeanour. In the lower right corner, a bald man bends over a slate, while a group of eager young men cluster around him; the figure is Euclid, the Father of Geometry, in the likeness of Bramante. The reference to the architect is further proclaimed in the vast architectural space featuring coffered

▲

Raphael (1483–1520)
The School of Athens
1509–11, fresco, 500 x 770 m (197 x 303 in)

barrel vaults and a soaring central dome. Light fills the interior, as if the architecture opens to the sky. Raphael's familiarity with the plan – and even his connection with Bramante – cannot be precisely stated, but they were both working towards the same end: to celebrate the papacy and the reigning Pope.[3] When Bramante died, Raphael took over as supervising architect until his own death. Other architects followed in the century-long project, and Bramante's original idea was subsumed into a design just as majestic but far more conventional.[4] It is through Raphael's depiction, however, based on a building yet to be built, that we can still admire Bramante's own grand design. ●

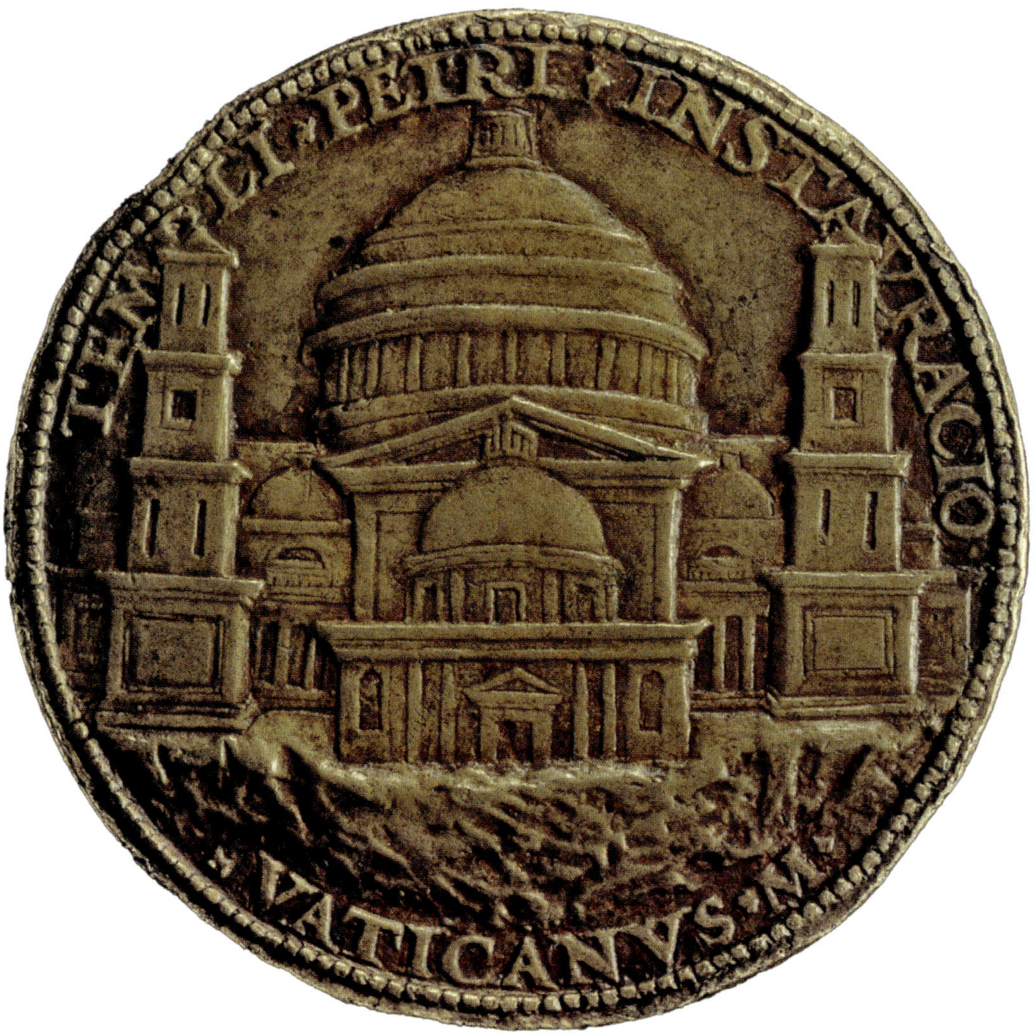

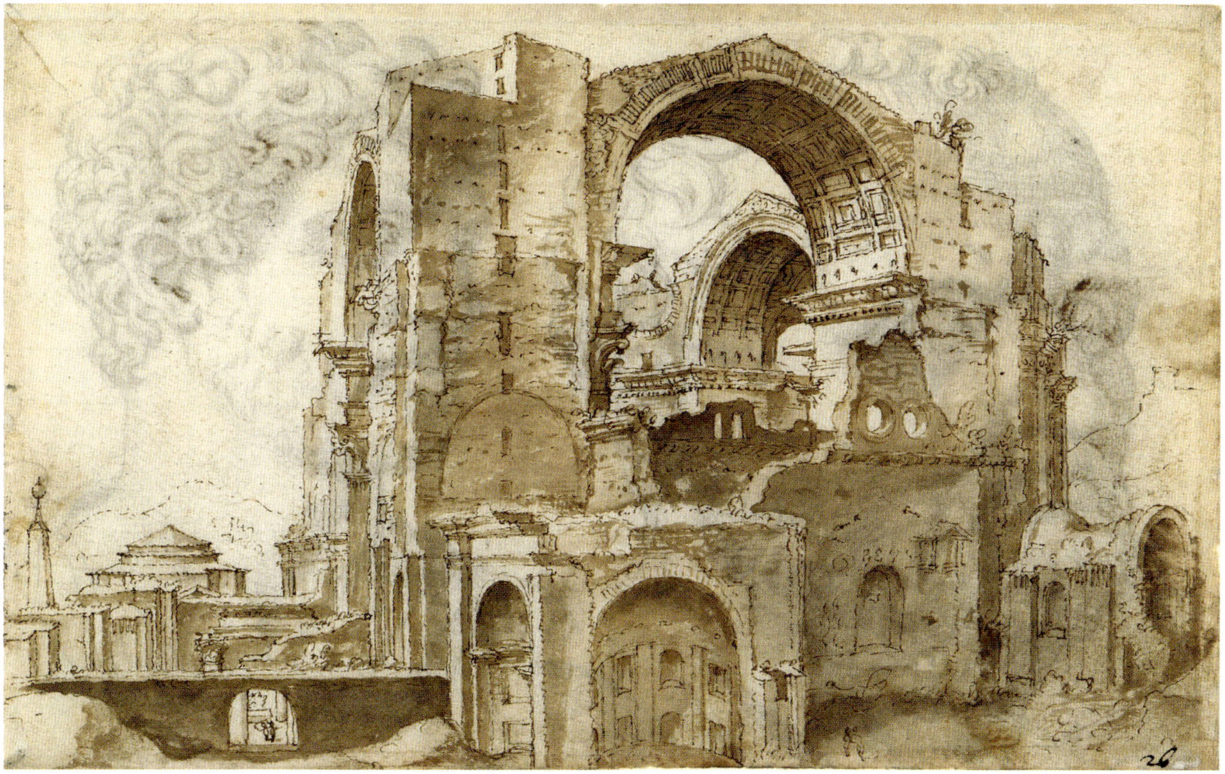

◀

Attributed to Caradosso Foppa (1445–*c.* 1527)
Medal featuring a view of St Peter's Basilica, after Bramante's design
c. 1506, cast bronze, 6 cm (2 in) diameter

The reverse of this commemorative medal depicts Bramante's concept for St Peter's Basilica, featuring a Greek cross plan crowned with a dome resting on a colonnade. The Latin inscription describes the design as a 'restoration'. In fact, the plan was to replace, not renovate, the fourth-century cruciform basilica. There is no known image of the interior design aside from a partial floor plan. A portrait of Pope Julius II is on the obverse of this medal; as the patron he is given pride of place.

▲

Maarten van Heemskerck (1498–1574)
Crossing Pillar of St Peter's Basilica (Roman Sketchbook)
c. 1532–36, brown ink, pen and brush, brown and grey wash on paper, 14 x 20 cm (5 x 8 in)

Van Heemskerck visited the Vatican shortly after the Sack of Rome (1527–28), when, due to lack of funds, construction was nearly at a standstill. While the site itself was in disarray, this wash and pen rendering offers a good view of coffered vaults and supporting piers (for the dome) similar to those in *The School of Athens*. Compared to Raphael's majestic depiction, the building seems, in the drawing, to be more a ruin than a work in progress. At the time, Antonio da Sangallo the Younger presided as architect.

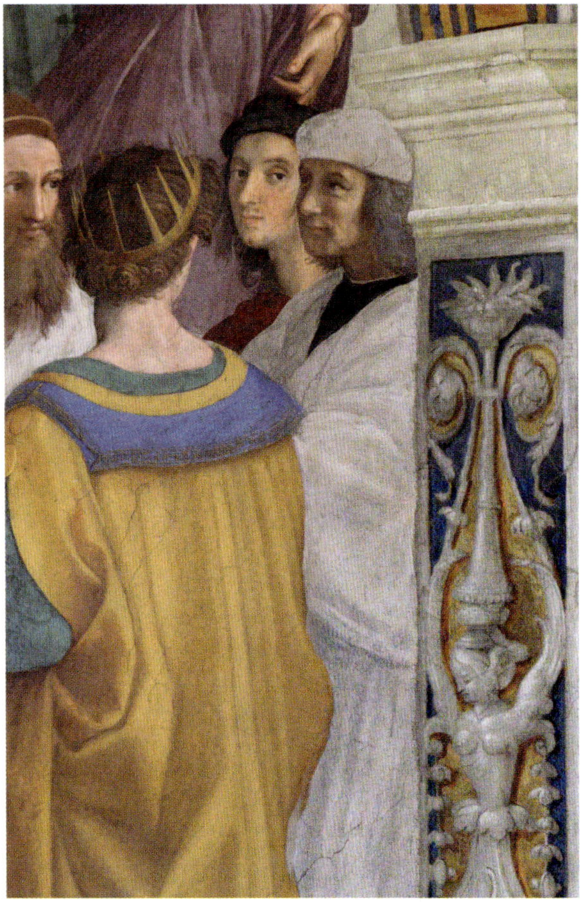

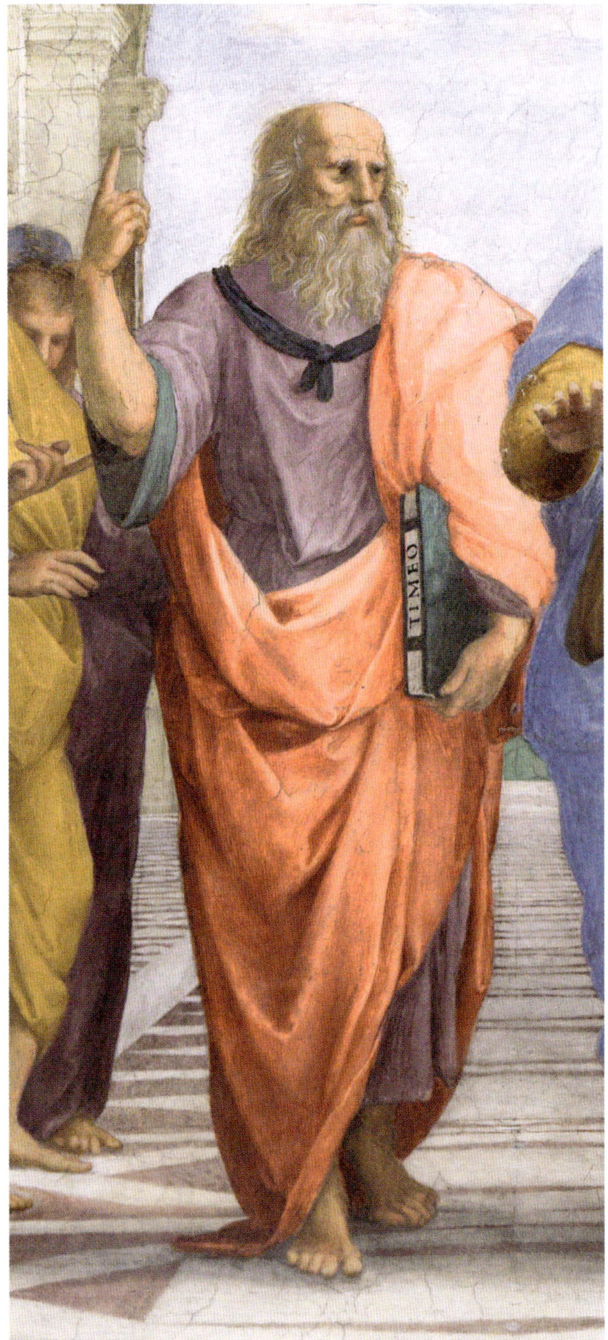

▲

Raphael
Detail of a self-portrait of Raphael from
The School of Athens

Raphael included his own likeness, tucked into a narrow space roughly a third above from the lower right corner. He wears a dark cap and peers out at the viewer. He is the only figure to do so; it was a common motif for a self-portrait at the time. The figure next to him gazes at the scene and smiles in approval. He is identified as Il Sodoma, Julius' first choice for the fresco commission; he had hardly begun when Julius fired him to replace him with Raphael.

Raphael
Detail of Plato from *The School of Athens*

With his bald pate and flowing beard, Plato bears a strong resemblance to Leonardo da Vinci. Raphael was among the many admirers who visited Leonardo's Florentine studio in 1504 when he was painting *La Gioconda* (*Mona Lisa*). Shortly afterwards, Raphael produced a drawing of a woman featuring a similar gown and headdress in exactly the same pose. Copying and adapting expanded Raphael's skill; perhaps this portrait is an acknowledgment to an unsuspecting master.

Raphael
Detail of Bramante as Euclid, drawing on a slate, from *The School of Athens*

The historical record implies a connection between Bramante and Raphael, but nothing can be verified. The sixteenth-century writer Vasari asserted that they were distant relatives, but did not specify the relationship. Bramante was born in Fermignano near Urbino; being much older, he had left the region before Raphael was born. Here, in contrast to the other scholars whose tools are books, Raphael depicts Euclid drawing, a tribute, perhaps, to the architect Bramante's profession.

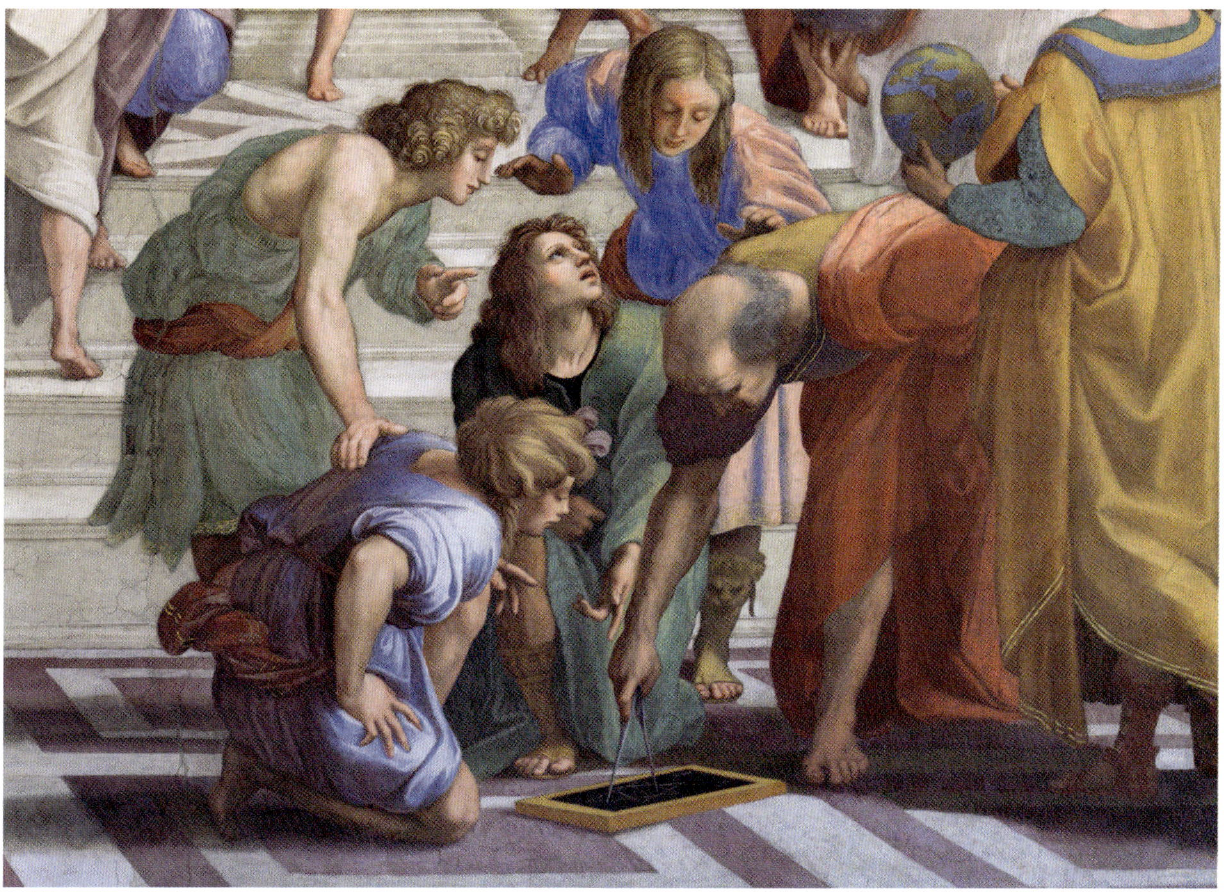

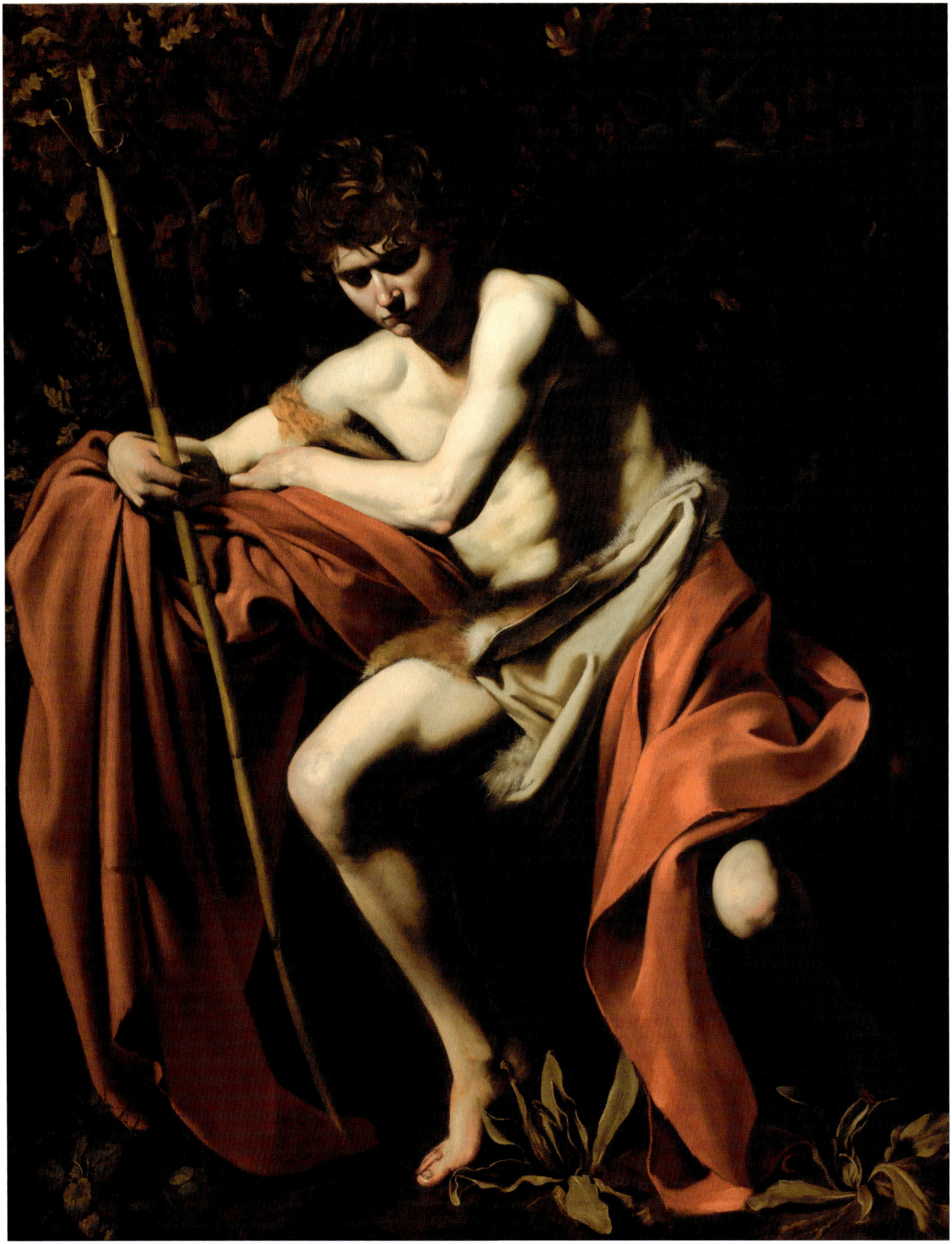

PASSING THE TORCH

How Caravaggio's dramatic use of light inspired generations

Prior to the opening of the Contarelli Chapel in San Luigi dei Francesi in Rome (1600), Caravaggio enjoyed a modest reputation for still life and provocative anecdotal paintings among a limited circle of patrons. His new scenes from the life of St Matthew startled the public with blunt storytelling, heighted by the dramatic play of blinding light and deep shadow. For the next ten years he portrayed saints and martyrs as they had never been seen before: rough, work-worn figures that could have walked onto the canvas straight off the Roman streets. Painted at the height of his popularity, this image of St John is almost unnervingly real. The wiry limbs and thick torso are those of a young ruffian rather than a holy hermit, and his intense expression is more sullen than devout. His tanned face, in stark contrast to the pale tone of his limbs, reveals that Caravaggio worked directly from real models, presenting them in character exactly as they appeared in life. Although Caravaggio's career was brief, his influence dominated religious art for decades, reaching far beyond those who encountered his work in Rome. Over the subsequent centuries, artists across the European continent could not resist stealing light from Caravaggio's torch.

Just as he supplanted Renaissance ideal beauty with the forms and flaws of reality, Caravaggio rejected the warm, suffused light associated with the followers of Leonardo, Raphael and Titian. Instead of the expansive vistas of Renaissance compositions, Caravaggio employed a shallow, undefined space, with the figures pushed to the surface of the picture plane and the background obscured in shadow. The light that sweeps across his canvas from an unseen source illuminates the figure for drama rather than definition; as seen in this depiction of St John, the bright glare sculpts the contour of his left arm and right thigh, while casting much of his brooding face in shadow. It is not fully known how Carvaggio achieved these effects in his studio, and in his day, as other artists tried to discover his secret, there was much speculation.

◀

Caravaggio (1571–1610)
Saint John the Baptist in the Wilderness
1604, oil on canvas, 173 x 133 cm (68 x 52 in)

It was said that he blocked the windows in the rooms where he painted. A rumour circulated that he broke open a hole in the ceiling to illuminate his models from above. This prompted one of his followers, Spanish artist Jusepe de Ribera, to request that his landlord provide a rooftop window for his studio.[1] While Caravaggio's placement of the light source remained a mystery, artists imitated its compelling effects. Known as tenebrism (from *tenebroso*, or 'dark'), this concentrated interaction of light and dark offered a powerful alternative to the more naturalistic illumination of chiaroscuro ('light and shade').

The spread of Caravaggio's influence also defied tradition. He never cultivated students or mentored apprentices. However, his fellow painters, including Orazio Gentileschi and Bartolomeo Manfredi, regularly visited his studio to see his current work and assimilated his innovations into their own styles, sharing them, in turn, with their assistants. In the brief time that his public career flourished in Rome, Caravaggio was outstandingly productive; his paintings could be seen in church chapels and, through invitation, in the homes of his collectors. One of these, the Genoese banker Ottavio Costa so admired *Saint John the Baptist in the Wilderness*, which he had commissioned to display in a family oratory in Liguria, that he had it replicated for the original site and kept the original in Rome. And, as the reigning cultural capital of Europe in the early seventeenth century, aspiring artists flocked to Rome to see important new works, learn new techniques and – if fortunate – launch their careers with Roman patronage. From 1600 to 1630, of the 2,700 artists registered in Rome, nearly 600 had foreign origins.[2] For several decades after Caravaggio's death, artists from all over Italy, as well as from Flanders, Spain, the Netherlands and France, were drawn to Rome to study his realism, intensity, drama and light. And when they returned to their homelands they introduced new audiences to Caravaggio's ideas by making them their own. ●

▶

Artemisia Gentileschi (1593–1654)
Judith and Her Maidservant with the Head of Holofernes
c. 1623–25, oil on canvas, 187 x 142 cm (74 x 56 in)

Gentileschi's father, Orazio, was a close friend of Caravaggio. While she may have visited the painter's studio with her father, she more likely learned of Caravaggio's innovations through her father's interpretations. In a double steal, she took up one of her father's subjects and Caravaggio's lighting, the biblical heroine Judith after she has assassinated the Assyrian general Holofernes to save the forces of Israel from his assault. The small, flickering candle provides enough light to illuminate Judith's gesture as she cautions her maidservant to wait until is safe to escape.

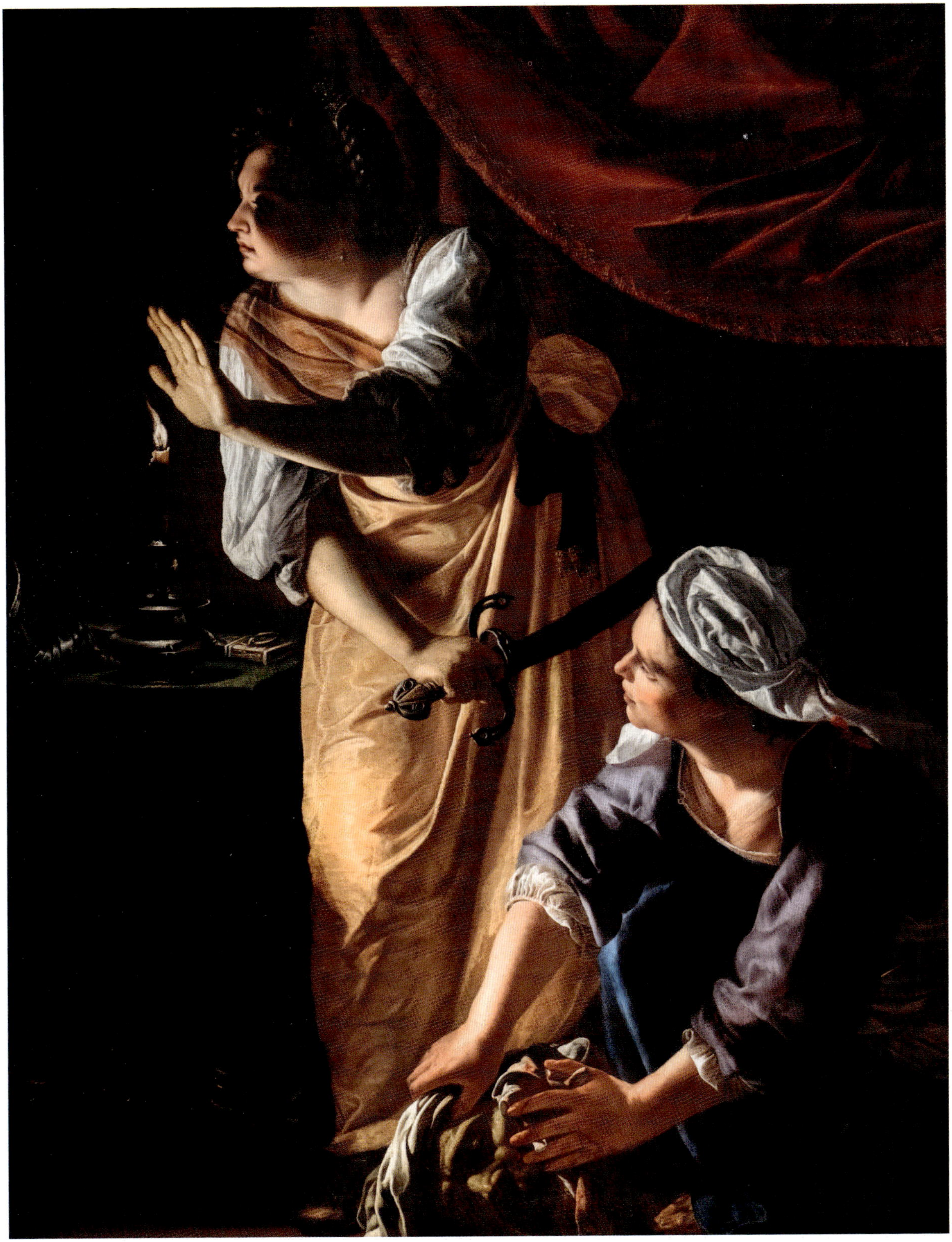

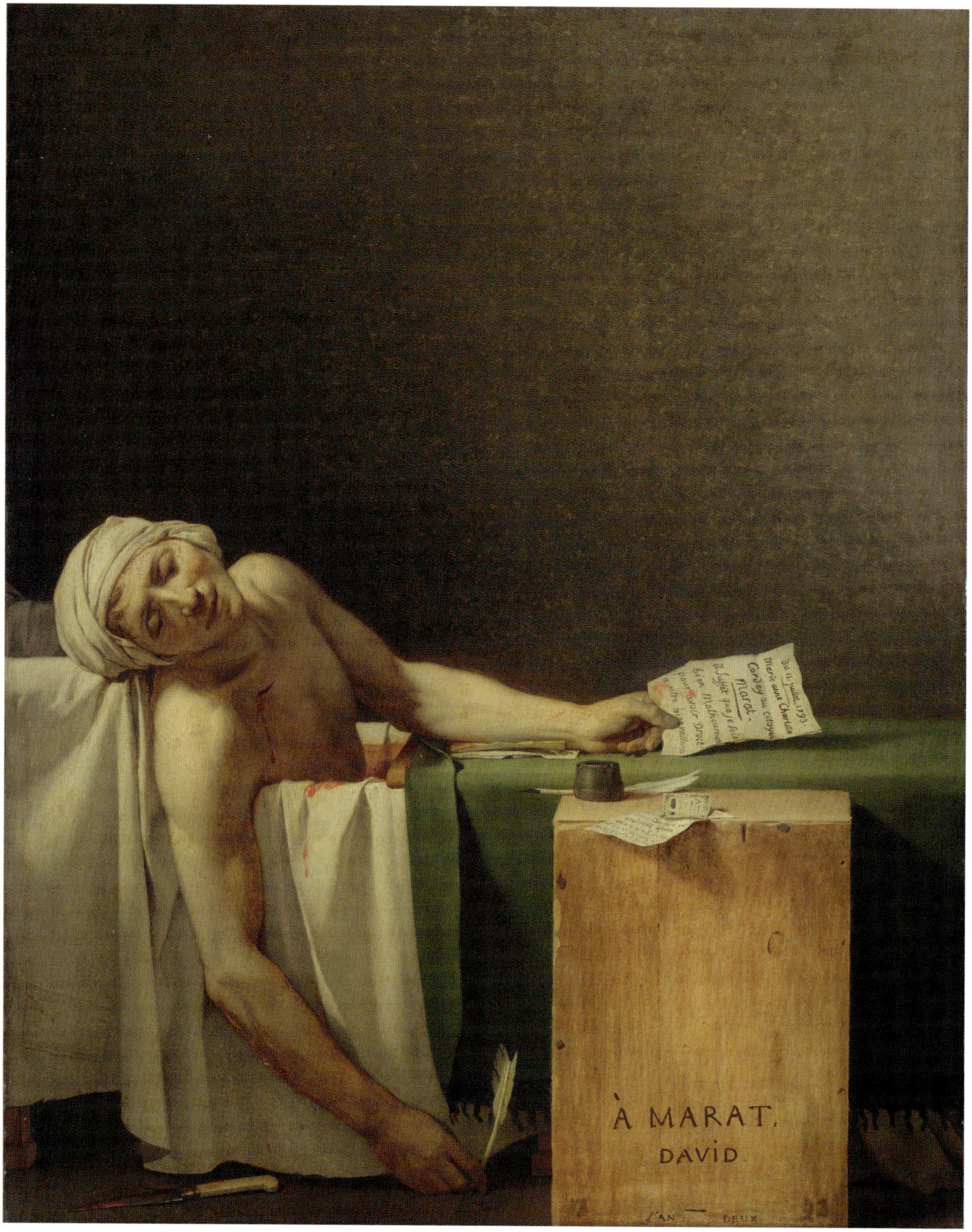
À MARAT,
DAVID

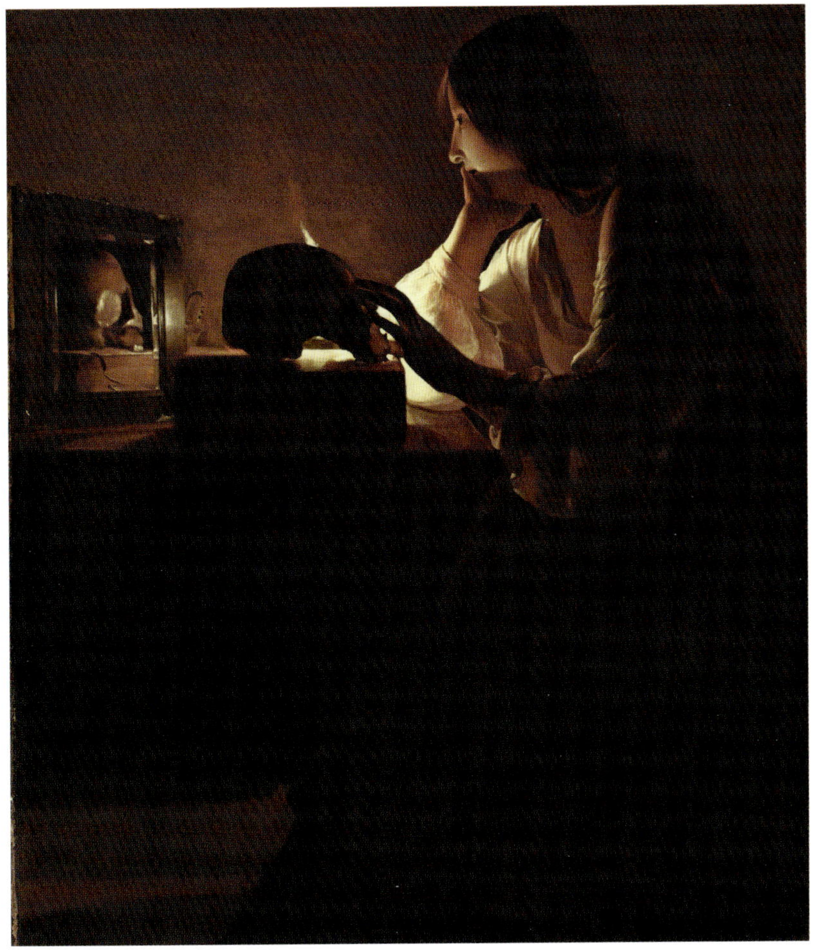

◀

Jacques-Louis David (1748–1825)
The Death of Marat
1793, oil on canvas, 162 x 128 cm (64 x 50 in)

David spent five years in Italy (from 1775 to 1780) studying ancient sculpture and the techniques of the Renaissance masters. While in Rome he also made note of Caravaggio's extraordinary manipulation of light and dark. Nowhere is this more boldly evident than in David's commemorative portrait of his friend, the publisher and fellow radical, Jean-Paul Marat. Murdered in his bathtub, he holds a paper that names his assassin. Although an invalid in life – plagued with a skin disorder – David presents Marat as a magnificent martyr, illuminated by the raking light from an unseen source.

▲

Georges de la Tour (1593–1652)
The Penitent Magdalene
c. 1635–40, oil on canvas, 113 x 92 cm (44 x 36 in)

The light source need not be hidden to unleash the full dramatic power of tenebrism. In De la Tour's depiction of Mary Magdalene, the trembling flame reveals the silhouetted form of a skull (representing vanity and transience). The Magdalene's pensive expression is in partial shadow, strongly contrasting with the harsh glare on her right arm and shoulder. As soft and subtle as it is dramatic, De la Tour's use of light casts a mood of mournful meditation. Despite speculation, there is no evidence that De la Tour ever travelled to Rome; his knowledge of Caravaggio's innovations came second hand.

A NEW VIEW

How Masanobu modernized perspective in the *Ukiyo-e* print

Okumura Masanobu's seemingly infinite capacity for innovation fuelled his rise to fame as his generation's master of the *ukiyo-e* ('pictures of the floating world') print. His prints captured the latest trends in the 'Floating World' – beautiful courtesans, cutting-edge fashions, scenes from theatrical productions and reigning celebrities – to cater to the sophisticated yet ever-changing taste of the wealthy, male patrons who frequented the Yoshiwara entertainment district of Edo (modern-day Tokyo). Masanobu's flair for novel interpretations of popular subjects secured his favoured status among collectors. However, what set him apart from rival artists in this genre was his inventive approach to woodblock printing techniques. He dusted prints with brass powder to simulate the appearance of a lacquered surface. He tinkered with traditional formats, producing large-scale horizontal prints and tall, narrow pillar prints that could be posted to advertise upcoming events. He added colour to the conventional black-on-white palette, favouring a delicate rose-red paired with subtle sage-green. His most novel creation was the *uki-e* ('perspective print'), derived from literature known as *Rangaku* ('Dutch knowledge') long-forbidden during the self-imposed isolation of Edo-era Japan (1603–1868).

The initial trade relations established by Japan with western nations in the mid-1500s were cordial, but within decades the nation adopted a policy of shunning foreign contact. In the first years of the 1600s, after centuries of conflict between warring samurai clans, the Tokugawa family seized and held power until 1868. The Tokugawa shogunate established order through military discipline, class hierarchy and rigid regulations; the clan's capital in Edo gave the era its name. To guard against alien interference – especially through religious conversion – the shogunate expelled all foreigners and banned outside trade and travel. By 1639, to all intents and purposes, Japan closed itself off from the wider world. Despite strict laws and isolation, the Edo era was notable for its prosperity, sophistication and a flourishing popular culture. And there was a singular exception to the restrictions on foreign contact; Dutch merchants were allowed to maintain a post on the artificial island of Dejima, built off the Nagasaki port, and once a year, under armed guard, a small delegation left Dejima to trade on Japanese soil. Along with western goods, the Dutch envoys introduced western technology – anatomy, astronomy, cartology, horology and weaponry – through examples of newly invented devices and illustrated manuals that explained how they worked and how to make them. This forbidden yet fascinating information became known as *Rangaku*, combining the words '*ran*' for Holland and '*gaku*' for learning.[1]

Masanobu's career coincided with the reign of the reformist shogun Tokugawa Yoshimune (ruled 1716–45) who encouraged *Rangaku*, particularly through the importation and translation of select

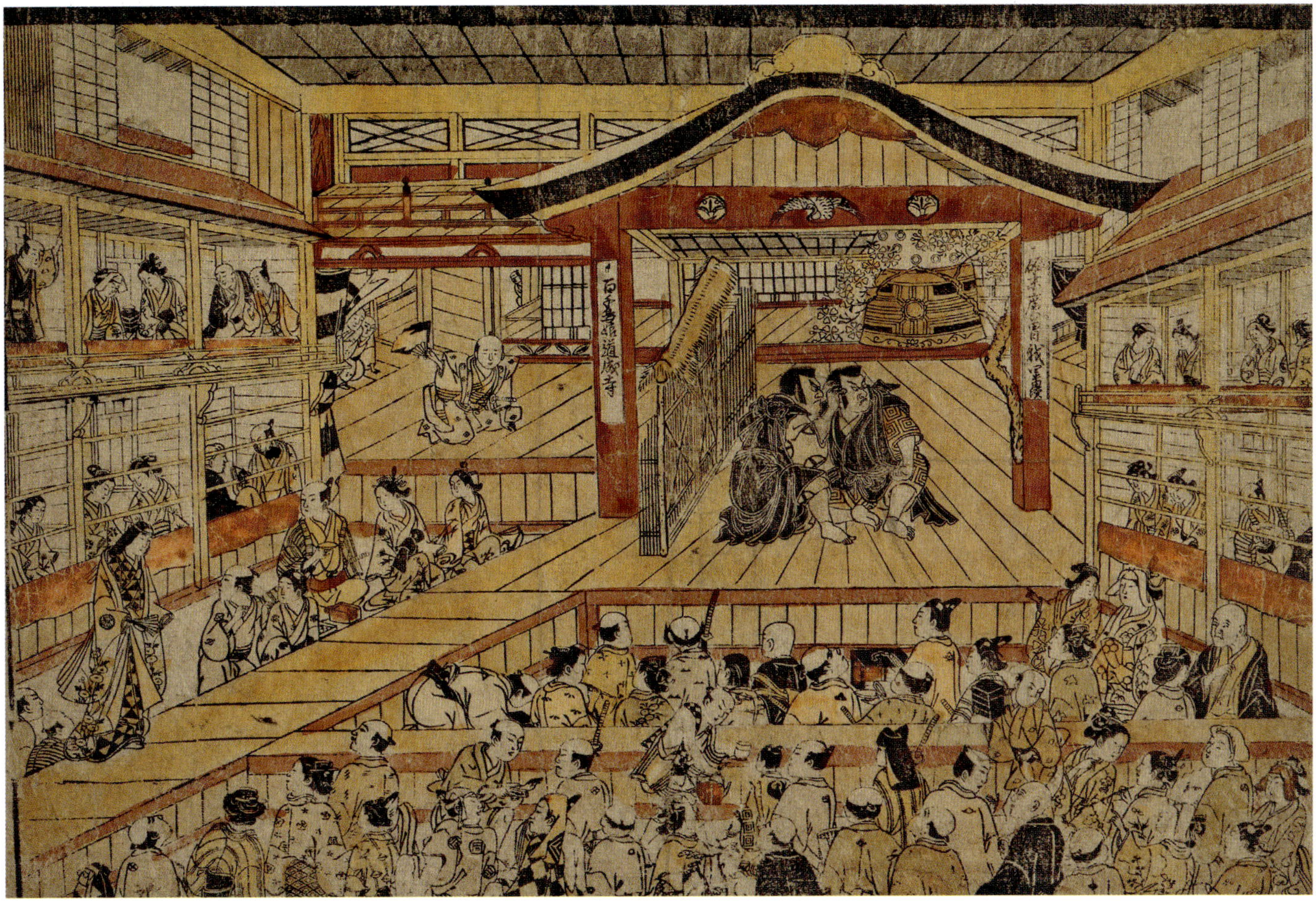

western books. The extent to which Masanobu had access to these books is not known, nor has a specific treatise on western perspective that he might have seen been identified. However, typical illustrations in books on western crafts depicted busy workshops. These may have provided an example of three-dimensional depth on a two-dimensional plane in the western manner. Masanobu's earliest *uki-e* subjects were theatrical, such as this scene from a popular *joruri* (a play with a sung narrative) presented at the Nakamura-za theatre. This type of print would have been purchased as a souvenir of a notable performance. The boards of the stage, the beams of the ceiling and the flanking balconies appear to converge on a single point located behind the actors. But further analysis reveals that there is no single vanishing point; Masanobu arranged his composition to simulate linear perspective instead of following perspectival theory. Rather than adopting the western practice, Masanobu created an illusion of it, giving his 'Floating World' patrons yet another novel experience. And he would continue to play with perspective, including the portrayal of landscape in *uki-e* and influencing print artists for several generations. ●

▲

Okumura Masanobu (1686–1764)
Scene from the joruri play 'Momochidori musume Dojoji' at Nakamura-za theatre
1744, woodblock print with hand colouring,
29 x 43 cm (11 x 17 in)

After a design by Giuliano da Sangallo (*c.* 1445–1516)
The Ideal City
c. 1480–84, oil and tempera, 77 x 220 cm (31 x 87 in)

In linear perspective, converging lines (orthogonals) meet at a single spot (vanishing point) to create the illusion of depth. The system was developed and refined in fifteenth-century Italy to simulate natural perception. Here, the vanishing point is on the horizon, seen through the central opening of the triumphal arch, with the pavement patterns, the piazza stairs and the decorative columns arranged along the orthogonals. It is unlikely that Masanobu saw such a meticulous application of the technique; his approach is experimental, imitating the effect rather than following the system.

After Strandanus (1523–1605)
The Invention of Copper Engraving
from *New Inventions of Modern Times*
c. 1600, engraving, 27 x 20 cm (11 x 8 in)

Books like *New Inventions*, featuring illustrations to introduce ideas, formed the core of *Rangaku*. Masanobu's familiarity with such books is not known but the type suggests a likely source for his understanding of western perspective. The narrow, uptilted interior space of this busy workshop, as well as the use of more than one vanishing point, departs from the strict application of western perspectival principles. Masanobu would do the same in depicting theatre interiors, adjusting the elements until they looked right to his eye.

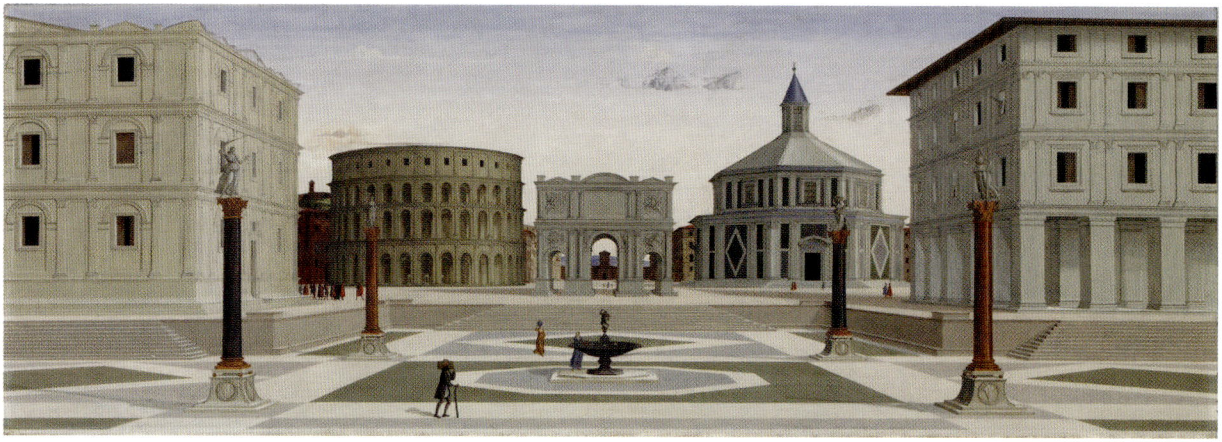

Kitagawa Utamaro (*c.* 1754–1806)
The Four Accomplishments of Women
c. 1788–90, woodblock print, 38 x 76 cm (15 x 30 in)

For several generations, print artists adopted Masanobu's innovative approach in their own *uki-e*. Here, known for *bijin-ga* ('pictures of beautiful women'), Utamaro transforms a traditional Chinese theme – the activities of the literati – by setting it in a pleasure house and replacing the scholars with courtesans. Equally striking is the illusion of depth, which he created by adapting Masanobu's method of using architectural elements to establish the orthogonals, drawing the eye to the hills in the distance.

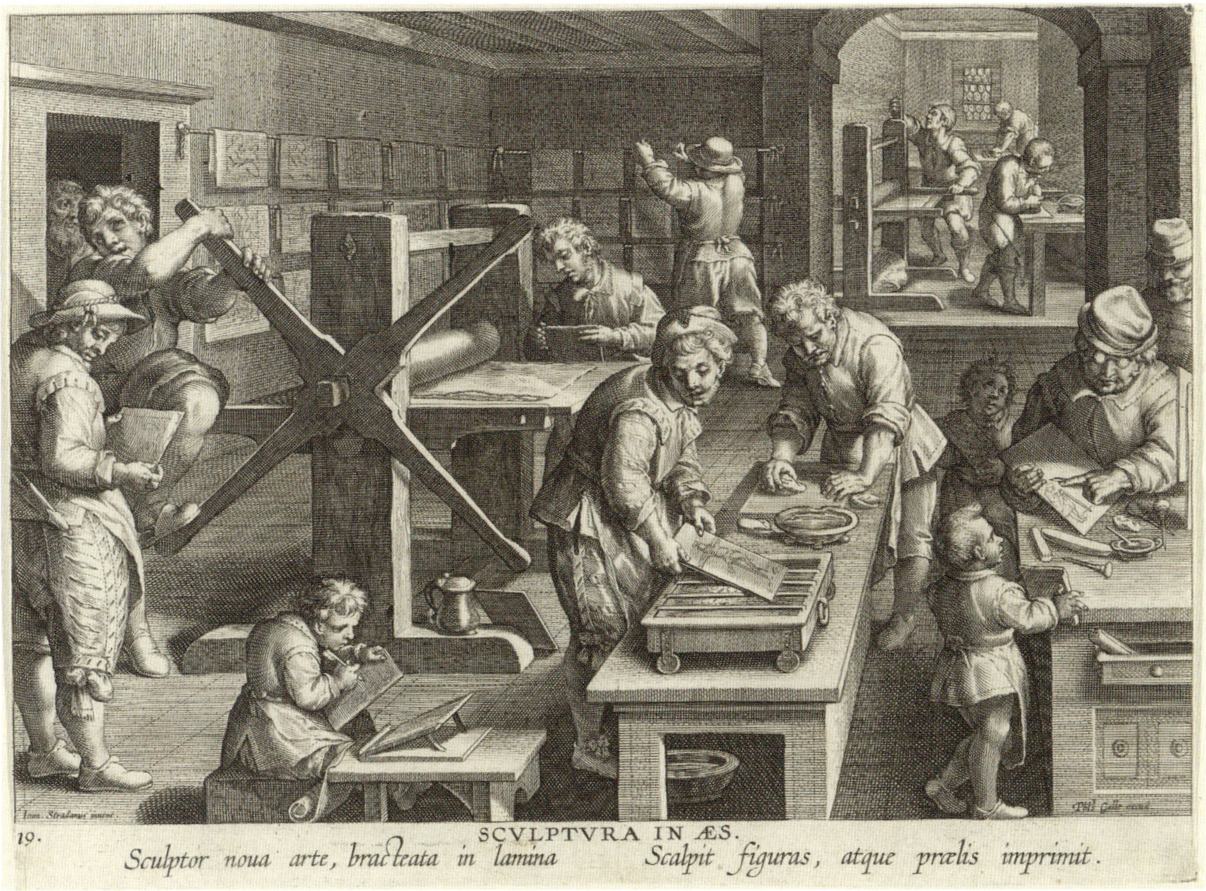
19.
SCVLPTVRA IN ÆS.
Sculptor noua arte, bracteata in lamina
Scalpit figuras, atque prælis imprimit.

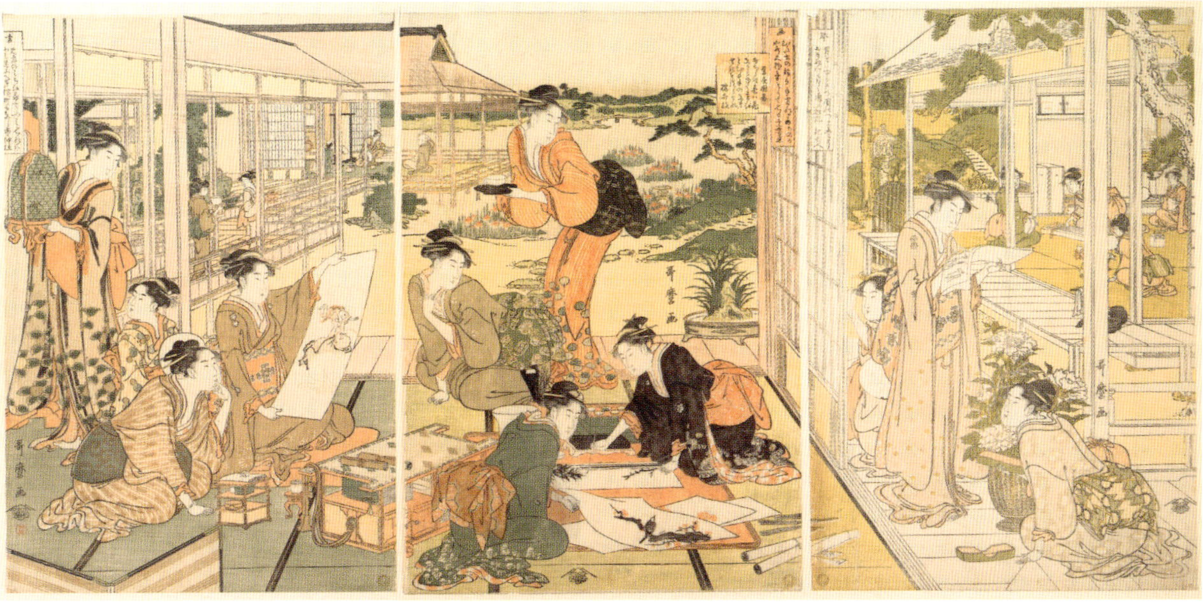

SIDE BY SIDE

How painting partners Monet and Renoir borrowed the same scene with different points of view

In 1862, as students in the École des Beaux-Arts, Monet and Renoir forged a friendship based upon their shared view that the art world was out of date. Both were frustrated with the path to recognition that required them to exhibit their works at the annual, juried Salon. Neither had an interest in traditional subject matter. Rather than the conventional repertoire drawn from history and mythology, they sought to portray the world they knew in vibrant scenes set in the public parks, cafés and the recreational resorts within a brief train ride from Paris. Monet's advocacy of *plein-air* painting convinced Renoir to sketch in oil out of doors as a means to capture the sensation of natural light. Late in the summer of 1869, Monet found the ideal subject for their objectives, and he invited Renoir to join him on the left bank of the Seine in Bougival, just a few miles west of Paris, to paint the crowds bathing and boating at La Grenouillère.

A summertime attraction located near the île de Croissy, La Grenouillère ('The Frog Pond') got its name for its easy access to the water. Visitors could rent a boat or take a swim near two floating entertainment facilities linked by narrow bridges: a café-bar and the Camembert, a small, round, raft-like structure with a tree growing out of the centre. Those who chose to swim could easily climb on to the Camembert, have a drink with the other patrons and then jump back into the water. Just a short, inexpensive train ride from Paris, La Grenouillère attracted a young crowd that flaunted class difference; that, and mixed gender bathing, gave it a raffish reputation. It offered precisely the type of entertainment that two financially strapped young artists would enjoy. During the last weeks of August and much of September, Monet and Renoir positioned their easels with a good view of the Camembert to create colour studies for a larger, more formal depictions to be completed in the studio with the intention of submitting them to the 1870 Salon.

Working side by side, the painters' subject is roughly the same: bathers bobbing in the water to the left, people crossing the bridge to the café on the right, and, in the centre the lively crowd on the Camembert. No doubt they stole glances of each other's canvas as they worked. However, the focus on the figures makes it appear that Renoir stood closer than his painting partner. Although Monet's figures – notably the bathers on the Camembert – add uncharacteristic anecdotal detail, he clearly found the expanse of water in the

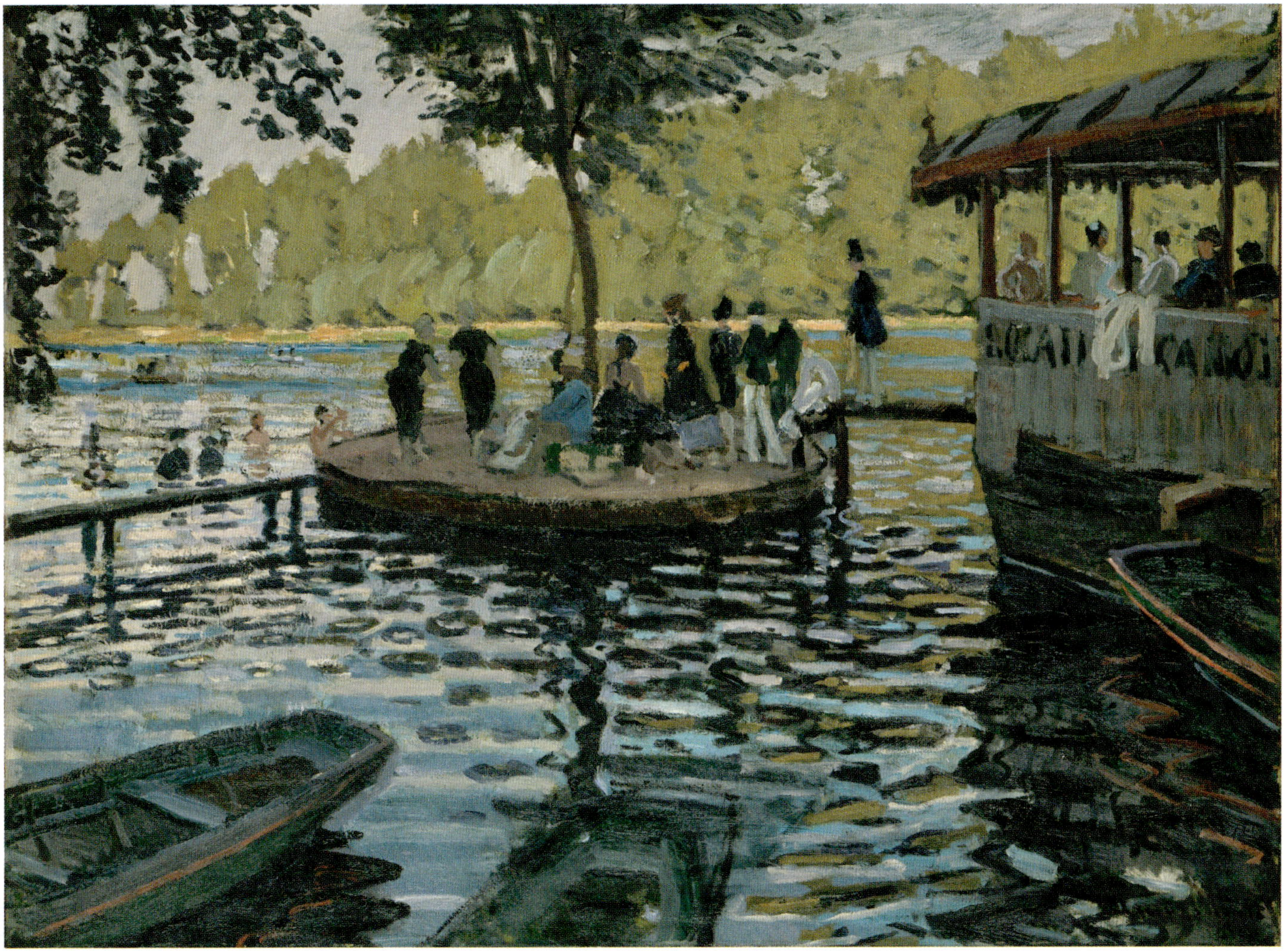

foreground more compelling. Ringed by the rowing boats, the river shimmers with colour, applied in long, broken brushstrokes of blue, pink, ochre and brown. Renoir uses similar hues, but his marks are more modulated, depicting an illustrative scene rather than evoking a visual sensation. Their shared subject reveals their aesthetic and intentional differences: Renoir was essentially a figure painter, while Monet favoured landscape. It does not appear that Renoir developed his study into a formal picture. Monet did create a large, more finished version of his sketch, but it was rejected by the Salon jury.[1] The real value to Monet's artistic development was in the freedom of stroke and tonality that he achieved in front of his subject, teaching him that a painter had to be present, right there on the scene and not in the studio, to represent the vitality of modern life under natural light and in glowing colour. ●

▲

Claude Monet (1840–1926)
La Grenouillère
1869, oil on canvas, 75 x 100 cm (30 x 39 in)

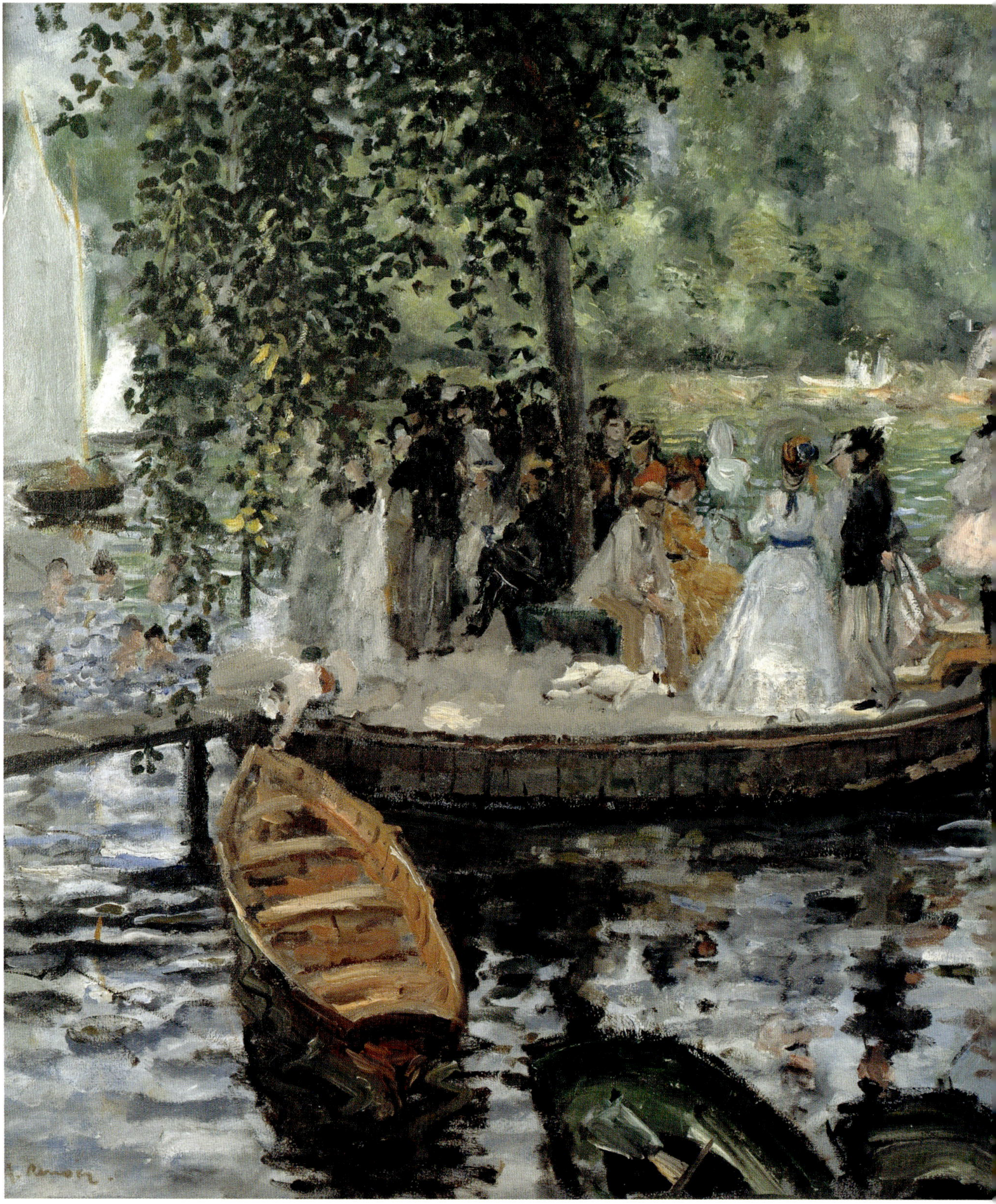

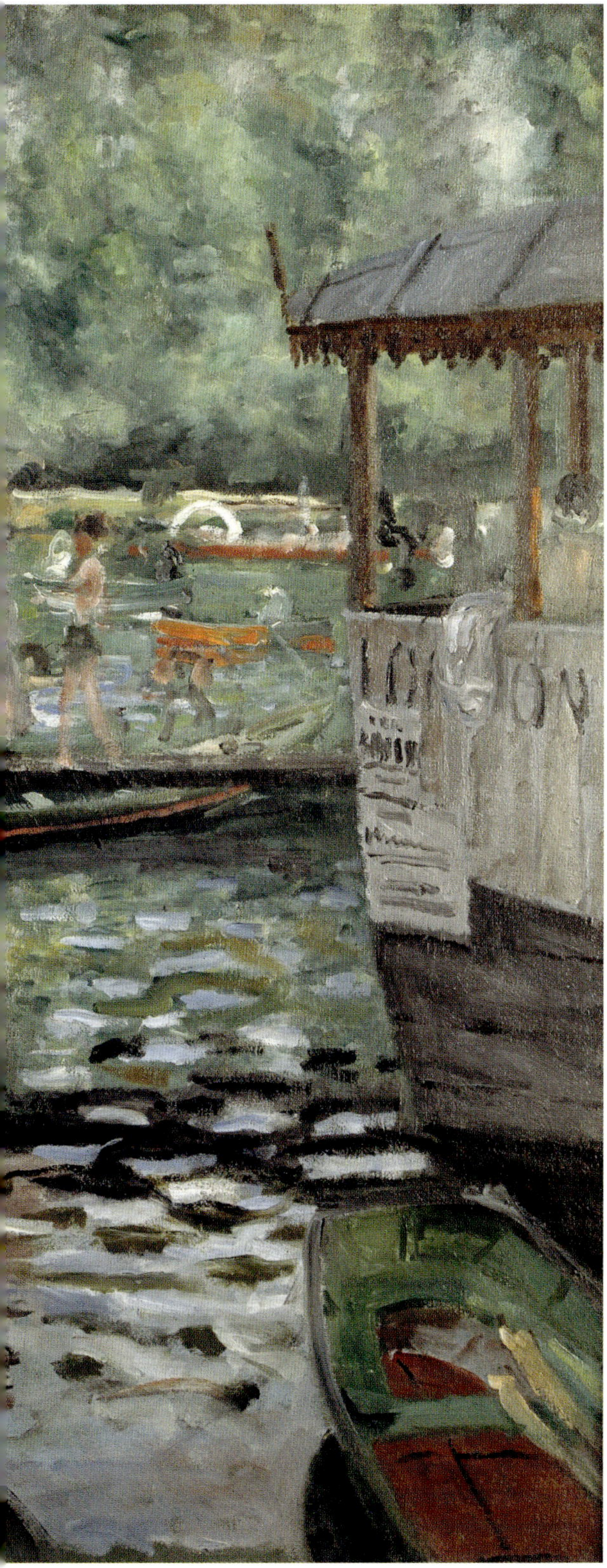

Pierre-Auguste Renoir (1841–1919)
La Grenouillère
1869, oil on canvas, 67 x 81 cm (26 x 32 in)

Renoir had previously posed figures in natural light, but in *La Grenouillère* he gave the setting unprecedented attention. His soft tonality simulates the sensation of warmth and mist on the riverside, and blurred brushstrokes catch the glimmer of the hot sun on the cool water. In contrast to Monet's rendition, Renoir focuses on the figures from the details of their garments to their lively interactions. The line of rowing boats in the foreground – a watery expanse in Monet's painting – leads the viewer's eye directly to the crowd on the Camembert.

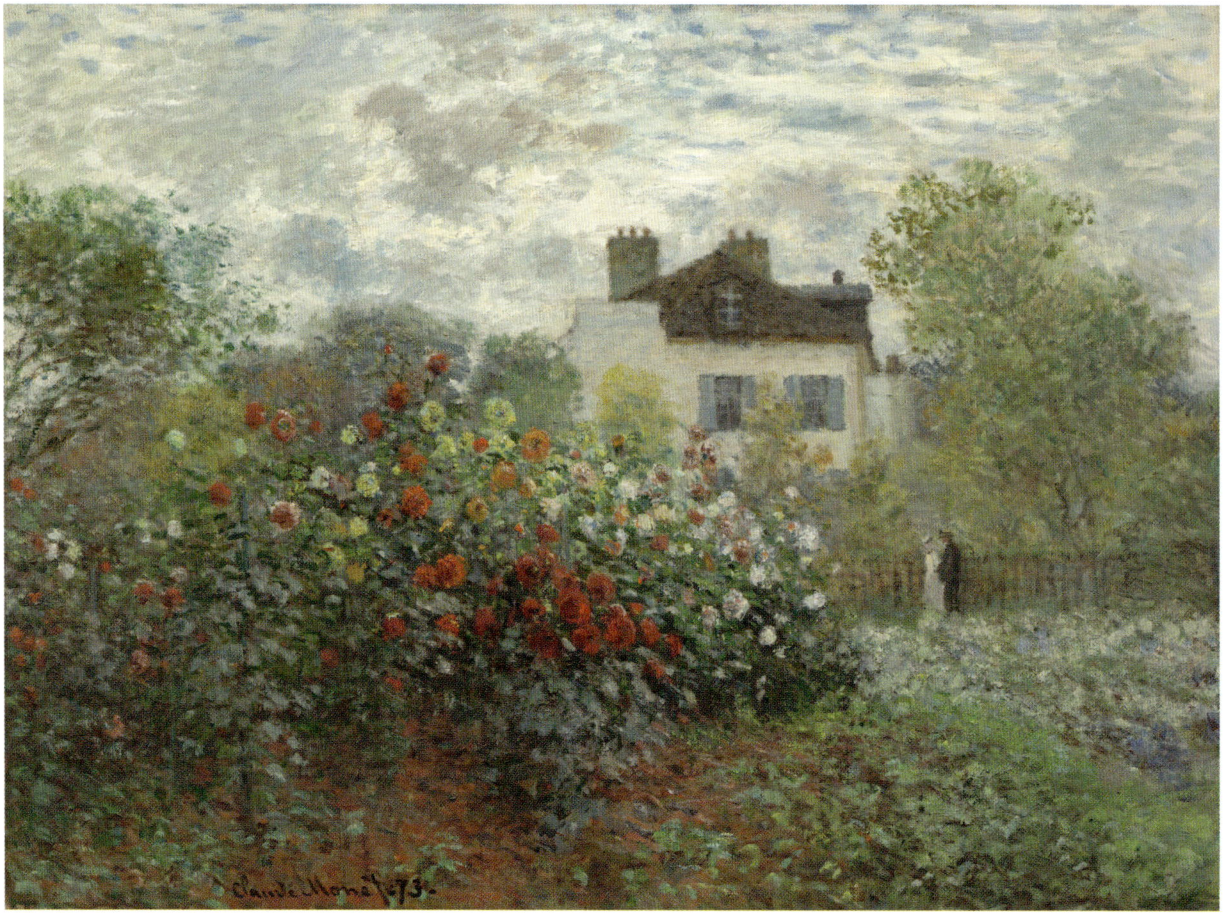

▲

Claude Monet
The Artist's Garden in Argenteuil (A Corner of the Garden with Dahlias)
1873, oil on canvas, 61 x 83 cm (24 x 33 in)

Monet moved to Argenteuil in December 1871. He was seeking a quiet, suburban setting surrounded by gardens where he could raise his family and paint. This magnificent stand of dahlias in front of the fence of his rented house presented an ideal subject; he used pure pigment and dabbing brushstrokes to heighten the beauty of the flowers in full bloom. The solid form of the whitewashed house is seen against the broad vista of a summer sky. The couple seems almost incidental, briefly pausing on their stroll to appreciate the blooming spectacle.

Pierre-Auguste Renoir
Claude Monet Painting in his Garden at Argenteuil
1873, oil on canvas, 46 x 58 cm (18 x 23 in)

With Argenteuil on the northwest train line out of Paris, Monet's friends often came to visit, bringing their paints and easels. While Monet painted the dahlias, Renoir painted Monet. Both stand outside the fenced-in property, offering a different perspective of the dense stand of flowers, which, in Renoir's depiction, are clearly diminished in scale. And in a striking contrast to Monet's vision, Renoir portrayed the suburban density of the area. Monet's secluded garden house was, in fact, surrounded by others just like it.

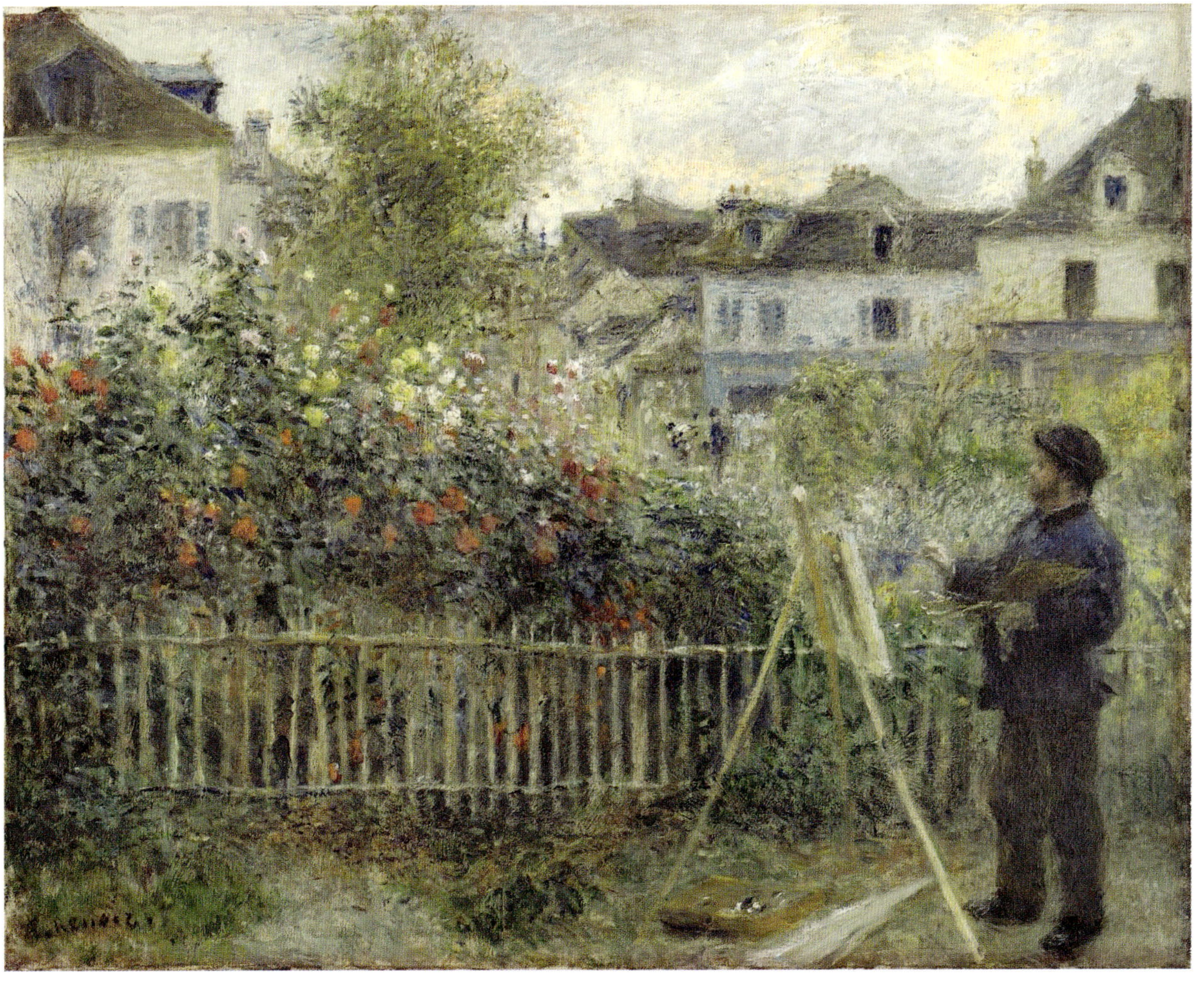

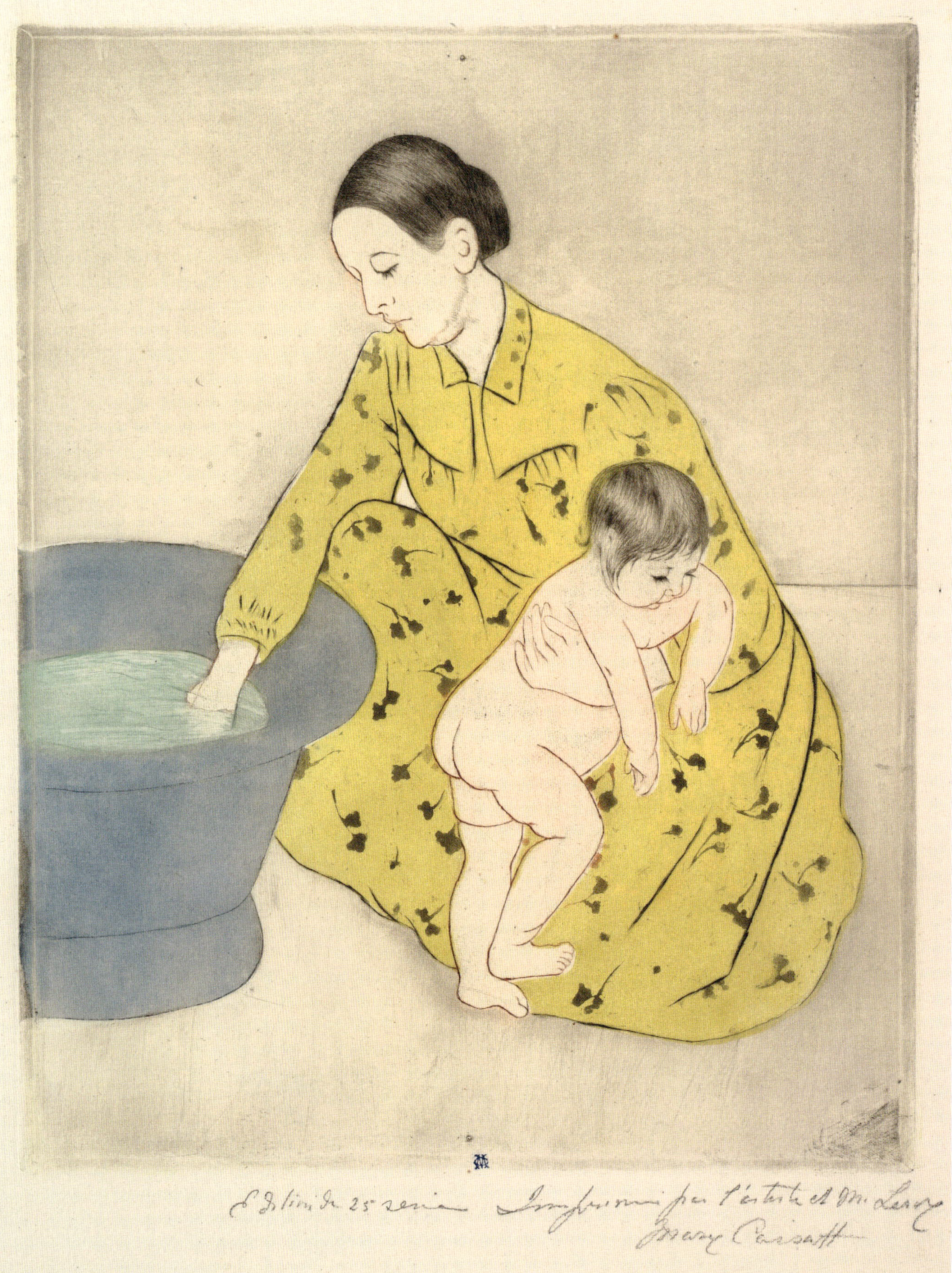
Mary Cassatt

INSPIRED ADAPTATION

How Cassatt was inspired by Japanese colour block printing

In the spring of 1890, Mary Cassatt asked her friend and fellow Impressionist, Berthe Morisot, to join her at an exhibition of Japanese art at the École des Beaux-Arts. Morisot had been experimenting with colour lithography and Cassatt believed that the prints on display would inspire her: 'You who want to make colour prints couldn't dream of anything more beautiful.' Just decades before, after centuries of self-imposed isolation, Japan had opened to broad trade with western nations, and the distinctive form of print known as *ukiyo-e* was widely admired and avidly sought by European collectors. The subjects featured worldly pleasures – actors, celebrities, courtesans, erotica and cutting-edge fashion – enjoyed by the elite class, as well as city views, tourist sites and scenes of everyday life. The printing technique surpassed any form of western practice, creating images in ink with the subtle handling of watercolour. Cassatt's enthusiasm was boundless, for as she told her friend, 'I dream of it and don't think of anything but colour on copper.'[1]

Both women were skilled in printmaking, so it may have struck Morisot odd that Cassatt referred to 'colour on copper'. *Ukiyo-e* printmakers employed wood blocks – up to twenty per image – to print the colours in an elaborate, sequential process. Individual blocks, keyed for perfect registration, were used to print each stage of colour. The inks were applied to the block by hand, brushed and blotted to create the subtle gradation of tone. Creation of a single print was the work of many expert hands.

Cassatt, whose previous experience with printmaking included drypoint and soft-ground etching on copper, believed she could develop an equivalent technique based on the skills she had already acquired. Working from a pencil sketch on paper, she transferred her image to a copper plate covered in a soft ground, etching the contour lines and adding details in drypoint. To create a more tonal surface, she treated areas of the plate with a

◀

Mary Cassatt (1844–1926)
The Bath (seventeenth state of seventeen) from 'The Set of Ten'
1890–91, drypoint, soft-ground etching and aquatint, printed in colour from two plates, 43 x 30 cm (17 x 12 in)

resinous aquatint ground. Cassatt daubed ink on the treated plate *à la poupée* ('with the doll'), using twisted rags that allowed her to manipulate the tone. She used no more than two or three plates per image, printing several colours with the same plate.

Her only assistant was a professional printer who pulled the impressions. This method produced the results she sought: a bold, calligraphic line with subtle colour variations in ink. When Camille Pissarro saw the results, he wrote enthusiastically to his son that Cassatt achieved a perfect tone, 'subtle, delicate without stains on the seams', in clear colours 'as beautiful as Japanese work'.[2]

The Bath was printed from two plates, one for tone and the other for linear details. Cassatt conceived the depiction of a mother preparing to bathe her child in response to a similar scene by the Japanese printmaker Kitagawa Utamaro, who produced a twelve-part suite of prints depicting the mundane side of glamorous courtesans' lives. Cassatt owned a set of 'Twelve Hours in the Pleasure Quarter of Yoshiwara' (1794), and in her series, 'The Set of Ten', she transformed the daily tasks performed by the off-duty courtesans – dressing, bathing, childcare – into scenes from the lives of western, middle-class women. These were the subjects at the heart of her repertoire, and while she openly acknowledged her print series imitated Japanese art, she took great pride in the results. Years later, when American artist George Biddle visited Cassatt at her country estate, Château de Beaufresne in Oise, he noticed that she had hung the 'Set' near her display of Utamaro's prints, not only paying tribute to her inspiration but daring the viewer to compare them. ●

▶

Kitagawa Utamaro (1753–1806)
Bathtime
c. 1801, colour woodblock print, ink and colour on paper, 37 x 25 cm (15 x 10 in)

As a master of the colourful *nishiki-e* ('brocade prints'), Utamaro designed images for the wood carvers and printers to follow. His *ukiyo-e* repertoire included keenly observed nature studies, erotica and humour, with his most desired imagery featuring beautiful women at leisure. The prints in this suite explore the intimate world of women carrying out their daily routines, and the similarities between this composition and Cassatt's *The Bath* suggest her knowledge of the print. Perhaps she saw the image as a challenge to create her own.

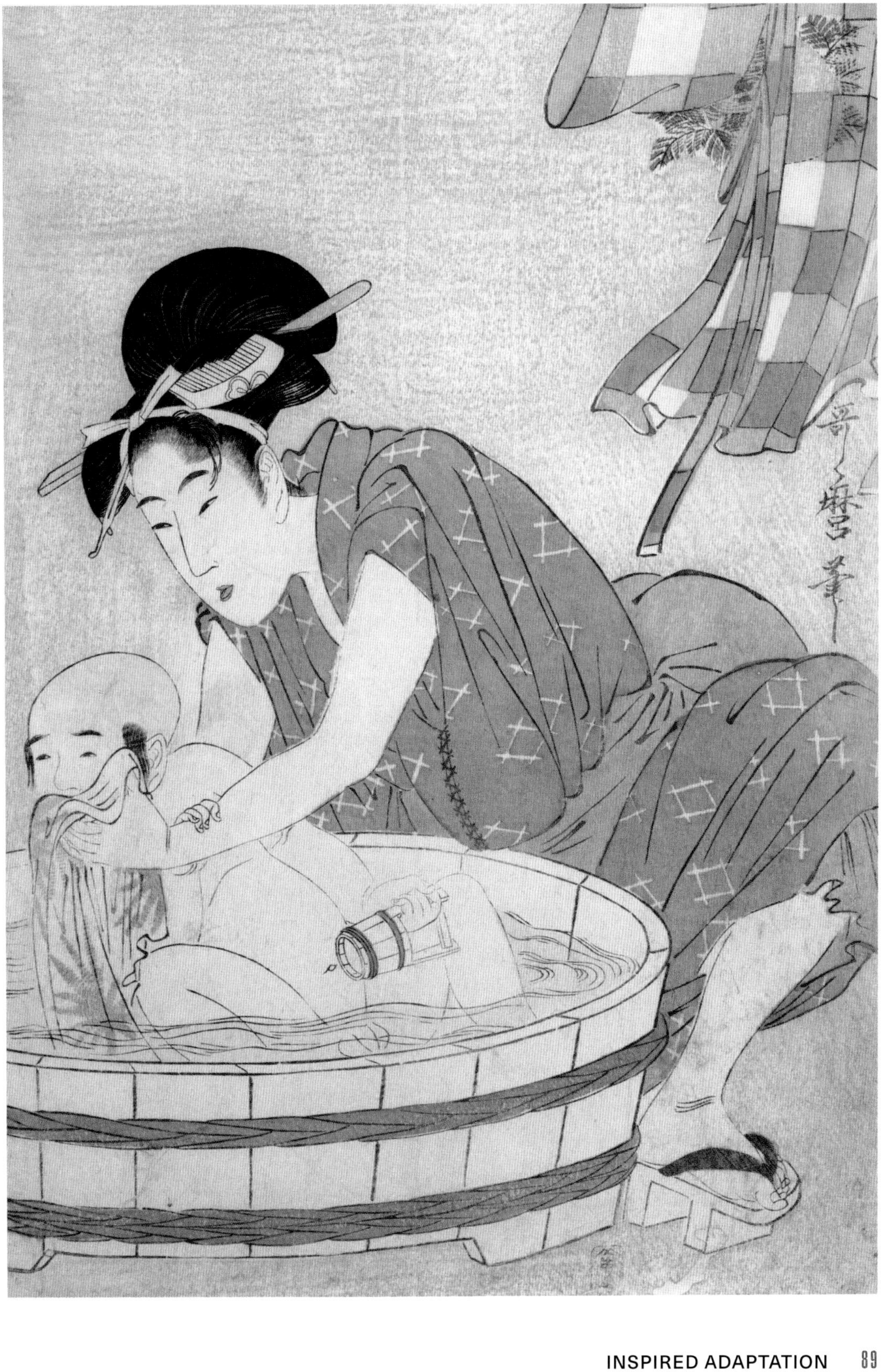

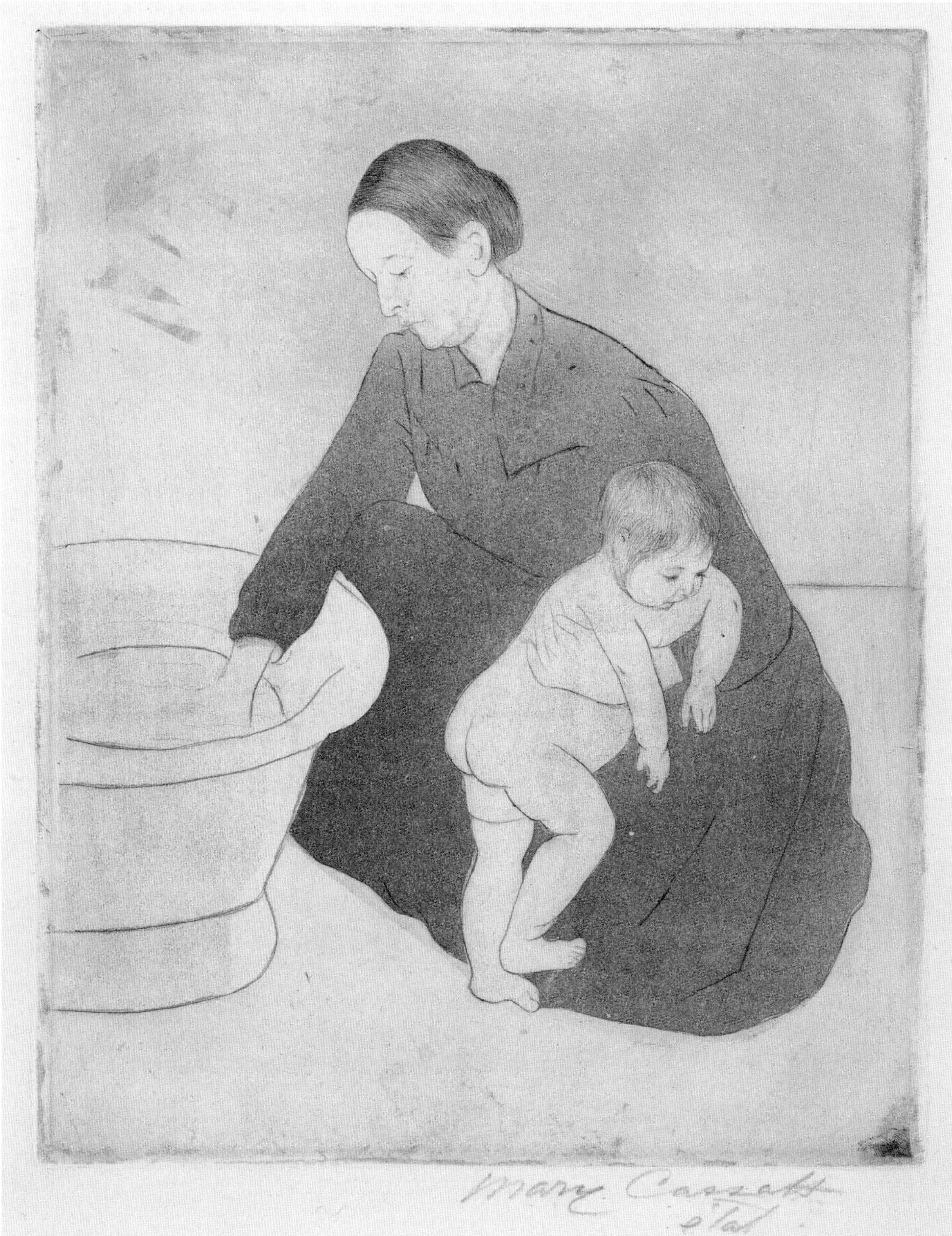
Mary Cassatt

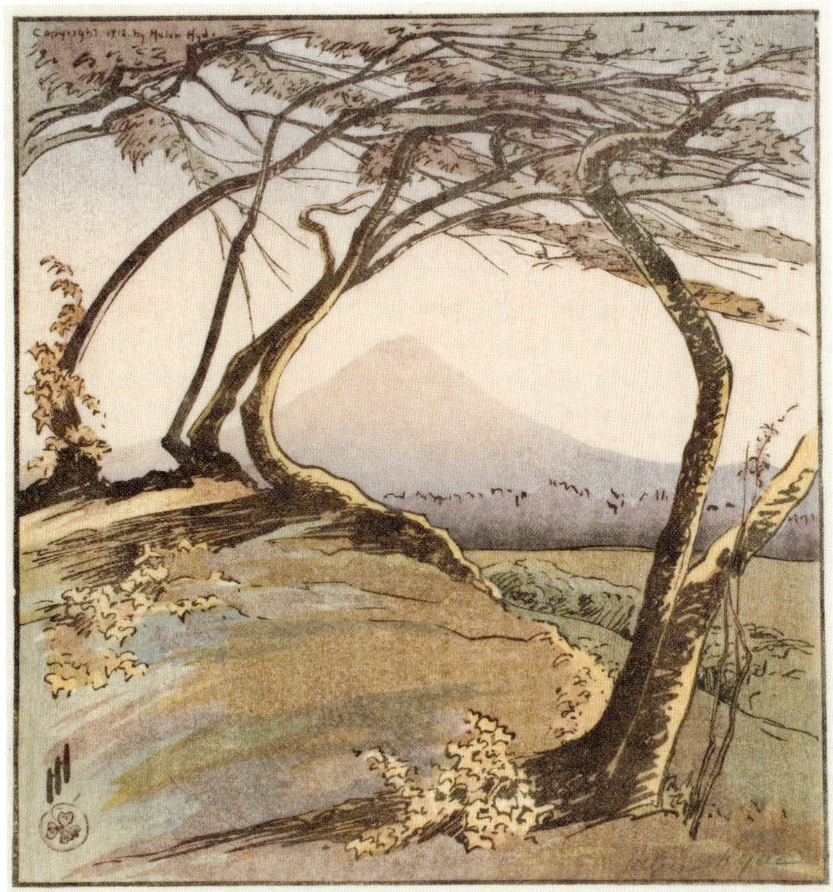

◀

Mary Cassatt

The Bath (fifth state of seventeen)

1890–91, drypoint, soft-ground etching, black ink, 41 x 30 cm (16 x 12 in)

In the process of modifying her plate, Cassatt tested her design by pulling impressions. These individual images are called states, recording a change to the plate that is permanent. In this rare monochrome image, Cassatt uses the grey ink to gauge the effect of tone and the clarity of the drypoint lines, created by incising into the surface of the plate to emphasize the contours and details. This is the sole impression of this state, pulled as an interim study rather than a departure from her technique of 'colour on copper.'

▲

Helen Hyde (1868–1919)

Mt. Orizaba from Jalapa, Mexico

1912, colour block print, 25 × 23 cm (9 × 9 in)

In 1893, Hyde attended an exhibition featuring Cassatt's 'The Set of Ten' in Paris. Within the decade she travelled to Japan to learn more about Cassatt's inspiration, *ukiyo-e*. Over two extended stays (1899–1901 and 1902–14), Hyde tried her hand at carving and inking blocks, but when she made her own prints, she followed tradition, providing the design and leaving the rest to skilled professionals. Many of her subjects feature Japanese settings and characters, but this vista was captured during a stay at a health resort in Mexico. Even so, the looming Mount Orizaba evokes the distinctive form of Mount Fuji.

LITTLE CABINET OF STEALS

How Rauschenberg combined found objects and purpose-made art

The myth of the thieving magpie offers an analogy to the way artists gather influence. Just as the bird is said to procure shiny objects for its nest, throughout the ages artists have mined their surroundings to expand their repertoire of imagery and ideas. Scientific observation of the bird now refutes the myth; magpies, in fact, demonstrate neophobia (fear of unfamiliar objects). However, in developing the 'combine', Robert Rauschenberg embodied the magpie's folklore, using found items as material for his art. He coined the term to clarify the often enigmatic works he made between 1954 and 1964; works in which he combined objects plucked out of ordinary life – often worn or discarded – and placed them in new configurations and contexts. Aside from adding scrawled lines and strokes of paint, he did not alter the components.[1] Rauschenberg's combines dissolve the notional divide between painting and sculpture, forcing the viewer to rethink their presumptions about what is and what is not art. Nowhere is this better seen than in his groundbreaking combine *Short Circuit*, an assemblage of found and purpose-made objects that is, in its craft and content, a little cabinet of steals.

Rauschenberg created *Short Circuit* for an exhibition at the Stable Gallery in New York City. It was not his first hybrid work. He had incorporated unorthodox materials – newspapers, metal, latex – into his practice from the start of his career, and in 1954 he created a collaged screen for his friend Merce Cunningham to be used in a dance performance. However, *Short Circuit* appears to be one of the earliest works deliberately conceived as a combine. Using scrap wood, he constructed a box with compartments, filling the lower half with a seemingly random collection of textiles and paper ephemera, including a lace curtain, a square of polka-dot print fabric, a picture of Abraham Lincoln, Judy Garland's autograph, an art postcard and a programme from a performance by John Cage. He affixed these to the surface with a thick layer of putty-coloured paint, adding bold strokes of light green, black and orange at the top. Two doors enclosed most of the top half of the box. The command 'OPEN', along with an arrow that points upwards, towards the left, is written on a thickly brushed red background in the space below the right door. Following the instructions reveals two small paintings: on the right a colourful scene painted by Susan Weil and on the left an American flag painted by Jasper Johns.

By hiding the little paintings behind the doors, Rauschenberg sneaked works by his former wife and his current partner into a curated exhibition from which they were excluded. The history of *Short*

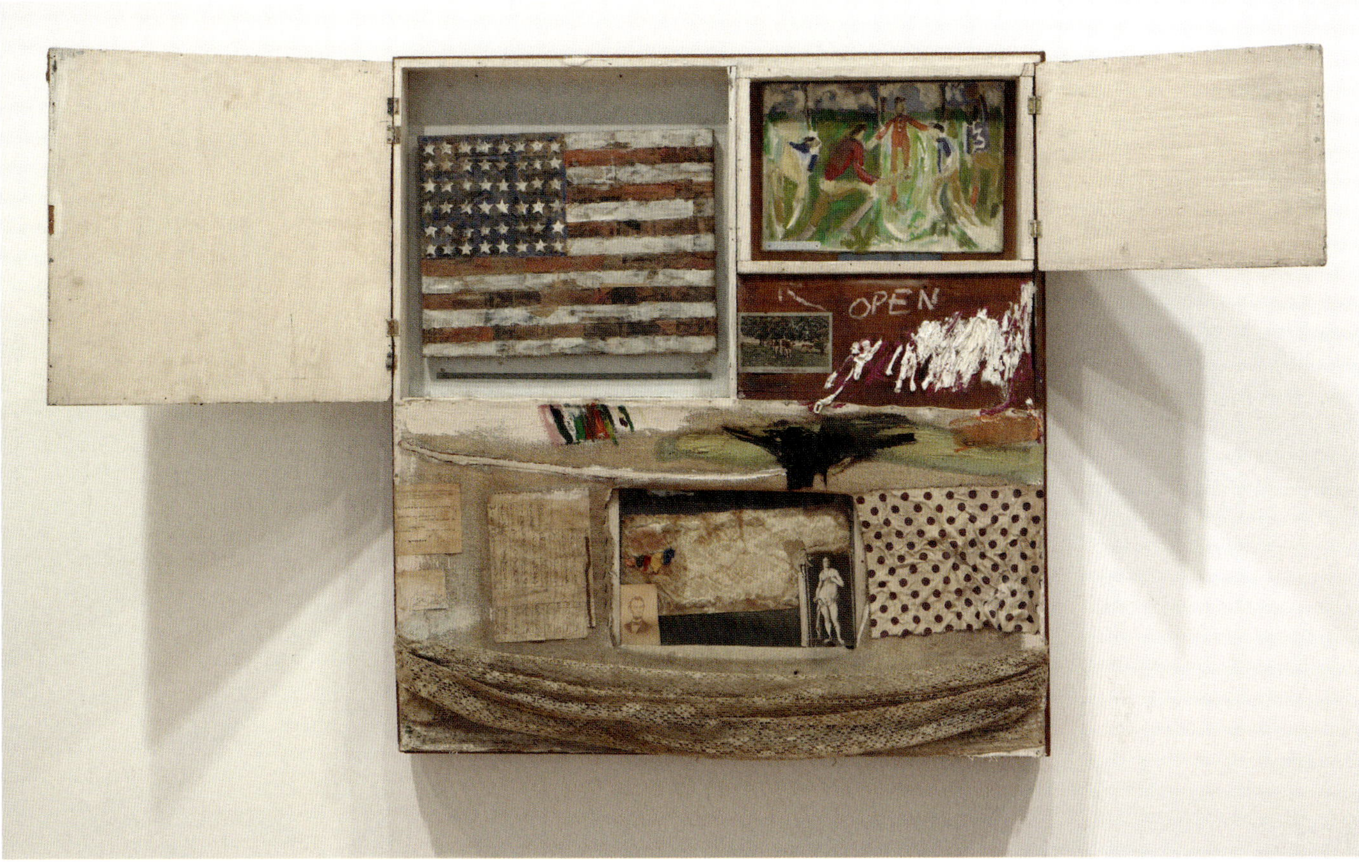

Circuit also involved a theft in the more conventional sense. Rauschenberg kept the work and rarely exhibited it, but in 1965, supposedly under the safe care of the gallerist Leo Castelli, Johns' *Flag* was stolen and has never been recovered. Two years later, with the consent of Johns, Rauschenberg asked their friend, Elaine Sturtevant, to replicate the purloined work. He positioned it slightly higher in the composition, leaving room for a label that explains, 'The original Jasper Johns Flag was stolen in 1965. It is replaced by an original Sturtevant 1967.' Rauschenberg was by no means the first artist to bridge the worlds of life and art with found objects; just decades earlier Pablo Picasso pasted chair caning on a canvas, Marcel Duchamp defaced a postcard with a moustache (see p.186), and Kurt Schwitters adopted torn train tickets as his signature medium. However, Rauschenberg's approach surged beyond the intention of simply bridging the worlds of art and life through assemblage. Appropriative action was part of his process and, despite the doors, he made no attempt to cover the thefts. ●

▲

Robert Rauschenberg (1925–2008)
Short Circuit
1955, mixed media (oil, fabric, notebook paper, postcard, printed reproductions, concert programme and autograph on canvas, wood supports and cabinets with paintings by Susan Weil and Elaine Sturtevant), 104 x 95 x 11 cm (41 x 37 x 4 in)

Jasper Johns (b. 1930)
Flag
1954–55, encaustic, oil and collage on fabric mounted on plywood, 107 x 154 cm (42 x 61 in)

Johns took up his iconic motif around the same time that Rauschenberg created *Short Circuit*. Although much smaller in scale than most of the works in his well-known series, the version made for the combine is most likely one of the first of what would be at least forty iterations of the subject. John claimed that he dreamed about painting a flag and then did just that. He did not assign any particular meaning to the subject, explaining that it appealed to him because it was something familiar to everyone.

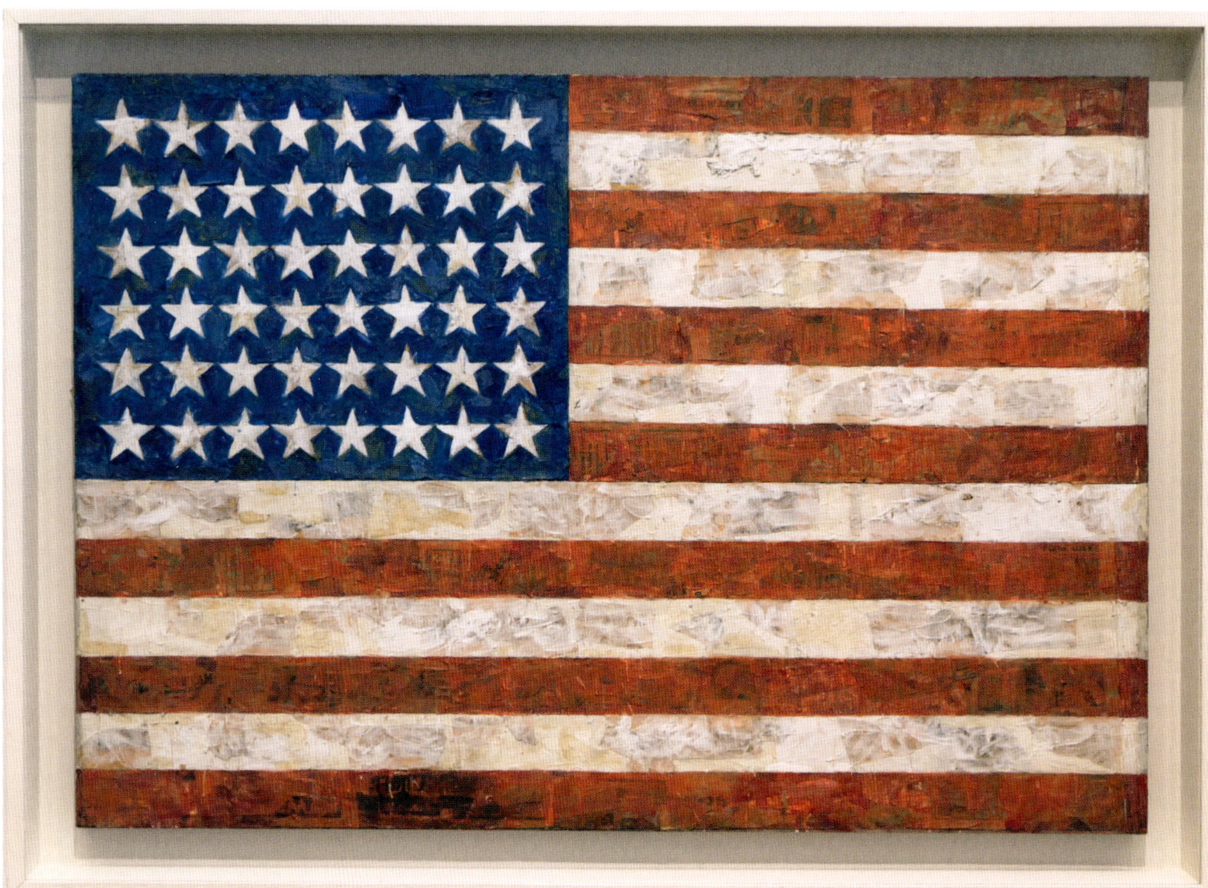

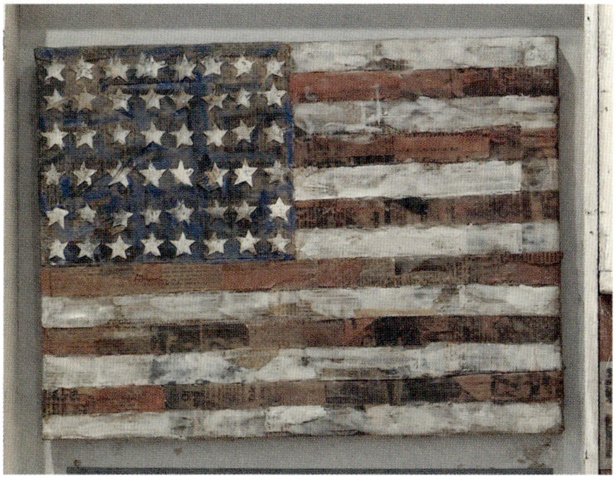

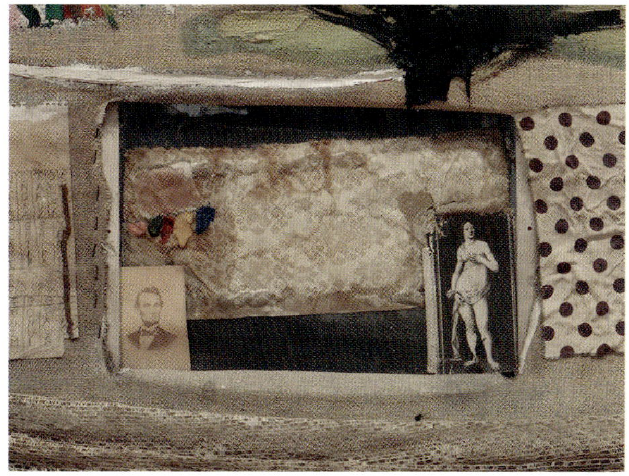

▲

Robert Rauschenberg
Detail of *Short Circuit*

The history of the small *Flag* painting's theft and replication is riddled with hearsay. The circumstances under which the original painting was removed are simply not known, and rumours aside, the work has yet to be traced. Both Johns and Rauschenberg were friendly with Sturtevant, but it is unclear who suggested that she make the replica or why they chose her. And given the fact that she replicated a lost work, she must have assembled the details from other examples of the motif, creating a new one out of various renditions.

▲

Robert Rauschenberg
Detail of *Short Circuit*

Rauschenberg's choice of objects in this section are all either scraps or ephemera. Their relationship may be random, but the assembly is not. The centre ensemble of a photographic image of Lincoln and a postcard of a sculpture of Venus form an off-kilter triangle with the image of a cow. The lace curtain below suggests a swag-draped stage, with the concert programme and the polka-dot swatch creating wings. There is a lot of wit in Rauschenberg's mixing and muddling, simultaneously elevating everyday objects while mocking the conventional methods and materials of art.

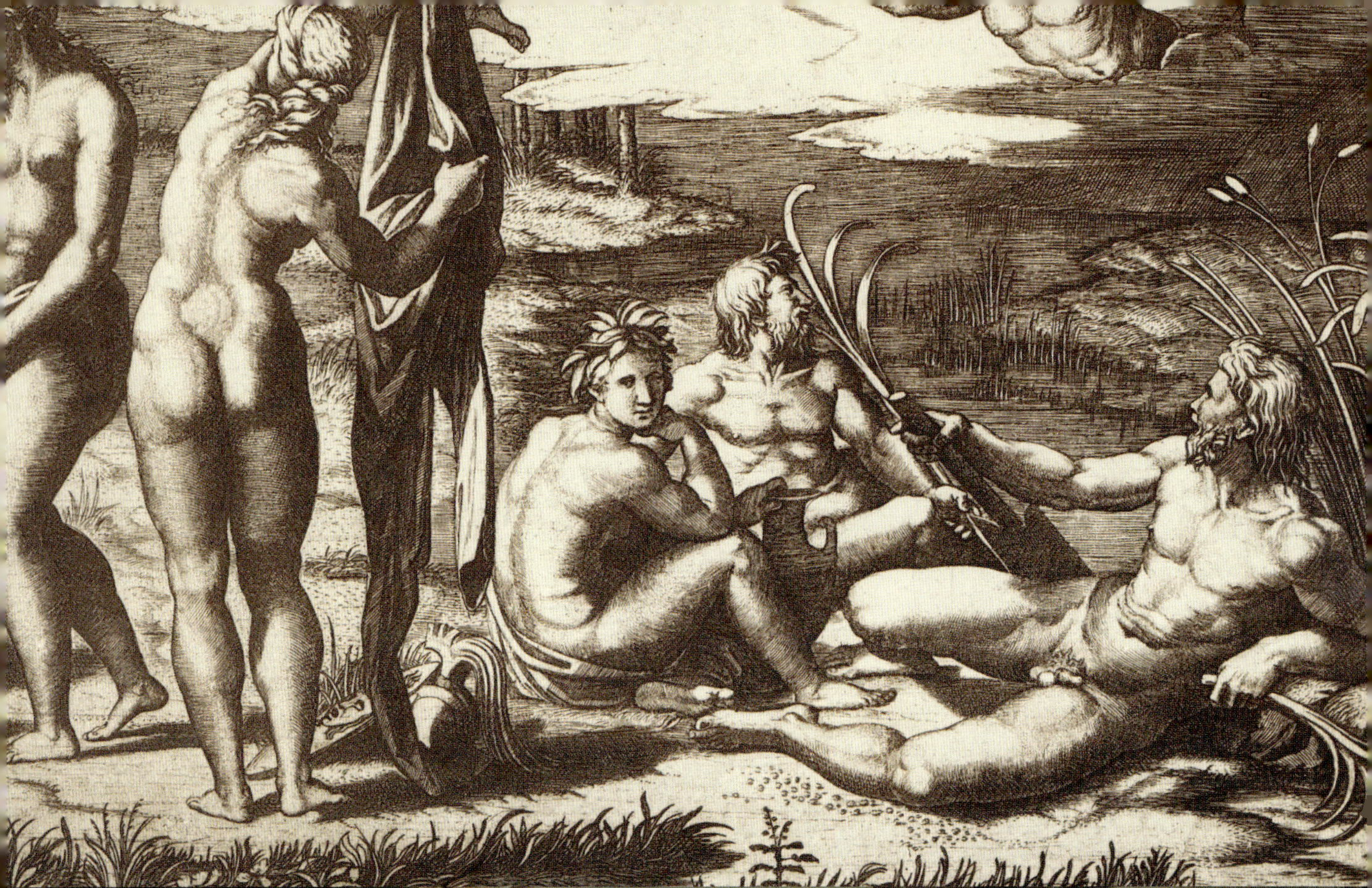

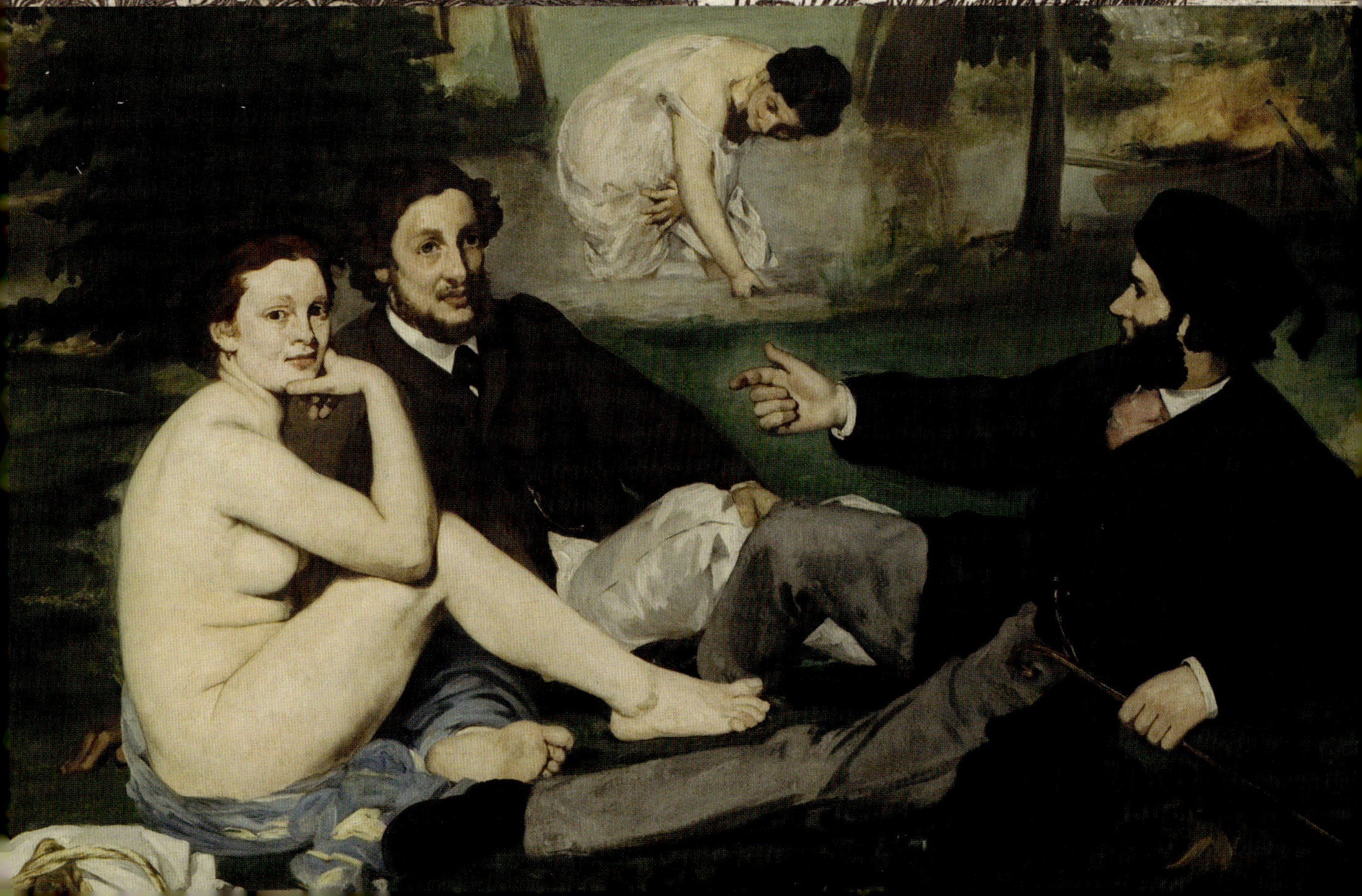

INFLUENCE & INNOVATION

No artist can avoid influence. Picasso punctured the myth of originality by observing that there was nothing new in the arts since the cave walls were painted at Lascaux. He openly embraced a wide range of influences from works imported from Africa to those painted in Parisian studios. In their pursuit of individual expression, great artists build upon influence to create innovative work, something significant and startlingly new. From physical beauty to ephemeral effects, from spatial perception to the way paint is applied to the canvas, the artist adept at stealing turns influence into innovation.

BODY LANGUAGE

How Michelangelo's Adam embodied the classical ideal of ancient sculptures

In 1496, Michelangelo astonished the Florentine art world with a marble figure of a sleeping Eros. According to historian Giorgio Vasari, the pre-eminent art patron Lorenzo di Pierfrancesco de' Medici was so impressed by the sculpture's classical beauty that he urged the young artist to 'bury it underground and then send it to Rome'.[1] This tale survives in many versions; in others it is the art dealer Baldassarre del Milanese, or even Michelangelo himself, who devised the forger's trick. No matter the source, the ruse worked. Burial gave the smooth marble surface an aged patina, convincing Cardinal Raffaele Riario, a nephew of the late Pope Sixtus IV, to purchase it. Rather than feeling duped when Michelangelo confessed to the scheme, the cardinal proudly displayed the work in Rome, leading to Michelangelo's first, significant church commissions and establishing his reputation as an artist who possessed all the genius of the ancient masters. Within a decade, Michelangelo obtained papal patronage, and in 1508 he began painting the ceiling of the Sistine Chapel with scenes from Genesis, centred by an unsurpassed image of human perfection: the *Creation of Adam*.

As an adolescent, Michelangelo trained as a sculptor in an informal atelier located in the Medici Palace gardens. It was there that he first encountered classical sculpture, having ready access to the collection of Pierfrancesco's cousin and guardian, Lorenzo de' Medici. Known as 'Il Magnifico' for his generosity, the eminent art patron took the young artist under his wing and introduced him to the poets and philosophers of the Neo-Platonic circle, who sought to revive the classical concept of a human-centred universe within Christian beliefs. Human beauty symbolized this new outlook, a beauty based upon the symmetrically proportioned, athletic form celebrated in the arts of the ancient world. This belief was the core of the Italian *renovatio* ('renewal' or 'rebirth'), an era of humanistic expression in all the arts we now call the Renaissance. Michelangelo thrived in this environment, but in 1492 the death of Il Magnifico left him without a benefactor at a crucial stage in his career. Although he employed duplicity to have his work acknowledged in Rome in 1496, it was his ability to rise to expectations that attracted prestigious commissions, and in 1503, when Giuliano della Rovere came to the papacy as Pope Julius II, Michelangelo acquired a patron whose ambitions matched the scope of his talent. In 1505, the Pope sought the design for a three-storey, multi-figured tomb from the sculptor, but within three years he redirected his attention to the decoration of the ceiling of the Sistine Chapel, built by the Pope's late uncle, Pope Sixtus IV, in the previous century.

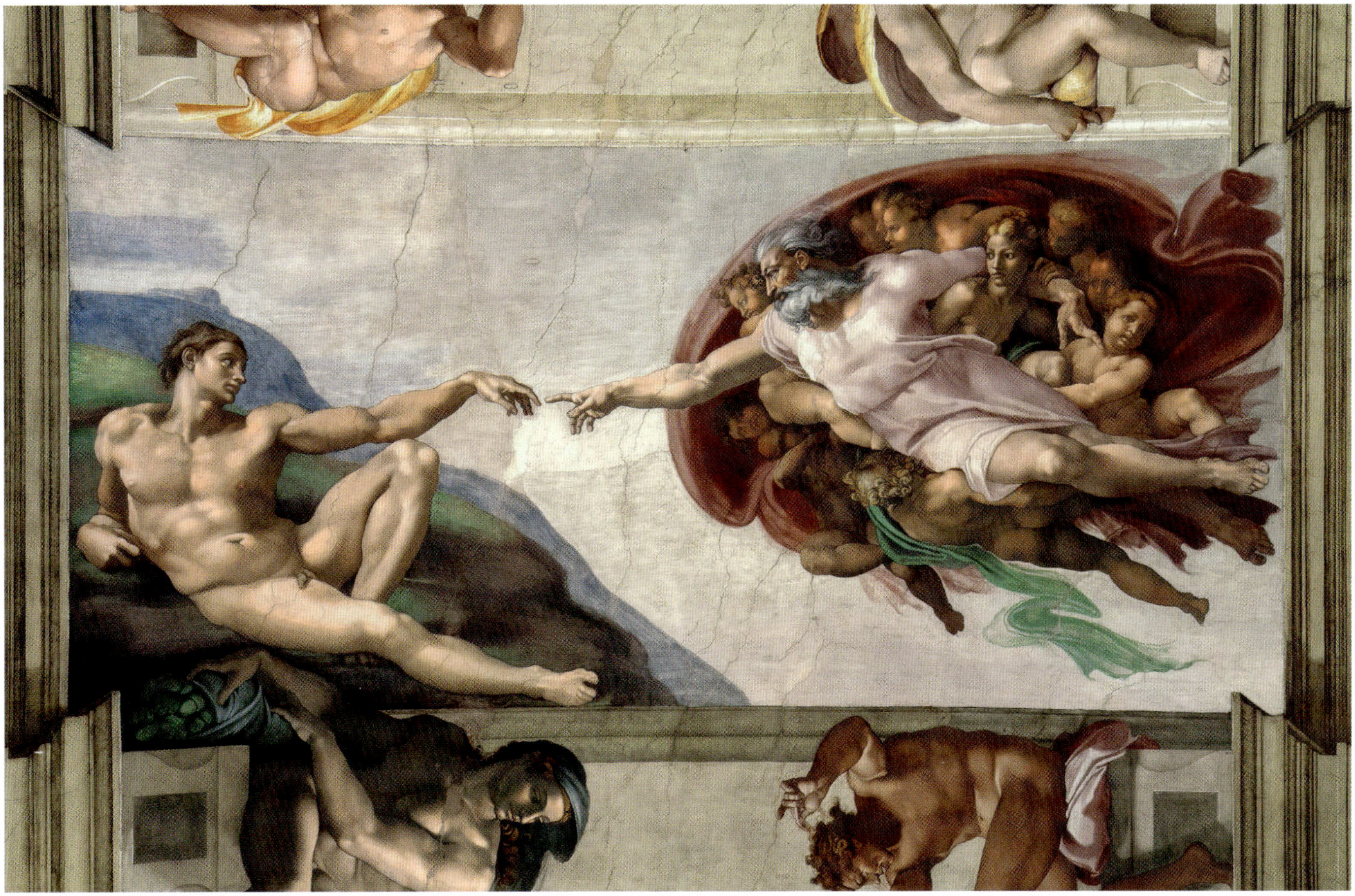

Michelangelo convinced the Pope to expand the commission from painting illusionistic antique sculptures on the chapel's pendentives to a multi-scene illustration of the Old Testament account of the creation of the world. At its centre, Michelangelo positioned the figure of God transferring the spark of life to his ultimate creation, Adam. The nude figure, portraying the first human being as a reflection of the image of the divine, is magnificently proportioned in accord with the classical ideal. It has not been possible to link the image of Adam to a single source, but the torque and flex of Adam's torso reflects Michelangelo's command of the classical form that he gained in Rome. Not only did he now have access to the collection of antique sculpture possessed by the papacy, but his reputation opened the doors of private collectors.

Michelangelo emulated the antique ideal with a full understanding of how the body worked and how to represent that in paint as well as marble. However, his own classicism reached beyond mere imitation; Adam's beauty is that of the perfect balance of classical physicality and Christian spirituality, a vital beauty that gives form to the essential beliefs of the *renovatio*. ●

▲

Michelangelo (1475–1564)
The Creation of Adam, Sistine Chapel ceiling
c. 1512, fresco, *c*. 230 x 480 cm (91 x 189 in)

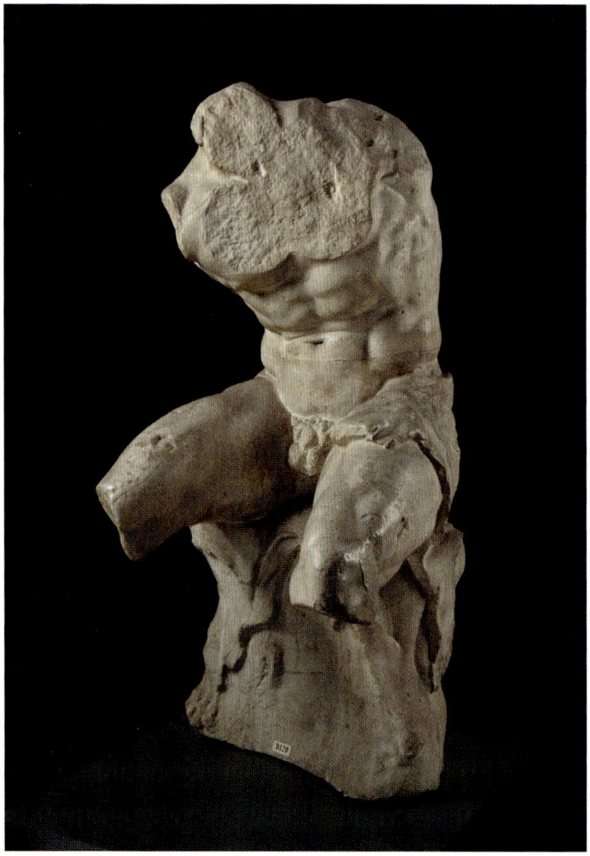

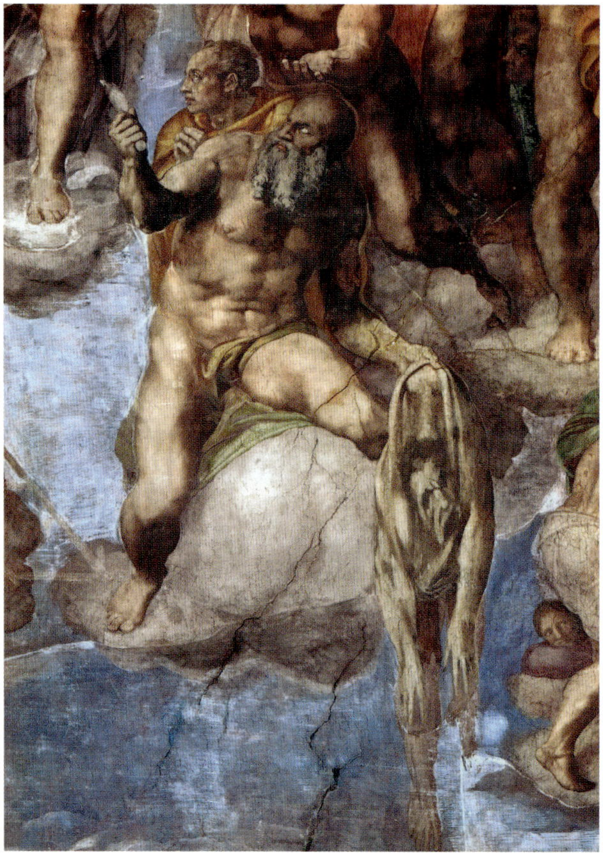

▲

Apollonius of Athens (fl. first century BC)
The Belvedere Torso
c. first century BC, marble,
157 x 90 cm (62 x 35 in)

This fragment – variously identified as Hercules, Marsyas or Polyphemus – came into the Roman collection of Cardinal Prospero Colonna in 1443. It did not enter the Vatican collection until the 1530s, but Michelangelo was known to have held a long-standing admiration for it, purportedly refusing Pope Julius II's request to replace the missing head and limbs. Even as a fragment, Michelangelo regarded it as an ultimate example of expressive muscular movement and repeatedly mirrored the form in his own portrayal of emotional physicality.

▲

Michelangelo
St Bartholomew, detail from *The Last Judgment*, the Sistine Chapel
1535–41, fresco, full artwork: 14 × 12 m (50 x 40 ft)

In 1534, Pope Clement VII commissioned Michelangelo to complete his work in the Sistine Chapel by painting a vast scene of the Last Judgment on the altar wall. Among the martyred saints he depicted Barthlomew, holding his flayed skin. The torque of the torso and the position of the saint's legs echo that of the *Belvedere Torso*, and while many scholars interpret the self-portrait of the artist within the skin as a testament that Michelangelo, too, felt martyred, the body of the saint acknowledges his deep debt to the antique.

Angelica Kauffman (1741–1807)
Design
1778–80, oil on canvas, 126 x 149 cm (50 x 59 in)

To personify the idea of 'Design' for an allegorical ensemble in the Royal Academy's Council Room, Kauffman portrayed a young woman sketching the *Belvedere Torso*. Since the time of Michelangelo, artists mastered the human figure through the close study of classical examples. To that end, art academies acquired plaster replicas of the works regarded as the most indicative of the antique ideal. And for women, barred from life class, these replicas provided the best opportunity to study the male form.

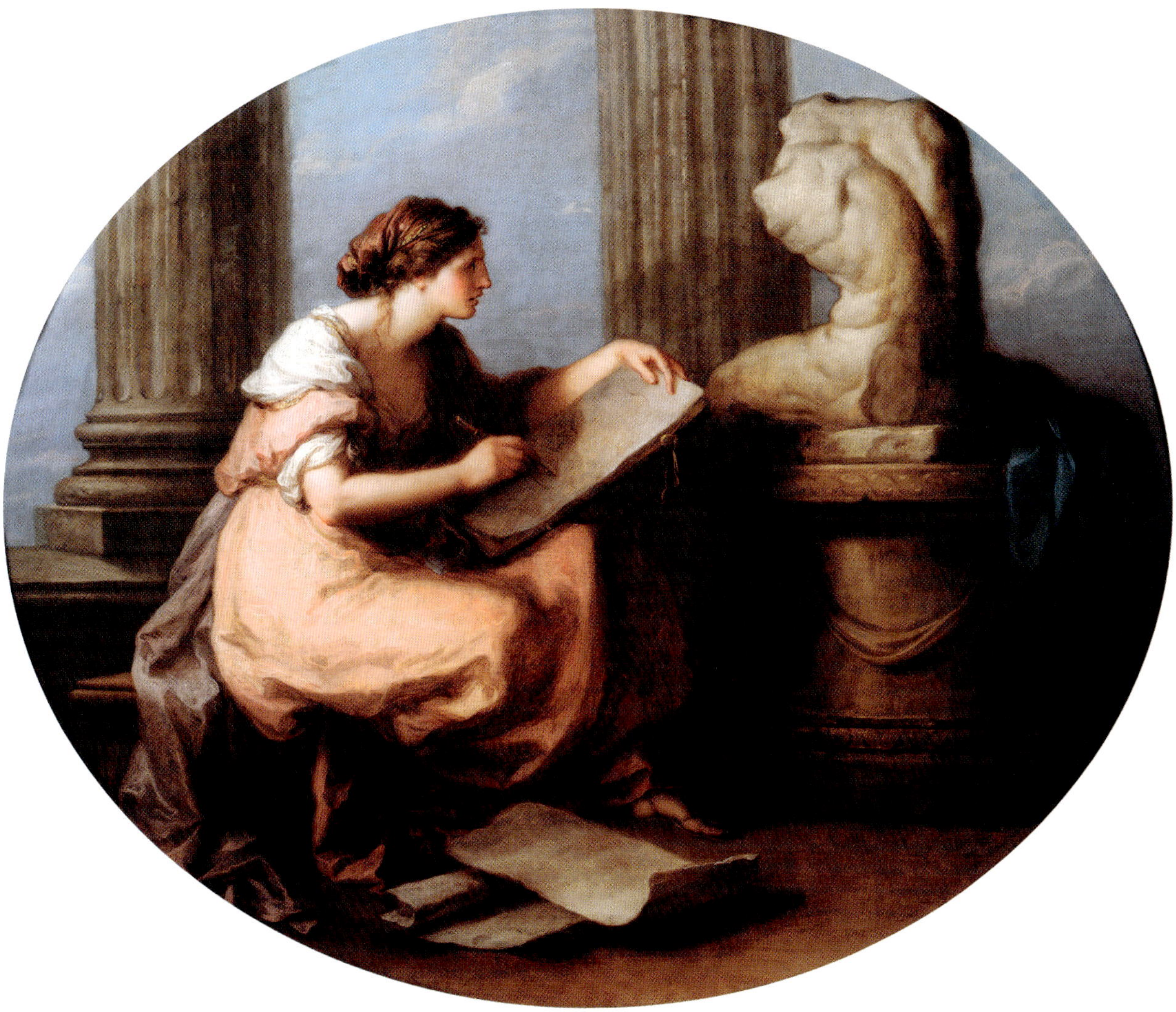

HONOURING TRADITION BY BREAKING THE RULES

How Manet interpreted Renaissance open-air gatherings for modern times

Few works at the Salon des Refusés drew more attention than Manet's *Le Bain* (*The Bath*).[1] Critics faulted Manet for crude execution and brushstrokes applied with a 'floor mop'.[2] The figures seemed lifeless – more mannequins than models – with the foreground nude lacking classical contours. More than anything, the subject baffled the critics. Rustic gatherings had a long and noble history in western art, from royalty relaxing in the countryside to flirtatious shepherds. However here, in a clearly contemporary setting, decorum was breeched by one woman bathing in her chemise while the other has shed her clothing completely. To make matters worse, three of the figures were easily identified: Manet's younger brother Gustave on the left, his brother-in-law, Ferdinand Leenhoff, on the right, and the nude Victorine Meurent whose distinctive features could be seen in the artist's *Mademoiselle V. in the Costume of an Espada* at the same exhibition. Louis Etienne accused Manet of perpetrating a 'young man's practical joke' as a bid for attention.[3] But Manet, over thirty, was hardly young and had already enjoyed success at a recent Salon. And he did not regard the work as a joke; the painting, later retitled *Déjeuner sur l'herbe* (*Luncheon on the Grass*), represents his struggle to forge a bond between honoured art traditions and a modern sensibility.

Throughout history, reference to precedent connected contemporary creative endeavours with tradition. In literature, allusion to previous works – whether in format or phrasing – grounded a new work in authority. The practice played an even wider role in the visual arts, preserving material forms and practices. Masters encouraged their apprentices to copy their works, and as the apprentice matured to master, the incorporation of these images proclaimed their lineage. Familiar configurations – a setting, a group of figures, a pose – added meaning to narrative expression, allowing the viewer to read the subject through established visual vocabulary (see p.132). These practices continued through Manet's day, most notably that of copying significant works of art to develop a visual repertoire, as well as to hone skills. Manet regularly sketched at the Musée du

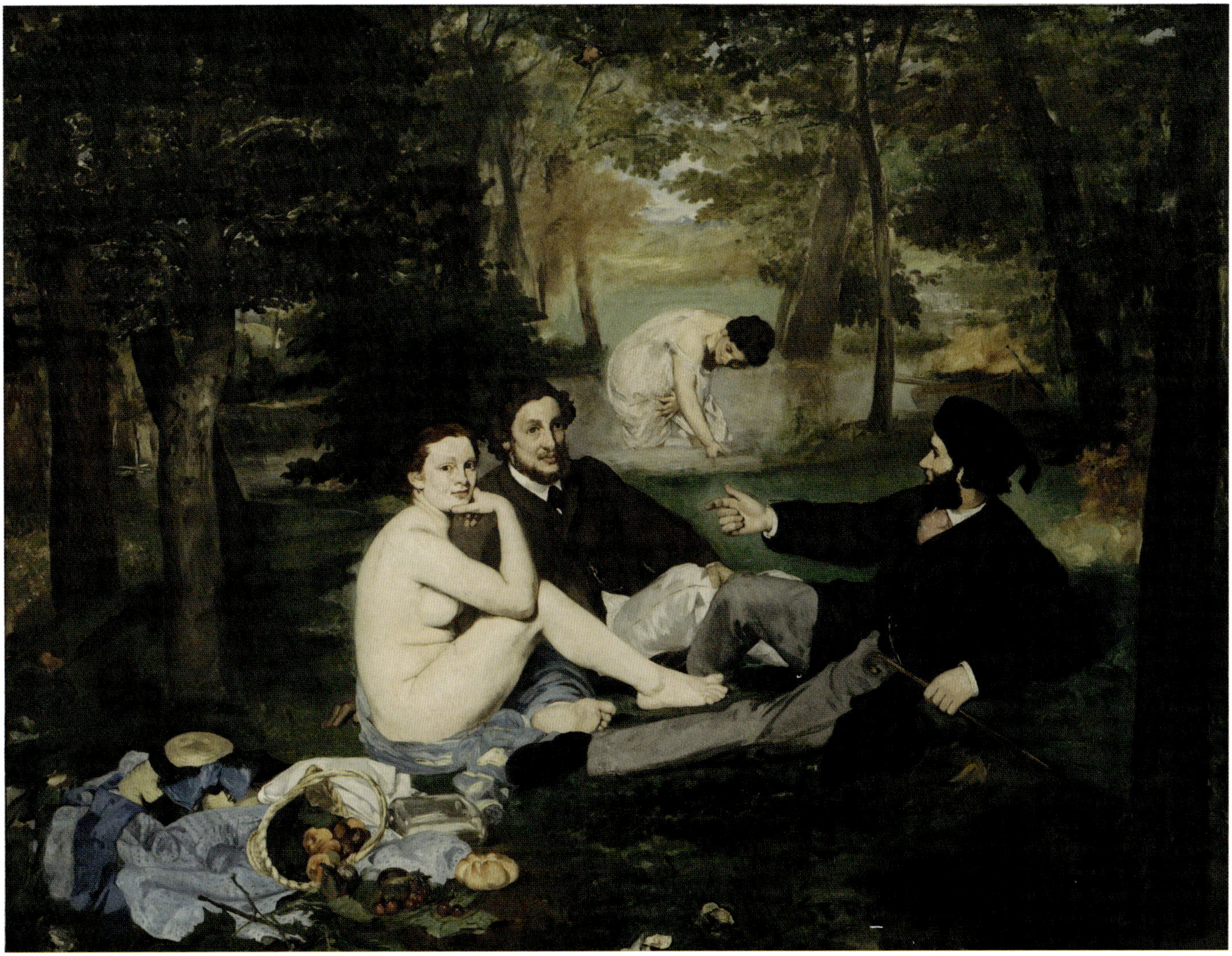

Louvre, and his interest in the sixteenth-century oil painting *Le Concert champêtre* (first attributed to Giorgione but now attributed to Titian) is clearly evident in *Déjeuner sur l'herbe*. Indeed, his long-time friend, Antonin Proust, recalled that Manet had copied 'Giorgione's women, the women with the musicians' with the intention to 'redo it' 35, although Proust may have embellished the memory.The older composition is a meditation on music and friendship; two young men compose a song, graced by the serene presence of Echo and Inspiration in the personified forms of female nudes. *Le Concert champêtre*, well known and widely admired, provided an authoritative template for an open-air gathering; while the reference seems obvious, not a single critic of Manet's painting mentioned the connection.

▲

Édouard Manet (1832–83)
Le Déjeuner sur l'herbe
1863, oil on canvas, 207 x 265 cm (81 x 104 in)

Perhaps Manet's translation of a traditional masterpiece into contemporary terms just went too far for public acceptance. After all, the nude was a real woman, and she, as well as the man behind her, gazed out of the frame, directly at the public. And, at double the size of Giorgione's revered painting, Manet's intention appeared audacious rather than aspirational. He never again attempted such a blunt convergence of the old and new, but his efforts influenced a rising generation of modernists, including Claude Monet who reprised the theme – now with figures fully dressed – on a grander scale two years later. In subsequent years, *Déjeuner sur l'herbe* developed its own authority, inspiring artists from Pablo Picasso to photographer Jeff Wall. It has been reset in popular culture, including fashion photo shoots and record album covers. Manet's manipulation of influence became iconic, demonstrating that at times to honour tradition an innovator has to break the rules. ●

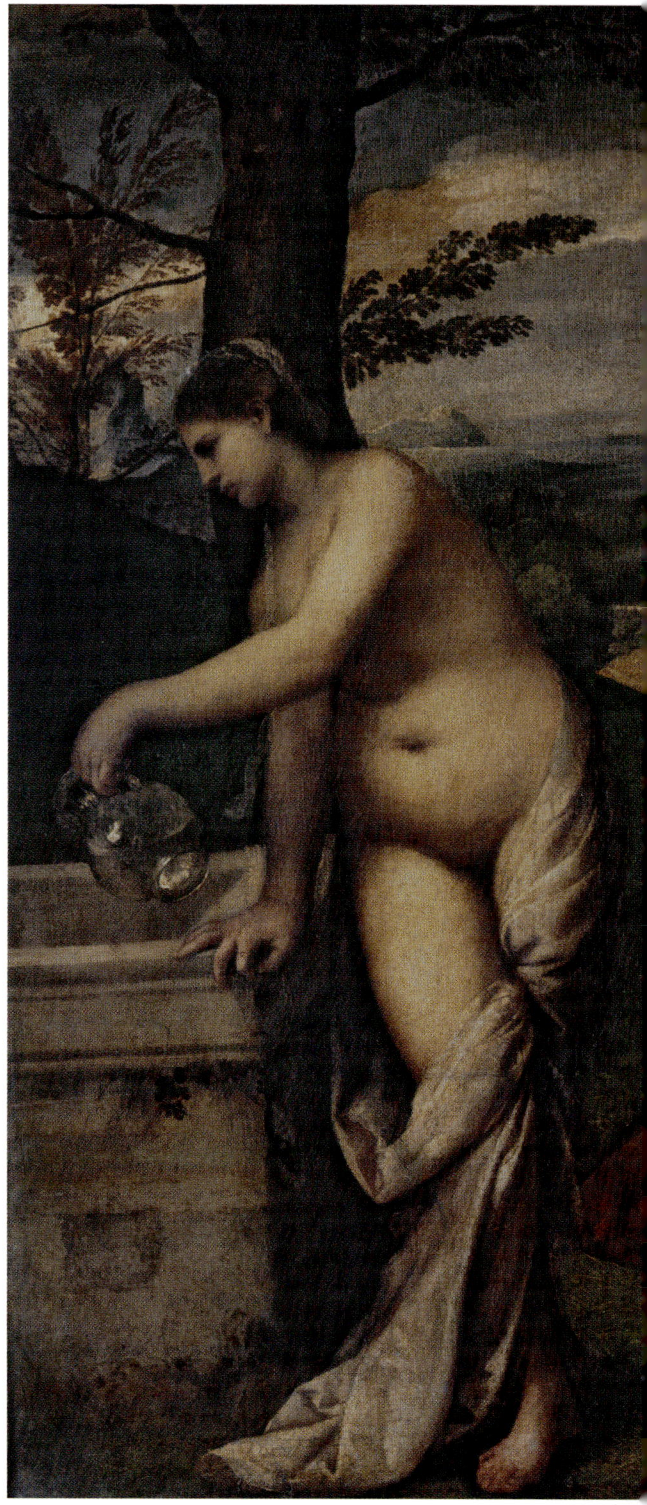

▶

Titian (*c.* 1488/90–1576)
Le Concert champêtre (*The Pastoral Concert*)
1509–10, oil on canvas, 105 x 137 cm (41 x 54 in)

Long attributed to Giorgione, Titian's rustic idyll offers a meditation on creativity. The two young men wear contemporary clothing; the lute player's garments identify him as an aristocrat, while his companion is dressed for agricultural labour. Rather than human women, the female figures embody ideas, recognized as such by the objects they hold – Inspiration fills the well with her pitcher while Echo repeats the melody of the composers' song – as well as their unself-conscious nudity. Manet's choice to substitute real women for the personifications violated the time-honoured convention for depicting the female nude.

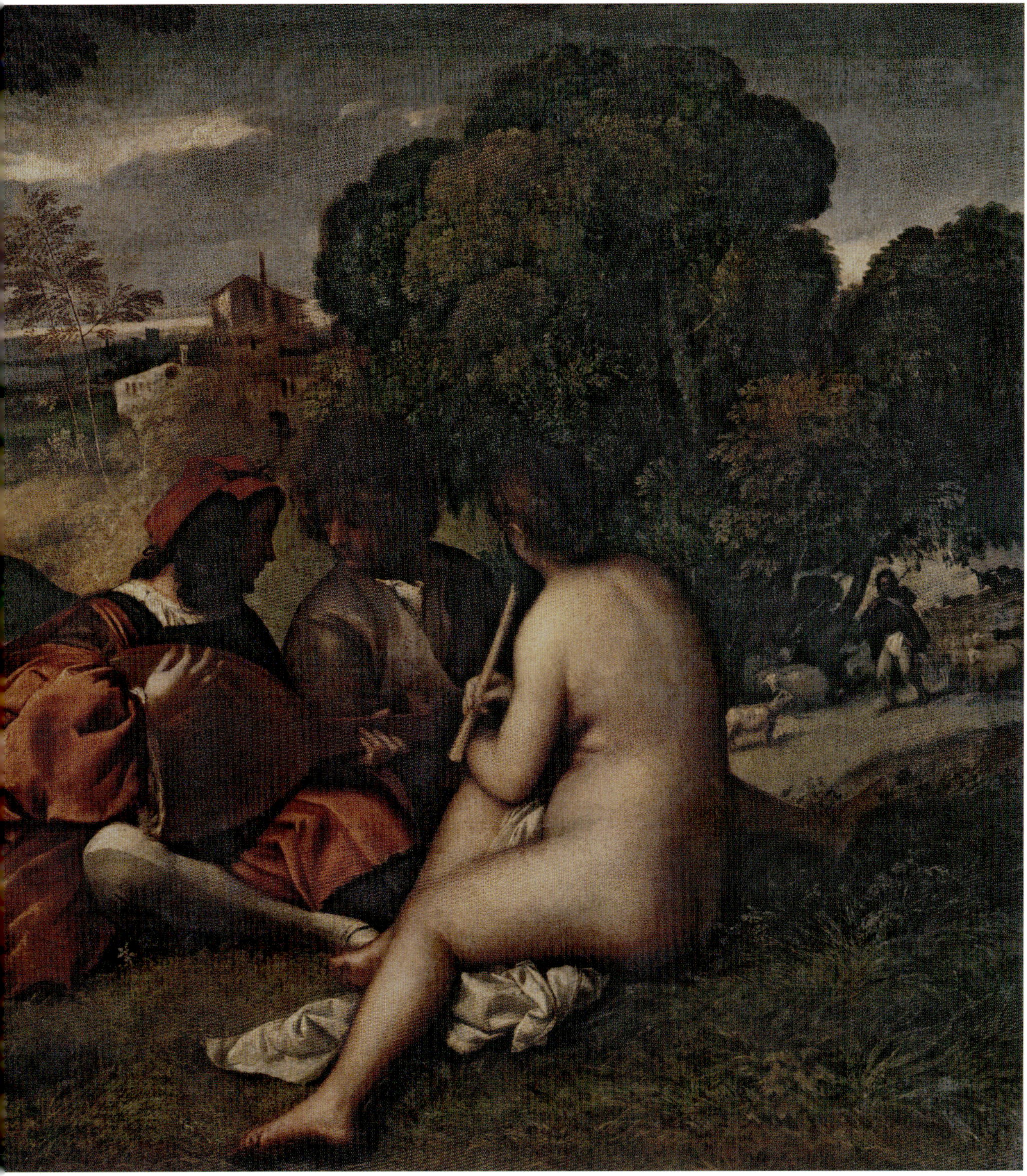

Marcantonio Raimondi (*c*. 1480–before 1534), after Raphael (1483–1520)
The Judgment of Paris
c. 1510–20, engraving, 29 x 44 cm (11 x 17 in)

This print documents a lost painting by the Italian Renaissance master, Raphael. Although the central group of figures represents the subject – the beauty contest that led to the Trojan War – it was the grouping at the right that influenced Manet. He directly quoted the positions of the two river gods and a naiad and wittily substituted contemporary objects for mythological iconography: a walking stick for the River God's reed and a picnic basket atop the abandoned blue gown for Athena's cast-off helmet.

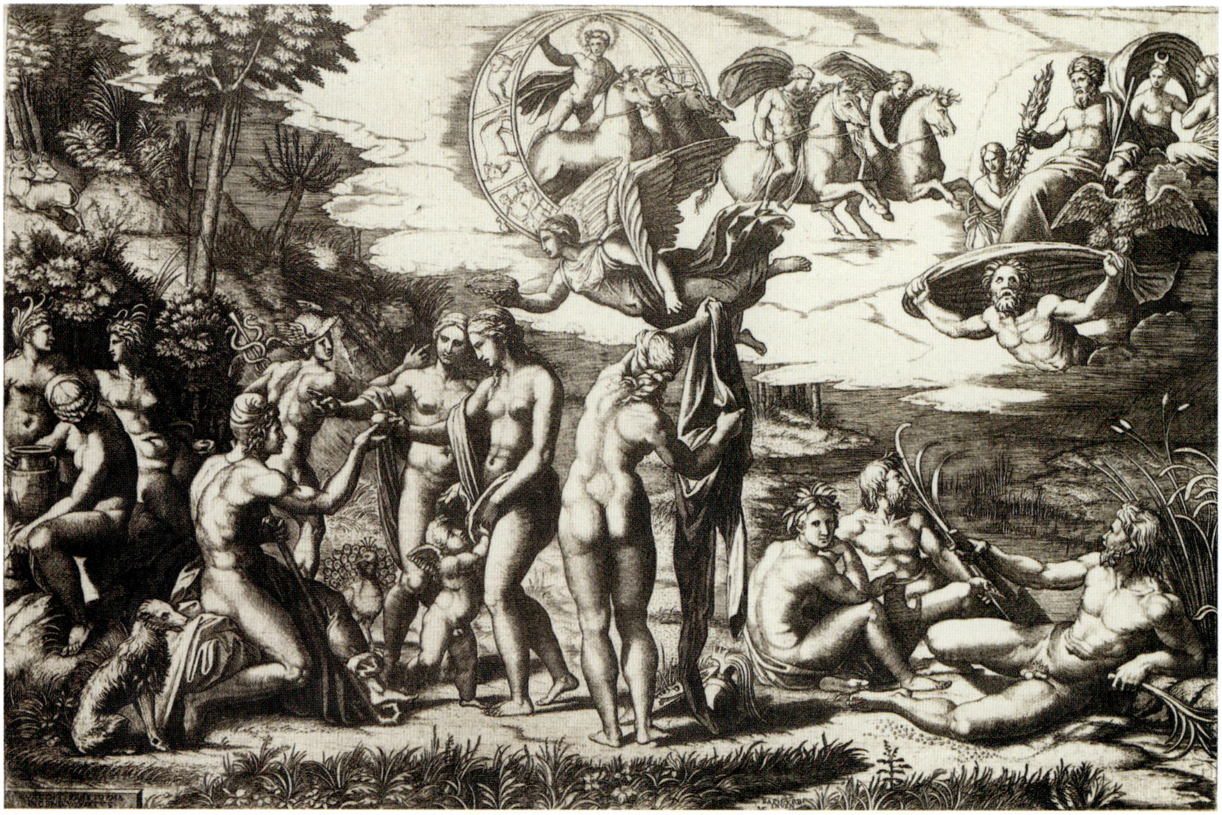

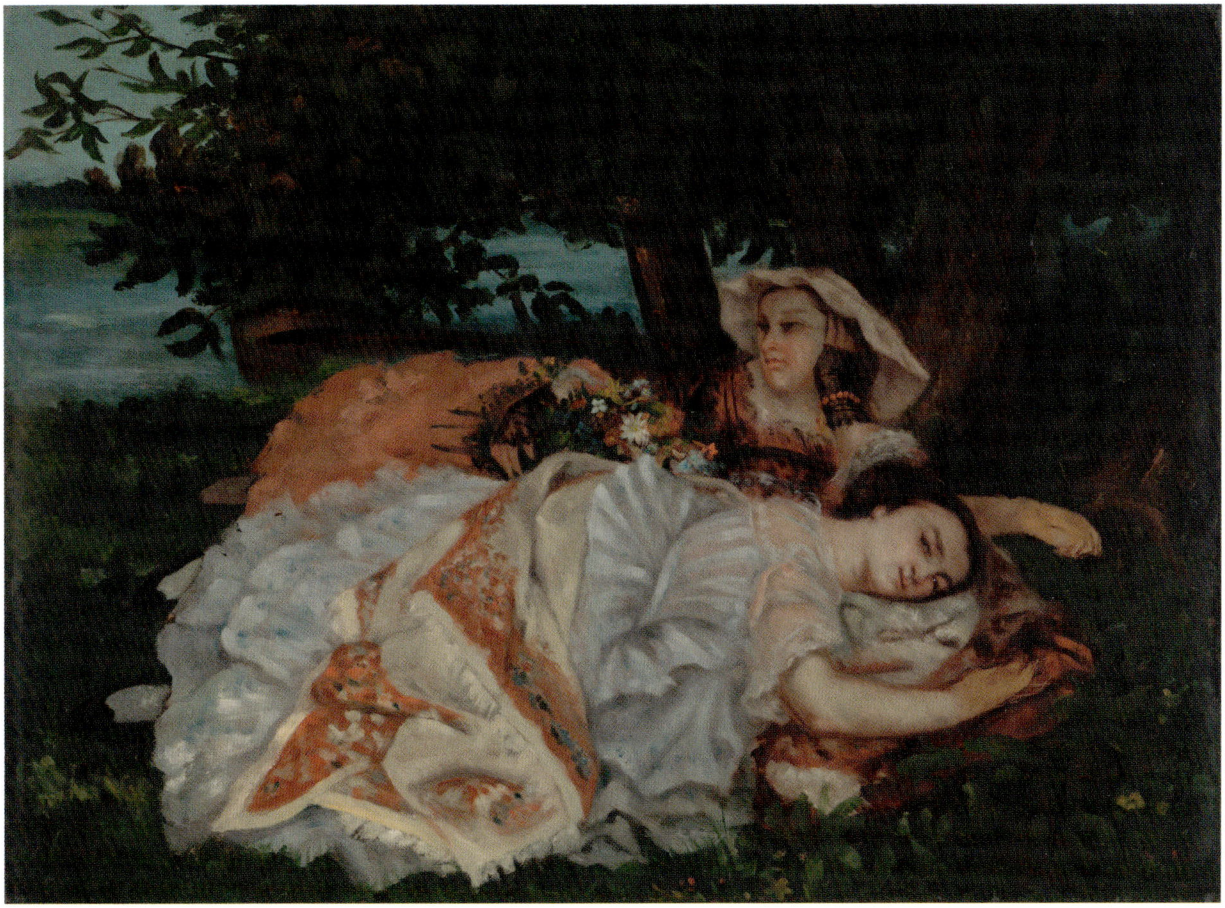

▲

Gustave Courbet (1819–77)
Young Ladies on the Banks of the Seine
1856–57, oil on canvas, 174 x 206 cm (69 x 81 in)

Courbet faced his own critical barrage when he exhibited this painting at the 1857 Salon. Updating the concept of an outdoor idyll by featuring two women sprawled on the banks of the Seine on a hot summer's day – one has removed her bodice and skirt – prompted viewers to wonder about the women's reputation, profession and even their relationship. Manet deeply admired Courbet's realist approach and, no doubt, drew inspiration from his efforts to invigorate tradition with a modern sensibility.

LOOKING THROUGH A DIFFERENT LENS

How Degas' spatial dynamism was inspired by the nascent age of photography

Edgar Degas celebrates the urbane spirit of contemporary Parisian street life in *Place de la Concorde*. The building façades and the walls of the Tuileries Gardens mark the site as the large public square at the eastern end of the Champs-Élysées. The impeccably dressed man in the foreground is Degas' friend Ludovic Napoléon Lepic, and he is accompanied by his daughters Jeanine and Eylau. However, rather than portraying known individuals in a specific place, Degas evokes the ambience of the world in which they live. This is modern Paris, and by using daring angles and a bold composition, Degas renders the dynamic visual character of modernity that poet Charles Baudelaire described as 'the ephemeral, the fugitive, the contingent'.[1] The scene appears unplanned – immediate and spontaneous – as if seen in the blink of an eye or at the click of a camera's shutter.

By the time he painted *Place de la Concorde*, Degas had demonstrated a keen and well-established interest in photography. He had sat for several professional studio portraits and collected *cartes-de-visite* (card-sized photographs) of celebrities and friends. He kept a selection of photographs in his studio and repeatedly studied photographic portraits – of his sitters and of himself – to sharpen the quality of likeness in his own work. There were a number of photographers in his circle, most notably Gaspard-Félix Tournachon, better known as Nadar, who hosted the First Impressionist Exhibition (1874) in his studio. With its sense of visual accident – the random movement of the figures, the emptiness of the central space, the carriage entering the scene in the left midground, the cut-off figure of a man turning to look at Lepic who strides right out of the picture plane – Degas' depiction of spatial dynamism appears to have been directly taken from photographic imagery. However, while his fascination with new ways of seeing eventually led him to take his own photographs, he did not do so until at least a decade after he painted this scene, and he did not own a camera until 1895.

Degas resisted any element of the accidental in his art. He famously stated, 'No art was ever less spontaneous than mine.'[2] Throughout his career he maintained the disciplined practice that he had learned as a student at the École des Beaux-Arts: sketching from life, making preparatory drawings and perfecting his motifs by repeating them in pencil, pastel, charcoal and even clay. While his method was deliberate and rigorous, and his respect for traditional mastery genuine and deeply rooted, he was always

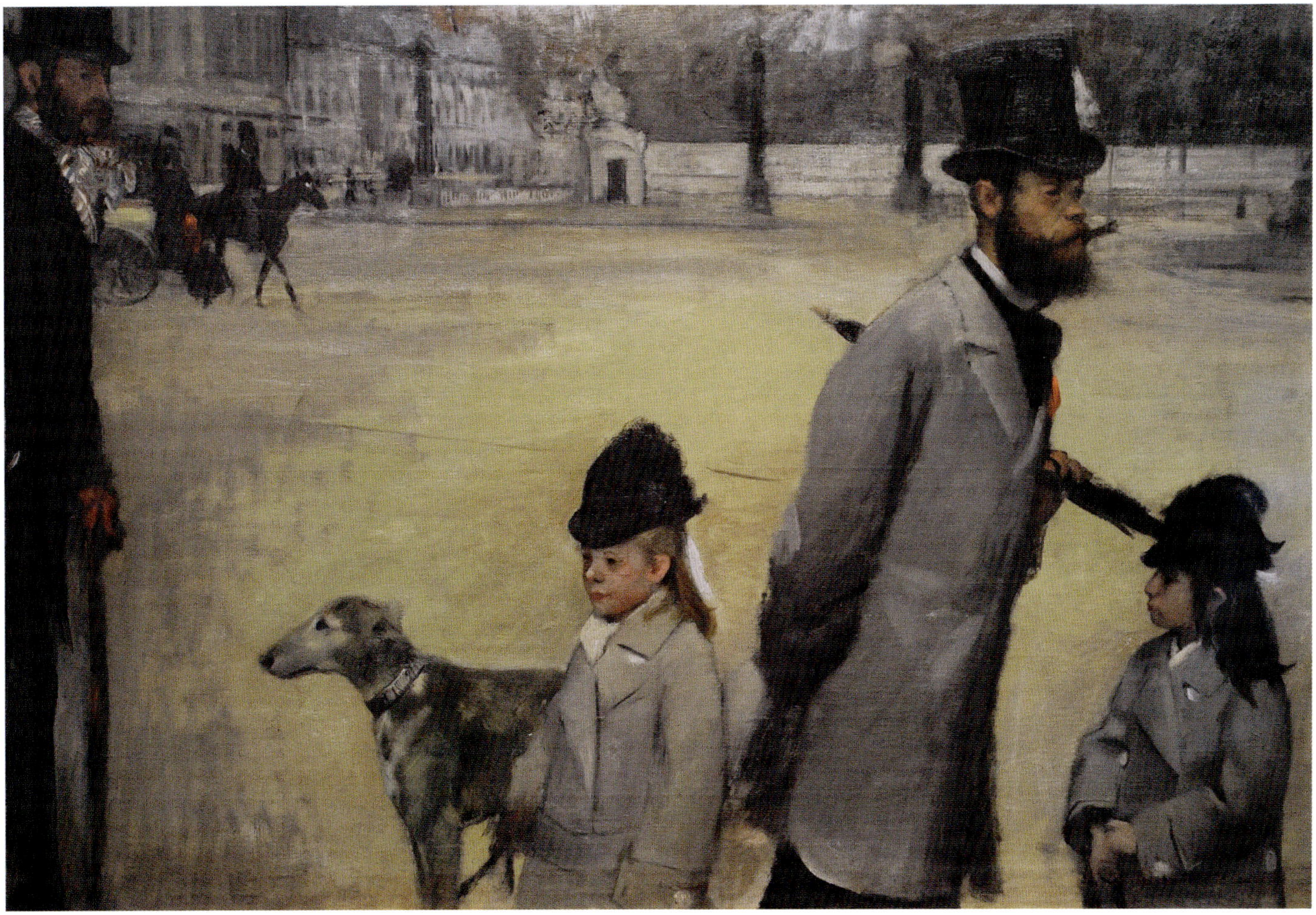

interested in innovation. This is clearly evident in the range of visual strategies he incorporated to create the freeze-frame effect in *Place de la Concorde*. Certainly the foreground figures – caught in motion and cropped at the edges of the picture plane – echo the compositional suggestion of capture in photography, but the placement of Lepic, as well as the man on the left, also recall the seventeenth-century device known as a *repoussoir* figure. Literally translated as 'pusher', this refers to a large figure positioned in the right or left foreground that defines and contains the space as well as heightening the sense of depth within the picture plane, providing the effect of an inverted proscenium. The dynamic angles and empty space, as well as the cut-off forms, also may draw upon Degas' knowledge of *ukiyo-e*, the Japanese prints that he, like his fellow Impressionists, avidly collected. Along with photography, these sources demonstrated different perspectives and alternative methods that enhanced representation. And while photography was an influence, it is more apt to regard Degas' approach in *Place de la Concorde* as in tandem with, rather than in imitation of, the medium in a shared quest to capture the spirit of modern life. ●

▲

Edgar Degas (1834–1917)
Place de la Concorde
1875, oil on canvas, 78 x 117 cm (31 x 46 in)

Louis Daguerre (1787–1851)
Boulevard du Temple
1838, daguerreotype

This bird's-eye view of a boulevard is believed to be the earliest surviving example of the daguerreotype, a process Daguerre first began to develop with Joseph Nicéphore Niépce nearly a decade earlier. To capture the image, a copper plate coated with polished silver and treated with light-sensitizing iodine was exposed for up to 15 minutes. As a result, the carriage and foot traffic on the street did not register; only the boot black and his client in the near left foreground held still for a sufficient time. Like Degas, Daguerre crafted an accidental view through a deliberate technique.

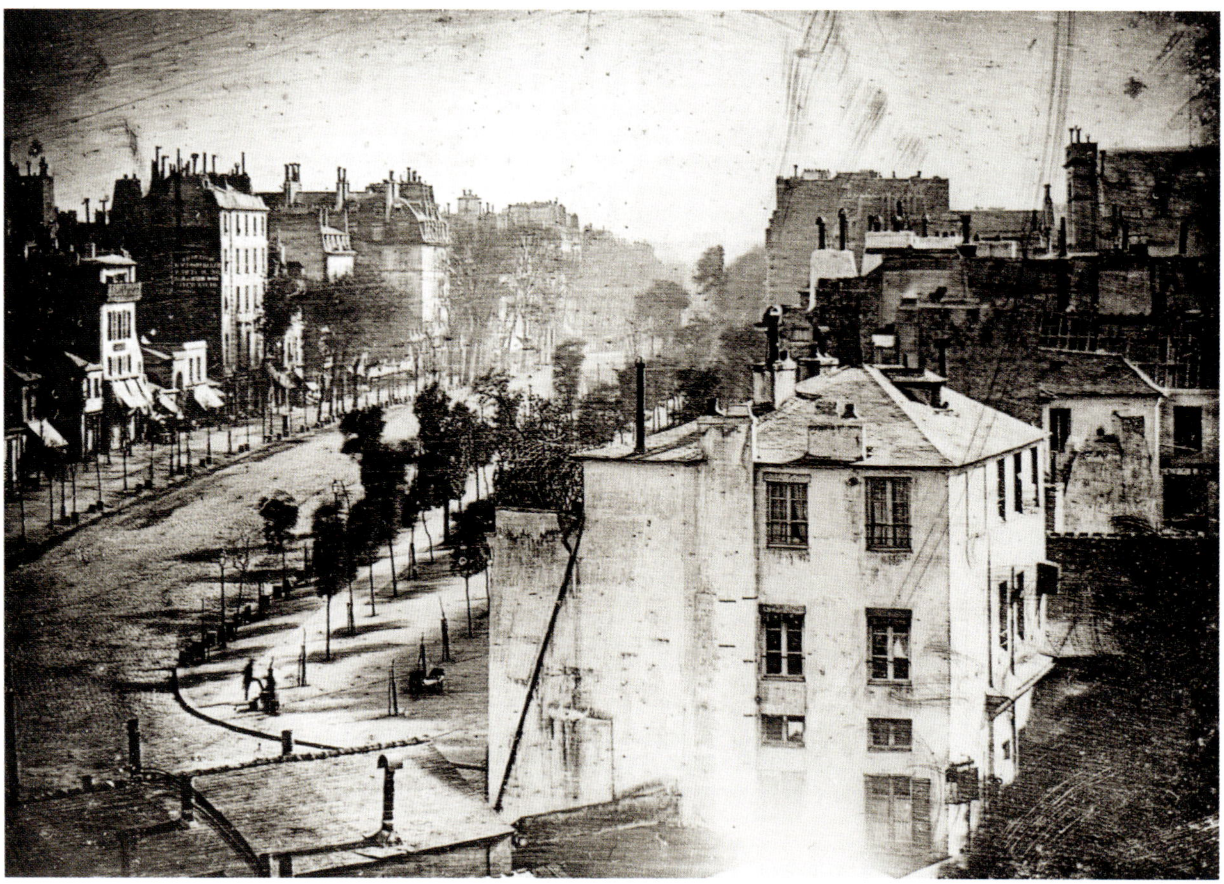

Johannes Vermeer (1632–75)
Officer and Laughing Girl
c. 1655–60, oil on canvas, 51 x 46 cm (20 x 18 in)

The figure of the officer, filling the left foreground corner, guides the viewer's eye to the focal point of the painting: the light-struck face of the laughing girl. Vermeer angled the man's position and cloaked him in shadow; like an inverted stage proscenium, the officer frames the scene. Known as a *repoussoir* (pusher) figure, and characteristic of seventeenth-century European painting, this device added dynamic depth to the picture plane. Degas adopted this practice in his own work, with the jaunty figure of Lepic in *Place de la Concorde* marking his most effective application.

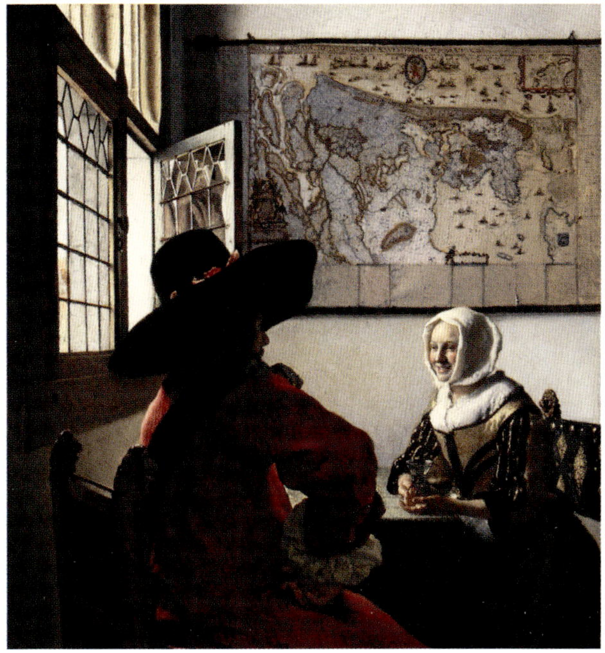

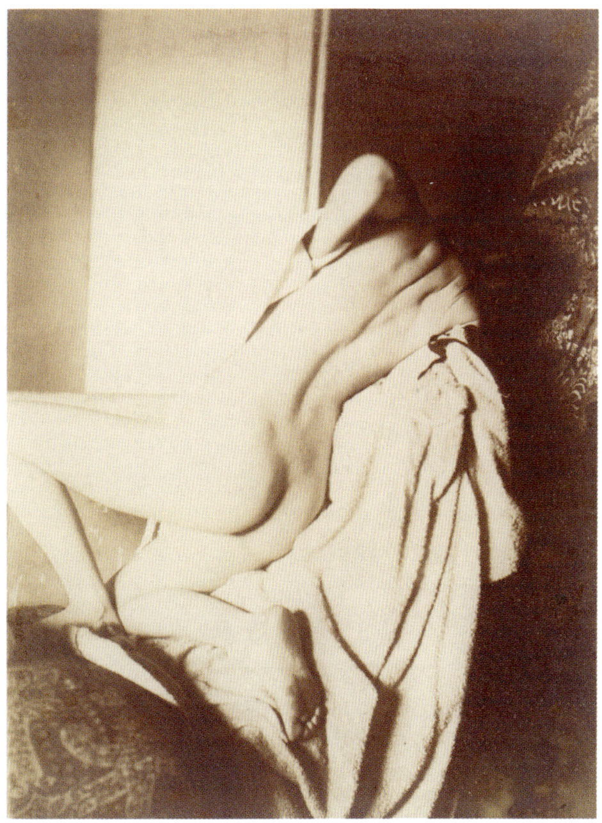

Edgar Degas
After the Bath, Woman Drying her Back
1896, gelatin silver print, 17 x 12 cm (7 x 5 in)

Degas acquired a camera in 1895, and many of his photographs comprise conventional portraits and posed tableaux. In contrast, *After the Bath* explores the play of light and shadow on a model's body. In fact, the image was part of a wider study in varied media of women drying themselves after bathing. This exact pose can be seen in an oil painting, now in the collection of the Philadelphia Museum of Art. While Degas may have regarded the photograph as a means to develop the painted image, it has a compelling photographic aesthetic all its own.

SHIFTING SENSATIONS

How Steer updated Constable's naturalism

Before launching his career in London, Steer spent time in Paris where he followed a well-established path of training: a round of preparatory sessions at the Académie Julian and then classes at the École des Beaux-Arts. While his studies were thoroughly conventional, the art world beyond the official institutions introduced him to a full range of advanced ideas, especially in Steer's chosen field of landscape. During his stay (1882–84) he discovered the fresh, atmospheric aesthetic of Impressionism, and although there was not an Impressionist exhibition while he was in residence, works by the artists associated with the movement – notably Claude Monet and Camille Pissarro – were on view in contemporary galleries. Upon his return to England, Steer applied the spontaneous, *plein-air* technique to local views, which quickly earned him acclaim as the foremost British practitioner of what was dismissively labelled by an anonymous critic in the *Art Journal* as the 'dab and dot school'.[1] But Steer's approach was only partly inspired by Impressionism. The foundation for his naturalistic style owed as much to two masters of an earlier generation that had influenced Monet and Pissarro: J.M.W. Turner and John Constable.

In the early 1890s, Steer visited a number of sites that Turner had depicted throughout his career, ranging from Richmond Hill to Chepstow. Rather than reprising the renowned painter's subjects, Steer wanted to immerse himself in the atmosphere that Turner had so powerfully captured on canvas, shifting his attention from the topography of the locale to the visual sensations of light and weather conditions. In this, Steer forged an alignment between British naturalistic landscape and the modernist motivations of the Impressionists, for, as he explained in a lecture to the Art Workers' Guild in 1891, 'The Impressionist is inspired by his own time because he is inspired by nature.'[2] In his paint handling – loose, with heavy impasto – he followed Constable, but Steer had a distinct advantage. Prior to the development of pre-mixed oil paint in collapsable tubes in 1841, artists who desired to work outdoors had to mix the pigment in the studio and carry it to the site in clumsy, resealable bladders. Keen to make oil sketches, Constable limited his on-site palette to a modest range of white, black, blue and red. When he returned to the studio, he reworked his studies into larger sketches, which he then used for the

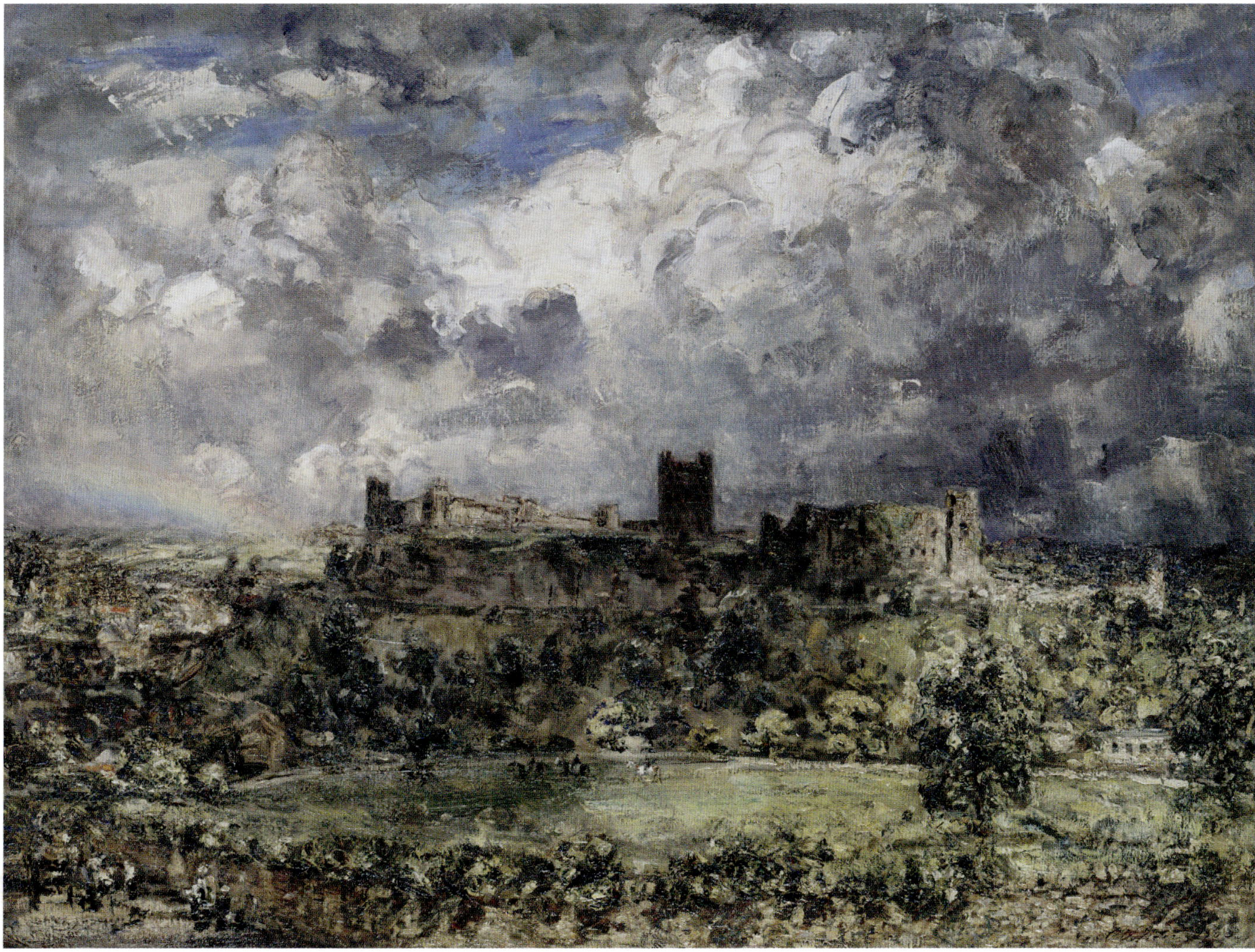

monumentally scaled paintings – his six-footers – that he created for formal exhibition. With tubes of paint and a portable easel, Steer was not limited to the studio; he could work directly on his canvas at the site.

Steer first visited Richmond in North Yorkshire, a location he associated with Turner, in 1895, making some sketches of the medieval keep. He returned in the summer of 1903 and created a makeshift studio in an abandoned chapel on high ground with a panoramic view of the castle from across the River Swale. The chapel also served as a handy retreat from the near constant inclement weather. With a heavily loaded brush and a palette that strikingly contrasts the land and sky, Steer captured the thick, roiling clouds breaking to reveal a patch of blue. His treatment of the ground below evokes the glistening aftermath of a downpour; the sensation of cooling humidity cloaks the details of the vista.

▲

Philip Wilson Steer (1860–1942)
Richmond Castle
1903, oil on canvas, 77 x 102 cm (30 x 40 in)

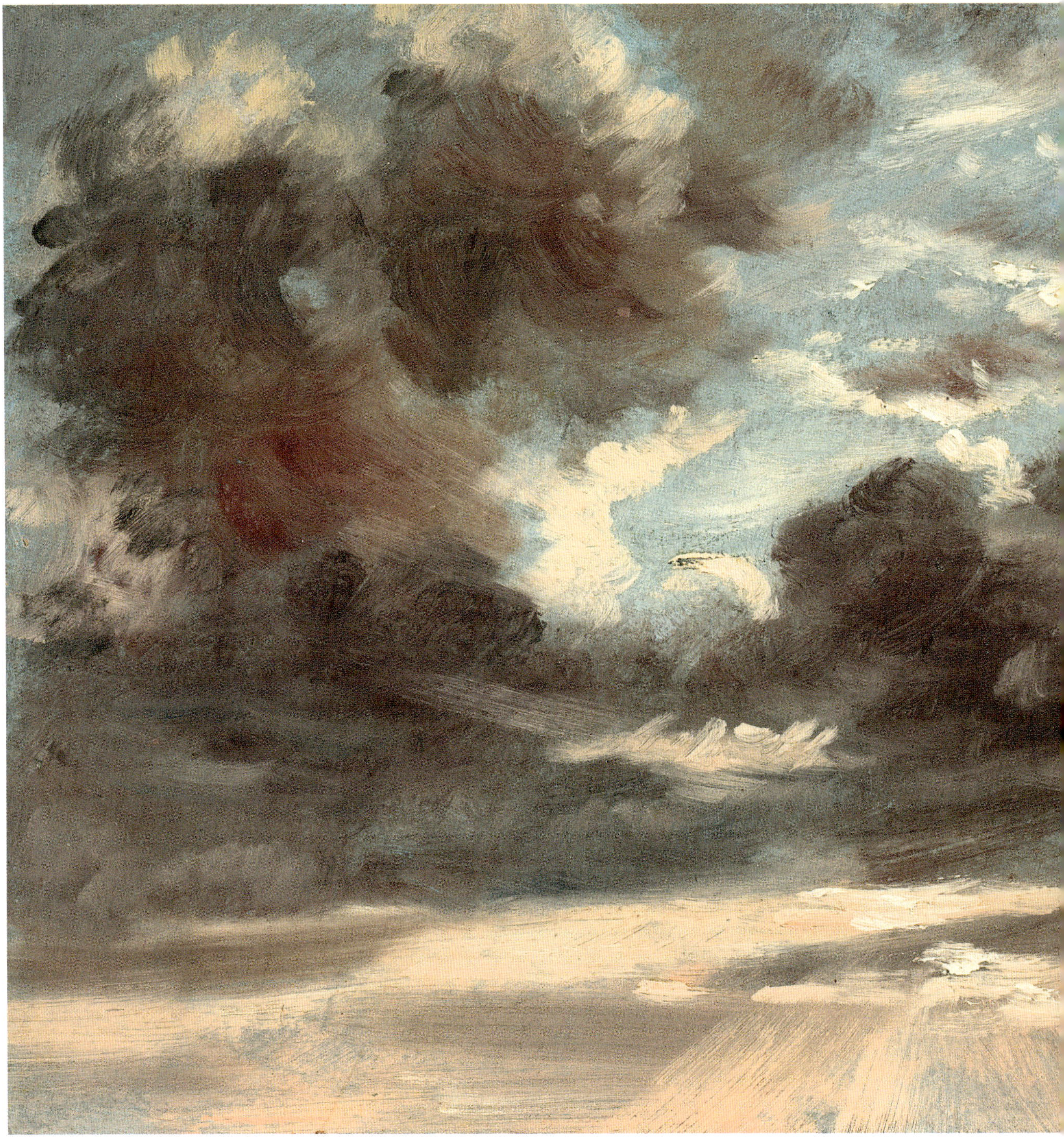

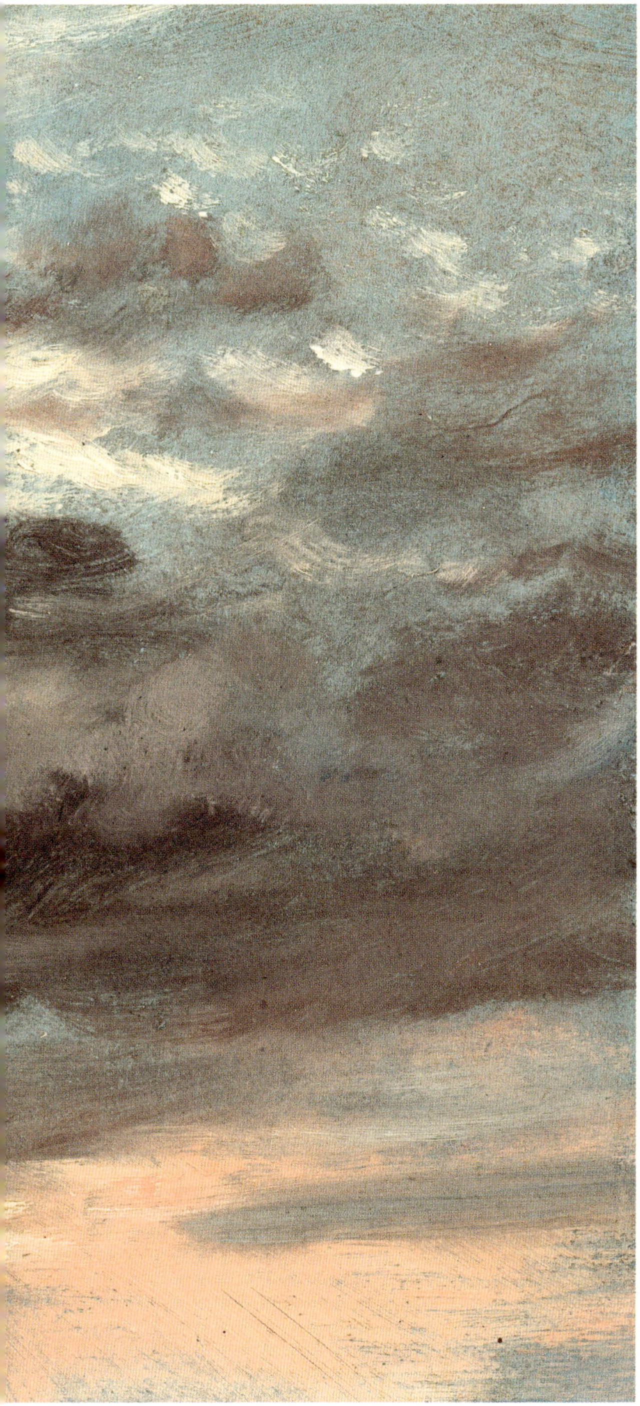

The castle complex is softly rendered, anchoring the composition while muting the building's architectural character. The stabilizing placement of the building, the descriptive brushstrokes and, most importantly, the volatile sky, all echo Constable's studio sketches, many of which, by this time, were held in museum collections. By working fully outdoors, recording immediate observations rather than relying on memory in the studio, Steer updated British naturalism through the innovations of Impressionism, fusing the practices he most admired at home and abroad. ●

◀

John Constable (1776–1837)
Cloud Study: Stormy Sunset
1821–22, oil on paper on canvas, 20 x 27 cm (8 x 11 in)

Long fascinated by the movement of clouds, Constable took up a practice he called 'skying'. He prepared a limited palette of oil pigments in the studio and headed outdoors with brushes and absorbent paper. Looking up, he worked quickly, blending wet colours to capture such changing effects as this rose-tinted, clearing sky. He often identified the cloud types, as well as the date and time, on the back of the sketch. He made around forty of these sketches between 1819 and 1824, which he used as visual references in his studio work.

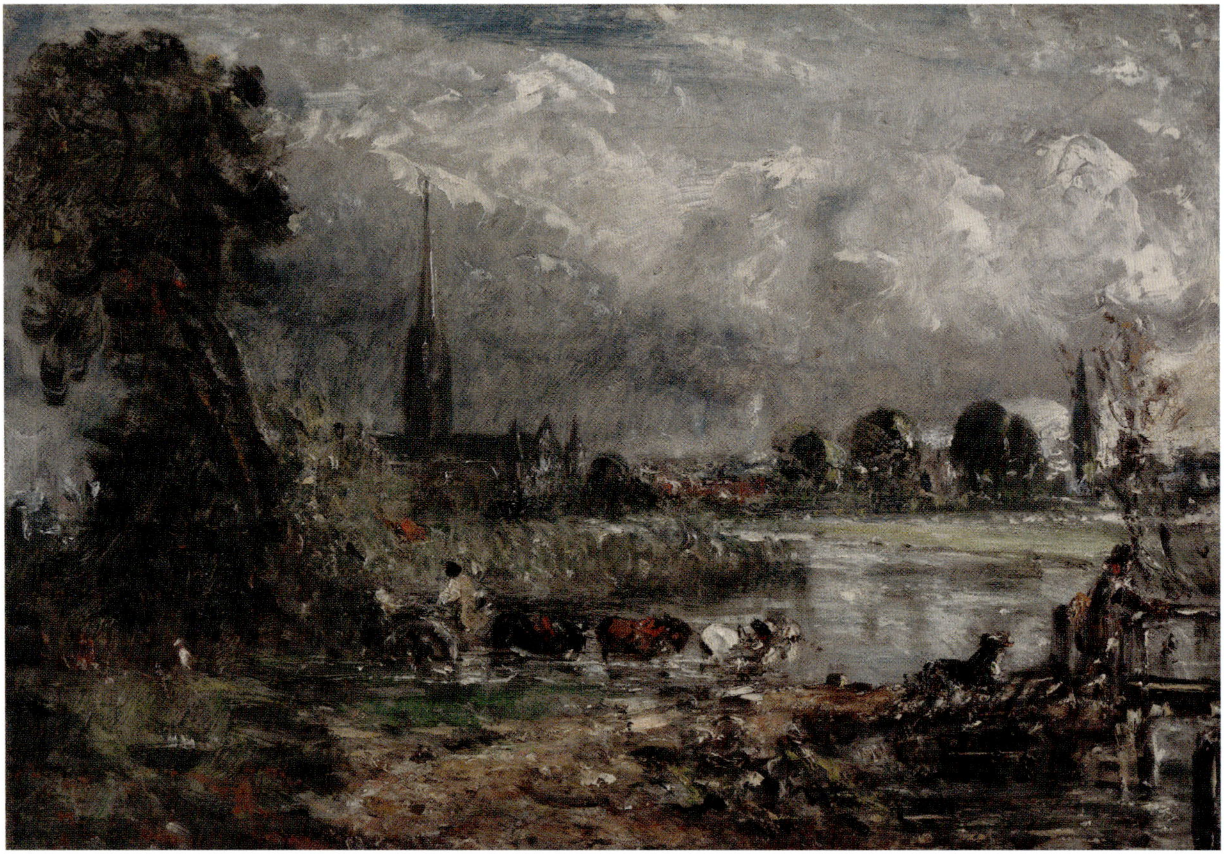

▲
John Constable
Salisbury Cathedral from the Meadows
c. 1829, oil on canvas, 36 x 51 cm (14 x 20 in)

This studio oil sketch is believed to be the last of many studies for the finished version of the subject which Constable exhibited at the Royal Academy in London in 1831. His process encompassed many stages, including on-site sketches. Never intended for public display, this type of study allowed Constable to collect and render his visual impressions using a full palette applied with unrestricted freedom. Charged with the vitality of first-hand observation, these sketches appealed to a new generation of painters – as well as collectors – who sought a more authentic vision of nature.

Camille Pissarro (1830–1903)
The Crystal Palace
1871, oil on canvas, 47 x 74 cm (19 x 29 in)

During the Franco-Prussian War of 1870–71, Pissarro took refuge in London. Already a committed *plein-air* painter, Pissarro often set his easel up on the streets of Sydenham. Pissarro found inspiration in the mundane: the ever-present fog, the play of light and shadow, and the low-lying clouds in an active sky. These were the building blocks of what would become the Impressionist landscape, giving the sensation of light and atmosphere precedence over the setting. While in residence, Pissarro also studied the works of Constable and Turner, admiring their expressive portrayal of the natural landscape.

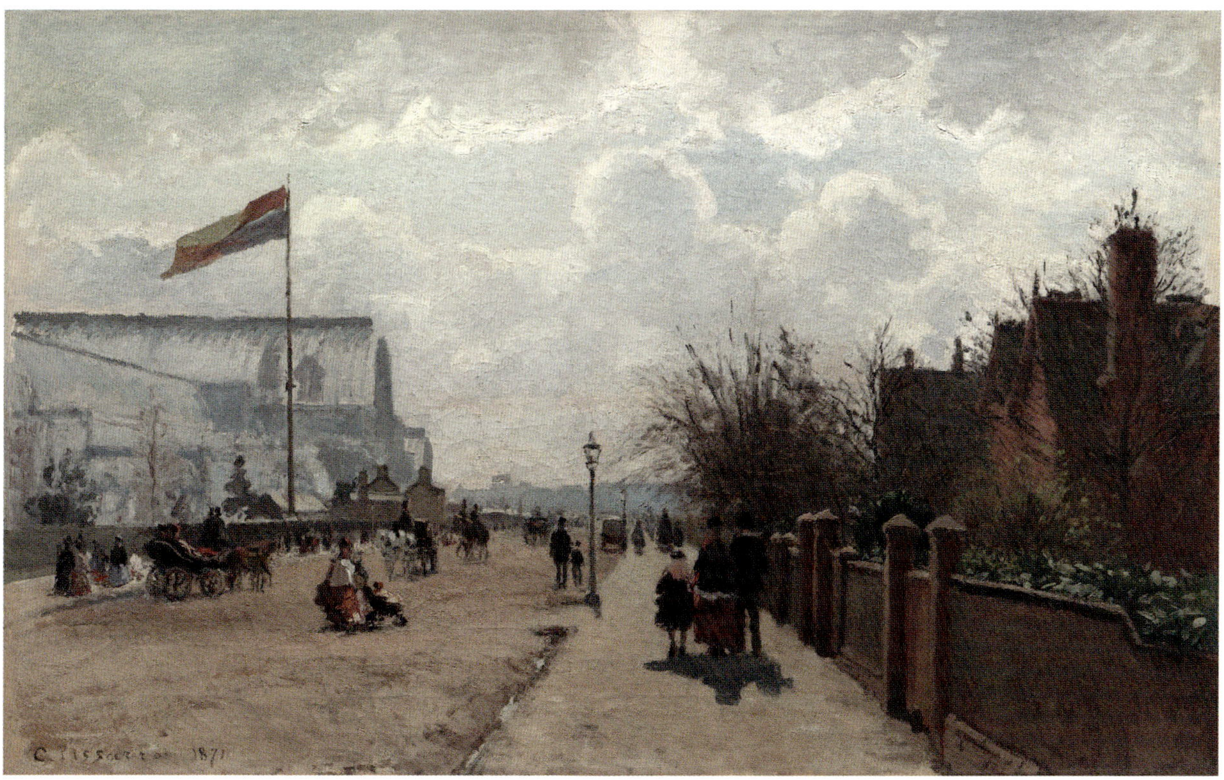

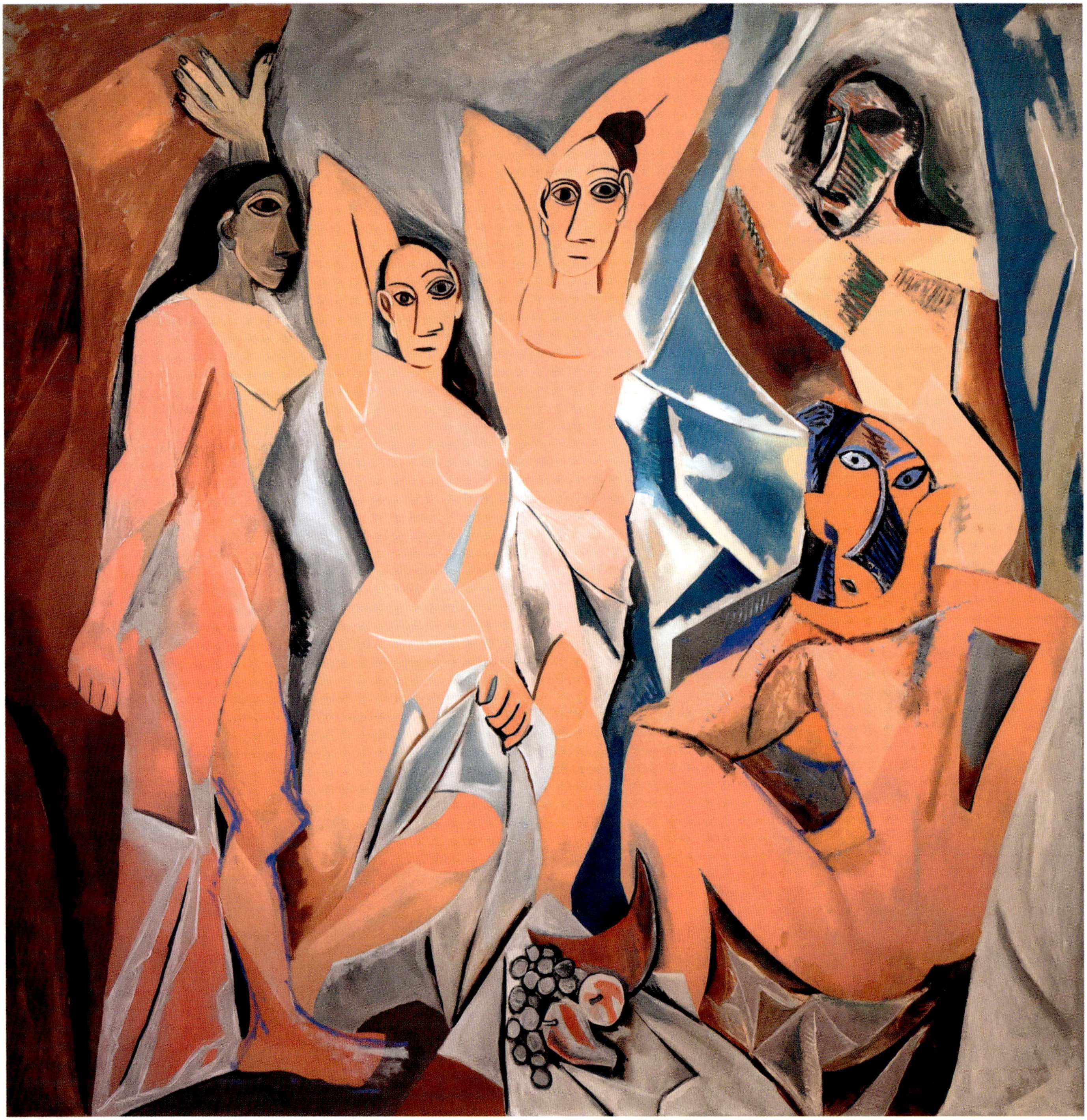

▲

Pablo Picasso (1881–1973)
Les Demoiselles d'Avignon
1907, oil on canvas, 244 x 234 cm (96 x 92 in)

THE MASTER THIEF

How Picasso's *Les Demoiselles d'Avignon* borrowed from Cézanne

On 27 April 1907, Pablo Picasso invited Leo and Gertrude Stein to his studio in the Montmartre district to view an unnamed painting that had preoccupied him since February.[1] The young Spanish artist was keen to exploit the support of the wealthy, expatriate American siblings, but they did not record the details of their visit nor anything about the work they saw. In the following months, a small number of artists and critics also came, and those who did comment found the painting confusing, even disturbing. The grand-scale canvas portrayed five nude women in aggressive postures – arms raised or akimbo, fists clenched – so dynamic that they seemed ready to burst out of the shallow, flattened space. Each figure was statuesque and strongly proportioned; the central two were naturalistically rendered, but the others' limbs and torsos fractured into faceted planes. And rather than conventional facial features, these flanking figures' heads appeared mask-like, as if carved from stone or wood, evoking cultural origins that were not Picasso's own. The art dealer Daniel-Henry Kahnweiler recalled that everyone in Picasso's circle regarded the work as 'something mad or monstrous'.[2] Picasso ignored their reactions, but despite finishing the work mid-summer, he did not exhibit it until 1916. By then, the work had a new name, *Les Demoiselles d'Avignon*, and Picasso had secured a fearless reputation in his quest to redefine the objectives and aesthetics of painting. Ten years on the work still had the power to shock, prompting critic André Breton to remark, 'There is nothing left but to declare oneself for it or against it.'[3]

According to popular lore, Picasso once asserted that 'Good artists borrow, great artists steal.' When and why he said it is uncertain, but over his career Picasso proved himself a master thief. Through academic studies in Barcelona and Madrid, he learned the value of copying the Old Masters, and during his early visits to Paris, where he settled in 1902, he gleaned ideas from Impressionism, Post-Impressionism and Symbolism. The mask-like heads in *Les Demoiselles* signalled his growing fascination with the arts of Africa, the Iberian Peninsula and the southern Pacific, all grouped at the time in Europe under the disparaging descriptor 'primitive'. His earliest encounter with these works cannot be pinpointed; he might have seen an African mask acquired by Henri Matisse or consulted illustrated books, such as Leo Frobenius' *Die Masken und Geheimbünden Afrikas* (*Masks and Secret Societies of Africa*, 1898). Likely the most crucial connection was his visit to an exhibition at the Musée d'Ethnographie du Trocadéro (later Musée de l'Homme; the collection now absorbed by the Musée du quai Branly) in June 1907. Three decades later he told André Malraux that he found the experience unsettling, complaining of a smell of mould and comparing the installation to a 'flea market'. Yet, the masks were a revelation: 'I understood why I was a painter... *Les Demoiselles d'Avignon* must have come to me that day.'[4]

Art scholars have searched – without definitive results – for the masks that inspired Picasso, but he was more intrigued by aesthetics than anthropology, and his method of transformative appropriation is of greater significance than a precise source. The 'primitive' heads in *Les Demoiselles* are just one of many such steals, such as the long-lived theme of the female nude in western art and the structural approach of Paul Cézanne. Picasso even paid tribute to Cézanne by placing a little still life in the lower foreground of the finished painting, a motif that appears in many of his preliminary drawings. It is less significant that Picasso stole or even what he stole than how he openly deployed his theft, layering his art with the purloined references. And his daring prompted subsequent artists to steal ideas from *Les Demoiselles*, as seen in contemporary responses by Matisse and Duchamp, and later in pioneering works by such women artists as Sylvia Sleigh, Jenny Saville and Claudette Johnson. Whether or not Picasso actually said that 'great artists steal' is as of little consequence as the matter of which masks he copied; through his work he demonstrated the artistic potential in theft. ●

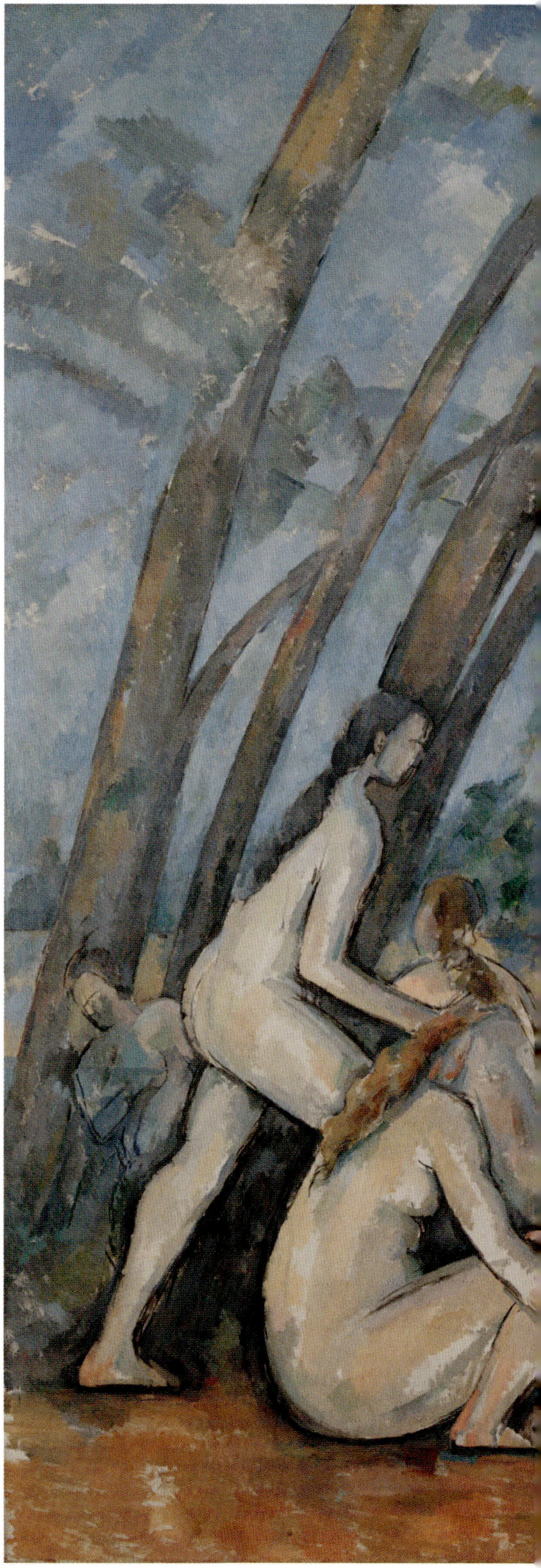

▶

Paul Cézanne (1839–1906)
Les Grandes Baigneuses
1900–06, oil on canvas, 211 x 251 cm (83 x 99 in)

Over the course of his career, Cézanne painted bathers more than one hundred times; Picasso would have seen this version in the memorial retrospective exhibition held at the Salon d'Automne in October 1907, a few months after he finished *Les Demoiselles*. However, it was Cézanne's experimental engagement with the elemental components of painting – compositional geometry, surface, colour, brushstroke – rather than subject matter that captivated Picasso. Whether a mountain, a still life or the nude in nature, studying Cézanne's work proved to be an essential step toward Cubism.

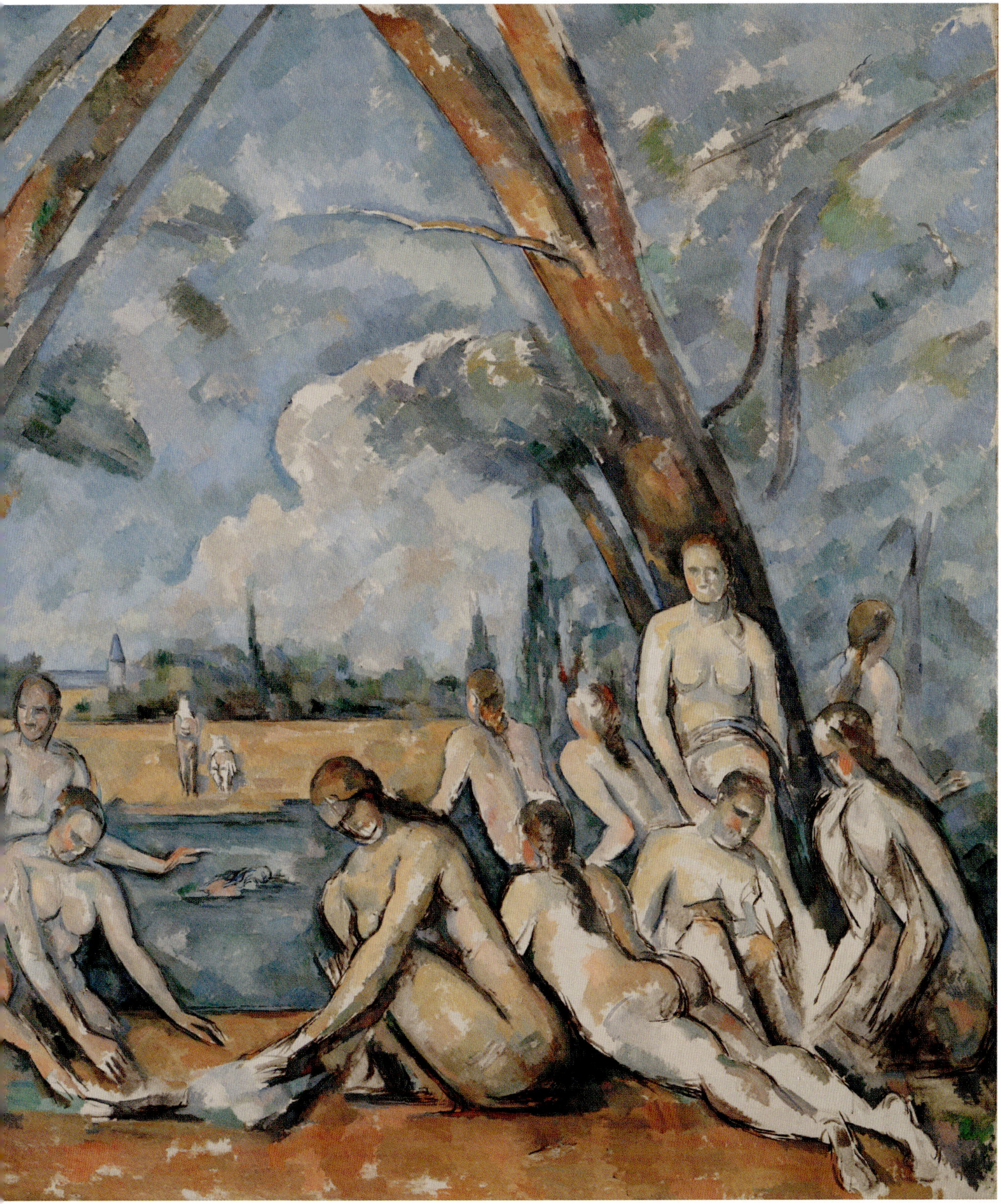

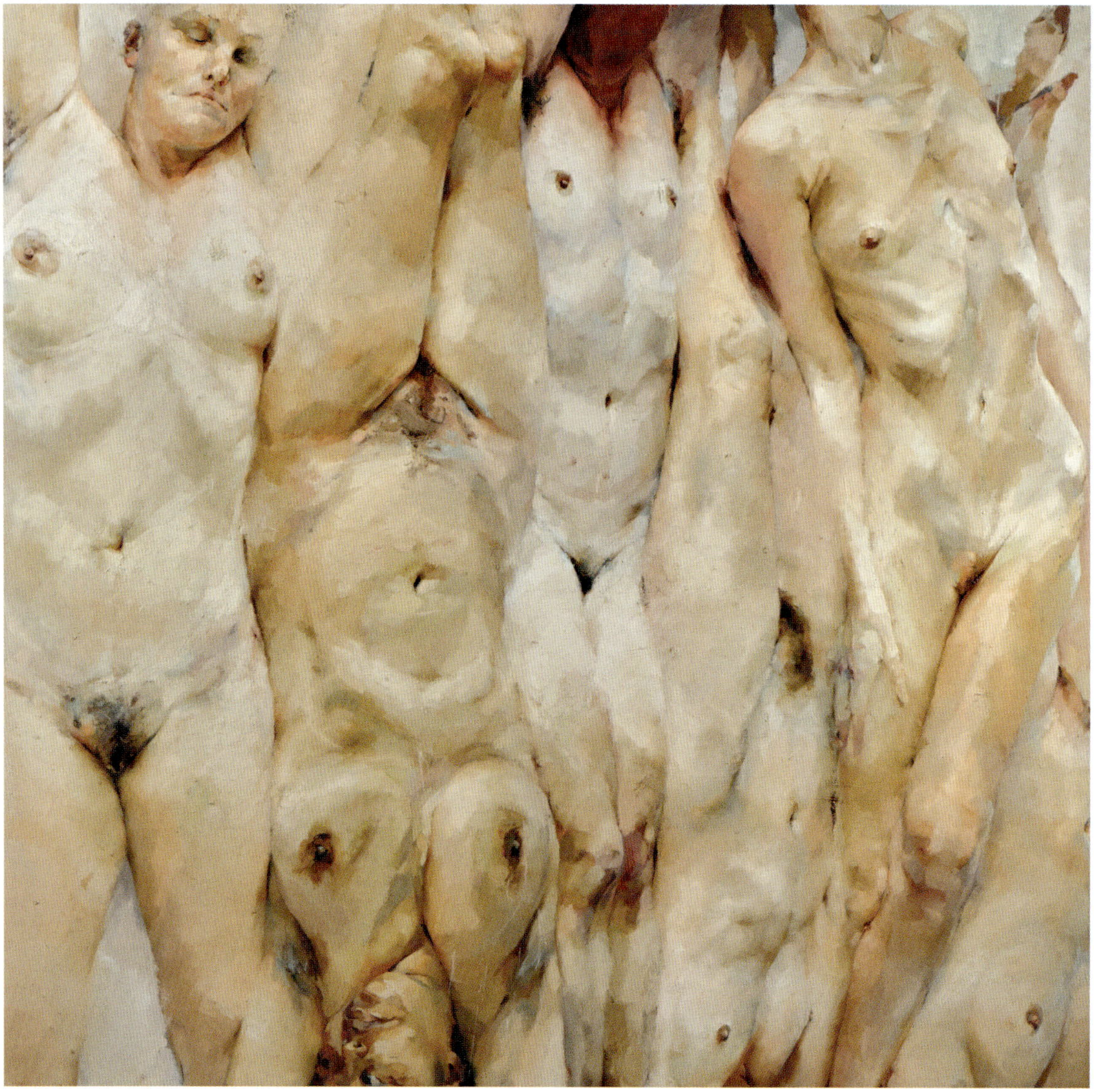

▲

Jenny Saville (b. 1970)
Shift
1996–97, oil on canvas, 330 x 330 cm (130 x 130 in)

Saville paints the female body with unparalleled scrutiny. She has acknowledged the influence of Picasso on her early work, and nowhere is this clearer than in *Shift*, where she fits the figures together in a faceted jigsaw, moving them to the very surface of the picture plane. However, unlike Picasso's treatment of the female form in *Les Demoiselles*, Saville retains the natural physicality of flesh, using her paint to express the undulating curves or lean bone structure of individual figures. For Saville, painting's purpose is to explore the integrity of the human form rather than deconstruct it.

Claudette Johnson (b. 1959)
Standing Figure with African Masks
2018, pastel and gouache on paper, 152 x 122 cm
(60 x 48 in)

Johnson recalls being struck by Picasso's use of masks in *Les Demoiselles* while still at art school, but it was the confrontational fearlessness of the women that motivated her to paint in response. Although she used her own image in this painting, gazing into a mirror propped on a chair, she does not regard it as a self-portrait. Dressed in jeans and a cropped shirt, the figure inhabits her body with confident power. Johnson's figure reorients Picasso's imagery from iconic to experiential, with the masks and fragmented female figures relegated to the background.

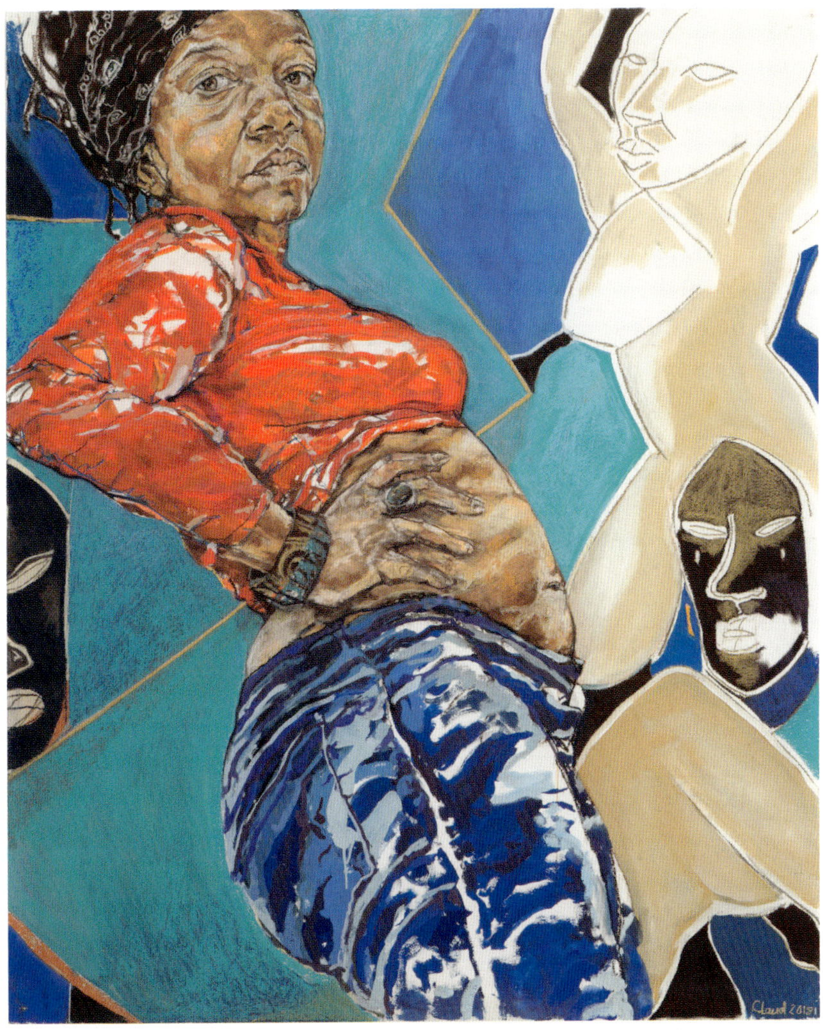

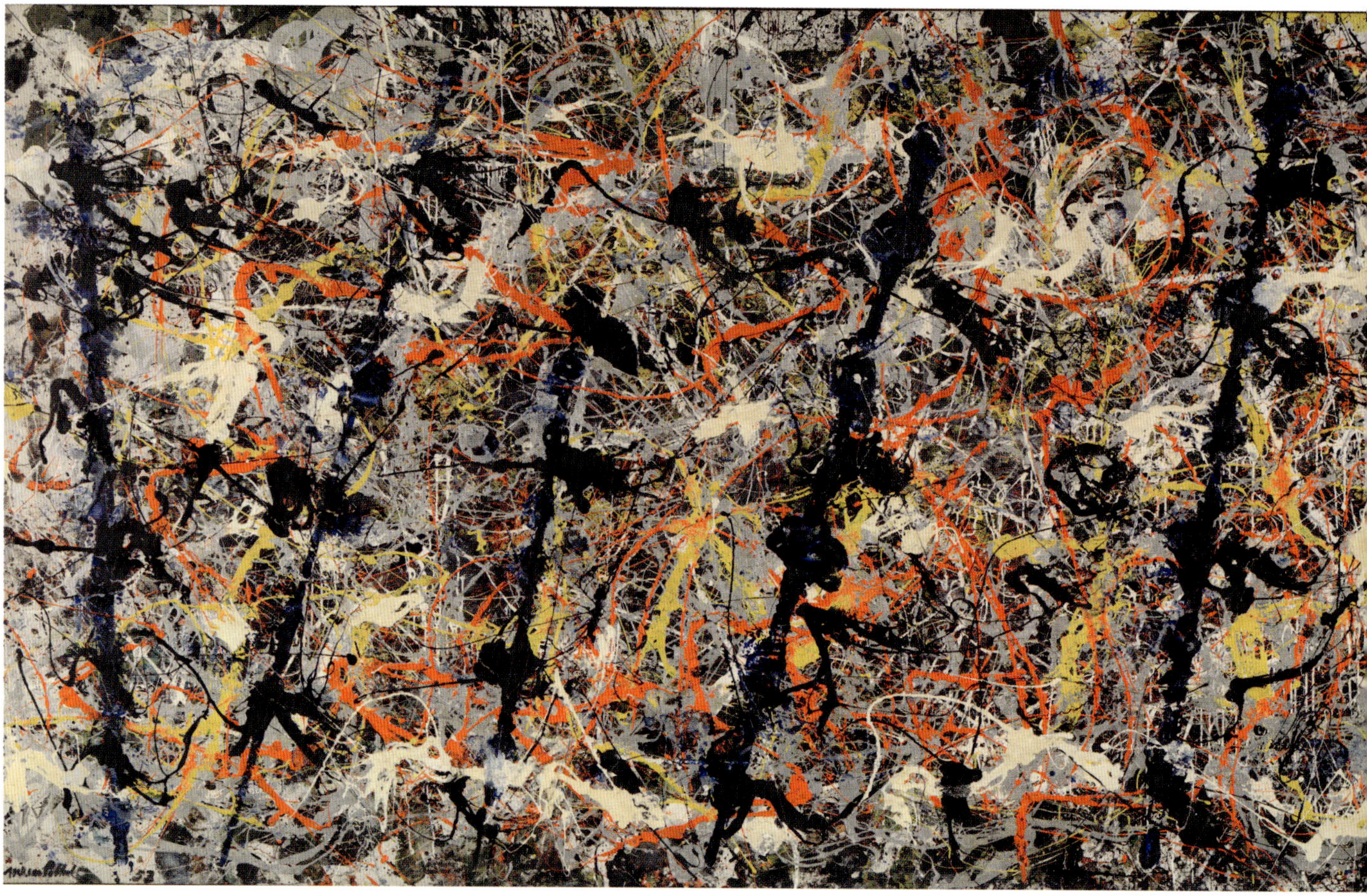

I TAUGHT JACK THAT

How Pollock learnt rhythm and flow from Benton

At first glance, the work of two figures who shaped American art in the twentieth century appear to have nothing in common. As a founder of American Regionalism, Thomas Hart Benton extolled a view of a country fuelled by industriousness, thrift and resilience. He set his narrative scenes in the farmlands and small towns of the agricultural Midwest, depicting homesteading and community gatherings. Naturalistic in form and national in content, Benton's paintings affirmed the populist view of America as a land of abundance and opportunity. Shedding both representational imagery and traditional technique, Jackson Pollock rejected Benton's form and content. He discarded figuration, conventional tools and the belief that painting should carry meaning beyond the

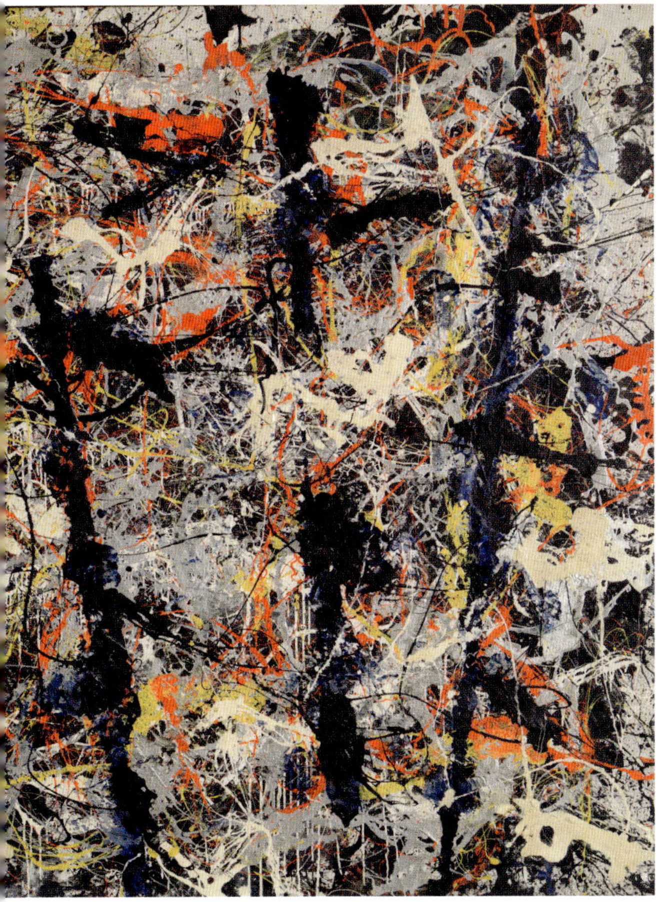

Jackson Pollock (1912–56)
Blue Poles
1952, oil, enamel, aluminium paint, glass on canvas, 212 x 489 cm (83 x 193 in)

object itself. He, too, is regarded as a founder of a movement – Abstract Expressionism – and his groundbreaking approach supplanted American Regionalism as the nation's distinctive contribution to modern art. Yet, in 1973, when Benton heard the news that the National Gallery of Australia had acquired Pollock's 1952 masterpiece, *Blue Poles*, he wrote to a friend, 'I taught Jack that.'[1]

Although tinged with irony, Benton's claim of credit was rooted in truth. From 1930 to 1933 Pollock studied under Benton at the Art Students League in New York City. Benton ran an unorthodox studio, where he replaced the standard curriculum with his own painting demonstrations. The free-wheeling atmosphere suited Pollock, who had been expelled from several schools in Los Angeles. He welcomed Benton's influence as a mentor, adopting his approach to scenes of farm life with the same rhythmic roll of the landscape and vigorous figure style. When Benton left New York to paint the mural *A Social History of the State of Indiana* for the Indiana Pavilion at the Century of Progress International Exposition in Chicago in 1933–34, Pollock floundered. He ended his art training, searching instead for guidance in the work of such international artists as Pablo Picasso, and the Mexican muralists José Clemente Orozco and David Alfaro Siqueiros, on view at the time in New York. Pollock also began to manipulate the form of his figures, giving brushstroke, line and colour the dominant role in his painting. Through the 1940s, his explosive, abstract approach obliterated the representational figure and by 1947, when he moved his canvas from the easel to the floor, the act of applying paint became as significant to his work as the result of the application.

Thomas Hart Benton (1889–1975)
The Hailstorm
1940, tempera on canvas mounted on panel,
84 x 102 cm (33 x 40 in)

No matter the subject or scale, Benton organized his compositions through a strong horizontal structure, anchored by vertical elements. However, undulating bands of landscape and angled placement of his upright forms obscured the underlying rigidity of his method. Here, in his depiction of an oncoming storm, every element pulses with energy, from the roiling clouds in the sky to the thickly curled leaves of the vegetation in the foreground. His figures embody the same dynamic energy, a quality that Benton regarded as exceptionally American.

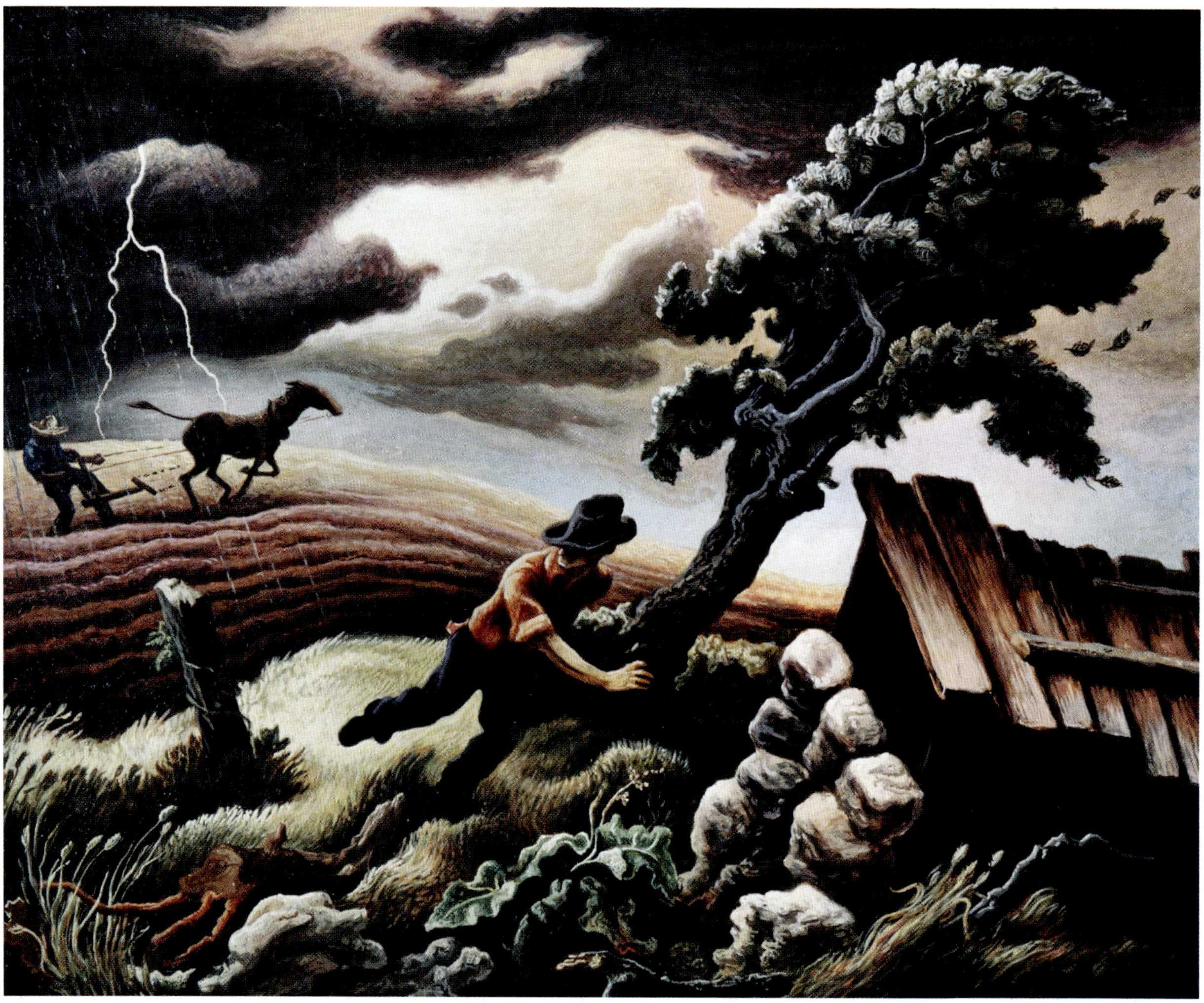

Jackson Pollock
Man with Hand Plow
c. 1933, oil on canvas, 55 x 70 cm (22 x 28 in)

Pollock found a generous mentor in Benton, who found him work and guided his early development. As well as emulating Benton's dress and swagger, Pollock adopted the rhythmic organization of his teacher's dynamic style. He also built a repertoire of regionalist subjects, although his own upbringing in California was far from the Midwestern experience that Benton regarded as definitively American. When Benton left New York in 1933, Pollock expanded his vision, abstracting his forms and figures under such new influences as the work of Picasso and the Mexican muralists.

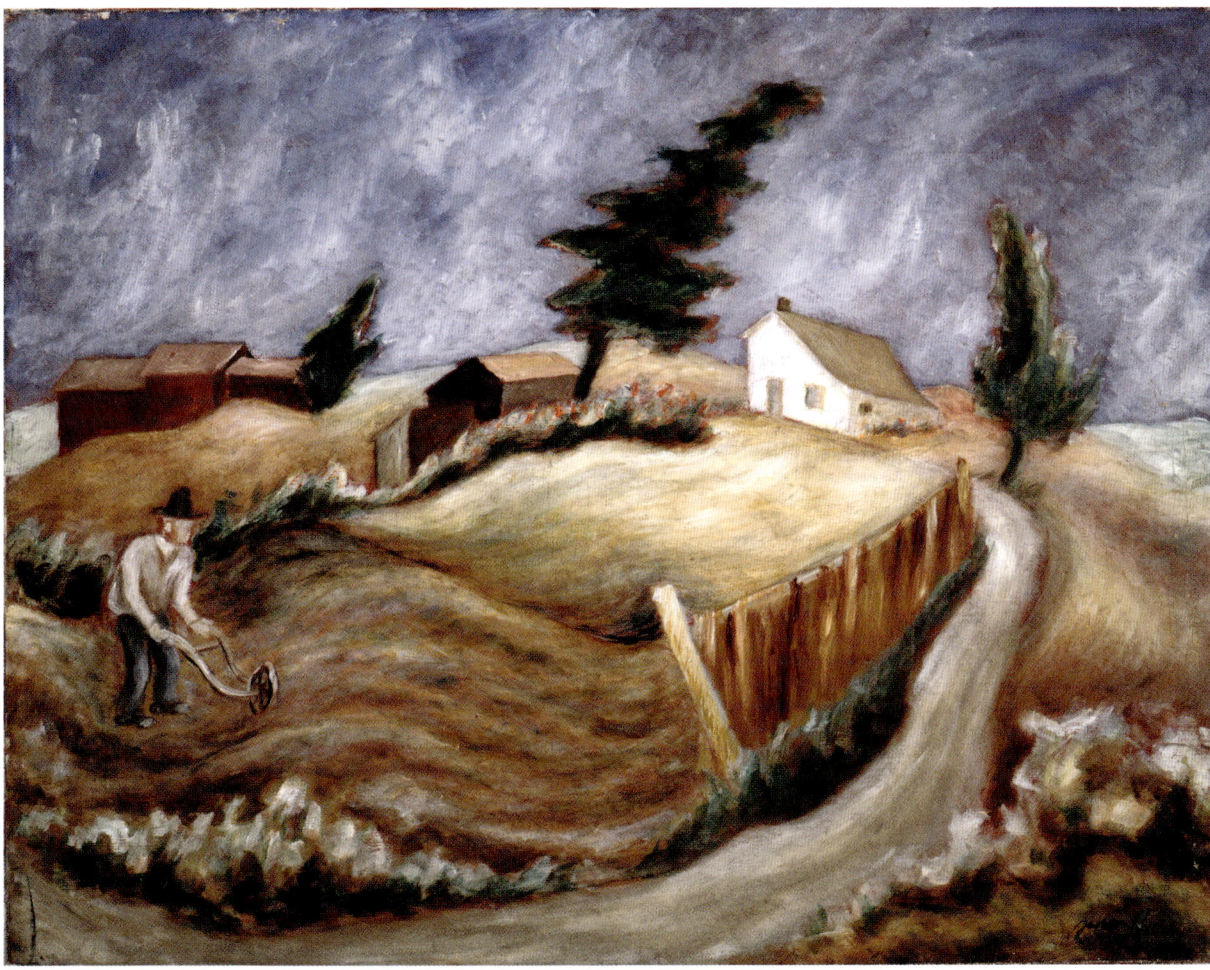

Blue Poles displays Pollock's signature process at its most evolved. Hovering over a length of untreated, unstretched canvas, he dripped enamel and aluminium paints from a stick or stiff brush to lay down an initial structure. He worked around the canvas, layering more paint, even pouring it directly from the can. Pollock put the full force of his body behind the slashing movement of his arm; his unconscious, athletic motion was as crucial to the final work as the paint on the canvas. With tangled skeins of line and colour, Pollock's so-called 'action' paintings stand as a record of his physical performance as a painter as well as the pure visual imagery of a self-contained work of art. The throbbing, muscular style echoes the underlying dynamism of Benton's compositions, replacing the action expressed through figures with a purely formal track of gesture. In an interview in 1944, Pollock shrugged off Benton's influence, describing what he saw in his instructor's studio as 'something against which to react'.[2] But decades later, Benton recognized his own rhythm and flow in Pollock's abstract masterpiece and wondered if his former student tapped into 'some vague memory of my theory demonstrations'.[3] Pollock may have denied it, but he carried and transformed those studio lessons from emulation to innovation; the proof is in his painting. ●

▶

Jackson Pollock
Naked Man with Knife
c. 1938–40, oil on canvas, 127 x 91 cm (50 x 36 in)

Although Pollock deliberately pushed his approach away from Benton's influence, he continued to seek examples in the work of artists he admired. Here he adopted the subject and figural composition of a now lost image of Cain and Abel by the muralist José Clemente Orozco, but the twisted postures of the figures – rendered in swathes of colour and slashing lines – give his paint application dominance over the narrative. The bodies are abstracted into the representation of pulsating power; within a few years, Pollock would completely abandon figure and narrative for pure form.

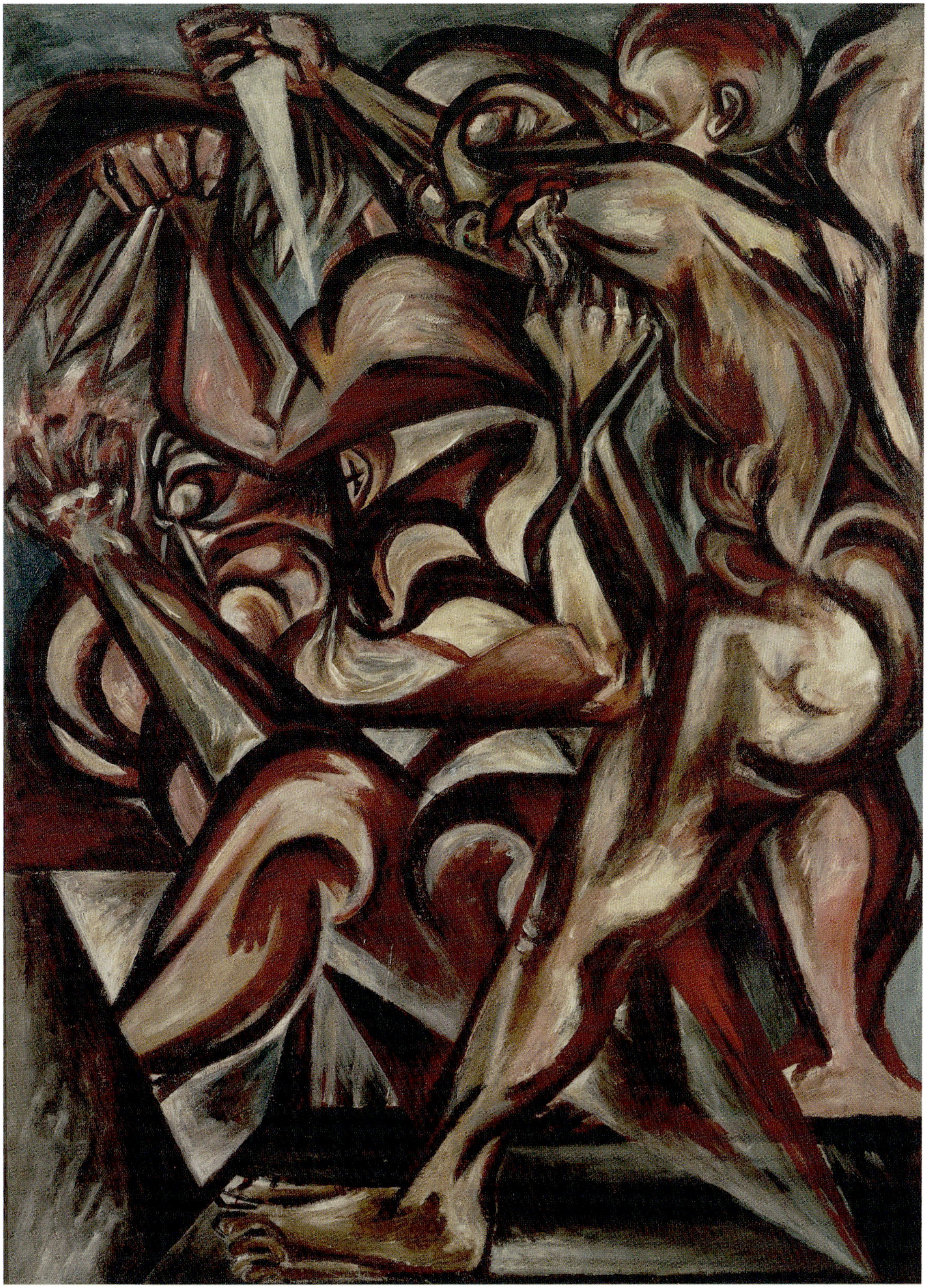

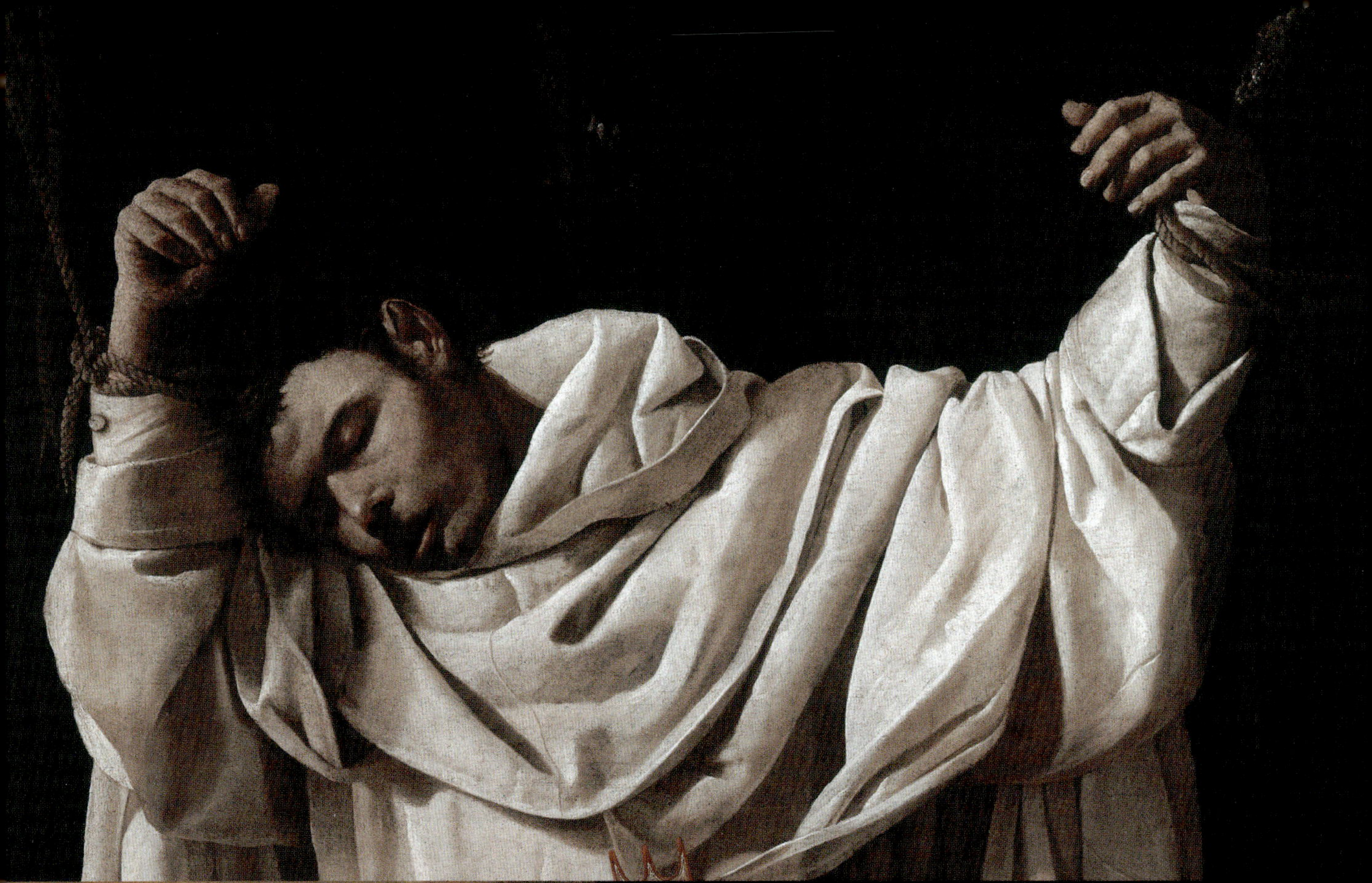

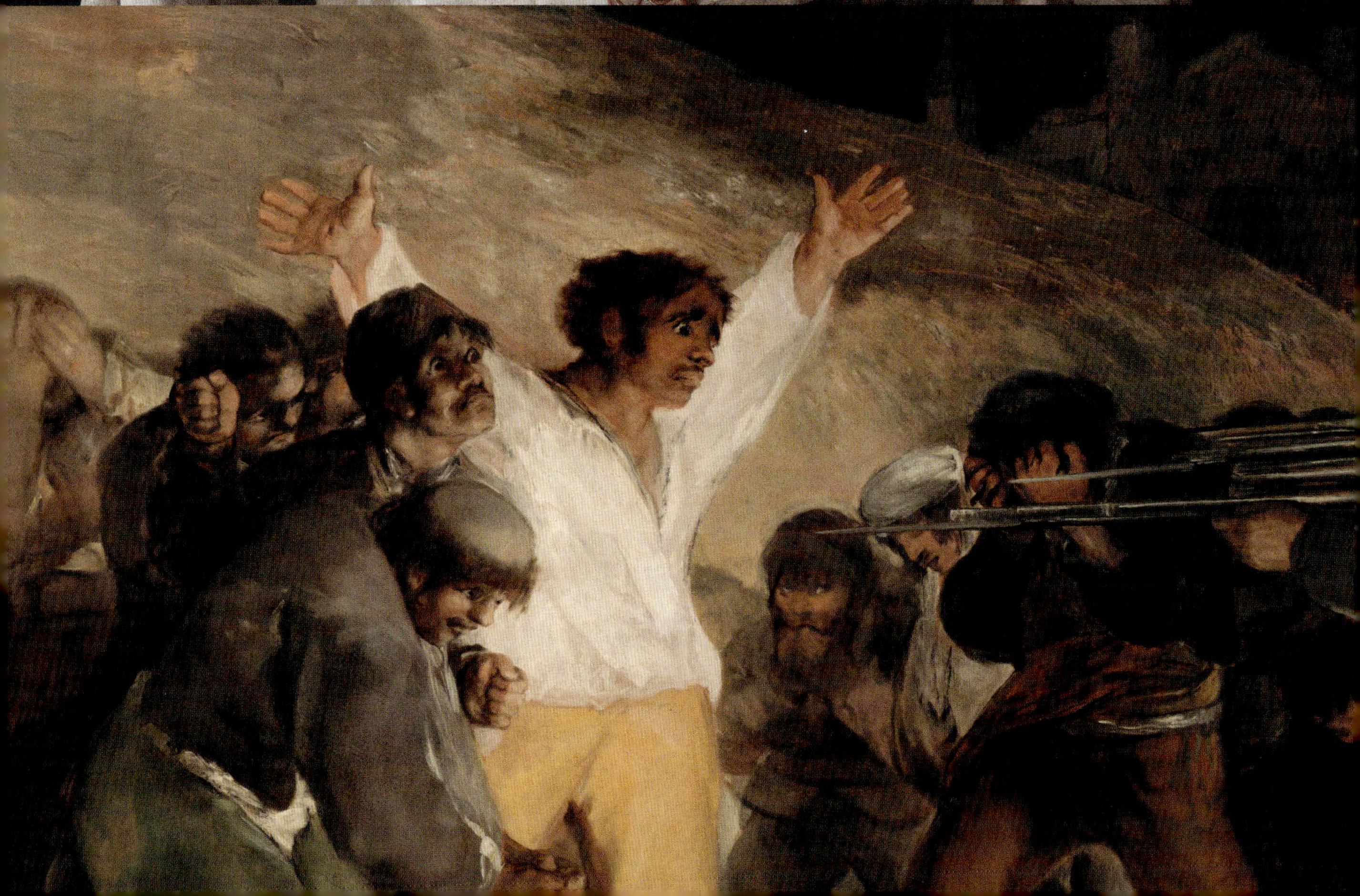

MEANINGFUL CONNECTIONS

A deliberate and easily recognized steal forges a meaningful connection between the artist's work and its source. In portraiture an artist can use costume, pose or even a gesture to elevate the sitter's status and character. They might incorporate a specific motif from another work as a tribute or to deepen the meaning of their own endeavour through association. Reprising a known subject with a shift in setting, medium, even gender, may question, criticize or lampoon the source. Or an artist may simply admire a work and want to reimagine it in their own distinctive style.

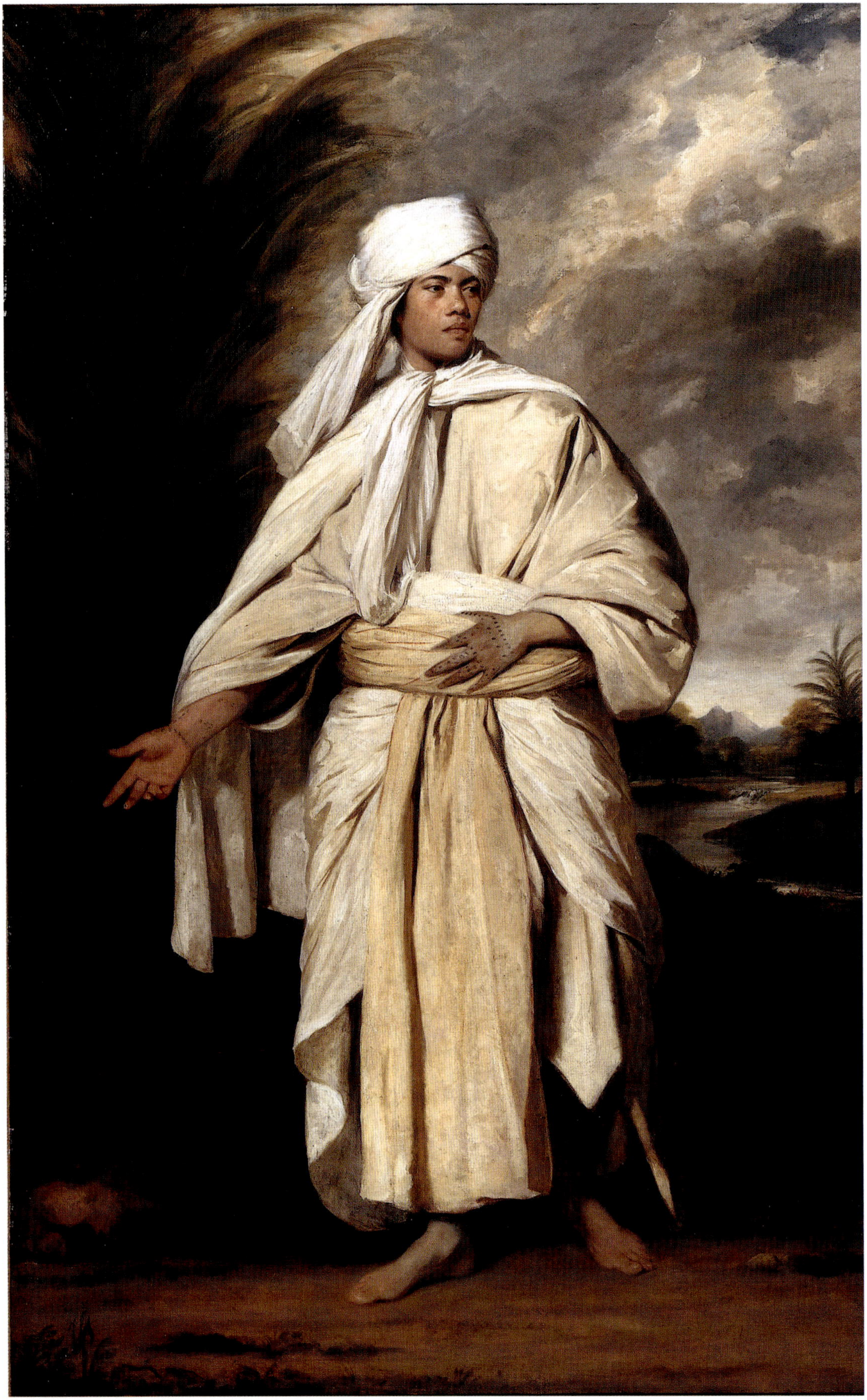

AN ANCIENT POSE FOR A CONTEMPORARY CELEBRITY

How Reynolds invoked the classical beauty of Leochares' *Apollo Belvedere*

When the young Polynesian Mai (*c.* 1753–80) asked Captain James Cook for a passage to England on the HMS *Adventure* in 1774, he had a clear purpose in mind: to seek the support of King George III in reclaiming his homeland Raiatea from occupation by Bora Bora. Recognizing that Mai would be the first known Pacific Islander to visit the British Isles, botanist Joseph Banks and naturalist Daniel Solander had another plan.[1] With the patronage of John Montagu, 4th Earl of Sandwich, they introduced Mai to elite society to gauge how a genuine 'noble savage' – the long-standing stereotype of the non-western man most recently romanticized as an uncorrupted state of virtue by Jean-Jacques Rousseau – fared in the 'civilized' world. Elegant and impressively savvy, Mai turned the experiment on its head, demonstrating ease in every social situation, proving to be a master at chess and, according to diarist Frances Burney, possessing 'manners so extremely graceful' that he seemed to have hailed from 'some foreign court' rather than 'primitive' Polynesia.[2] Mai quickly became a sought-after celebrity, and while it is not known exactly when he met the renowned society painter Joshua Reynolds, by 1775 they were frequenting the same social circles.

Always looking out for crowd-pleasing subjects, Reynolds invited Mai to pose for a monumental, full-length portrait in the Grand Manner to be displayed at the Royal Academy exhibition in 1776.

As President of the Royal Academy, Reynolds defined the Grand Manner in his annual discourses (1769–90). In portraiture, he stressed the importance of reaching beyond the mere imitation of nature to incorporate 'a more perfect idea of beauty' based on esteemed examples from Renaissance painters, who had built their concept of physical perfection on the surviving examples of ancient Greek sculpture.[3] This could be done by generalizing a sitter's appearance, but also through posture and bearing.

◀

Joshua Reynolds (1723–92)
Portrait of Mai (Omai)
c. 1776, oil on canvas, 236 x 140 cm (93 x 55 in)

Mai's youth and good looks needed little enhancement, so Reynolds incorporated a pose that instantly triggered meaning with his contemporary audience: that of the *Apollo Belvedere*, a lost, fourth-century bronze sculpture by Leochares known through a marble copy uncovered outside Rome in the late 1400s. The eminent German scholar Johann Joachim Winckelmann had recently cited the work as an unparalleled representation of youthful beauty and innate grace that, according to Winckelmann, defined Greek manhood. In his fulsome praise, Winckelmann saw the sculpture as the personification of 'noble simplicity and quiet grandeur', and the relaxed, balanced and open-bodied posture of the Apollo became a symbol of human perfection.[4]

Reynolds' likeness of Mai was consistent with preparatory sketches for the portrait as well as with the few other images of Mai made during his stay in London. The tattoos on his hands are clearly seen and his feet are bare. Mai's robes, tied with a sash suggesting tapa bark fibre (indigenous to Polynesia and neighbouring Pacific islands), drape gracefully over his body, allowing the pose to be easily read while maintaining a sense of decorum. Mai had worn similar robes in a portrait with Banks and Solander by William Perry; they resemble a Middle Eastern burnoose (a long, hooded cloak) more than any authentic garments from Polynesia. Mai likely invented this attire to enhance his air of exoticism; at social events he commonly wore fashionable, bespoke suits. With ethnically ambiguous garments and the power of a pose, Mai and Reynolds fused the image of the exotic other with an icon of refined western humanity. By the time Reynolds unveiled the portrait to universal acclaim, Mai, who had failed in his mission to secure monarchical support, had already sailed for home. ●

▶

After Leochares (Greek, fourth century BC)
Apollo Belvedere
AD 120–40, marble, 224 cm (88 in)

Uncovered at a site near Rome in the late fifteenth century, this grand-scale marble of the Olympian god Apollo provided a template for the ancient Greek ideal of male beauty for centuries. Even before it was installed in the Cortile del Belvedere of the Vatican Palace (1511), reproductive prints of the sculpture circulated throughout Europe. Artists adopted the relaxed posture, known as *contrapposto* (in which the weight of the body is supported on one leg, leaving the other free to bend naturally at the knee) and the extended arm as a display of masculine grace.

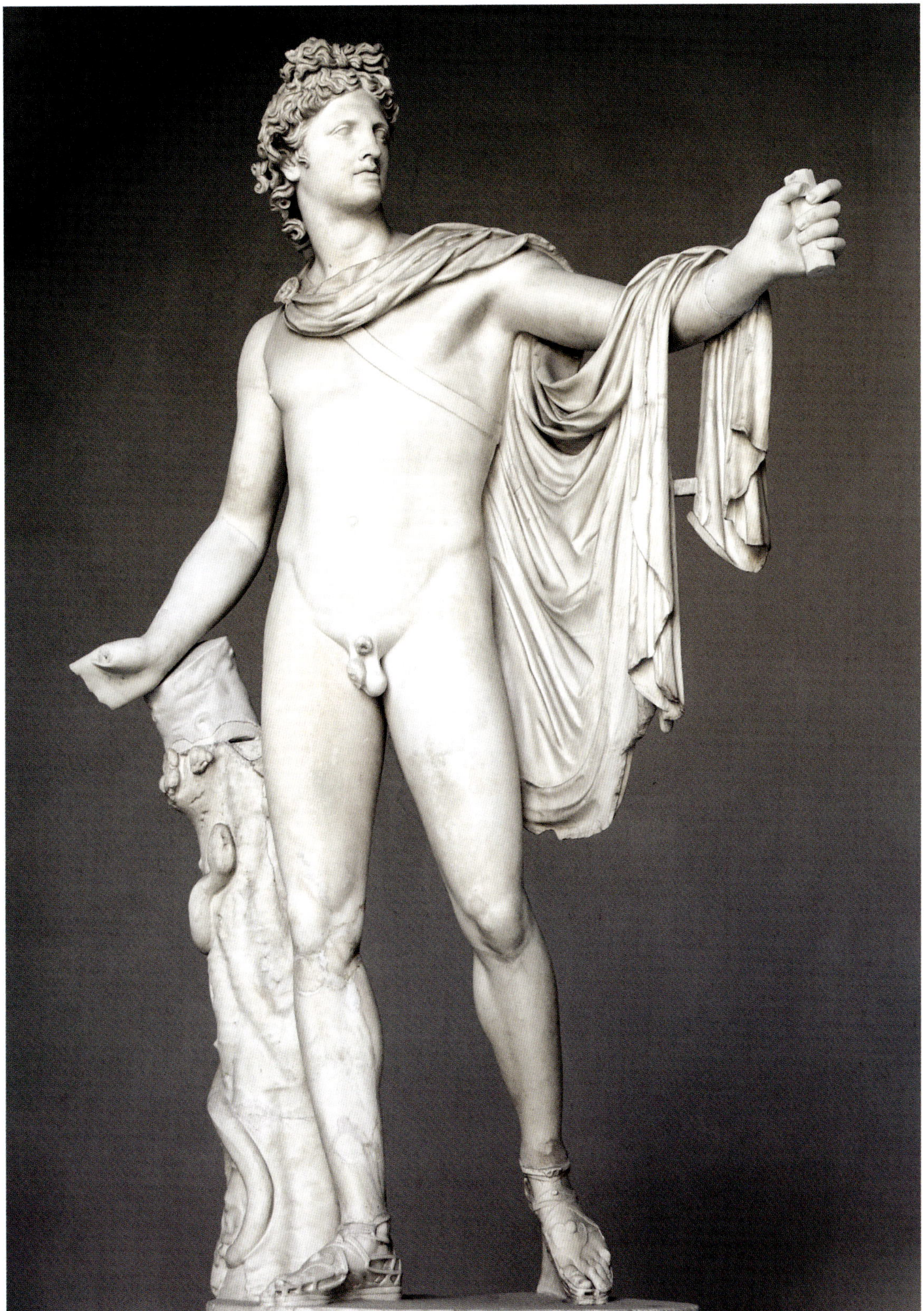

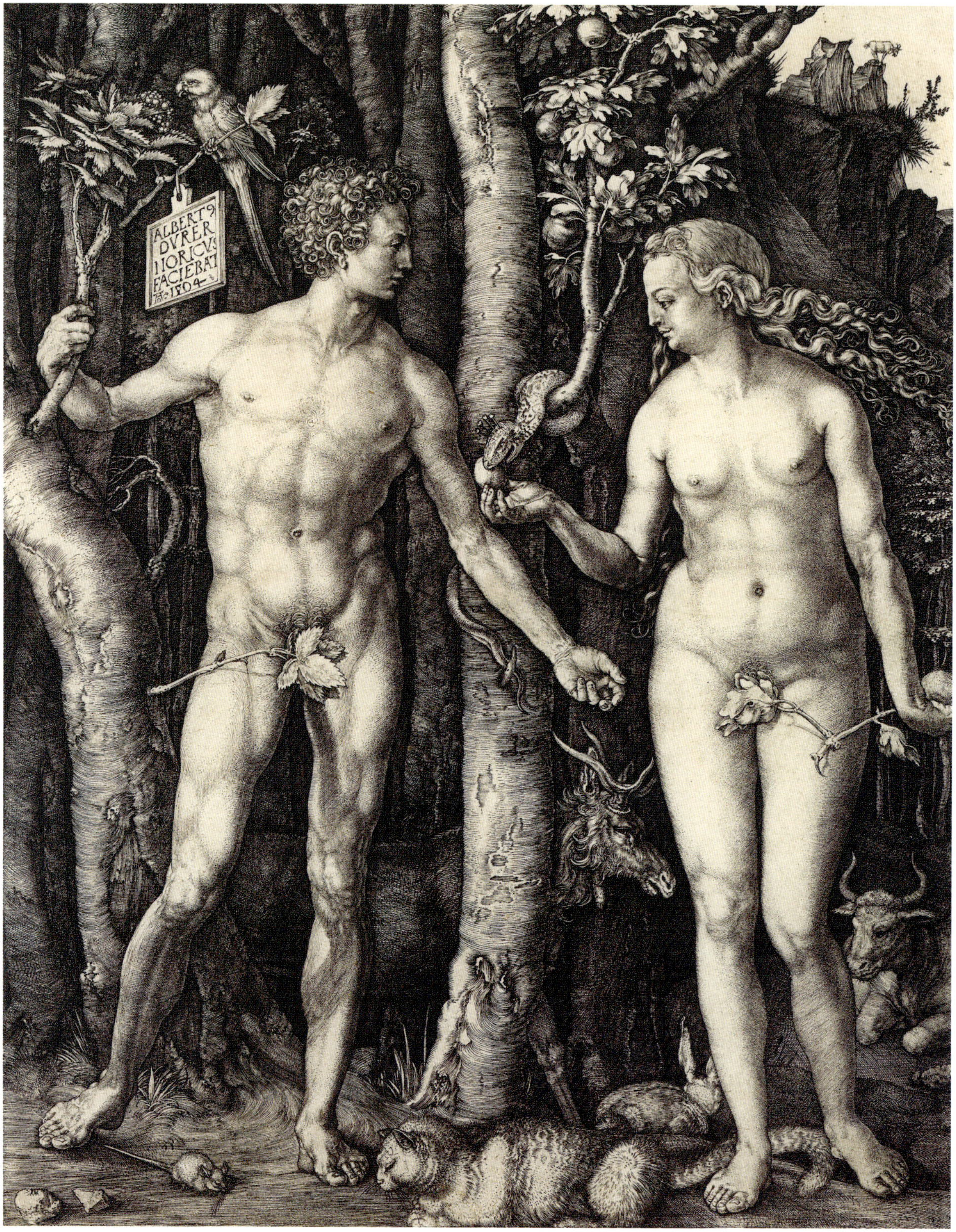
ALBERT9
DVRER
NORICVS
FACIEBAT
1504

◀
Albrecht Dürer (1471–1528)
The Fall of Man (*Adam and Eve*)
1504, engraving, 25 x 19 cm (10 x 7 in)

The influence of the *Apollo Belvedere* on Dürer's conception of Adam is clearly evident, but how he knew about the sculpture is not known. It is speculated that he visited Rome on his second trip to Italy (1505–06) after he made this print, and reproductive engravings of it were not available until after 1504. Most likely, he saw a drawing and modelled Adam after Apollo as an ideal of human beauty.

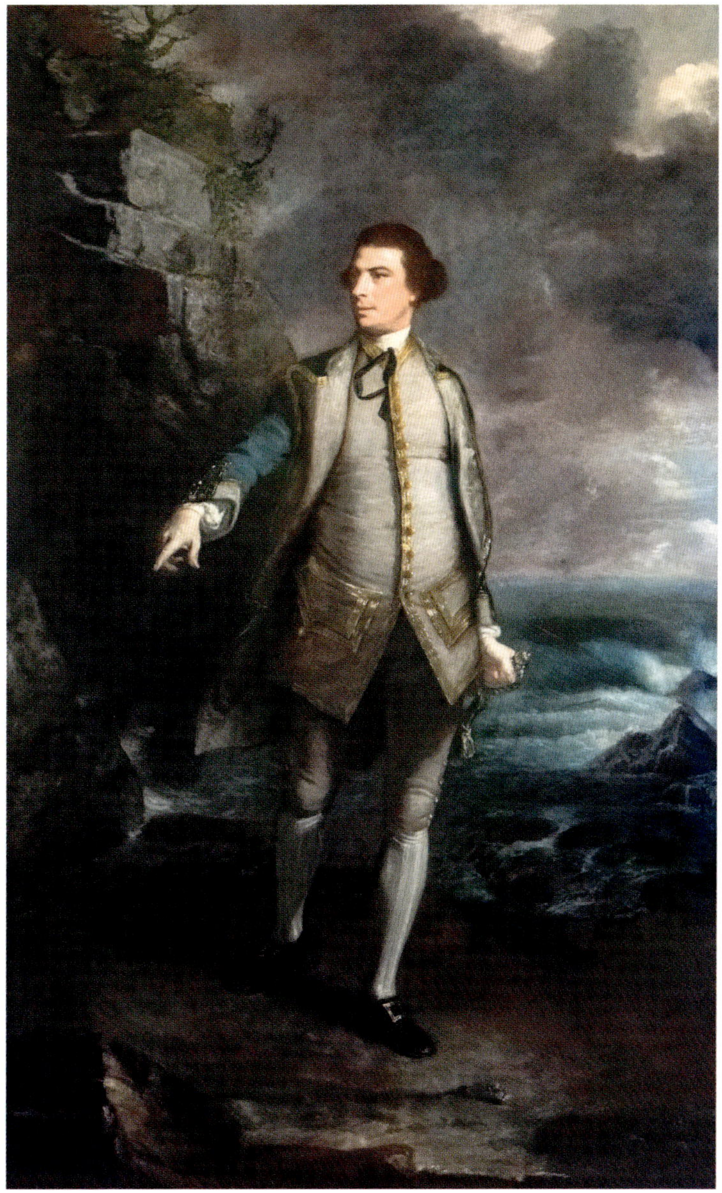

▶
Joshua Reynolds
Portrait of Captain Augustus Keppel
1752–3, oil on canvas, 239 x 148 cm (94 x 58 in)

Keppel, whose storied naval career began in childhood, funded Reynolds' first journey to Rome (1749–52). Reynolds' decision to portray Keppel in the famed pose reflected the artist's admiration for his patron. Here, the relaxed posture becomes a stride and the outstretched arm points the way, presenting Keppel as a commanding leader rather than an embodiment of male beauty. Reynolds had made a sketch of the sculpture while he was in Rome.

A MODEL FOR MARTYRDOM

How Goya reinterpreted an iconic image of sacrifice

Goya heightens the horror of execution through visual contrast. Dressed in uniform, the soldiers are anonymous. Their heads turn away from the viewer; shadows hide their faces. They move as a single force as they raise their weapons to fire. Flanked by the piled-up dead in the foreground and the next round of victims shuffling out of the background, the group of men that face the firing squad are distinguished from one another by dress and emotional reactions. One among them is fully illuminated. His white shirt and buff trousers reflects the faint lantern light. Fearful, yet resigned to his fate, he kneels and raises his arms in surrender to the impending gunfire. He forces the viewer to confront the difference between the human victims and their dehumanized executioners. However, there is another, more subtle, contrast that fuels Goya's interpretation. The painting amplifies the power of a recent event through association with a centuries-old symbolic figure: the *Christus triumphans*, a crucifixion that features Christ alive on the cross in triumph over a merciless death.

In the last months of 1807, Napoleon's French troops marched into Spain under the guise of protecting the Iberian peninsula from British incursion. When it became clear that this was an occupation rather than an alliance, the Spanish king, Charles IV, abdicated in favour of his son. Soon after, Ferdinand VII was deposed and replaced by Napoleon's brother, Joseph Bonaparte. Rumours erupted that the Spanish monarch would be put to death, and on 2 May 1808 citizens took to the streets of Madrid in protest. The uprising was brutally quelled by armed troops. Arrests were followed by executions, which began late in the day and carried on through the early hours of 3 May. For the next six years, Spain endured French rule. Late in 1813 Spain regained independence, and in early 1814, Ferdinand returned to the throne to head a conservative, Catholic government, dismissive of the liberal demands of the so-called *guerillas* – little warriors – that had led the resistance.

To celebrate the restoration, Goya, who had long enjoyed connections with the court, was commissioned to commemorate the events of 1808. He recounted the story of resistance in a pair of

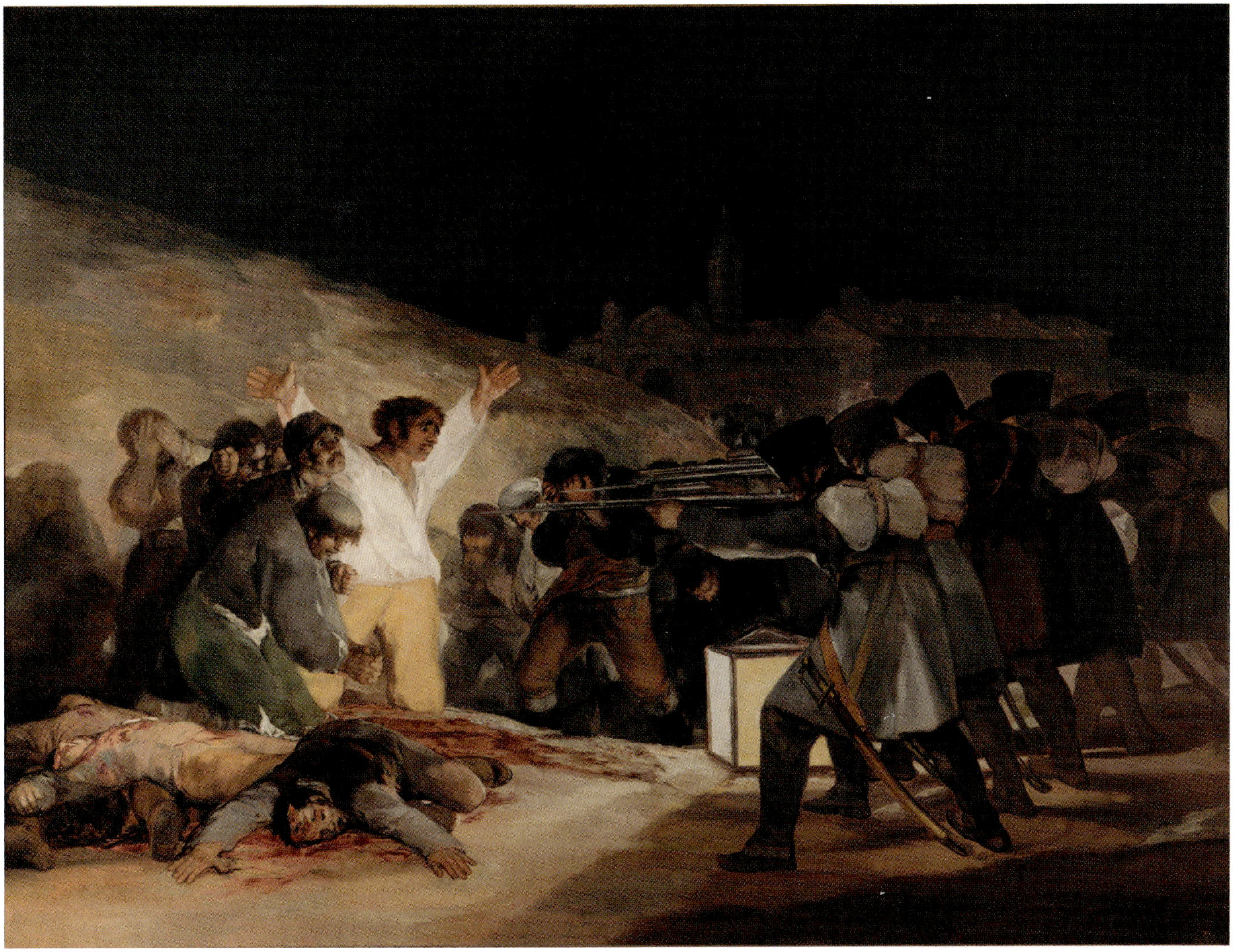

subjects: *The 2nd of May 1808 in Madrid* (*The Fight Against the Mamelukes*), a turbulent scene of the street battle between the *guerillas* and the French forces, and *The Third of May*. Goya's own horror at humankind's capacity for heartless violence was well known through his graphic work, but his patrons did not share his liberal views. Records for payment and framing exist, but the first public exhibition and the subsequent location of the works in the Prado Palace are a matter of speculation. It is fairly certain that the painting was not seen by the broader public during the time that their recollections of the events were still raw.

While both paintings record actual events and exhibit unprecedented realism for a royal commemorative commission, it is *The Third of May* that has been regarded as revolutionary. There is no sentimentality in Goya's presentation of the execution.

▲

Francisco Goya (1746–1828)
The Third of May 1808 (*The Executions*)
1814, oil on canvas, 268 x 347 cm (106 x 137 in)

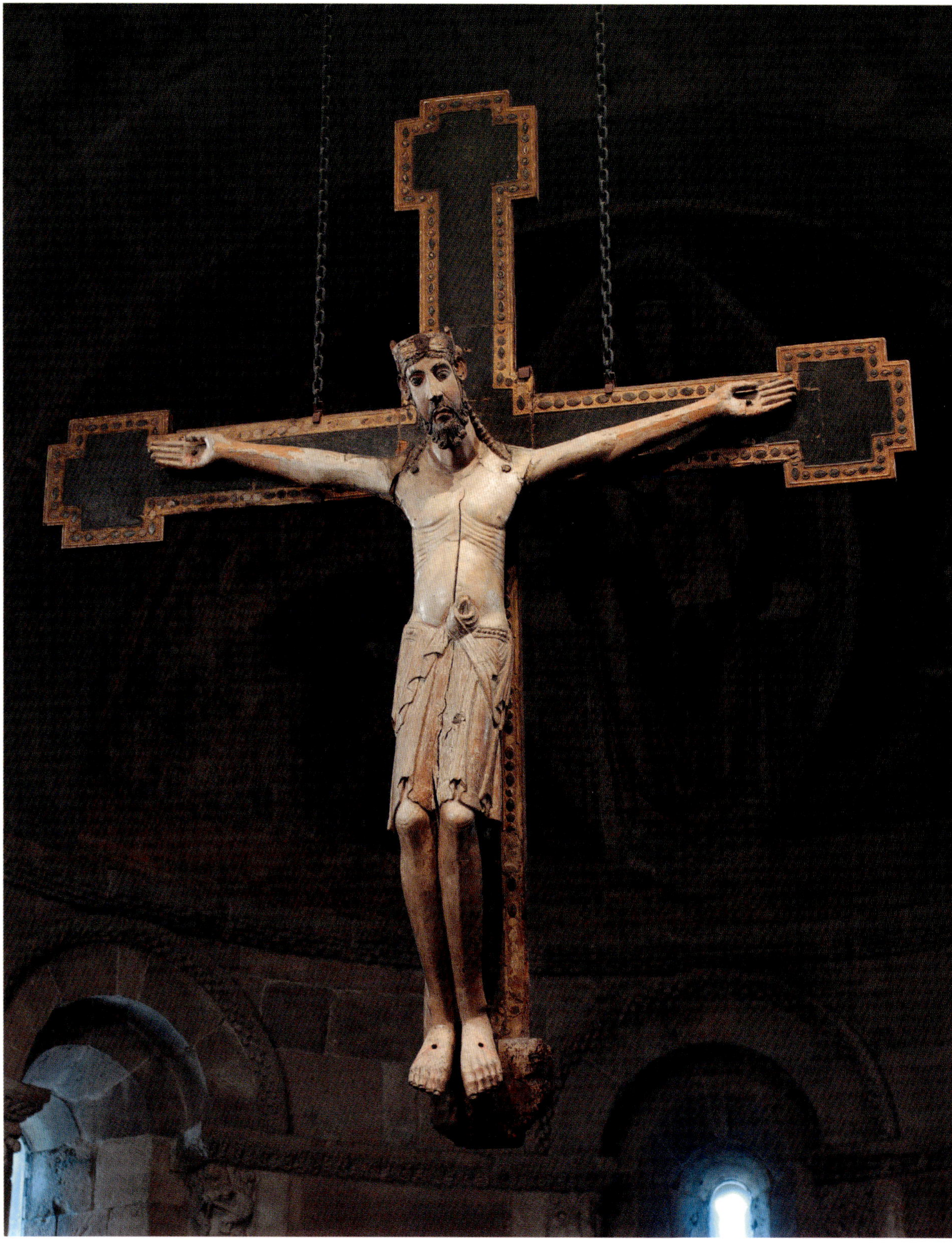

The victims are simply victims, and they face their fate with hopeless resignation rather than heroic resistance. However, to a Catholic audience, the valour in that passivity would be carried by the posture of the figure in the light. Based in Byzantine traditions, the image of a living Christ on the cross – eyes open, neutral expression and seemingly free of pain – embodied his transcendence over mortality. Death on the cross released him from his incarnation to rule in heaven as the saviour of humankind. By the twelfth century, monumental sculptures of the *Christus triumphans* were common in Spanish churches, and while it is not possible to cite an exact source for Goya's reference, the iconic pose with all its meaning would have been part of the artist's vernacular vocabulary and understood by his viewers. The open-eyed gaze of the *Christus triumphans* could be directed either to the heavens and his holy father or straight ahead to engage the faithful, but Goya's figure looks directly at his executioners, confronting inhumanity with divine justice. ●

◀

Castile-León, Spain
Crucifix
1150–1200, white oak with paint, gold leaf, tin leaf, 260 x 208 cm (102 x 82 in)

The body of Christ on this crucifix bears witness to torment. His wounds are fully displayed, but his head is upright, his face calm and his eyes open. Rather than thorns, he wears a golden crown. This is the *Christus triumphans*, a living Christ transcending mortal suffering and death to reign in heaven. This iconography was seen in painting, sculpture and the decorative arts from Byzantium to the nations of western Europe through the late Middle Ages, by which time this type of monumental crucifix was common throughout Spain.

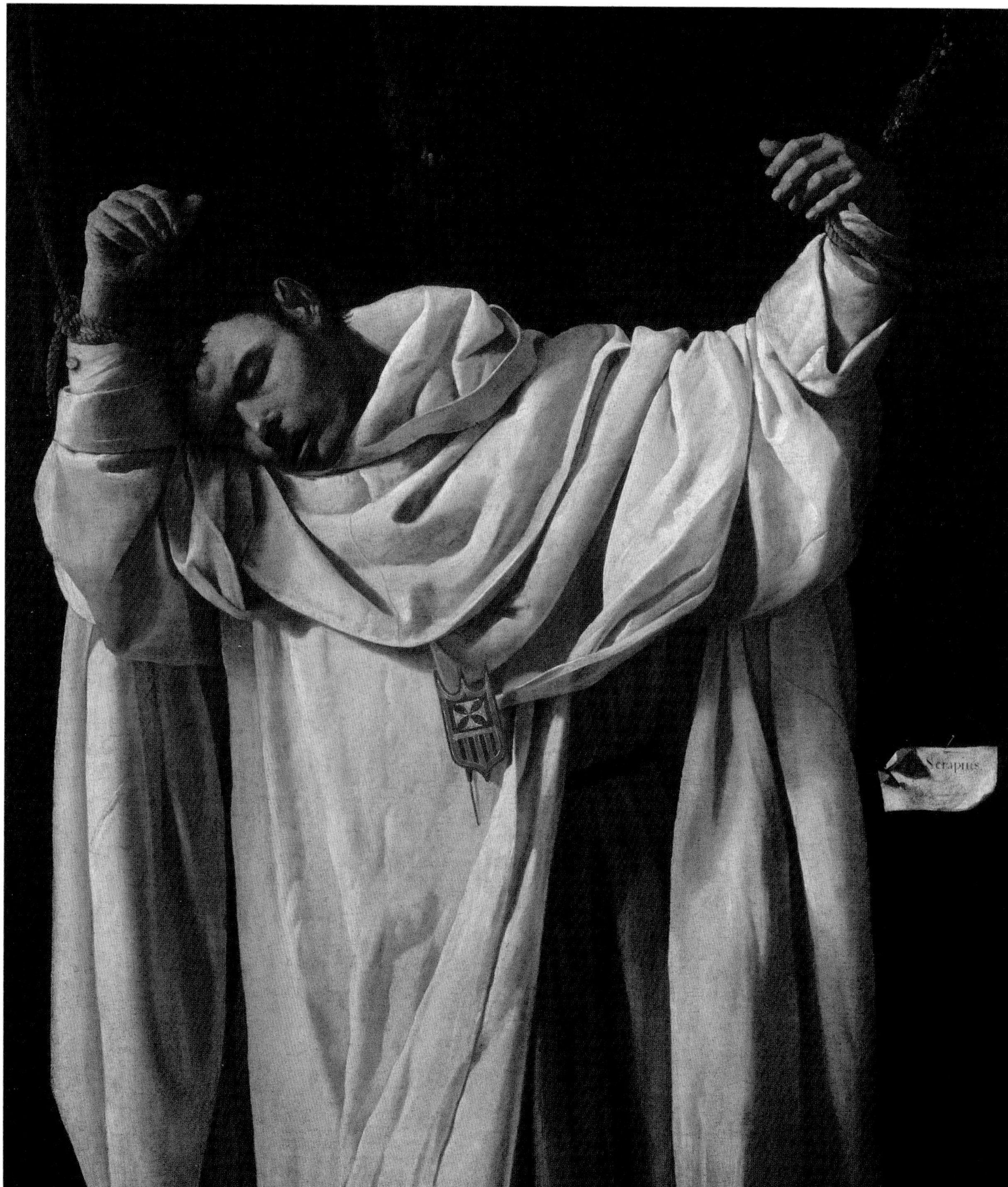
Serapius

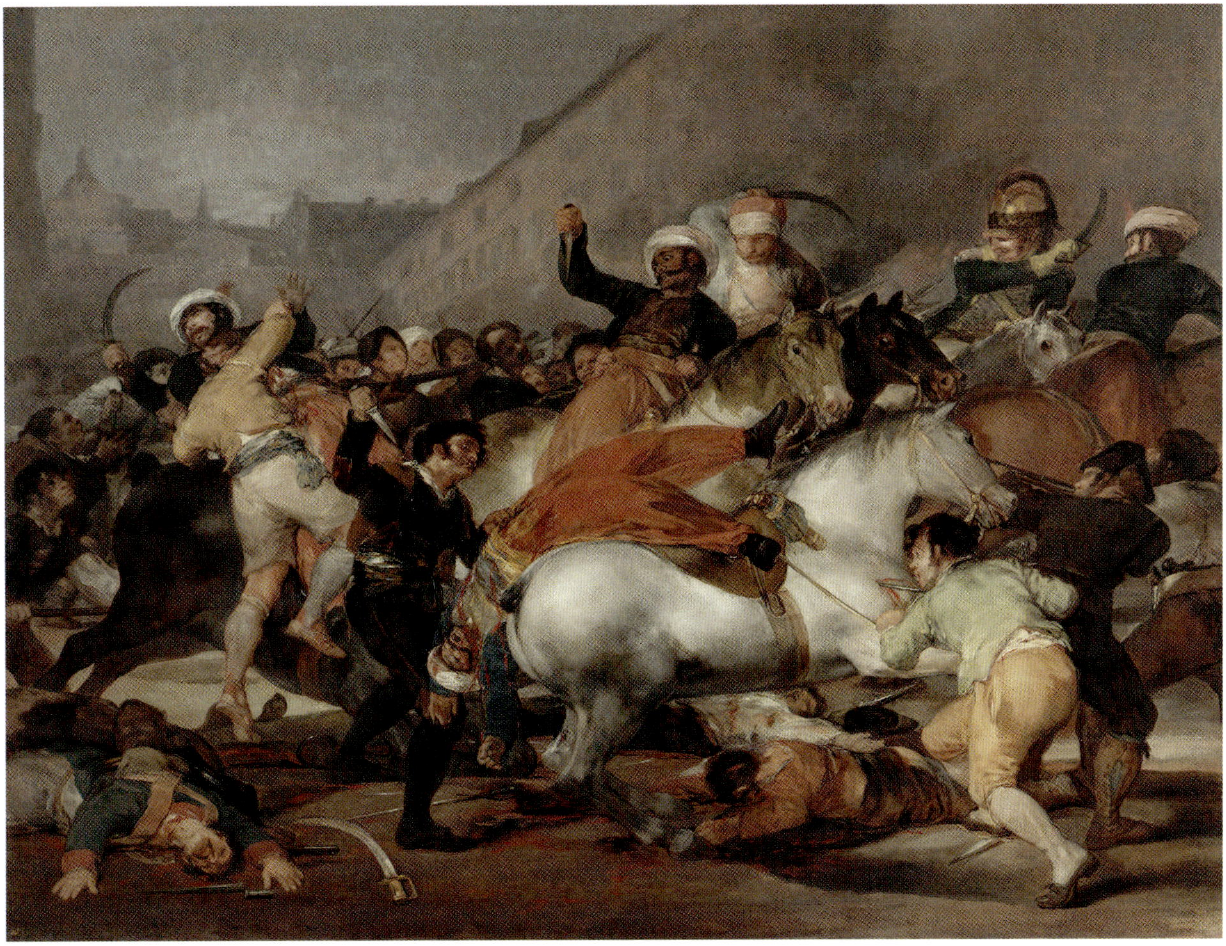

◀

Francisco de Zurbarán (1598–1664)
The Martyrdom of Saint Serapion
1628, oil on canvas 119 x 104 cm (47 x 41 in)

According to legend, St Serapion was tied to a cross and then disembowelled and beheaded. Zurbarán presents a less horrifying account of the saint's death; despite his bound hands, his body sags naturally, without strain. As much as martyrdom, the position evokes release as if Serapion's unwavering faith has delivered him from pain. Light from an unseen source illuminates the saint's immaculate white robe, connecting the painter's vision with Caravaggio's innovative approach to lighting as an emotional, as well as dramatic interpretation (see p.71).

▲

Francisco Goya
The 2nd of May 1808 in Madrid (*The Fight against the Mamelukes*)
1814, oil on canvas, 269 x 348 cm (106 x 137 in)

This riotous scene captures the events that led to the executions the following day. The uprising against the French occupation was crushed by the mounted and armed troops, including the Mamelukes of the Imperial Guard. Famed for their fearlessness and brutality, this division of the calvary had its origins in Egypt; their scimitars and uniforms, consisting of a turban, a short jacket and ballooning trousers, make them instantly identifiable. The *guerrillas*' garments vary, marking them as citizens of diverse origins and different social stations.

THE ATMOSPHERE IN THE ROOM

How Chase mirrored Velázquez's *Las Meninas* in his family portrait

This radiant pastel presents the artist's wife and eldest daughters in their summer house in Shinnecock Hills on south shore of Long Island. Chase first brought his family to the seaside hamlet in 1891, when he was hired as an instructor in the Shinnecock Hills Summer School; they stayed in a local inn. In 1892, they moved into a large home built by famed architect Stanford White, and it remained their annual retreat long after the school closed in 1896. The setting is the spacious, two-storey entrance that joined the domestic quarters with Chase's studio, and he filled it with antiques and imported ceramics, as well as comfortable furniture. Rather than a portrait of his family, the pastel is an intimate glimpse of familial contentment. This was the world Chase knew and loved, but *Hall at Shinnecock* also pays tribute to a work by the artist that Chase described as 'the greatest painter that ever lived', *Las Meninas* by Diego Velázquez.[1]

Like many American artists of his generation, Indiana-born Chase longed to study abroad. In 1872, after several years' training at the National Academy of Design in New York, he enrolled in the Academy of Fine Arts, Munich. The Bavarian city provided his home base for travel to other European art capitals until 1878, when he secured a teaching position at the Art Students League in New York. Having first seen the work of Velázquez in Munich, he visited Madrid in 1881, spending many hours copying the Spanish Baroque master's paintings in the Museo Nacional del Prado. Upon his return Chase exhibited his sketches at the Art Students League and later displayed them in his showplace studio on 10th Street. Over the next several years, Chase revisited Spain, and by 1885 the influence of Velázquez's style was evident in his approach to portraiture and his palette. Most notably, Chase tackled spatially complex interiors, seen in *A Corner in My Studio* (1885) and *Hide and Seek* (1888), forging a direct engagement with *Las Meninas*.

The airy, light-filled interior of *Hall at Shinnecock* strongly contrasts with the shadowed, burnished brown enclosure depicted in *Las Meninas*. However, by 1892 Chase's grasp of Velázquez's innovations went beyond copying atmosphere and palette. Now fully commanding Velázquez's approach to space, Chase weights the foreground with figures and objects and enhances the expansive depth through the rose-lit staircase landing in the background, a device directly adopted from the open door in

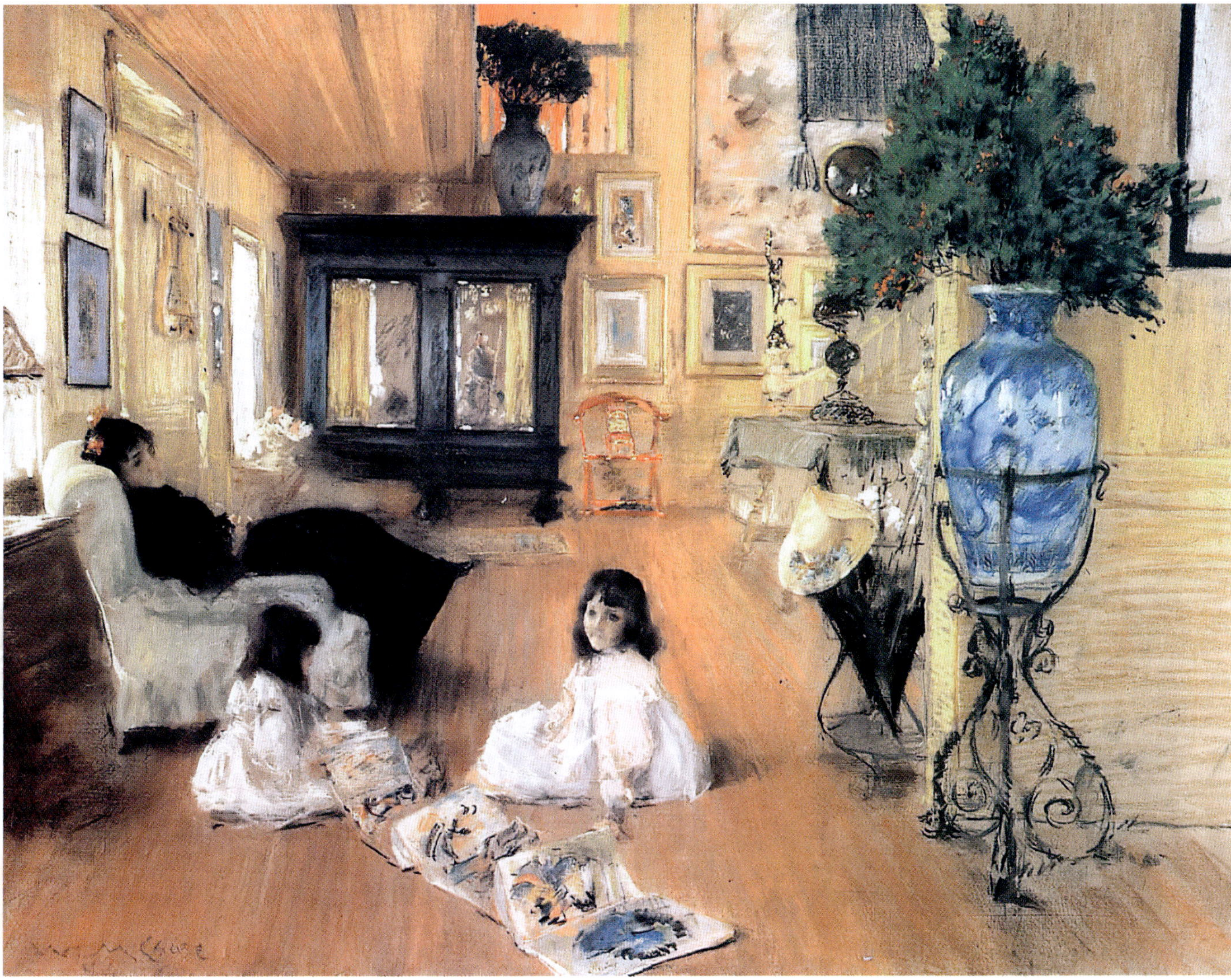

Las Meninas. The placement of his wife Alice and their daughters Koto and Cosy, echoes Velázquez's positioning of the handmaiden and the infanta on the left, without mimicking their exact poses and gestures. The branch-filled vase and the umbrella stand provide the same balance on the right as the group of the infanta's attendants. Chase handled his most overt reference with subtlety: his own image in the reflection on glass door of the Dutch armoire in the left background. Although his position standing at the easel connects him with the figure of Velázquez, the mirrored image is a direct tribute to the implied presence of the king and queen.

Chase's greatest tribute to *Las Meninas* is seen in the way he translated the inherent hallmarks of Velázquez's style into a vernacular all his own. Working in pastel, Chase equalled the fluidity and confident touch of Velázquez's brushwork.

▲

William Merritt Chase (1849–1916)
Hall at Shinnecock
1892, pastel on canvas, 81 x 104 cm (32 x 41 in)

He dissolved details – the diaphanous folds of the girls' dresses, the blue ribbon on the hat, the pattern on the tall vase – into strokes of pure pigment. Highlights of red – the flower in Alice's hair, the chair in the centre background – reprise Velázquez's signature accent. Most of all, he crafted a parallel moment in time. Like Velázquez's royal subjects, Chase's family stops what they are doing to take notice of the implied presence. It is a break in previous activity, obvious yet ambiguous, that involves the viewer in an unspoken narrative. In a lecture in 1903, Chase praised Velázquez's ability to build upon the great examples of the past with fresh forms and methods to more fully convey 'the time and place he was called on to depict'.[2] This is precisely what Chase achieved in *Hall at Shinnecock*. ●

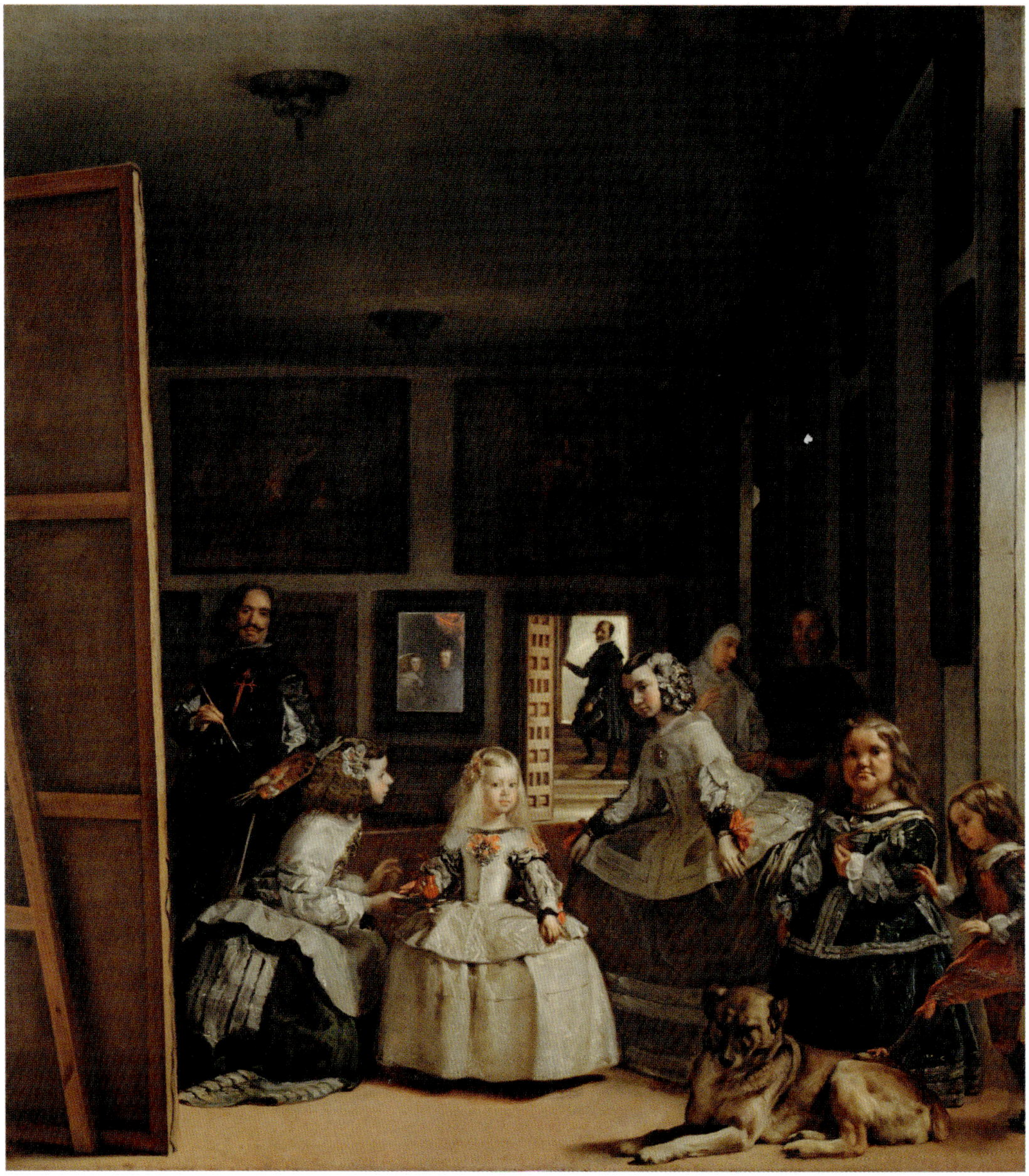

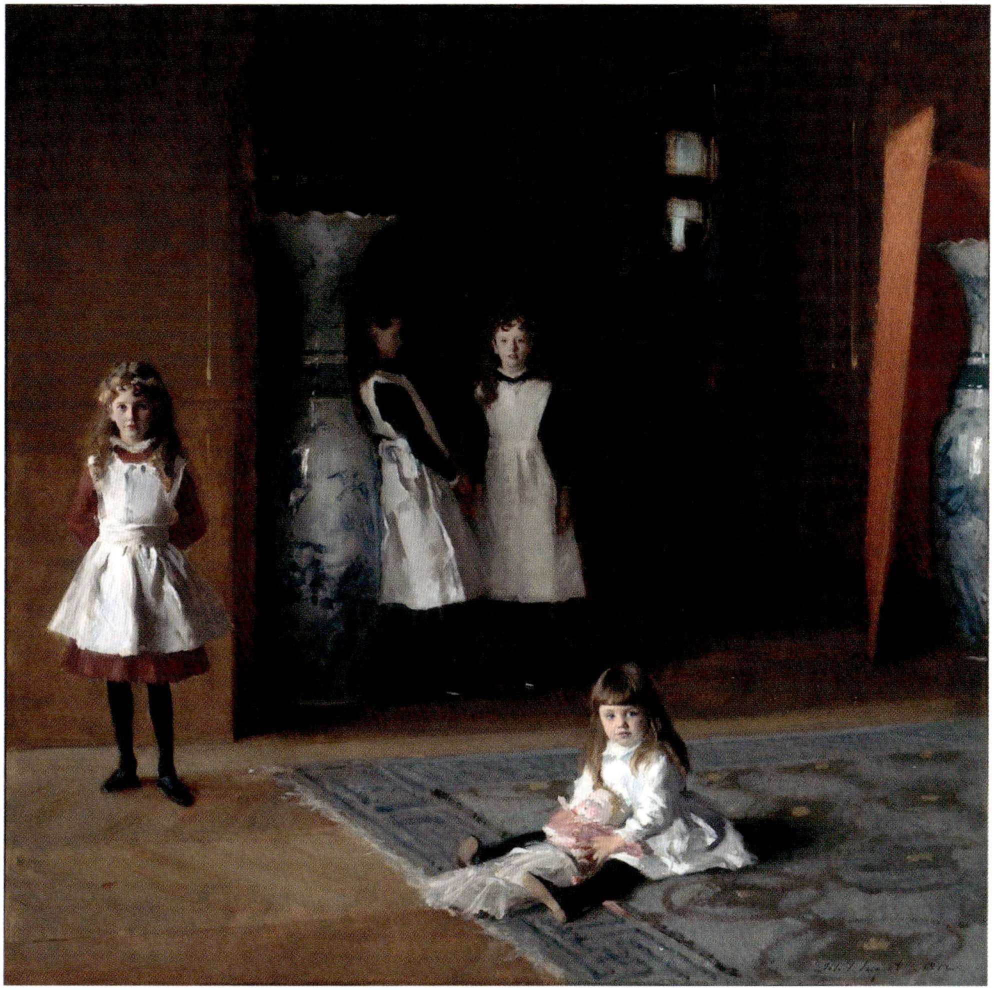

◀

Diego Velázquez (1599–1660)
Las Meninas
1656, oil on canvas, 321 x 282 cm (126 x 111 in)

Surrounded by her attendants (the 'Ladies in Waiting' of the title), the five-year-old Spanish Infanta Margarita Teresa gazes at her parents, King Philip IV and his wife, Mariana. However, their presence is only implied through a reflection in the mirror. Brush in hand, Velázquez stands ready at his easel, but who is he painting? The enigmatic subject, as well as the spatial complexity of this unorthodox family portrait has puzzled critics and intrigued artists over the centuries.

▲

John Singer Sargent (1856–1925)
The Daughters of Edward Darley Boit
1882, oil on canvas, 222 x 223 cm (87 x 88 in)

The daughters of a Boston ex-patriate living in Paris are depicted in the foyer of the family's apartment. The setting allowed Sargent to exploit the space and shadow, and each girl is portrayed as unaware or disinterested in the others' presence. In 1879, Sargent had made his own pilgrimage to Madrid to copy the work of Velázquez, and his tribute features the Spanish master's golden-brown palette, punctuated by black and white.

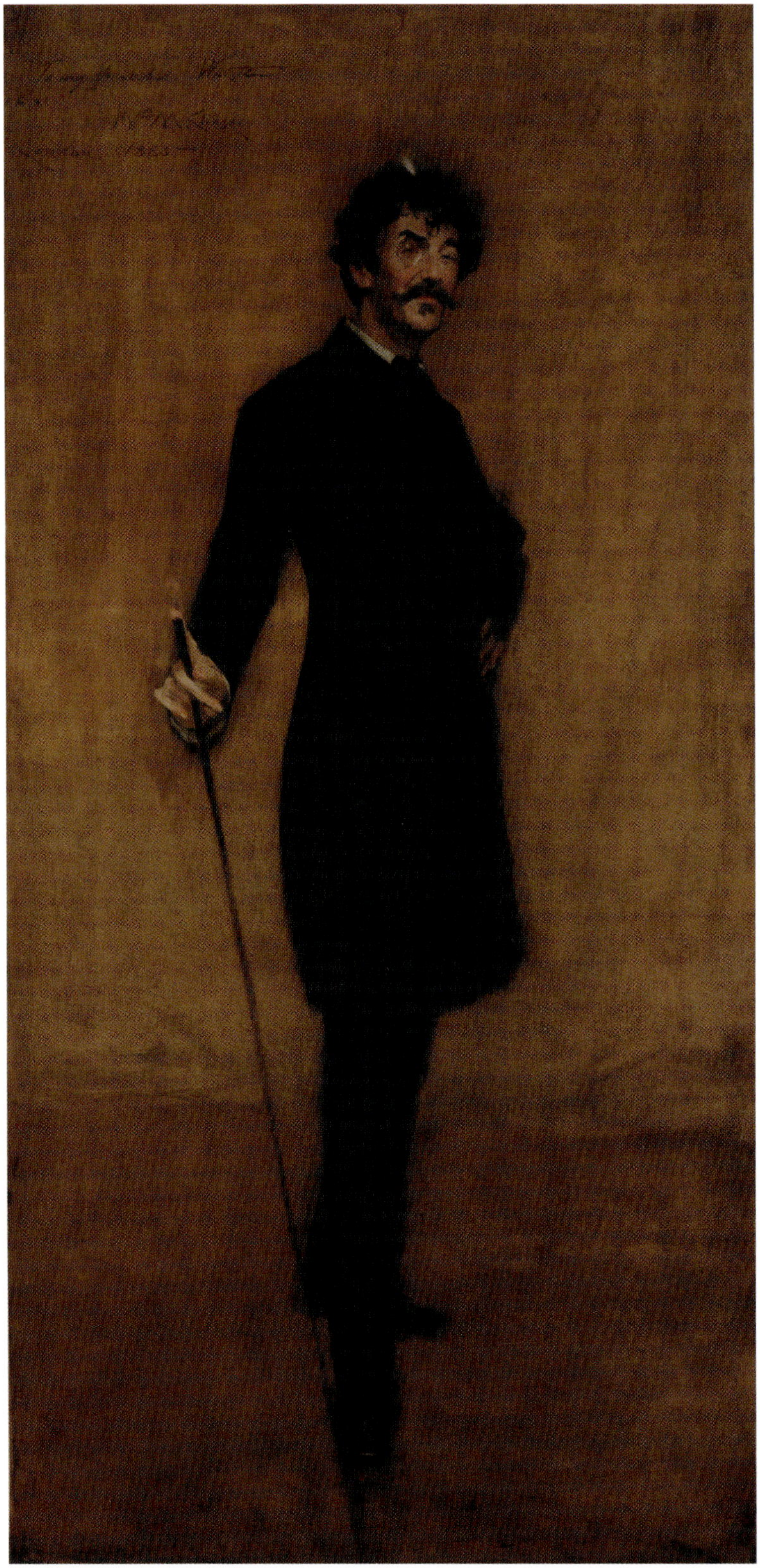

William Merritt Chase
James Abbott McNeill Whistler
1885, oil on canvas, 188 x 92 cm (74 x 36 in)

Prior to his 1885 journey to Spain, Chase stopped in London, where he sought out Whistler, whose style he compared to that of Velázquez. Chase paid tribute to this affinity in the burnished palette and loose brushstroke he used when Whistler suggested they paint each other's portraits. Whistler hated the likeness, deriding it as a 'lampoon'. It is believed that Whistler destroyed his portrait of Chase.

William Merritt Chase
Detail of *Hall at Shinnecock*

Chase appears in the family portrait as a shimmering reflection on the glass door of the armoire. In contrast to Velázquez's stillness in *Las Meninas*, Chase is at work, his head tilted toward the easel as he applies his strokes. His medium – pastel – gave him the most direct way to apply pure pigment on canvas, and while his dynamic handling echoes the brushstrokes of the Spanish master, his rose-gold hues evoke the sunlight of high summer.

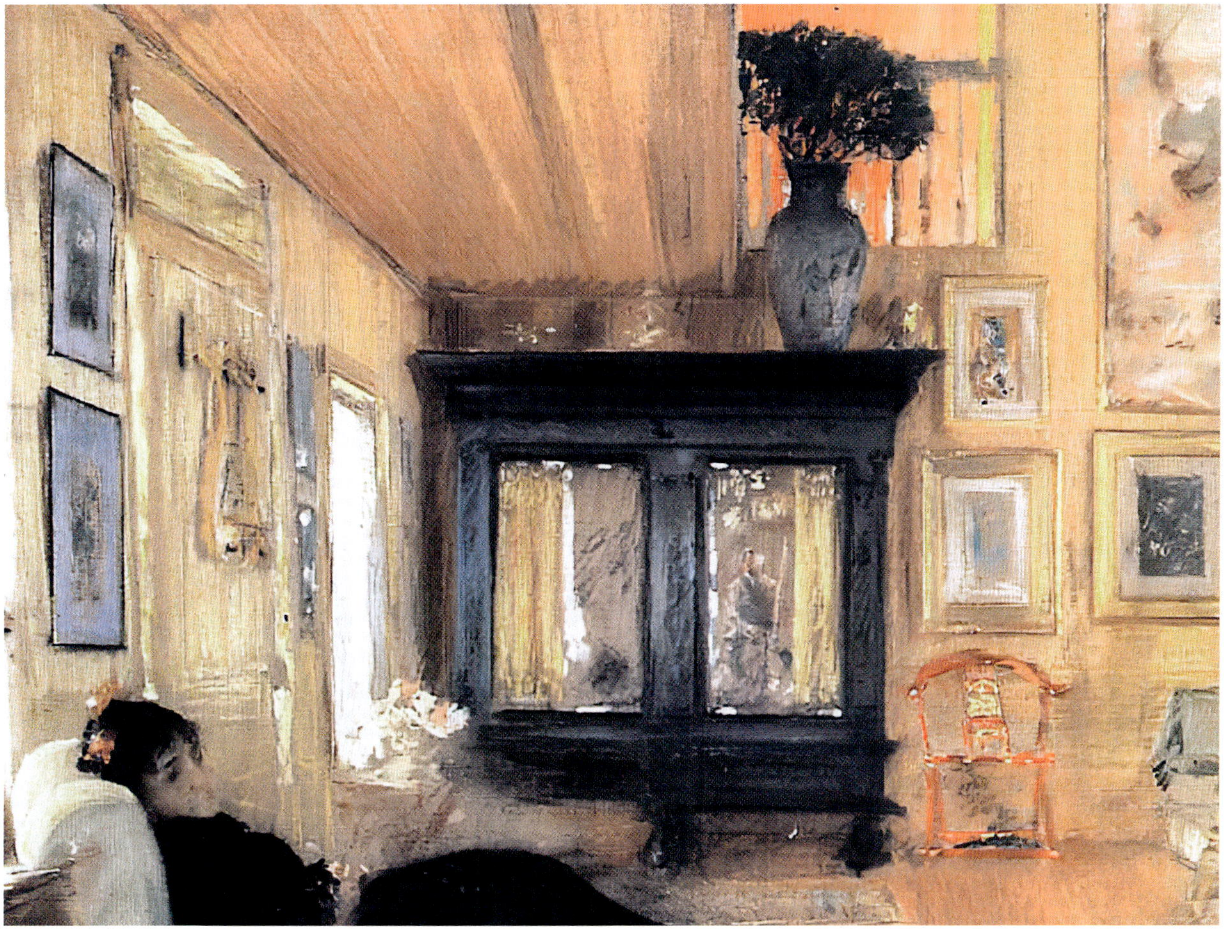

REORIENTING THE GAZE

How Sleigh turned Ingres' *Turkish Bath* from fantasy to reality

Sylvia Sleigh's figure compositions disrupt the western tradition of the idealized human body. Whether the sitter is female or male, her observation was unflinching. Her forthright approach – recording every distinctive feature and flaw – allies her work to such contemporary realist figure painters as Lucian Freud, Philip Pearlstein and Alice Neel. However, there is a difference in Sleigh's trademark honesty. Central to her quest to capture true and individualized form, Sleigh poses her sitters in familiar positions, evoking the recumbent goddesses and reclining odalisques of such artists as Giorgione, Titian and Velázquez. Her bold counter to the icons of art history is best seen in the male nudes that she painted between 1968 and 1976, often and rightly read as a feminist appropriation of the male gaze. However, Sleigh's own gaze is informed by more complex intentions than a mere turnabout to demand fair play. As much homage as revisionist critique, her nuanced response to the conventions of figure painting complicates her engagement with Jean-Auguste-Dominique Ingres' orientalist fantasy in her own version of *The Turkish Bath*.

In the simplest sense the designation 'orientalist' refers to the western representation of eastern culture in art and literature. Throughout the Middle Ages and the Renaissance, eastern examples acquired through contact and trade introduced the West to new materials, aesthetics and techniques, as seen, for example, in the rise of manuscript illumination painted with rare, mineral-based pigments. Over the centuries, such renowned artists as Rembrandt, Rubens and Reynolds collected imported textiles and garments to feature in fanciful portraits. By the eighteenth century, as travel eastward became less arduous, writers and artists joined diplomatic missions, enriching the anthropological record as seen in the descriptive travel letters of Lady Mary Wortley Montagu, wife of the ambassador to the Ottoman court, written during their stay in 1716–18 and published in 1763 after her death. Encyclopaedic documentation followed, mostly by the artists and scholars embedded with the French army during the invasion of Egypt in 1798. At the same time, despite this increasing body of cultural information, the rising spirit of Romanticism cast an exotic –

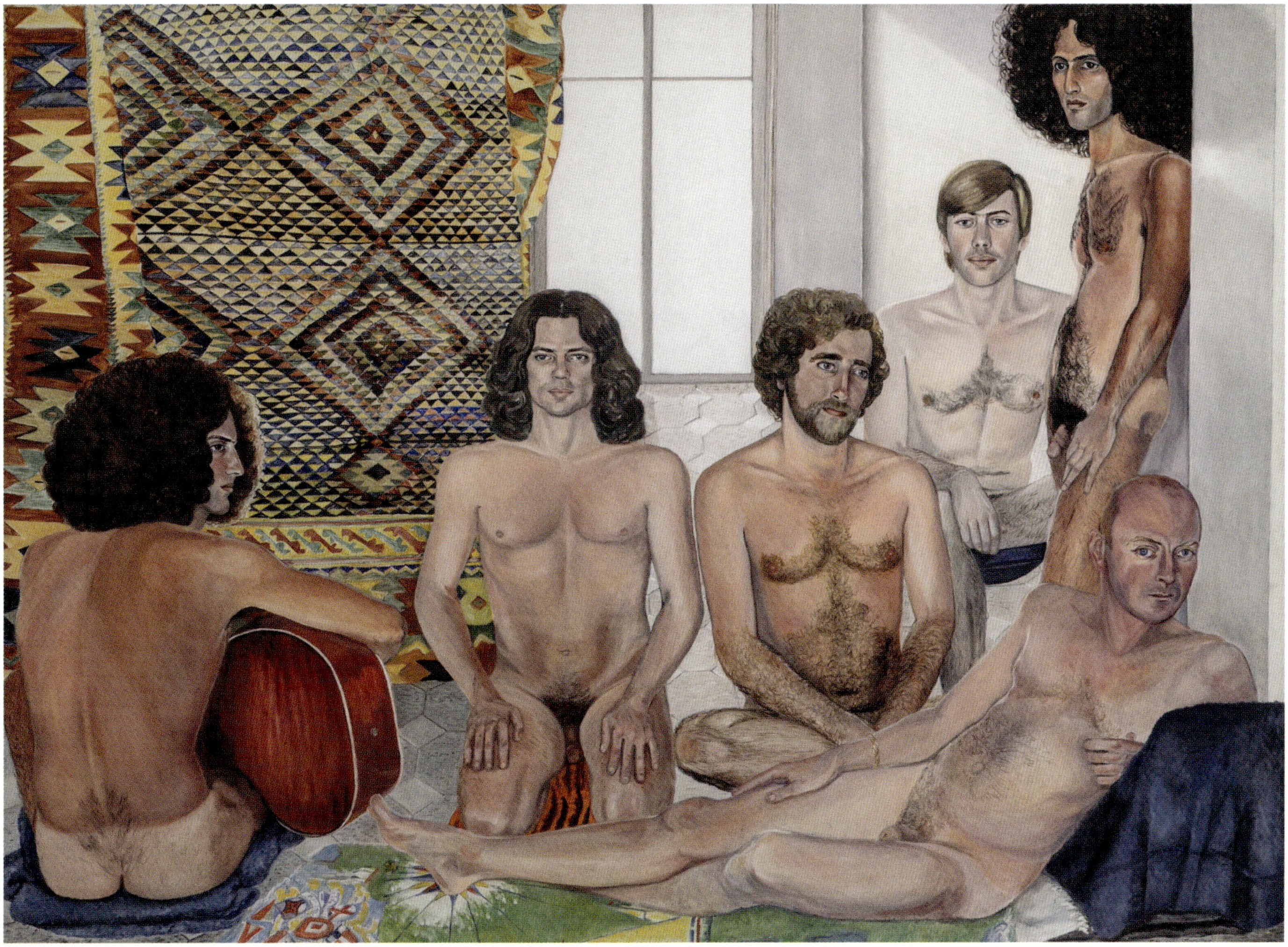

and often erotic – gloss on orientalist subjects, most notably those depicting life in the harem, the protected women's quarters in Middle Eastern and North African households. While many artists relied upon first-hand observation and anthropological sources to enhance the veracity of their orientalist interpretations, Ingres' view into a Turkish women's bath is pure fantasy, culled from his own imagined vision of the East.

In a 1978 interview, Sleigh openly acknowledged the influence of Ingres' *Turkish Bath*, stating she wanted to do 'exactly the opposite'.[1] Other than the rug hanging over the window, Sleigh rejects the decorative elements of orientalism. Her sitters are not in a steamy bath, but a well-lit, open space. Their postures betray none of the calculated eroticism of Ingres' figures; they sit and stand as they might if they were dressed. And, in contrast to what Sleigh described as Ingres' 'heap of flesh', her men are fully individualized: different body types, skin tones, body hair and even tan lines.[2]

▲

Sylvia Sleigh (1916–2010)
The Turkish Bath
1973, oil on canvas, 193 x 259 cm (76 x 102 in)

Their faces are equally distinctive; each, in fact, is a portrait of someone she knew. The man on the left, as well as the one standing on the right, is musician Paul Rosano, one of her favourite models. The men in the middle are Carter Ratcliff, Scott Burton and John Perreault, all art critics. The reclining man is her husband, the noted cultural writer Lawrence Alloway. Sleigh makes a sly reference to Ingres' composition in the framing figures; Rosano holding a guitar rather than a *tambur*, the recumbent Alloway and the standing depiction of Rosano mirror the placement and postures seen in Ingres' painting. Like the outward gaze of the men, this is deliberate on Sleigh's part. She wants the viewer to link her work to that of Ingres, not as a correction or a role reversal, but as a modern approach to an iconic subject, exposing its faults as well as its potential, with boldness, honesty and wit. ●

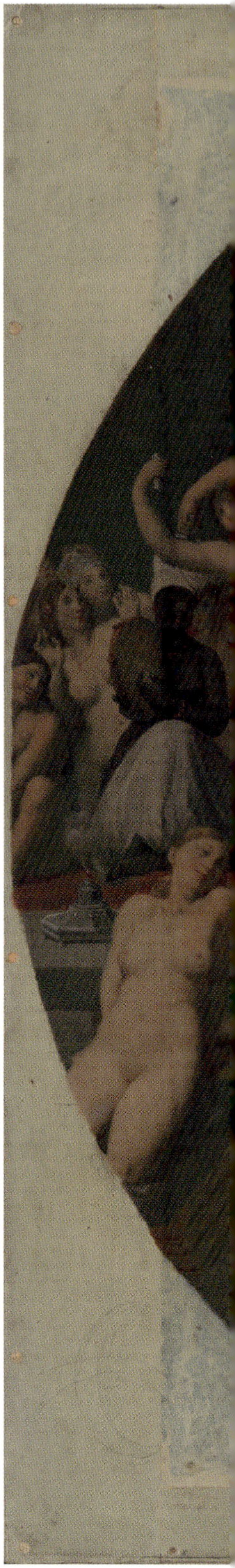

▶

Jean-Auguste-Dominique Ingres (1780–1867)
The Turkish Bath
1862, oil on canvas, glued to wood, D 108 cm (43 in)

Ingres never travelled outside Europe, but he was familiar with the letters of Lady Mary Wortley Montagu, having copied her description of the women's bath in Adrianople. His bathers, however, are pure fantasy, created out of the orientalist fascination with women protected from the male gaze. In fact, Ingres' bathers are not actual women, but idealized figures created to be surreptitiously observed. In this, the difference between Ingres' bathers and Sleigh's sitters is less a matter of greater male agency, than the distinction between what is imaginary and what is real.

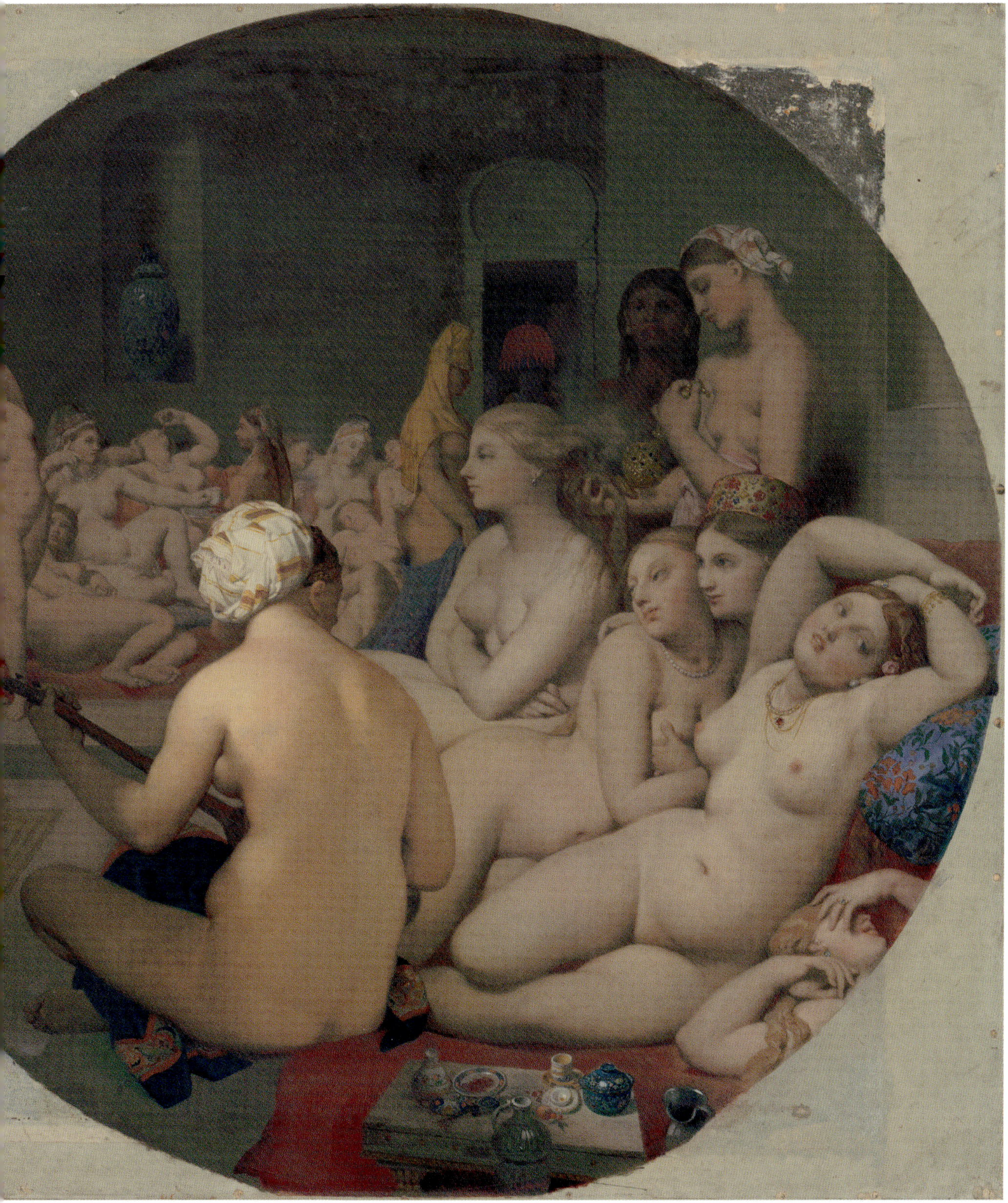

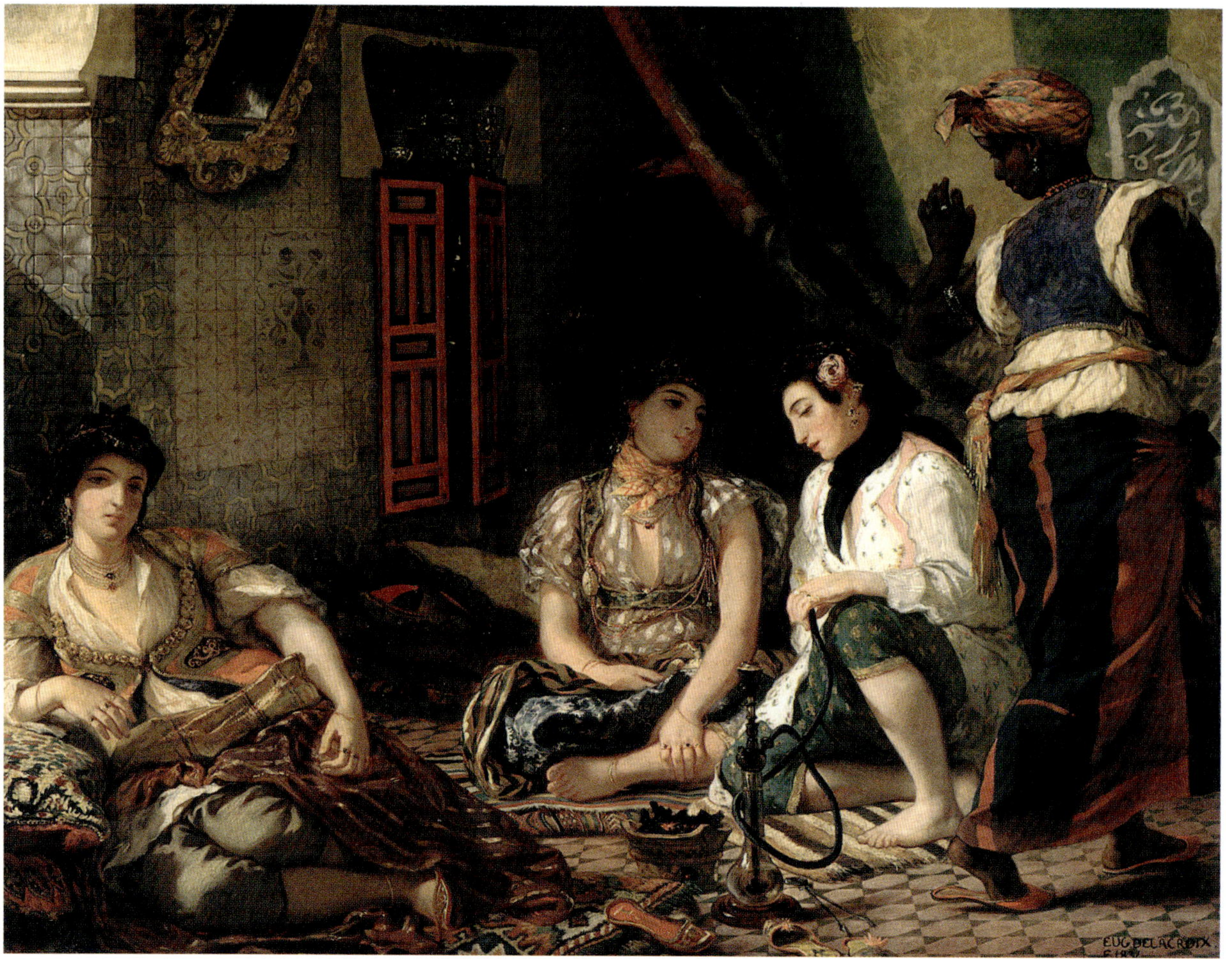

▲

Eugène Delacroix (1798–1863)
The Women of Algiers
1834, oil on canvas , 180 x 229 cm (71 x 90 in)

Delacroix travelled to Morocco with Charles de Mornay, who led a diplomatic mission to the court of the sultan in 1831. Returning home, the artist stopped in Algeria, where a merchant allowed him to sketch in the women's quarters of his household. *The Women of Algiers* was painted in Paris, based on sketches, notes and imagination. Although the interior and the garments are meticulously observed, the scene evokes an orientalist fantasy, presenting women in relaxed postures, exotic costume and the contrast between the fair-skinned concubines and their dark-skinned attendant.

Suzanne Valadon (1865–1938)
The Blue Room
1923, oil on canvas, 90 x 116 cm (35 x 46 in)

Valadon portrays a woman whose recumbent pose and revealing garments evoke the familiar form of the orientalist odalisque. Painted in response to Henri Matisse's *Blue Nude* (1907), Valadon engages her source in terms of colour rather than pose or composition. However, Valadon's sitter is a full contemporary woman, dressed in loungewear and relaxing on her bed as she smokes a cigarette. Her dispassionate attitude suggests a comfortable confidence; she is not there to be looked at but to luxuriate in a simple pleasure.

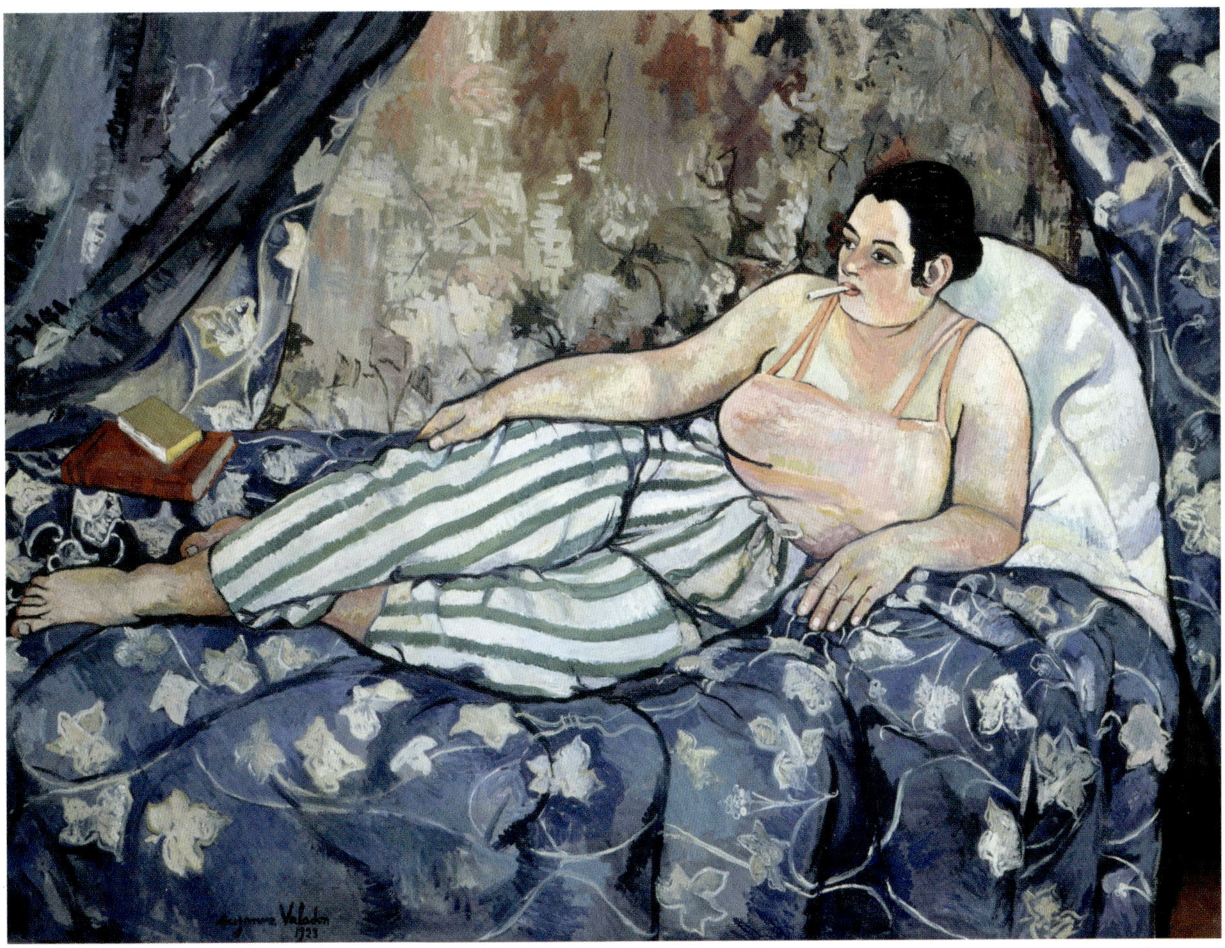

PICTURE WITHIN A PICTURE

How Lichtenstein paid homage to Matisse

Roy Lichtenstein's four-canvas series, 'Artist's Studio', displays his signature style. Strong outlines define flattened, simple forms. The high contrast and hard-edged clarity mimics popular print media: comic books, advertisements, product packaging. The colours are limited to black and white with primary accents. However, unlike his controversial Pop Art paintings of the 1960s, these canvases present imagery drawn from more traditional sources. Each painting offers a view into a room, complete with such mundane objects as a sofa or a table, a telephone, a radiator or decorative vases. And pictures are everywhere, hanging on the walls and propped upright on the floor. In three of the canvases – sub-titled *Look Mickey*, *Foot Medication* and *Model* – the images are self-referential, reprising Lichtenstein's earlier works. *The Dance* features an image by a painter of a very different era. Covering more than half the canvas, Lichtenstein reproduced a corner of Henri Matisse's iconic *The Dance (I)* of 1909, distilling the colourful, heavily brushed image into plain white figures rendered in sharp black lines against a grey background. Despite the difference in style, the reference is unmistakable. In *The Dance* Lichtenstein proclaims his artistic connections. Through references to Matisse's work – both overt and subtle – he proudly acknowledges his debt to art's history.

Like many of American artists of his generation, Lichtenstein cycled through established styles – figurative representation, Cubism, abstraction – to develop his own. In 1958, he started to incorporate popular cartoon characters in his work, including Mickey Mouse, Donald Duck and Bugs Bunny. By 1961, he had fully adopted the visual quality of his source material, limiting his colour palette, outlining figures in black and simulating the effect of Ben-Day Dots, a photo-mechanical process that simulates tonal gradation through closely-spaced dots or lines. His rigorous technique relied upon a skilled and steady hand. He made a preliminary sketch of his subject and used a perforated template to recreate the effect of Ben-Day Dots. Lichtenstein enlarged and transferred the sketch onto his canvas with a projector and then applied the paint with a flawless clarity that captured the mechanized anonymity of commercial printing.

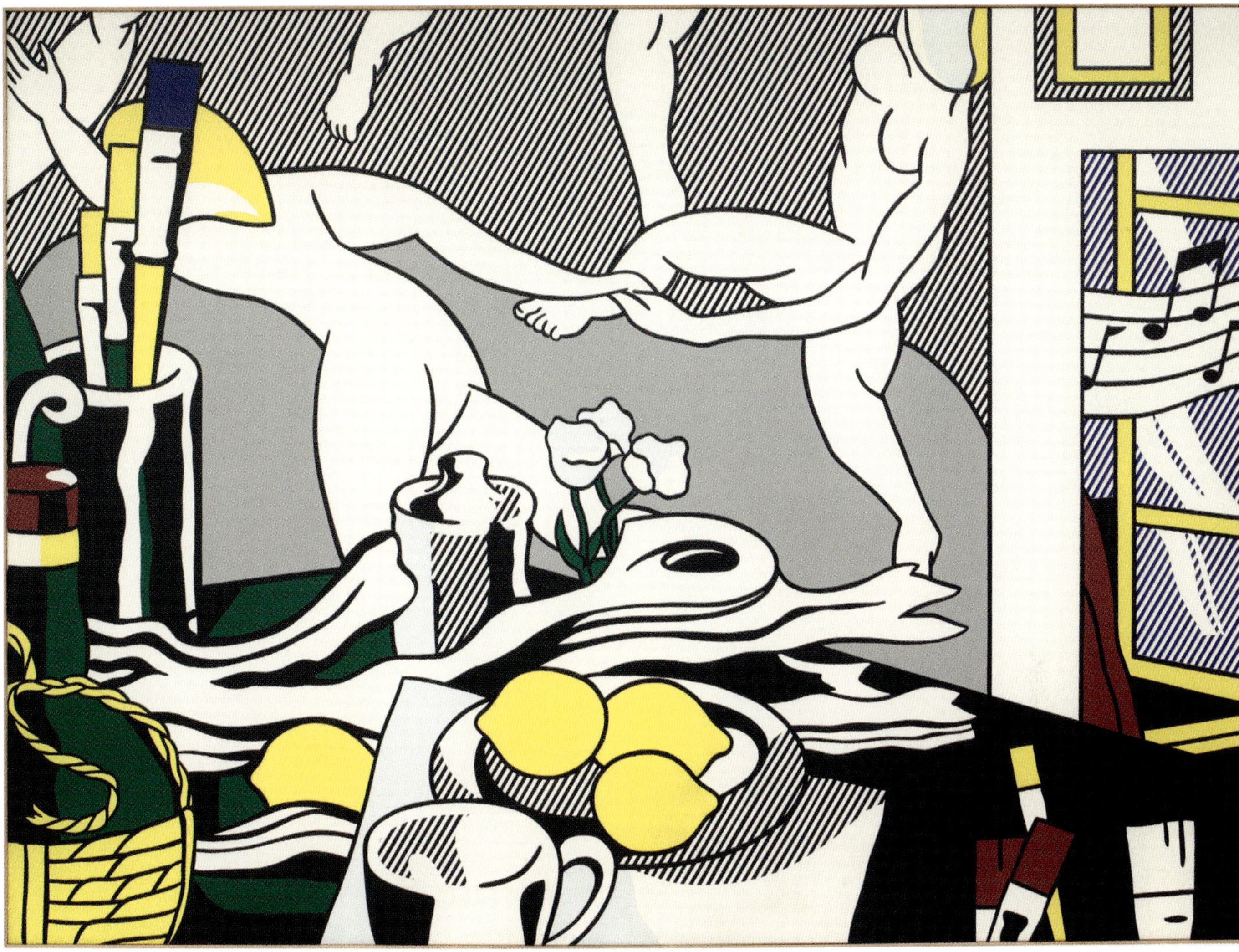

The result was a neutral aesthetic that obliterated the unique trace of the artist's hand: 'I want it to seem like I had divested it of quality,' by eliminating 'anything that was beguiling.'[1] As for content, Lichtenstein meticulously copied his source material, including the text bubbles in cartoons, jarring the art world with an unapologetic replica of comic book images on the grand scale of fine art.

The comic book images brought Lichtenstein recognition, as well as notoriety, but the history of twentieth-century art sustained him throughout his career. His interest was sparked in adolescence, when he received Thomas Craven's 1934 book, *Modern Art: The Men, The Movement, The Meaning*, as a gift. He copied the works of Pablo Picasso and Claude Monet, and later his wife Dorothy described his ongoing passion for museum

▲

Roy Lichtenstein (1923–97)
Artist's Studio 'The Dance'
1974, oil and magna on canvas,
244 x 326 cm (96 x 128 in)

visits: 'He was always looking at paintings,' and musing how he could 'transform them.'[2] His steal from Matisse in *The Dance* extended beyond the act of including a picture within a picture. Lichtenstein was well aware that Matisse had repeatedly painted his own studio; perhaps that inspired the series. However, the direct visual references to the older painter's own picture within a picture canvas, *Still Life with 'Dance' Panel* (1909), reveals the depth of tribute in this transformation. Along with the position of Matisse's *Dance*, Lichtenstein replicated the tilt of the tabletop, the placement of the window on the right, and the lemons, both in a dish and on the table. While Matisse does not depict a raffia-covered Chianti bottle, in Lichtenstein's painting it stands as a winking reference to an art world cliché. And the brushes that Lichtenstein gathers in the jars on the table are more than an allusion to the flowers in the vases; they signal Lichtenstein's readiness to observe and create, transforming visual history through his own concept of what was – and what could be – art. ●

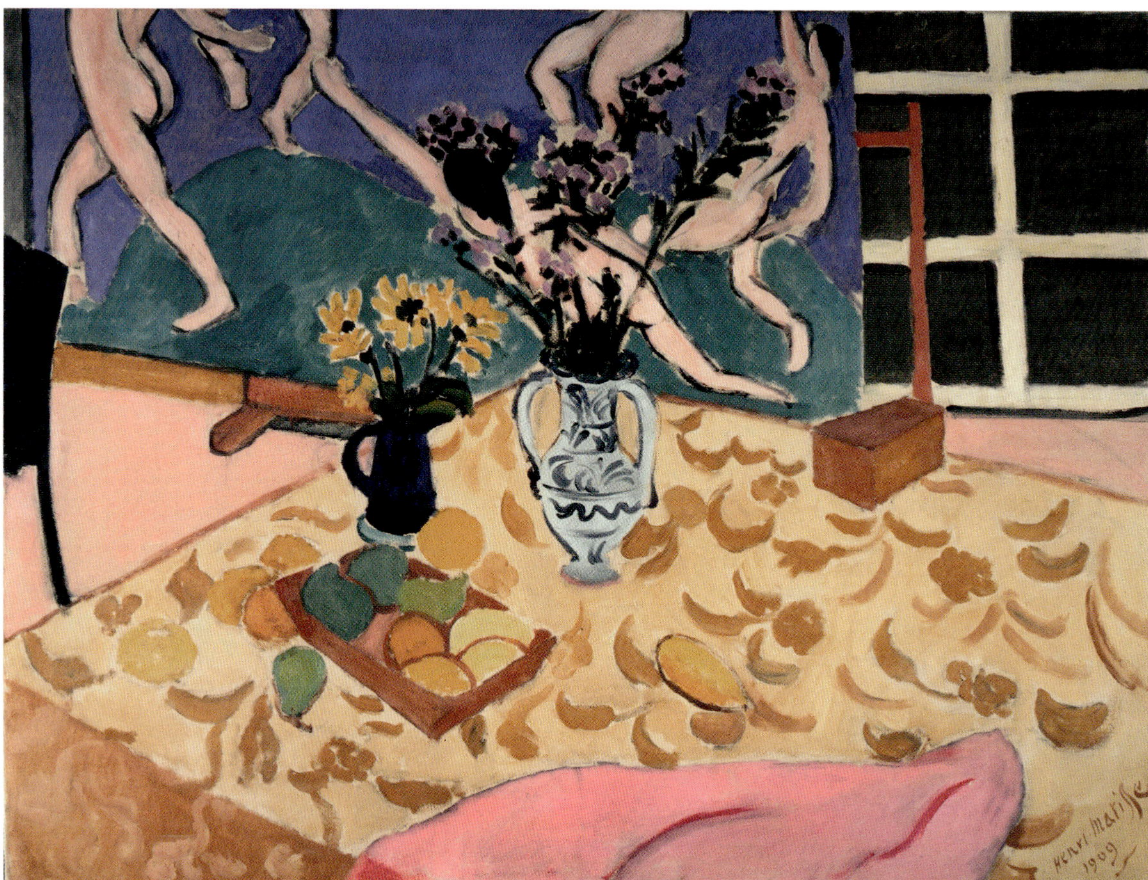

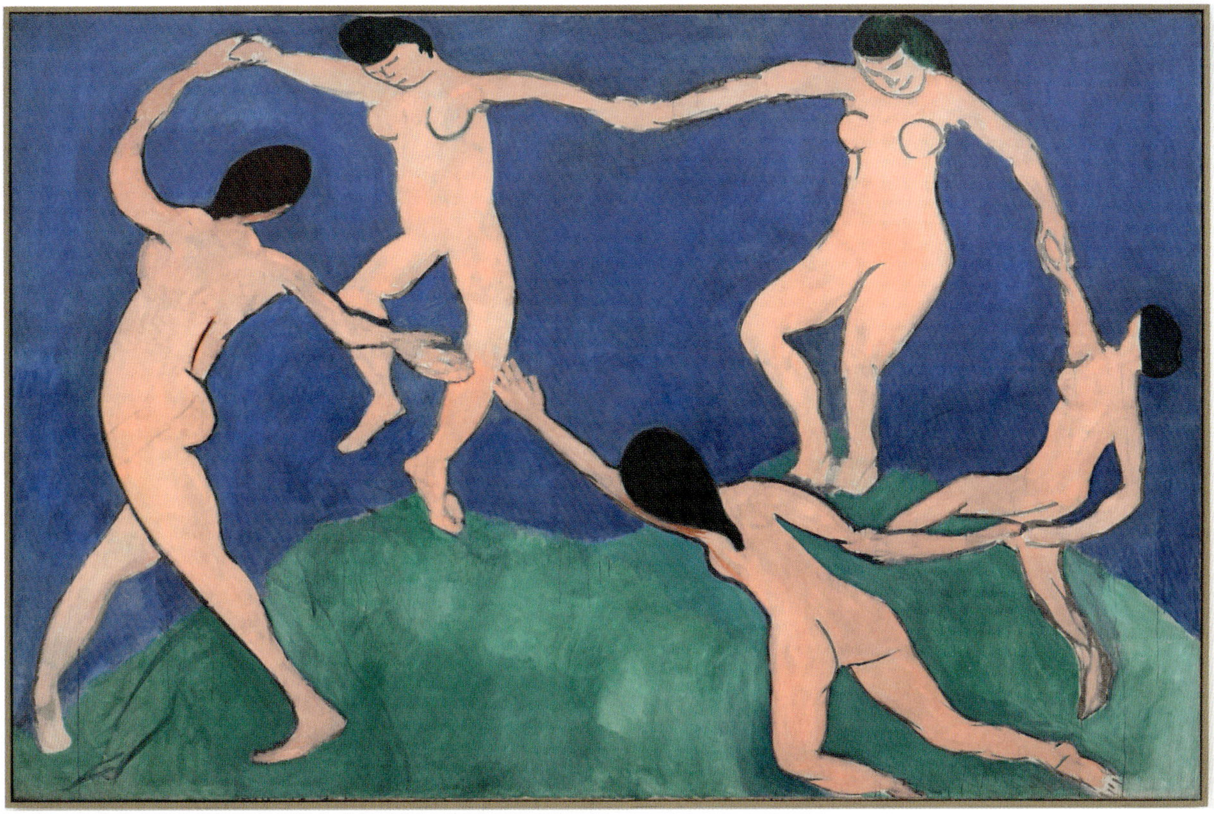

◀

Henri Matisse (1869–1954)
Still Life with 'Dance' Panel
1909, oil on canvas, 90 x 118 cm (35 x 46 in)

Still Life with 'Dance' Panel had long been in Russian collections when Lichtenstein painted 'Artist's Studio'. Lichtenstein likely knew the work through a reproduction. However, the similarities are striking. Matisse's work depicts a corner of his studio with *Dance (I)* on an easel. It is an actual space – the artist's studio in Paris on the Boulevard des Invalides – with all the clutter of daily life. Lichtenstein's clean, commercial style strikes a neutral atmosphere, and the space itself is imagined. However, the carefully chosen objects on view provide an intimate glimpse into the workings of Lichtenstein's imagination.

▲

Henri Matisse
Dance (I)
1909, oil on canvas, 260 x 390 cm (102 x 154 in)

Matisse painted *Dance (I)* as a study for a two-panel commission celebrating dance and music for his Russian patron, Sergei Shchukin. Although it differs in colour from the final version, which features red figures and a deeper-toned background, this work matches it in figural movement, rhythmic expression and vitality. It is likely that Lichtenstein used this work as his reference in 'Artist's Studio'; at the time he painted the series, *Dance (I)* was in the collection of the Museum of Modern Art.

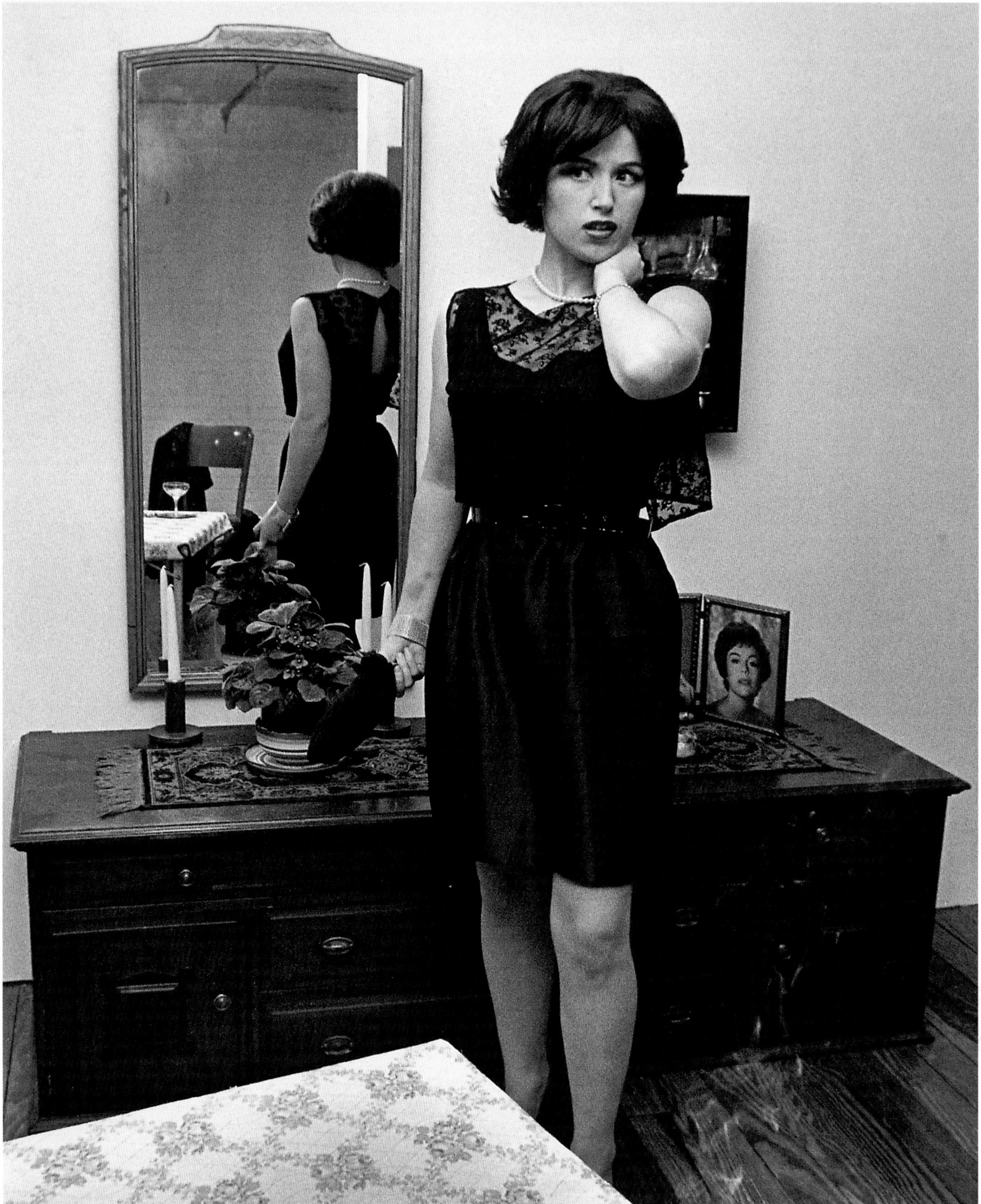

CINEMATIC SUGGESTION

How Sherman reimagined the B-movie heroine

Clad in a black lace cocktail dress, the woman in the photograph looks to her right with a wary expression, gripping a sheathed object in her right hand. The mirror's reflection implies another's presence; a half-filled martini coupe sits on the table and a man's jacket is draped over the edge of a pushed-out chair. The furnishings are spare and shabby; the mood is tense, but ambiguous. We sense something is about to happen, but what? Every detail seems unnervingly familiar, as if we have seen this scenario in a long-forgotten film about a woman trapped in a dangerous situation. However, rather than having its source in actual cinema, Cindy Sherman's photograph draws its inspiration from a once popular form of promotional ephemera: the glossy film still featuring a provocative image, shot on set and widely distributed. Sherman has curated objects that are suggestive and performs a character that taps into a female cinematic stereotype: a post-war, B-movie heroine – the girl in trouble. And while these visual details tap into a mass media memory of such characters and stories, it is the format that triggers the connection. In a daring act of stripping the medium of its original purpose, Sherman plays upon its inherent power to deliver a message.

Sherman began shooting her series 'Untitled Film Stills' in 1977. Over three years, she composed, performed and photographed tableaux of women in cinematic situations: the bored housewife, the jilted lover, the innocent in the city. She created a catalogue of characters based on female stereotypes, critiquing the reductive tropes of how women were portrayed in film while simultaneously exploring the power of costume and gesture to stimulate a network of connections that derived from popular cinema. The seventy prints in the series vary in setting, mood and level of suggestion, but two things remain consistent. Sherman, as the sole performer, disappears into the character without a trace of irony or self-identity. From image to image she is transformed. Even more striking is the consistency of format. Each photograph, a perfect replica of the high-volume, inexpensively produced film still distributed over the decades from the mid-1920s through its peak of popularity in the late 1950s and early 1960s. While she was appropriating the language of character, costume and gesture for her elusive narrative, Sherman relied upon the format to give her work its contextual significance: 'I wanted them to seem cheap and trashy, something you'd find in a novelty store and buy for a quarter.'[1]

◀

Cindy Sherman (b. 1954)
Untitled Film Still #14
1978, gelatin silver print, 25 x 20 cm (10 x 8 in)

In creating the 'Untitled Film Stills' series, Sherman adopted the role of the *auteur*. She controlled every aspect of the shoot, gathering the costume and props, staging the scene, creating her character and, whenever possible, using a shutter release cable to take the shot. Her attention to thought-provoking detail is particularly evident in *Untitled Film Still #14*. The woman's bouffant coiffure, the cinched waist and lace overlay of her inexpensive dress, and the above-the-knee hemline set the time in the early 1960s. The woman appears again in a photograph in the right half of the double frame behind her. Her hair is shorter, her look more open, as if from a more hopeful time. The taper candles, woven runner, artificial plant and printed tablecloth convey a half-hearted attempt to personalize a highly impersonal space. Sherman collected these items from thrift shops as a set designer would for an independent film. However, she cut out the scriptwriter and storyline, relying instead on the character and the configuration of objects to tease the viewer with a familiar ensemble, despite her claim that she had 'no film in mind at all'.[2] In fact, she regarded it as a mark of success when people insisted that they had seen the film. However, like the film still itself, Sherman's photographs were meant to tantalize rather than tell the story, putting viewers in the position of the unreliable narrator, mining their memories of movies for meaning. ●

▶

Richard Wallace (1894–1951; director)
John Meade's Woman (Francine Larrimore)
1937, photograph, 32 x 39 cm (13 x 15 in)

This film still depicts Teddy, the 'Woman' of the title, a country girl saved from the streets by John Meade, a ruthless lumber tycoon, a typical B-movie trope. Teddy is presented as a glamorous woman – marcelled hair and manicured nails – but she looks troubled as she turns away from the sumptuous meal before her. There is no indication of her modest past or her future as a labour leader, but the image is conceived to spark interest rather than tell the story. The *New York Times* critic Frank S. Nugent called the film a 'thoroughly absurd piece of theatrical clap-trap'.

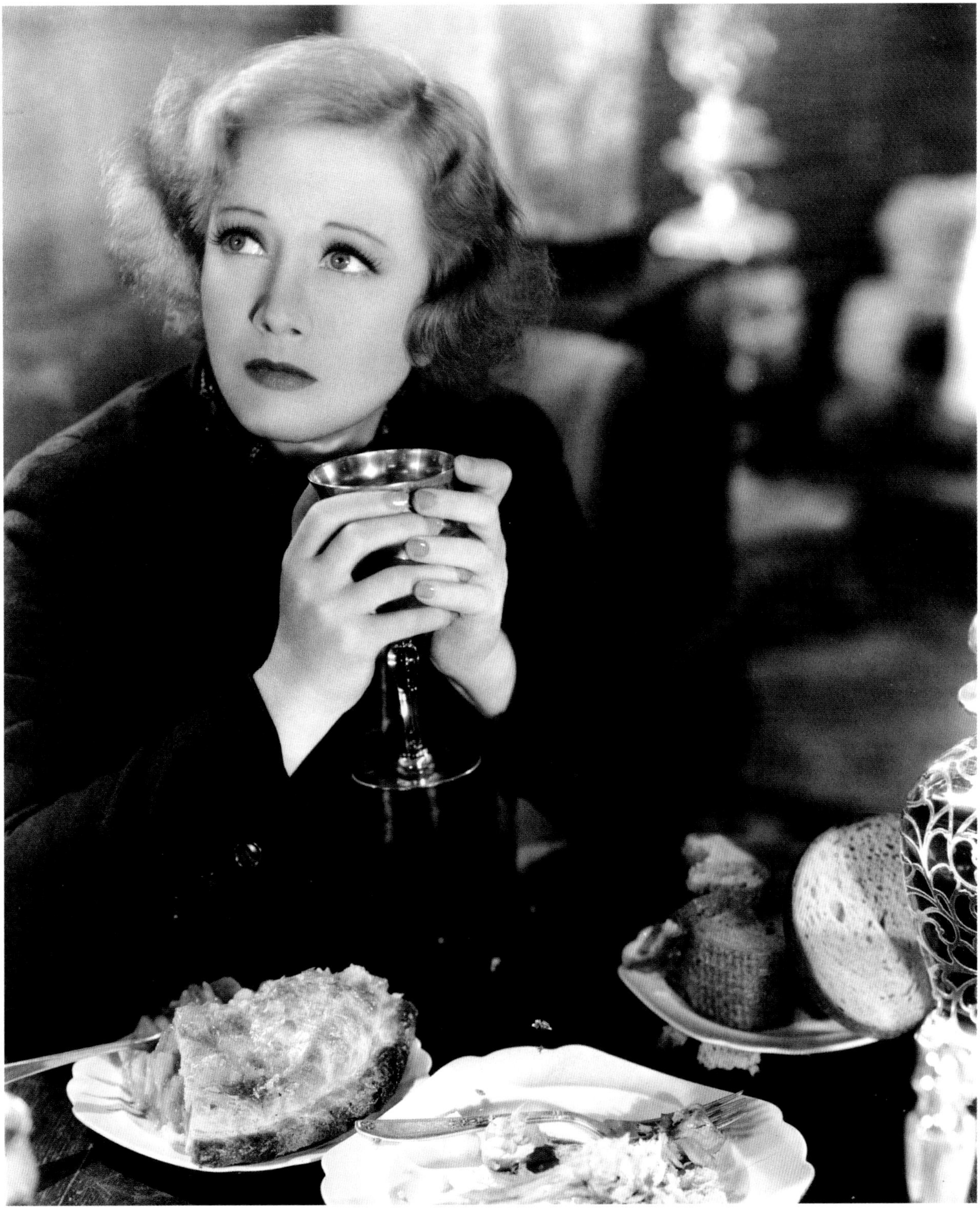

Edward Hopper (1882–1967)
Morning Sun
1952, oil on canvas, 71 x 102 cm (28 x 40 in)

When Hopper felt disinclined to paint, he went to the movies. He was a great fan of 1940s *film noir*, and his own work projected a similar vision of modern life, tinged by uncertainty and isolation. Whether deliberately or instinctually, he captured that evocative ambivalence in some of his best known works, including *Nighthawks* (1942). A work like *Morning Sun* conjures a single frame in a movie reel; in less than a second the light will change and the figure will move, advancing the story on the screen.

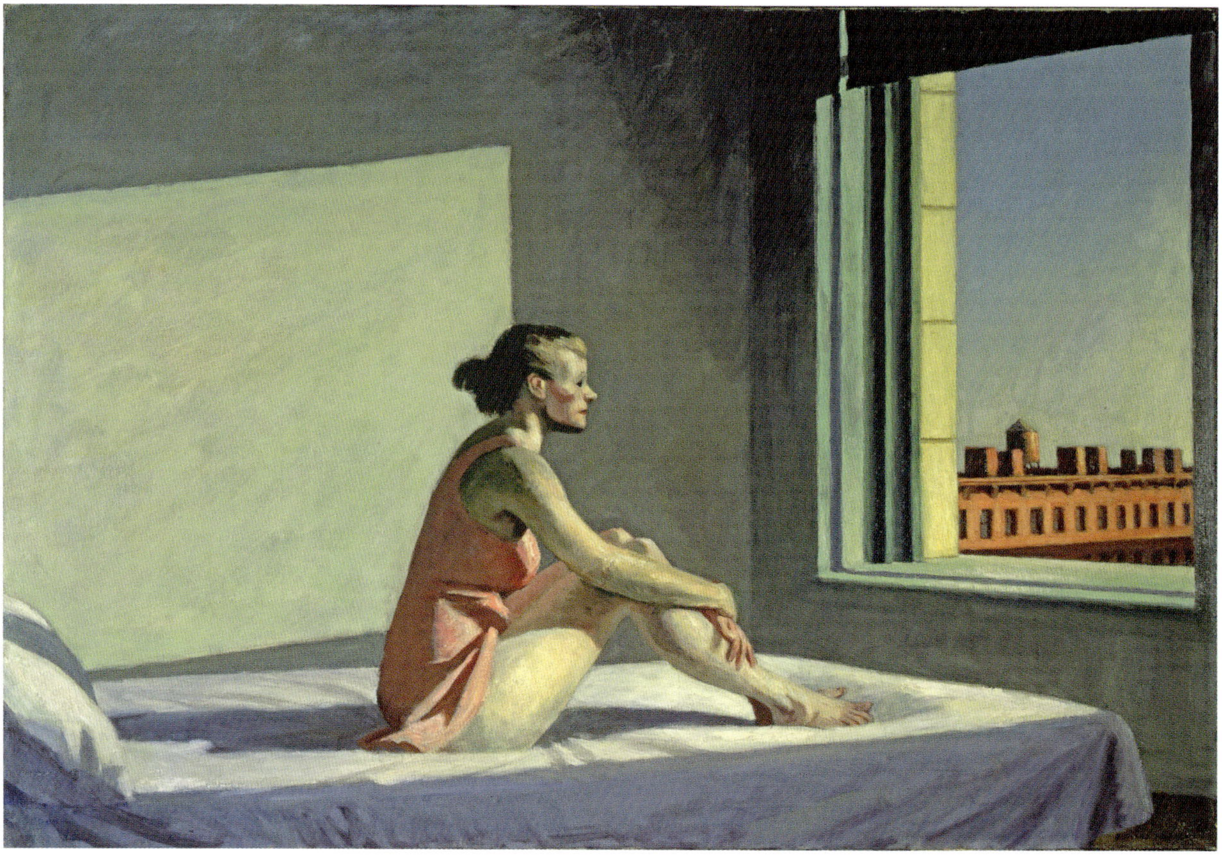

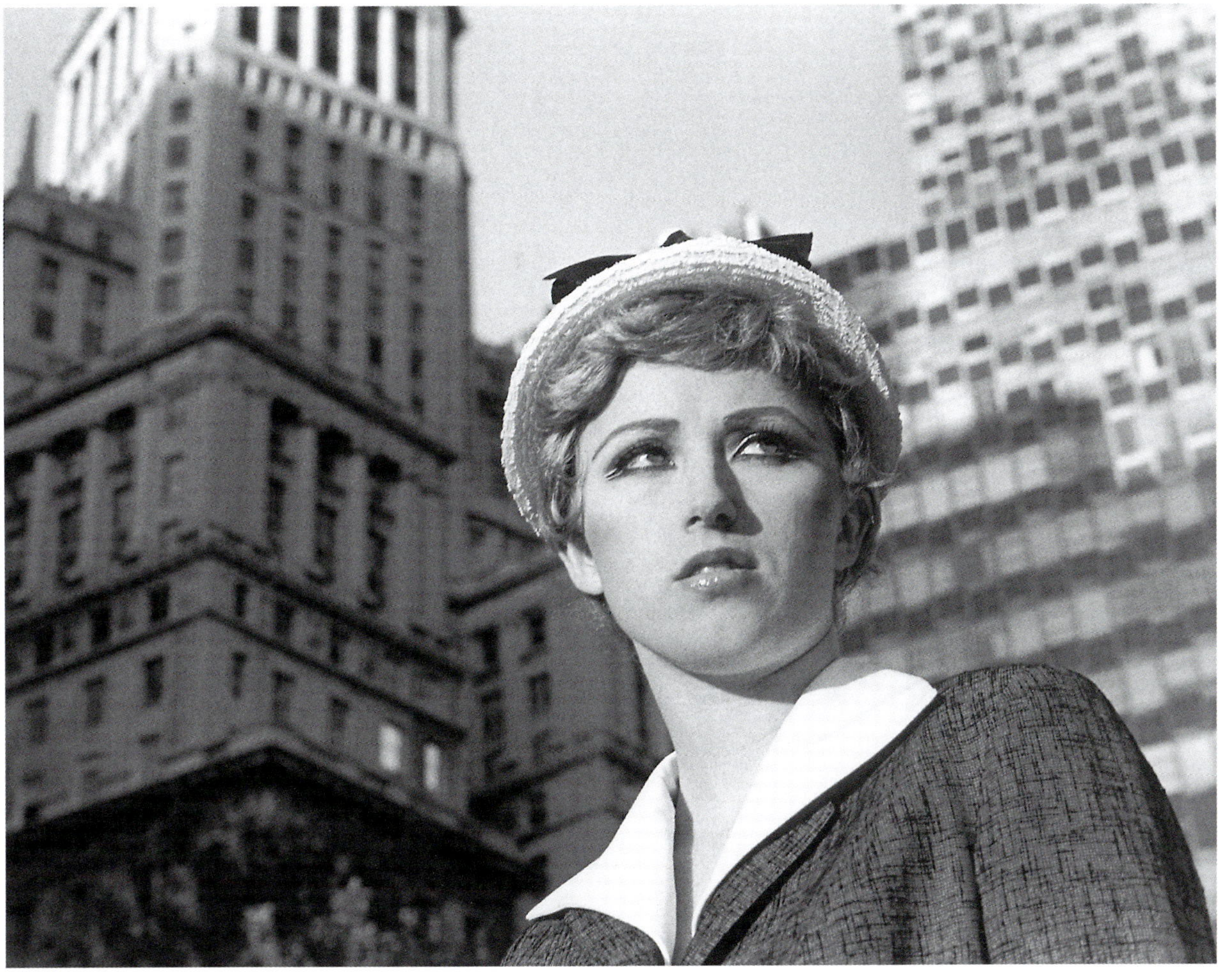

▲

Cindy Sherman
Untitled Film Still #21
1978, gelatin silver print, 20 x 25 cm (8 x 10 in)

The innocent ingenue was a popular B-movie stereotype. Sherman presents her in a tailored suit and a pert hat with a fearful expression. The looming skyscrapers in the background and the low angle of the shot emphasizes her vulnerability. Alone in the big city she will be at the centre of a story, but what that story will be remains to be told. Will she rise to an unknown challenge or will her hopes and dreams be crushed?

HYBRID INFLUENCES

How Shonibare transformed Raeburn's sombre figure with West African fashion

During his studies at the Byam Shaw School of Art in London (1984–9), Yinka Shonibare's tutor questioned why his work addressed Soviet politics: 'You are African, aren't you? Why don't you make authentic African art?'[1] To Shonibare – born in London, raised in Lagos and returning to London almost every summer throughout his childhood – cultural identity was not a simple matter. He saw himself as both African and British, and he embraced the duality as a potential enrichment rather than a dilution of his artistic selfhood. Instead of trying to produce 'authentic African art', Shonibare began to interrogate the concept of authenticity, seeking a visual means to explore the relationship between the colonized and the colonizer, one that would make a clear yet critical statement about the transformative power of exchange and influence. He found it in a distinctive fabric that he first purchased in a market in Brixton. Boldly patterned and brightly coloured, Dutch wax fabric – worn by his Nigerian relatives and neighbours – had a heritage even more complex than his own.

Dutch wax fabric, or *wax hollandaise*, embodied the colonial trade policies that bound the Dutch East Indies (now the Republic of Indonesia) to Holland. The Dutch East India Company introduced batik-dyed cottons – a resist technique, practised throughout Southeast Asia, that used wax to preserve patterns through multiple colour soaks – to Europe in the later eighteenth century. Western textile manufacturers, particularly in the Netherlands, soon produced an inexpensive version of the textile by replacing the labour-intensive, hand-application of wax with mechanized roller printing. The resulting fabric was vibrant with crisp, bold patterns but lacked the subtle surface effects of authentic batik. Rejected by customers in the Dutch East Indies, Dutch traders found an alternative market for the cloth in their nation's colonies in western Africa. The Vlisco Group, founded in 1846, quickly dominated the market by creating ranges of colourful prints tailored to African preferences. Within a century, Vlisco *wax hollandaise* became the signature textile of West African fashion; worldwide, the cloth proclaimed African authenticity.

▶

Yinka Shonibare (b. 1962)
Reverend on Ice
2005, semi-opaque synthetic polymer resin, cotton (Dutch wax), wool, leather, wood, steel, 160 x 402 x 602 cm (63 x 158 x 237 in)

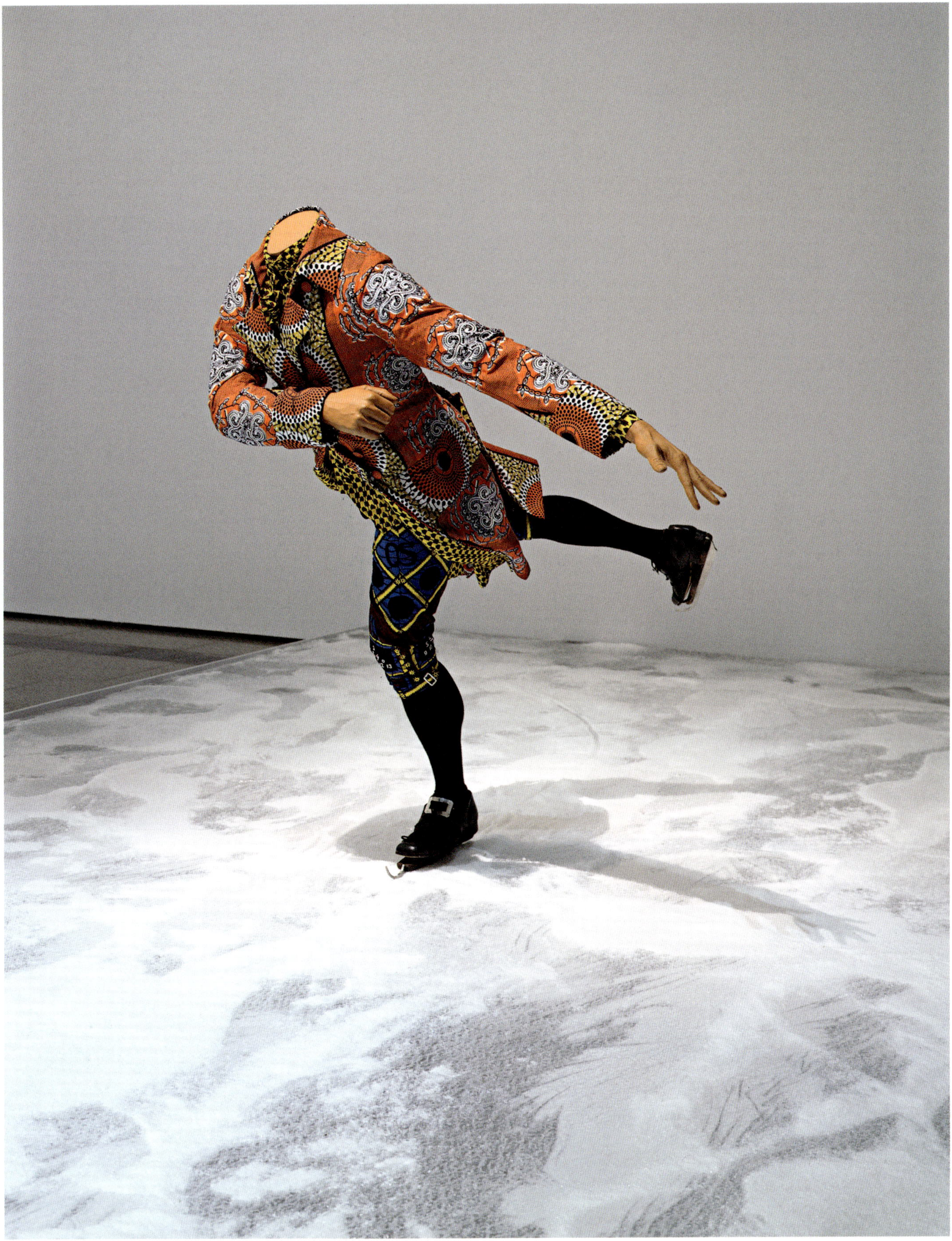

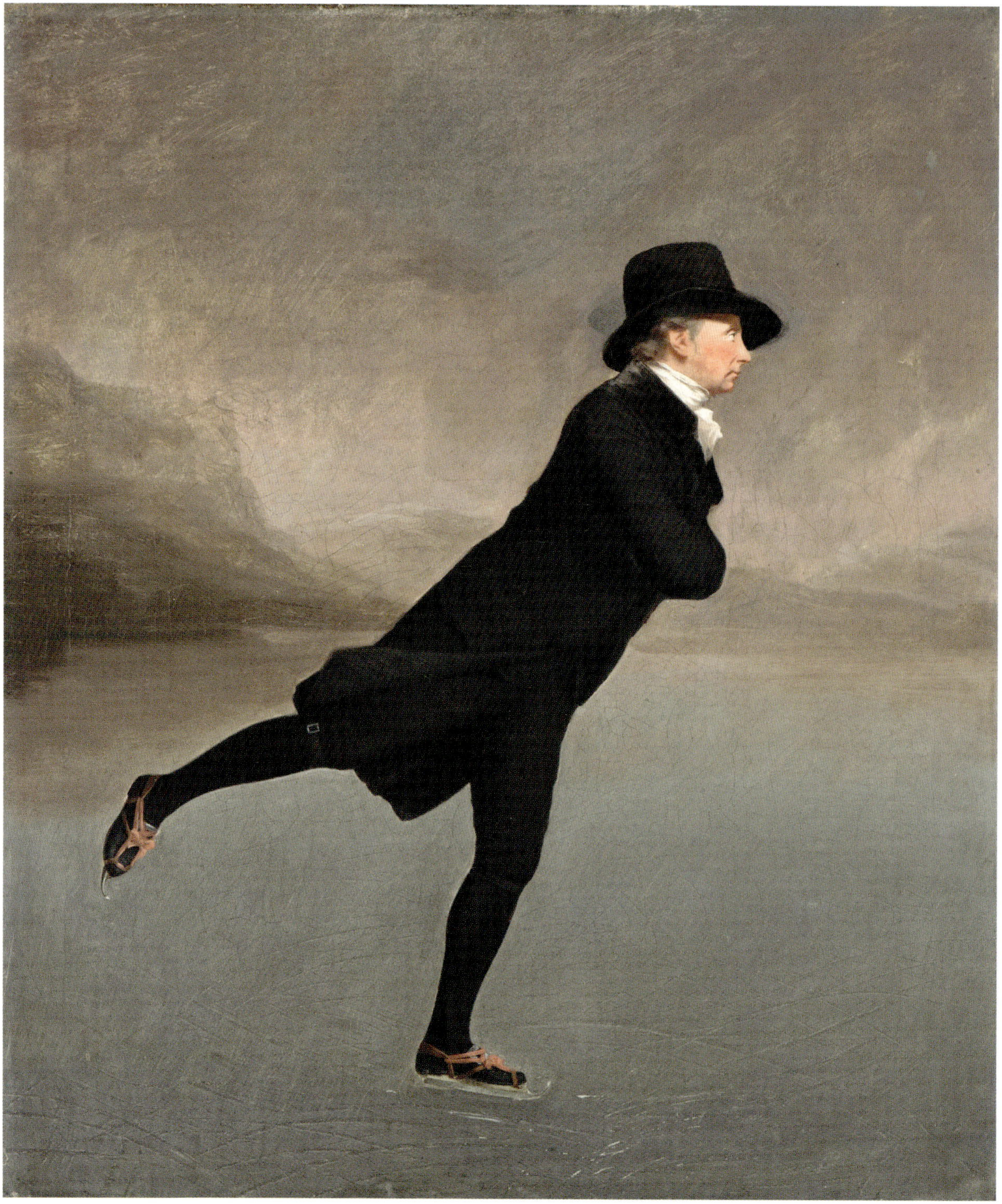

This 'cross-bred' history appealed to Shonibare, who took ironic delight that an emblematic African textile 'was actually fabricated in Europe'.[2] At first, he painted on it as a substitute for canvas, but turned to use it in a distinctive form of sculpture: near-life-sized, headless figures, dressed in Vlisco cloth. He appropriated poses from popular, late eighteenth-century European paintings, as seen in *Reverend on Ice*, his reprise of Henry Raeburn's popular depiction of *The Reverend Robert Walker Skating on Duddingston Loch*. The image of the sombre cleric gliding gracefully on a frozen pond struck Shonibare as inherently contradictory: a serious man engaged in a playful activity. The meticulously accurate recreation of the Reverend's severe garments in vivid, contrasting colours and patterns heightened the provocative sense of the figure's dislocation. Just as colonial trade drew upon the world as its market, Shonibare aggregated references, postures and materials to forge a global aesthetic of mixed origins and hybridity, blurring the notion of 'authentic' into obsolesce. Even without a head – the most conventional signifier of individuality in western art – Shonibare's Reverend asserts his singular identity. ●

◀

Henry Raeburn (1756–1823)
The Reverend Robert Walker Skating on Duddingston Loch
c. 1795, oil on canvas, 76 x 64 cm (30 x 25 in)

Portraying his friend the Reverend Walker flawlessly executing the 'travelling position' – gliding on one skate – Raeburn was not just lauding his friend's skill. The motif tapped into memories from his own childhood in Rotterdam, where his father served as the minister of the Scots Kirk. Shonibare encountered the painting in reproduction while carrying out research at the Cooper Hewitt, Smithsonian Design Museum in New York. He used the same pose for his depiction but replaced the cleric's plain, black attire with an exact replica crafted in multi-coloured and patterned *wax hollandaise* fabrics.

Multiple artists
Vlisco: African Fashion on a Global Stage
2016–17, installation at Philadelphia Museum of Art

Pieter Fentener van Vlissingen bought a textile factory in Helmond in 1846. His initial production of a wide variety of printed fabrics soon gave way to an industrial imitation of the hand-printed wax batiks produced in the Dutch Indies. He countered his failure to sell his cloth in the Dutch East Indies with new markets he cultivated in the West African supply ports along the route back to Europe. The name Vlisco now indicates the type of cloth as well as a brand name, the Vlisco Group, with four divisions located in the Netherlands and Ghana.

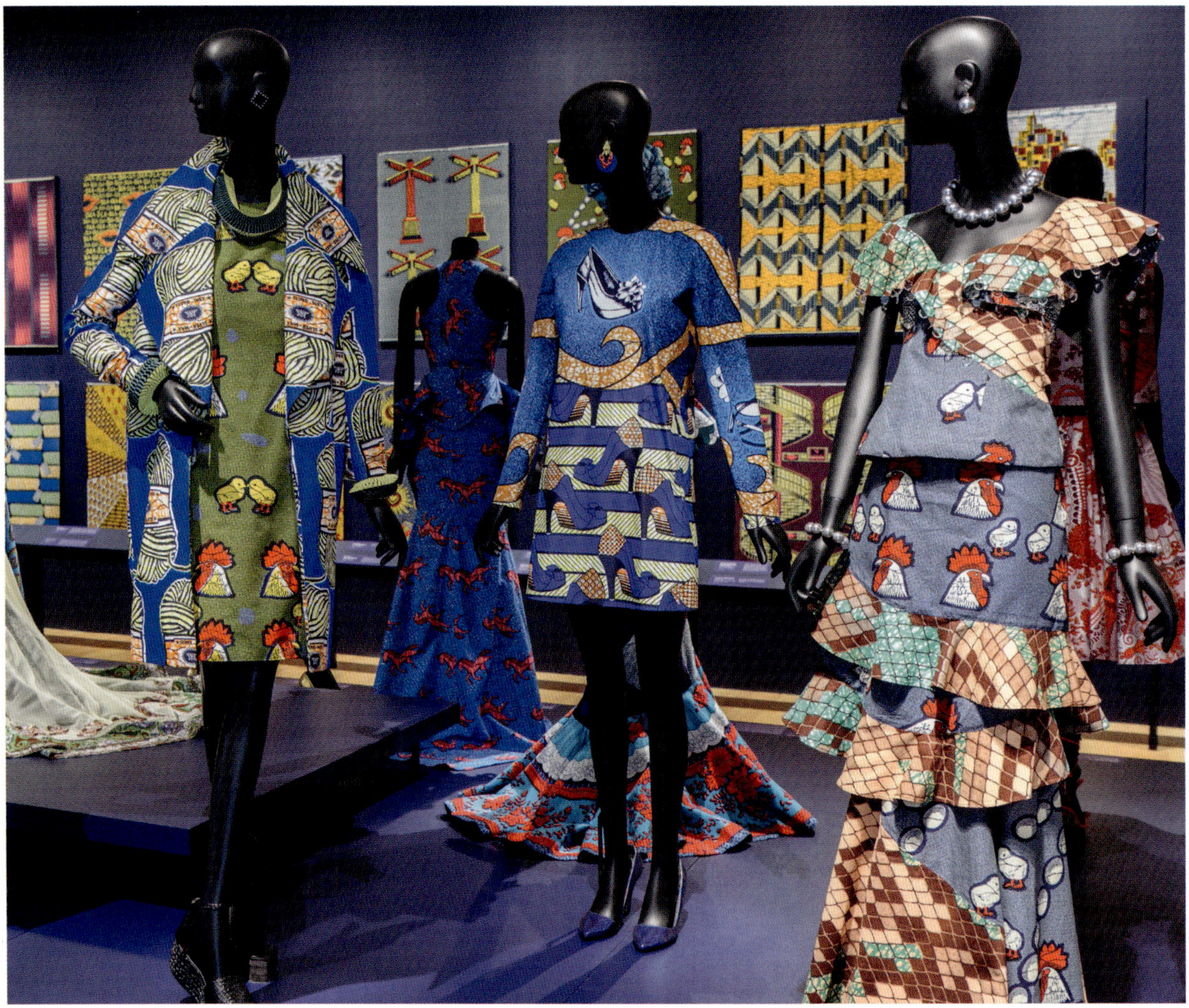

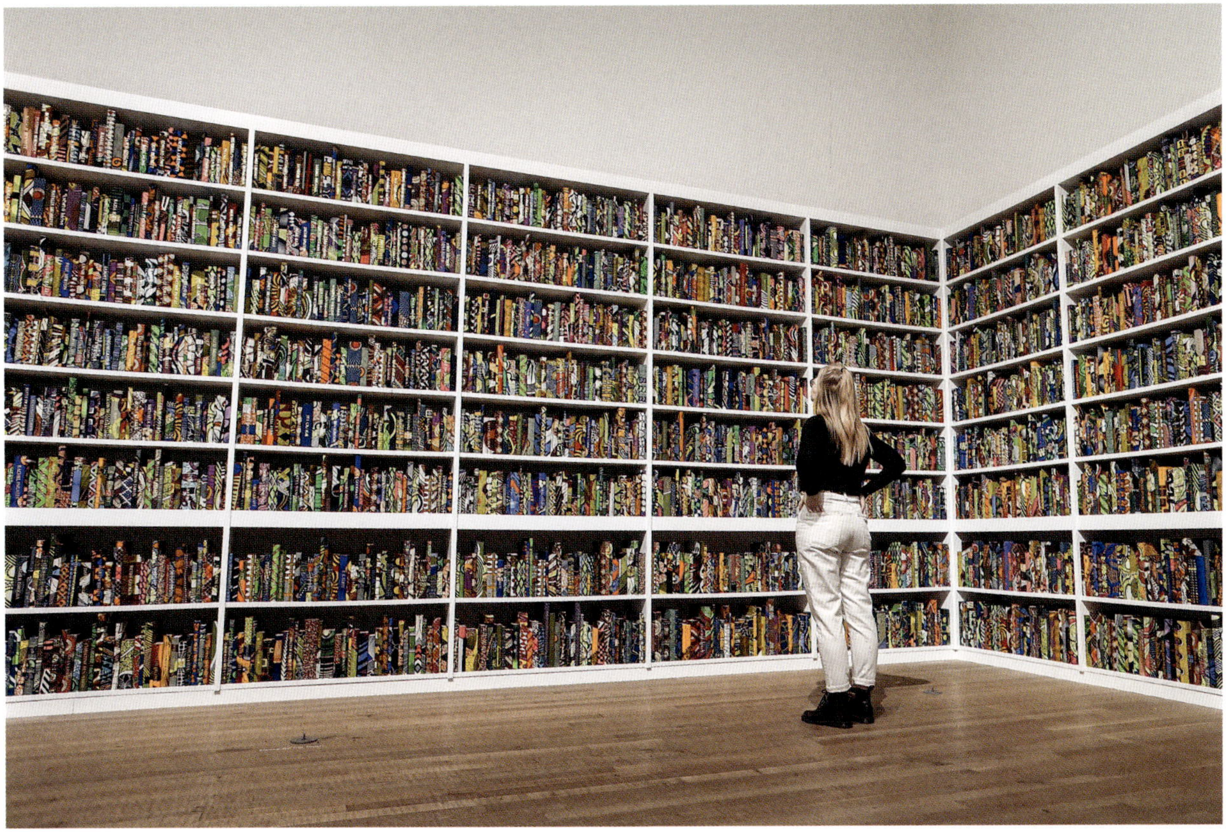

Yinka Shonibare
The British Library
2014 (this installation: 8 April 2019), books, Dutch wax print fabric, gold foil

The *wax hollandaise* cloth that Shonibare found in London's Brixton market reminded him of the special occasion garments worn by his female relatives in Lagos, Nigeria. When he learned of its hybrid history, he incorporated it into all of his work, including sculpture, film and photographic tableaux. *The British Library* features an installation of 6,328 hardback books, bound in Vlisco fabrics with titles painted in gold on the spines. He has since repeated the concept, varying the number of books and the titles, in such installations as *The African Library* (2018), *America* (2018) and *War* (2024).

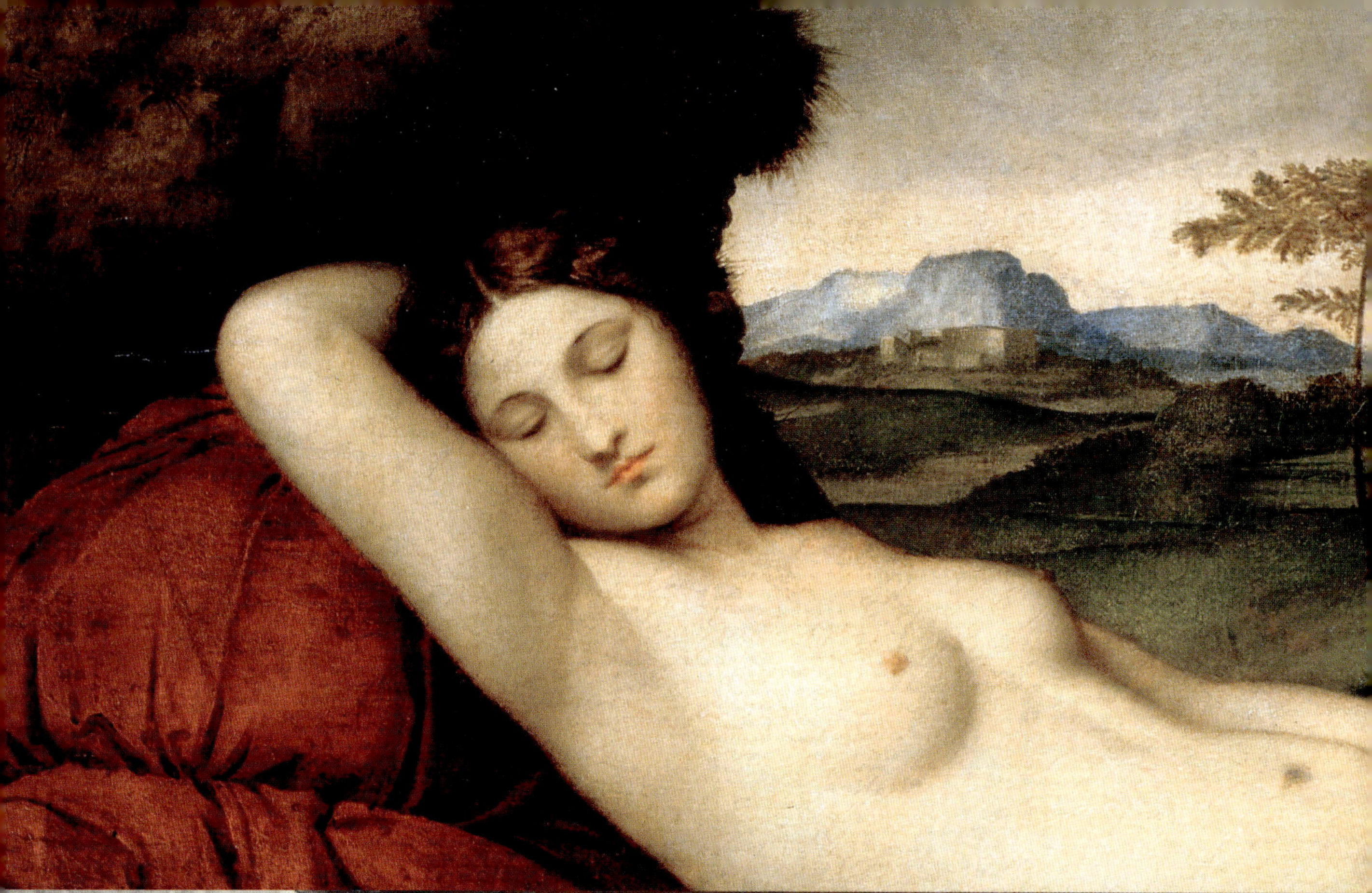
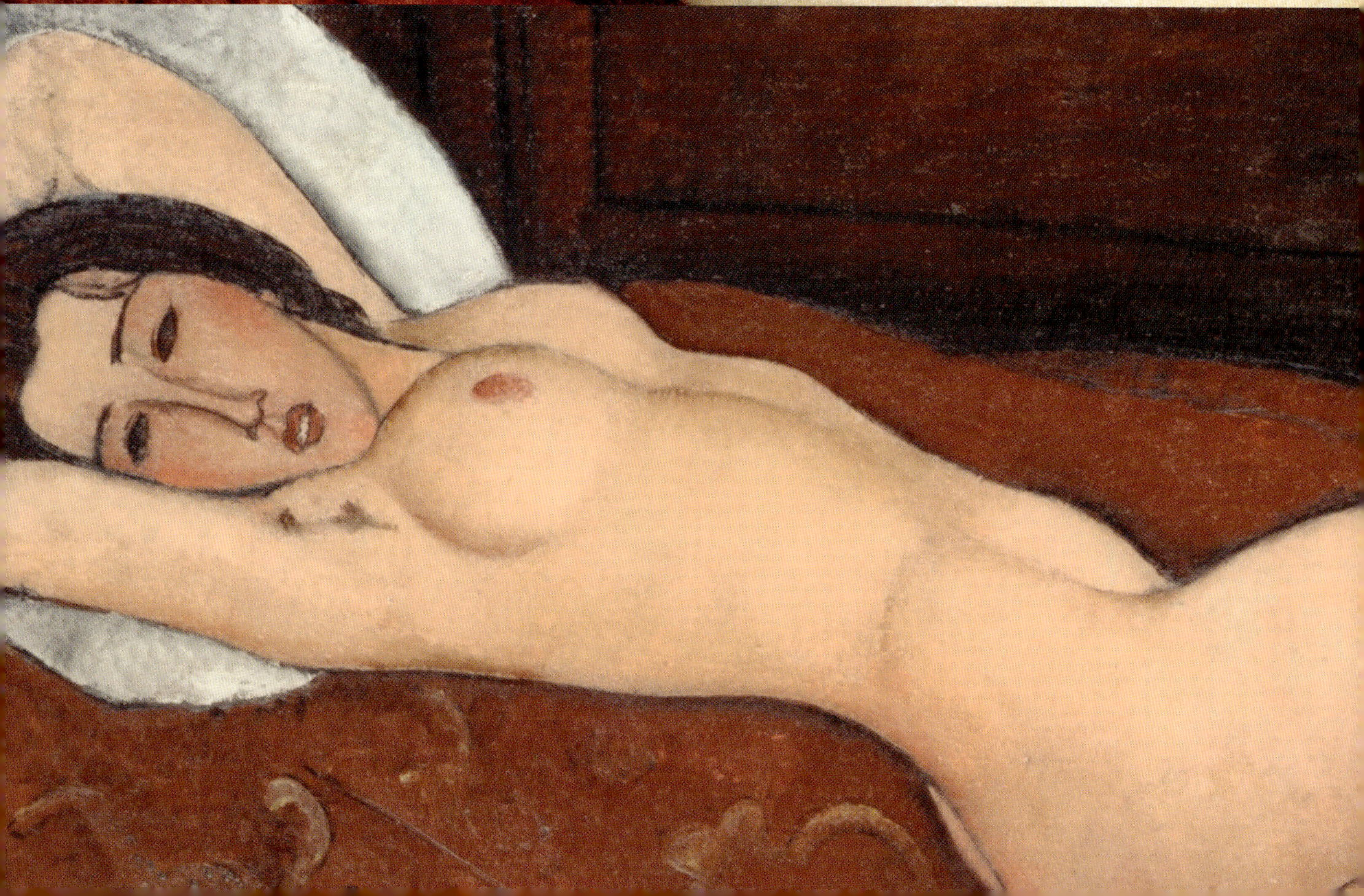

TRANSFORMATION

Through theft an artist can reclaim a heritage, right a wrong or undermine assumptions. A bohemian turns into an aristocrat through his pose. A woman can usurp a goddess and an icon can be knocked off its pedestal. Visual reference allows one artist to rouse ancestral spirits; another counters a symbol of oppression with a new vision of respect. And an old motif can be repurposed to give a contemporary community hope and resolution in a time of despair. When the transformation is powerful, the stolen source also acquires a new meaning and is never seen in the same way again.

STEALING SWAGGER

How Sargent was inspired by Van Dyck's portraits to give his sitters style

Of all the American artists who pursued their careers abroad, John Singer Sargent was a true cosmopolitan. Born in Florence, where his parents had moved in 1854, he and his family lived a sophisticated but unsettled existence, routinely visiting culturally rich European capitals and stylish summer resorts. From childhood, Sargent became fluent in several languages and social behaviour, adjusting with ease to new circumstances. He also demonstrated precocious – and prodigious – artistic talent, which was strongly encouraged by his parents. By the age of thirteen, Sargent was sketching Renaissance masterworks in the Bargello Museum in Florence, and five years later moved to Paris to pursue formal art training. He continued to copy renowned works, both in Paris and on his travels, collecting his drawings in a scrapbook for studio reference. Although immersed in European culture, he never lost his sense of American identity, which gave him the freedom to forge a style that melded Old World technique with New World innovation. It was this convergence of Old Master likeness executed in a bold, realist style that won an honourable mention for a striking portrait of his teacher, Charles Auguste Carolus-Duran, at his Salon debut in 1879. That portrait, in turn, led to his first portrait commission from the rising playwright Edouard Pailleron.

As a contemporary satirist, Pailleron was on the cutting edge of the Parisian art scene. His image was that of a bohemian, and his circle included urbane, like-minded artists, musicians and journalists, ever ready to critique convention through their work. With his long beard and dishevelled hair, Pailleron flouted the conformist masculine grooming standards of the day, announcing his sense of difference through his appearance. His choice of dress similarly challenged standards, as seen in the attire he chose for his portrait: a workman's jacket, a flowing open-necked shirt loosely tucked into his trousers and a braided cord in place of a tie. His daughter, Marie-Louise, would describe her father's ensemble as '*un peu débraillé*' ('a little scruffy') and a shock to the Parisian public 'accustomed to the protocol' of the 'black frock coat'.[1] Sargent captures these informal details, but at the same time he endows Pailleron with a poise and confidence that

▶

John Singer Sargent (1856–1925)
Edouard Pailleron
1879, oil on canvas, 96 x 39 cm (38 x 15 in)

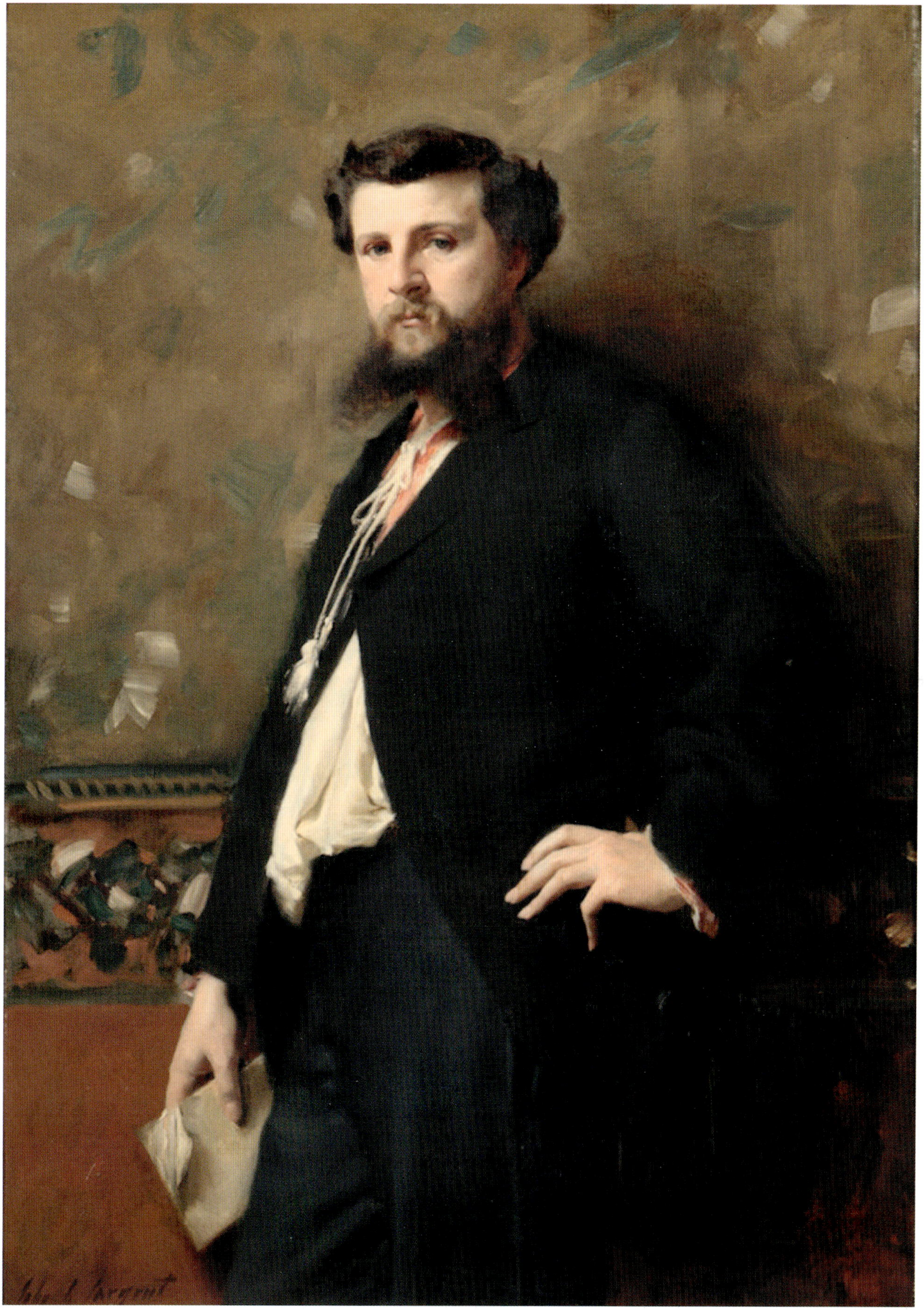

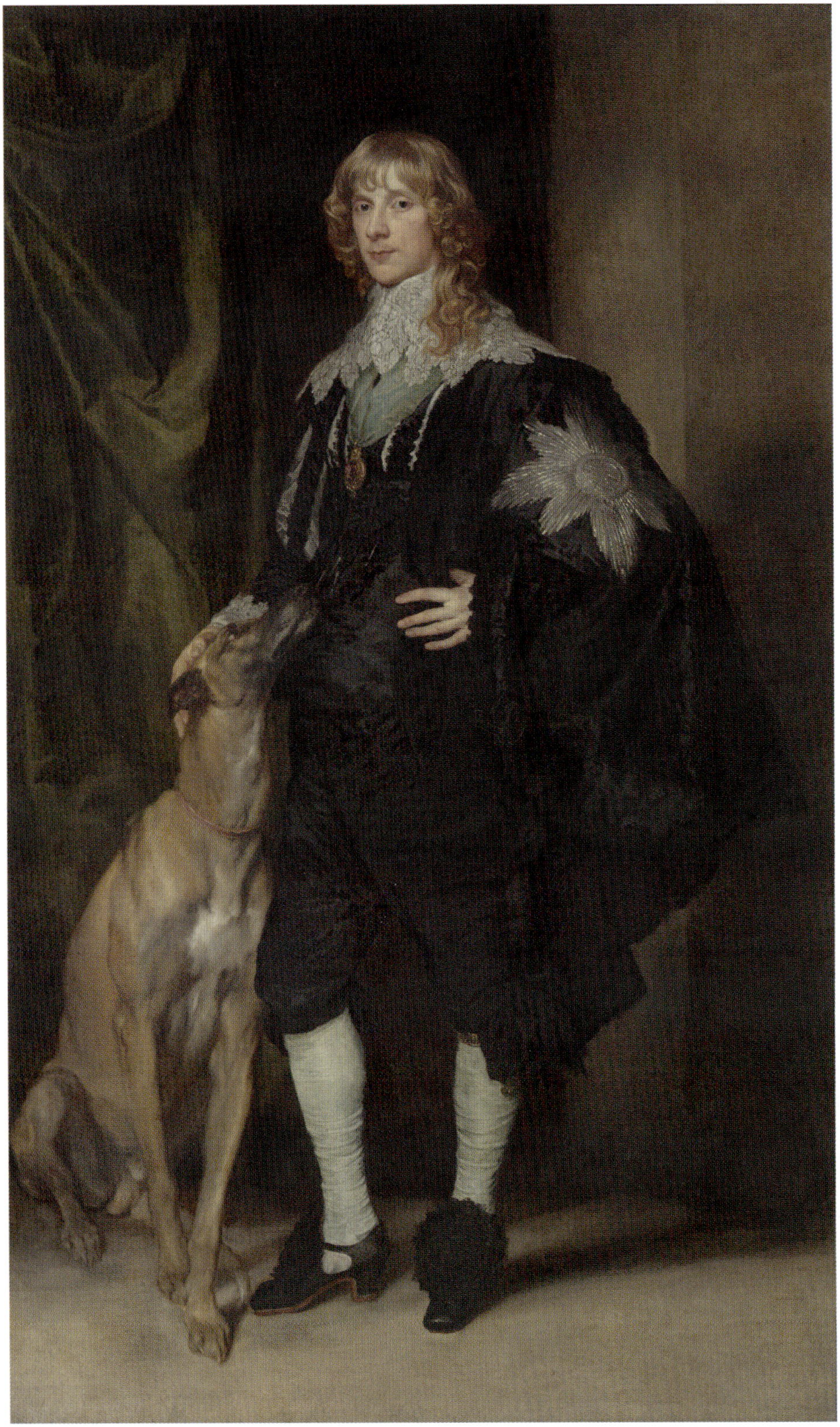

would be familiar to any astute viewer. It is the pose – relaxed yet commanding – long associated with aristocracy, particularly seen in the seventeenth-century portraits by the Flemish Baroque artist Anthony van Dyck.

As Sargent would centuries later, Van Dyck moved through the cultural capitals of Europe, settling in England as court painter to Charles I in 1632. He developed a distinctive formula for portraits of young, male aristocrats that emphasized their height, youth and glamour through elegant garments and a relaxed, yet assured demeanour conveyed through a *contrapposto* stance with shoulders, back and hips thrust forward. The slightly backward-leaning angle, with head held high, forces the viewer to look up the length of the sitter's body to meet his haughty gaze. The arrangement of the sitter's arms – one at his side, often holding an object, and the other on the lifted hip counterpoint to his bent knee – projected self-possessed elegance, indicative of the sitter's comfort with his social status. The distinctive stance defined what would later come to be known as a 'Swagger portrait', an iconic representation of male power and privilege.[2] Sargent's adherence to time-tested templates led him to Van Dyck's formula, which he could study in public collections or any number of reproductive engravings. However, rather than reserving the pose for young aristocrats, Sargent applied it to a new elite – financiers, politicians, artists, writers – transforming the swagger to proclaim the social hierarchy of the modern era. ●

◀

Anthony van Dyck (1599–1641)
James Stuart, Duke of Richmond and Lennox
c. 1633–5, oil on canvas, 216 x 128 cm (85 x 50 in)

Van Dyck portrayed his aristocratic sitter's confident nonchalance through a specific stance. The duke's bent right knee shifts his weight to his left leg, giving a natural ease to the disposition of his limbs. He places his hand on his left hip, all the better to display the embroidered insignia of the Order of the Garter on his mantle. While Sargent may not have seen this exact portrait, the stance was a hallmark of Van Dyck's depiction of aristocrats. In painting Pailleron, he mirrored the elegance and swagger for a new type of elite sitter.

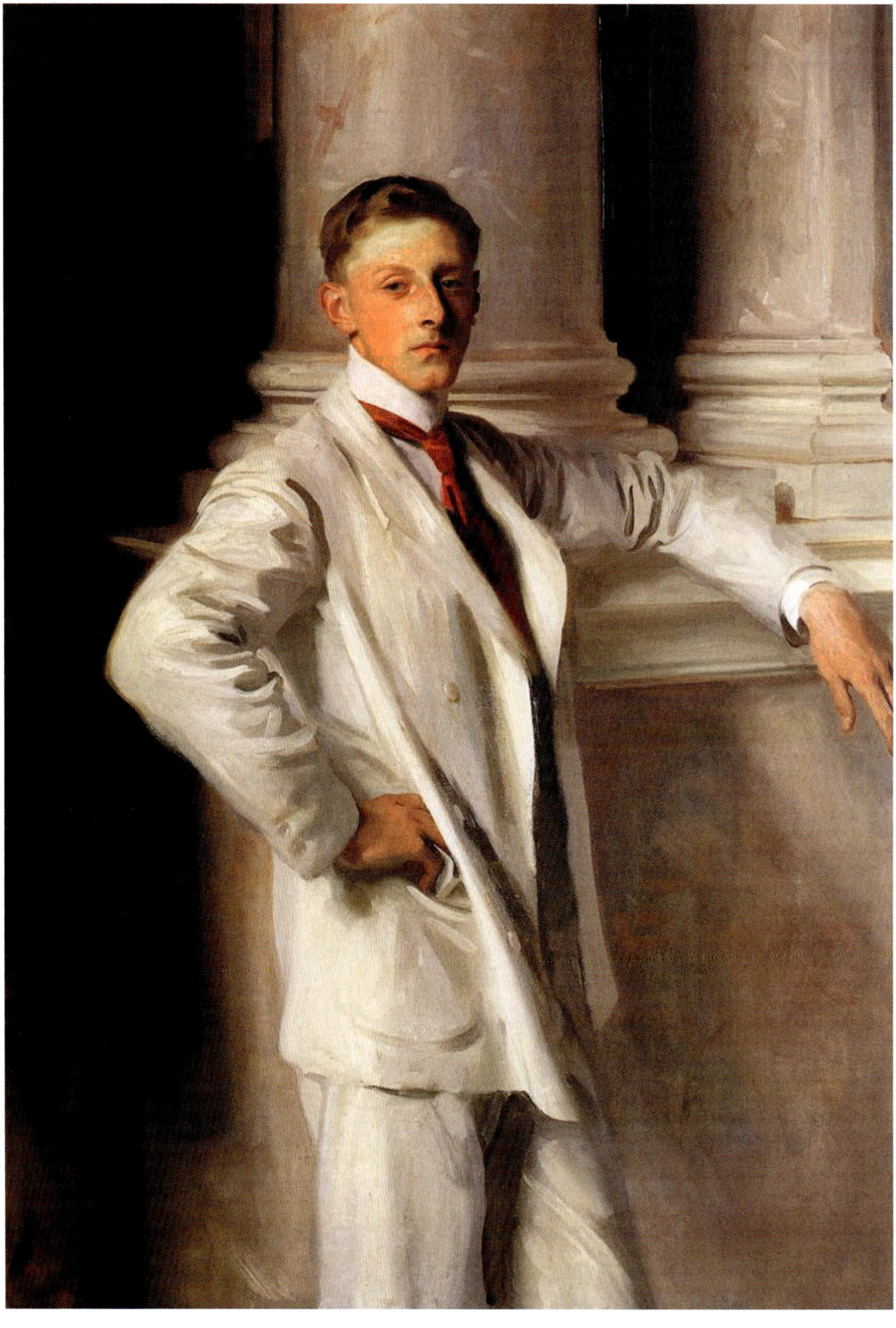

◀

John Singer Sargent)
Arthur Ramsay, 14th Earl of Dalhousie
1900, oil on canvas, 152 x 102 cm (60 x 40 in)

Throughout his career, Sargent evoked masculine poise through Van Dyck's characteristic stance. In this portrait of Dalhousie, he adds a subtle reference to aristocratic precedent: the architectural backdrop. While Pailleron stands in front of what might be a sitting room wall, Dalhousie rests his elbow on the plinth of a colonnade evoking his venerable family's estate. Dalhousie's immaculate white suit – undeniably modern – drapes his slender physique, further emphasizing his long-limbed proportions and innate grace.

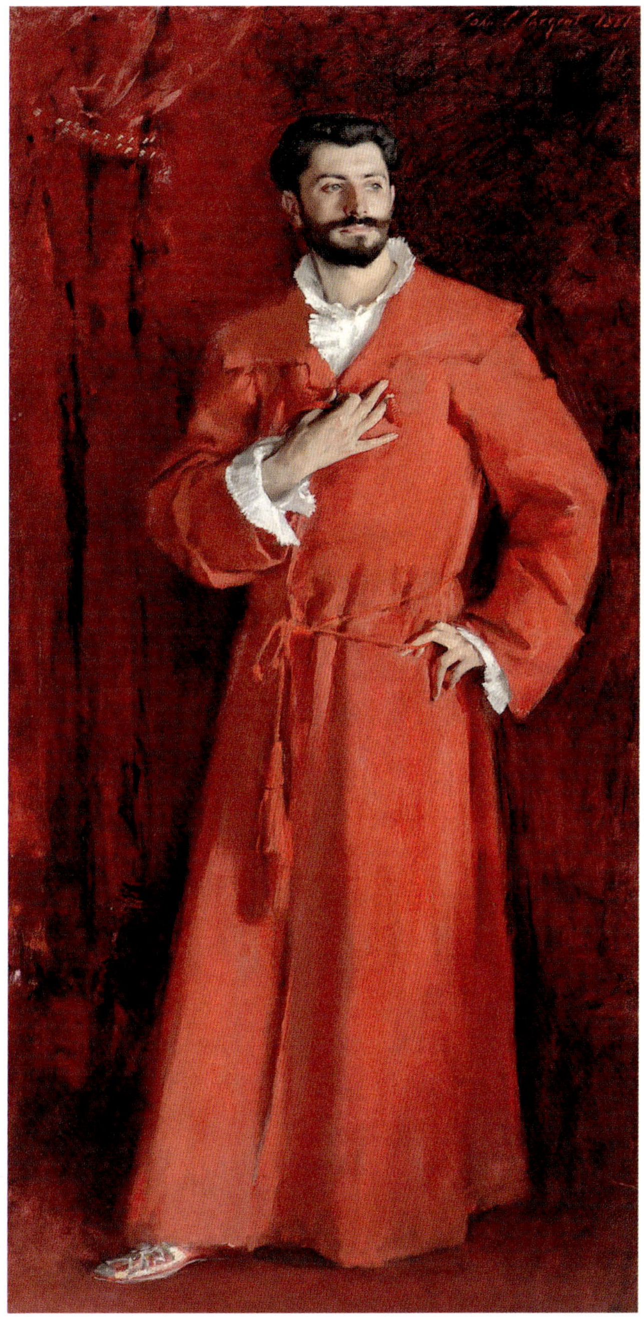

▶

John Singer Sargent (1856–1925)
Dr. Pozzi at Home
1881, oil on canvas, 201 x 102 cm (79 x 40 in)

In his portrait of the pioneering gynaecologist, Sargent used a palette of contrasts – pale skin, black hair and beard, and a scarlet robe accented with white collar and cuffs – borrowed from the Spanish Baroque. Pozzi presses his right hand to his heart, a traditional European gesture of respectful reverence, the *sincerità*. His left hand tugs at the loosely tied cord of his dressing gown; dubbed 'Doctor Dieu' ('Doctor God') by Sarah Bernhardt for his brooding good looks, Pozzi was a notorious seducer. If the robe opened it would reveal a more intimate garment, his dazzling nightshirt.

GROUNDING THE GODDESS

How Modigliani looked to the Old Masters' depictions of the female form

Amedeo Modigliani's nudes occupy a signature place in his career. While the poses vary – standing, sitting, reclining – the format is consistent. The figures are large, filling the canvas from edge to edge; the limbs of the figures often stretch beyond the picture plane. There may be a bed or a pillow to support the figure, but the background space dissolves into a tonal field of warm, dark colour, often deep red in hue. In contrast, the skin is pale and luminous, defined by a black contour line that draws attention to movement: a twist of the torso, the crossing of limbs. Although the figures are anonymous – and conceived through formal emphasis on surface, line and colour – they are, at the same time, disturbingly real. Their faces are individualized, often turned to meet the gaze of the viewer, and their bodies, while beautiful, are not idealized. Their physicality projects an unprecedented sexuality; when debuted, these works ignited a firestorm of reaction, ranging from admiration for Modigliani's bold reimagining of a standard motif, to shock and scandal. However, in painting these nudes, Modigliani did not set out to break the rules. Rather, this late-life series reveals his deep connection to a revered tradition: how nudity transforms a woman into a goddess.

The oldest known female nude figures date back thirty thousand years and are believed to have embodied fecundity. In subsequent times, nudity often signified the divine, proclaiming purity or power, as well as procreation. In the Olympic pantheon, Aphrodite (Venus), the goddess of love, often appeared in the nude celebrating human beauty and desire. During the Middle Ages, a nude figure came to signal female shame and male transgression as depicted in morality tales of voyeurism: King David and Bathsheba; Susanna and the Elders. The revival of classical culture, as well as a human-centred perspective, returned the female nude to a revered status in later fifteenth-century Italy, with a distinctive motif emerging in Renaissance Venice near the turn of the century: the reclining or sleeping Venus. In the work of such masters as Giorgione and Titian, the unclad female body in repose represented the epitome of divine loveliness, a representation of the Neo-Platonic belief that in beauty lies truth. Over the centuries artists repeated the motif, forging an unmistakable convention as well as providing an unassailable justification for exhibiting the naked figure of a woman in public; after all, Venus was a goddess and nudity was her natural state.

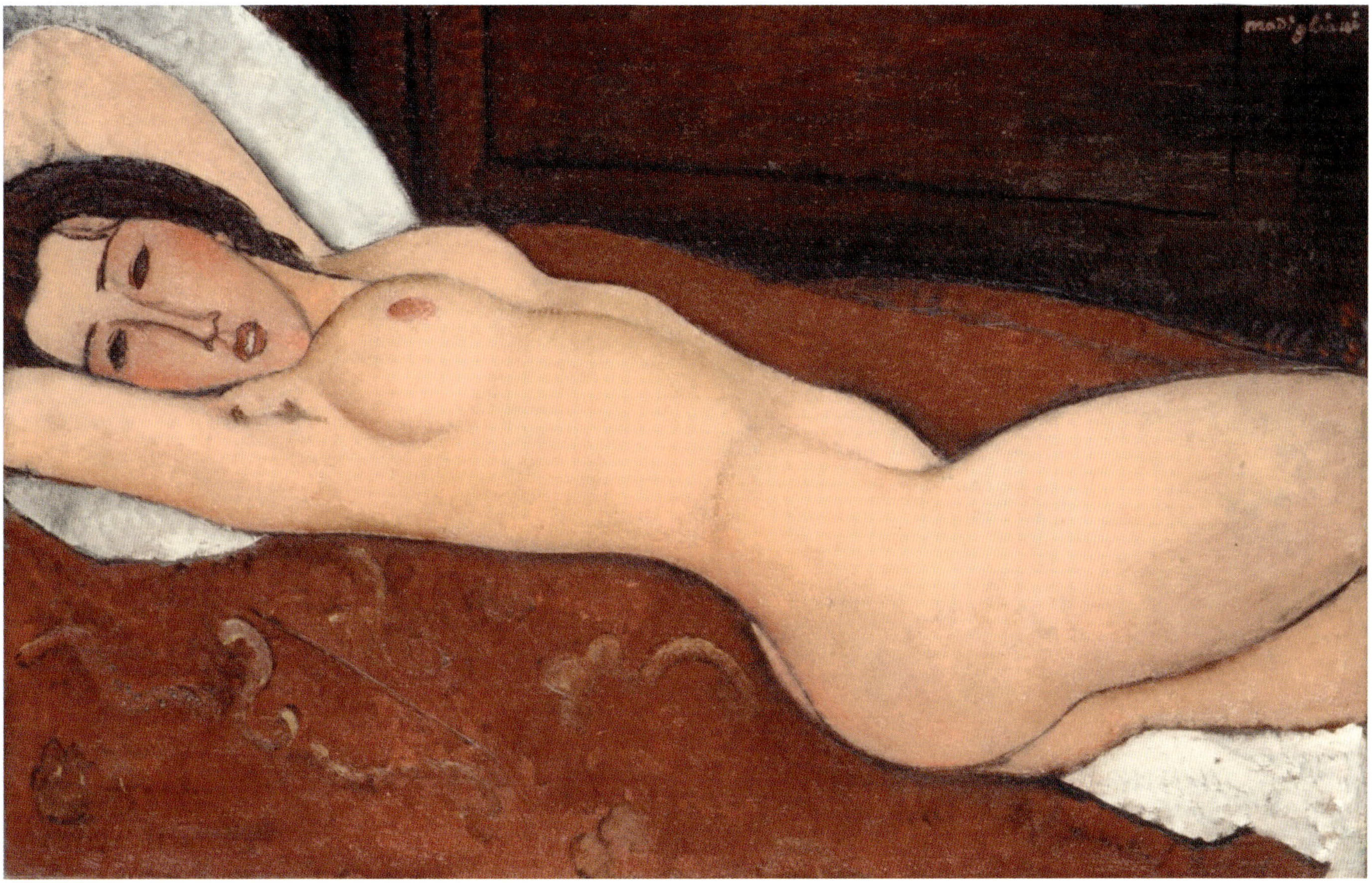

Despite the defining role that the female nude plays in Modigliani's career, the image is rare in his earlier work, appearing mostly as life study practice in his sketchbooks. He took up the subject in earnest late in 1916 as a commercial endeavour encouraged by the art dealer Léopold Zborowski, and over the next three years Modigliani produced roughly thirty paintings that share compositional elements of figure placement and palette, as well as subject. The reclining figures also share their origins in the motif of the sleeping Venus; each represents a reprise of a renowned example by Titian or Giorgione or Velázquez. Modigliani knew these works through his studies in Paris, Florence and Venice. Unlike many of his contemporaries, notably Picasso and Matisse, Modigliani explored the motif to pay tribute and extend the convention rather than disrupt it. While his nudes have shed the pretence of idealism and seem to revel in their own physicality, they are as serene as the goddesses that inspired them. And like those goddesses, they are comfortable in their bodies, acknowledging nudity as a natural state, whether the woman is human or divine. ●

▲

Amedeo Modigliani (1884–1920)
Reclining Nude
1917, oil on canvas, 61 x 93 cm (24 x 37 in)

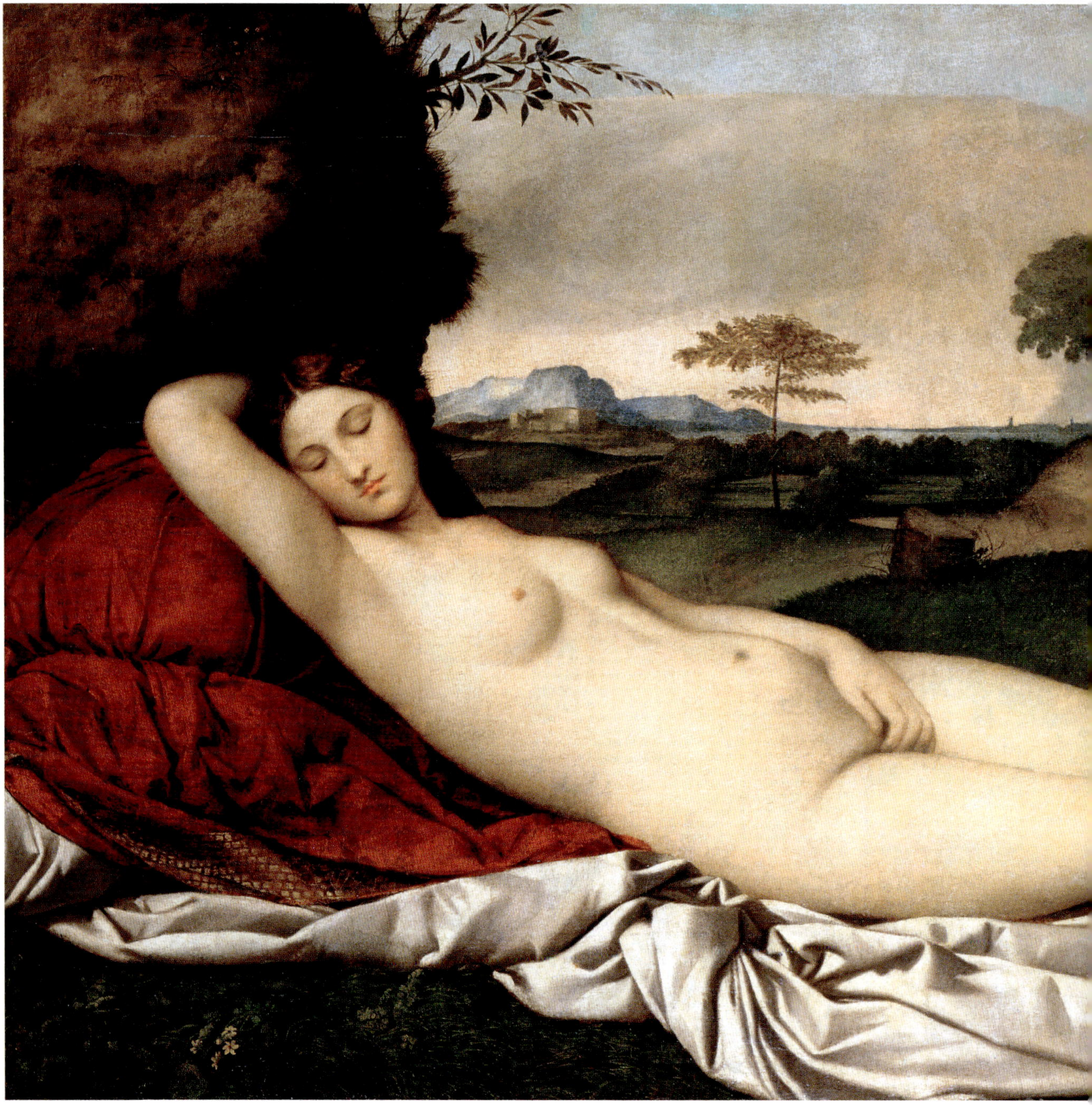

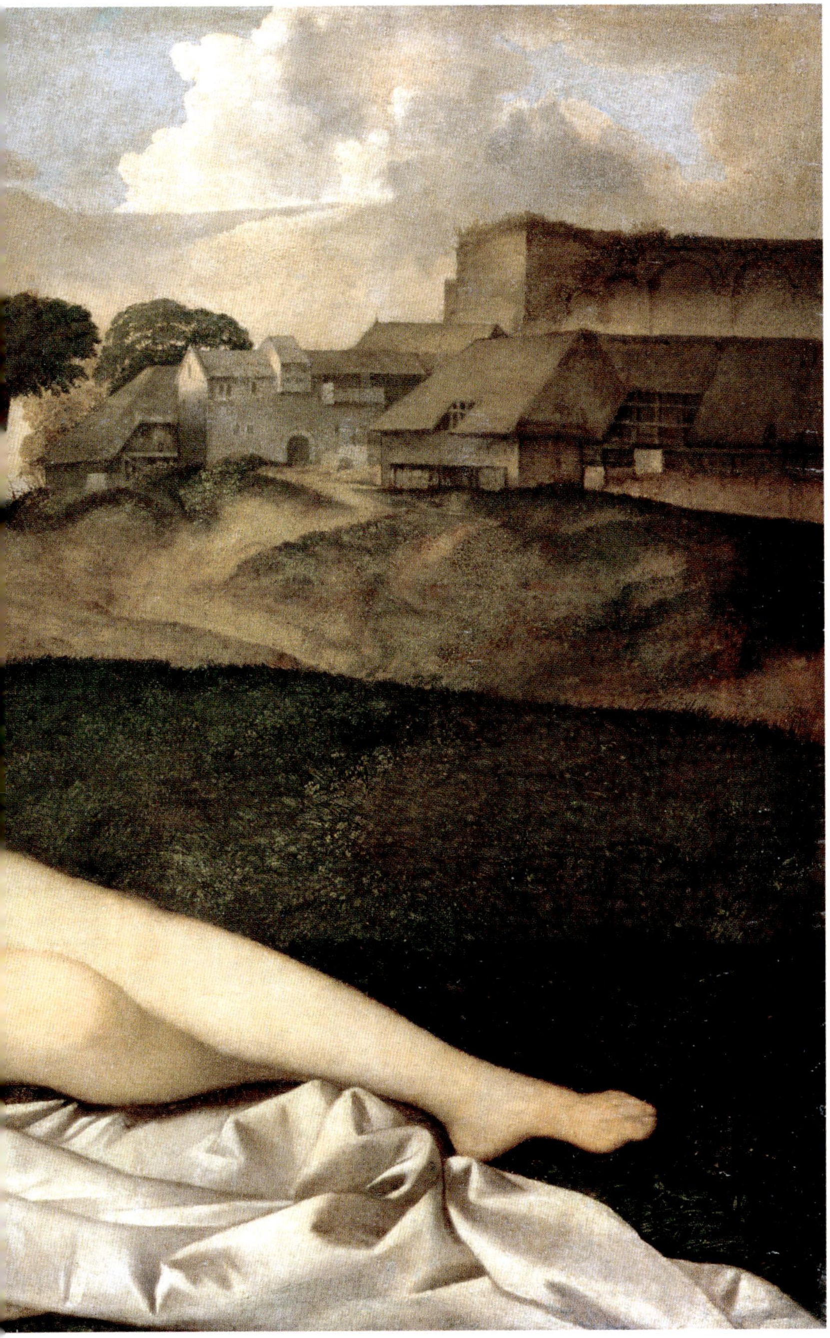

◀

Giorgione (*c.* 1477–1510), with
Titian (*c.* 1488–1576)
Sleeping Venus
c. 1508–10, oil on canvas, 109 x 175 cm
(43 x 69 in)

While it is not possible to state whether Modigliani had seen this work, its fame was such that he likely knew it through reproductions. In his late series of nudes, he deliberately adapted poses from well-known paintings, and the similarities here establish a strong visual connection. However, the differences are also significant. Giorgione's figure is fully relaxed, but Modigliani's model arches her back and twists her torso. Her eyes are open and her lips part. With both arms behind her head, her body is fully displayed without the conventional hand placed for modesty.

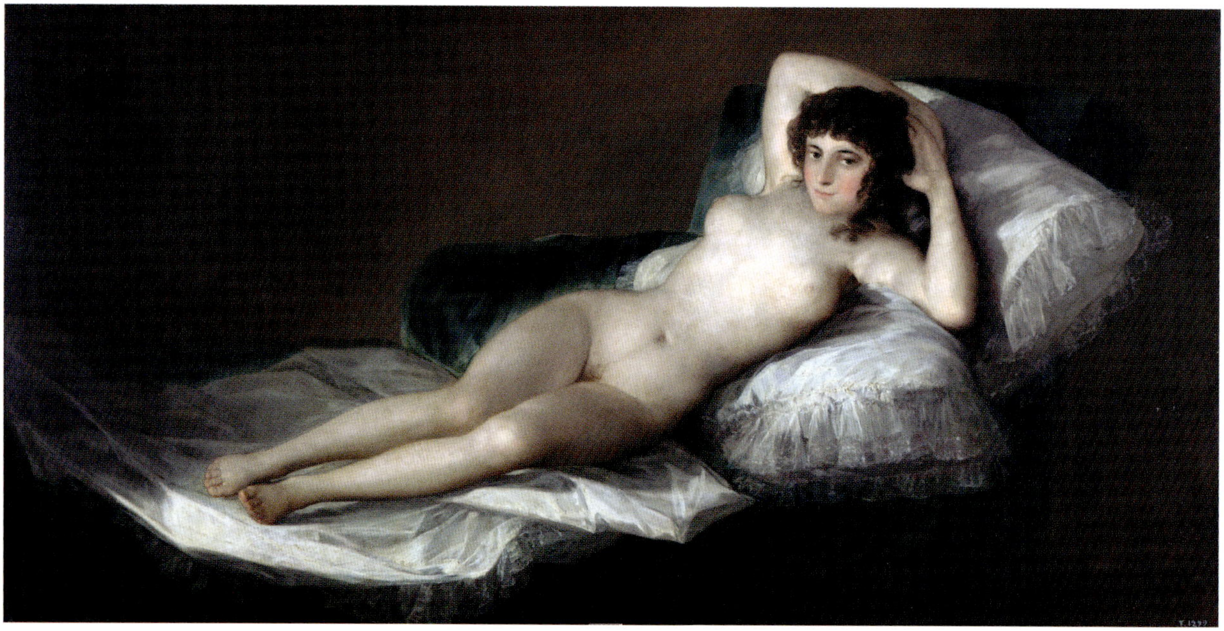

▲

Francisco Goya (1746–1828)
La Maja Desnuda
1795–1800, oil on canvas, 97 x 190 cm (38 x 75 in)

Goya's nude was likely commissioned by his longtime patron, Manuel de Godoy, Spain's powerful First Secretary of State. Overtly sexual, the painting was for his private collection, shown only to close friends. A clothed version, *La Maja Vestida*, depicts the same woman in the same pose. Modigliani admired Goya's work and the influence is clear. As with Giorgione's Venus, Goya's *Maja Desnuda* provided a template for *Reclining Nude* and, like Modigliani, Goya portrays an unidealized woman who boldly engages the viewer.

Alexandre Cabanel (1823–89)
The Birth of Venus
1863, oil on canvas, 130 x 225 cm (51 x 89 in)

Although Cabanel presents Venus in an enduring context – born in sea foam and ushered to her domain on the Isle of Cythera by attendant cherubs – he stripped the subject of its philosophic content. Here is a compliant and complicit goddess, aware of her beauty and willingly posing for the viewer's gaze. And she slyly stares back, hiding her eyes with her hand. The painting received an enthusiastic reception at the official Salon of 1863 and was purchased by Emperor Napoleon III for his private collection.

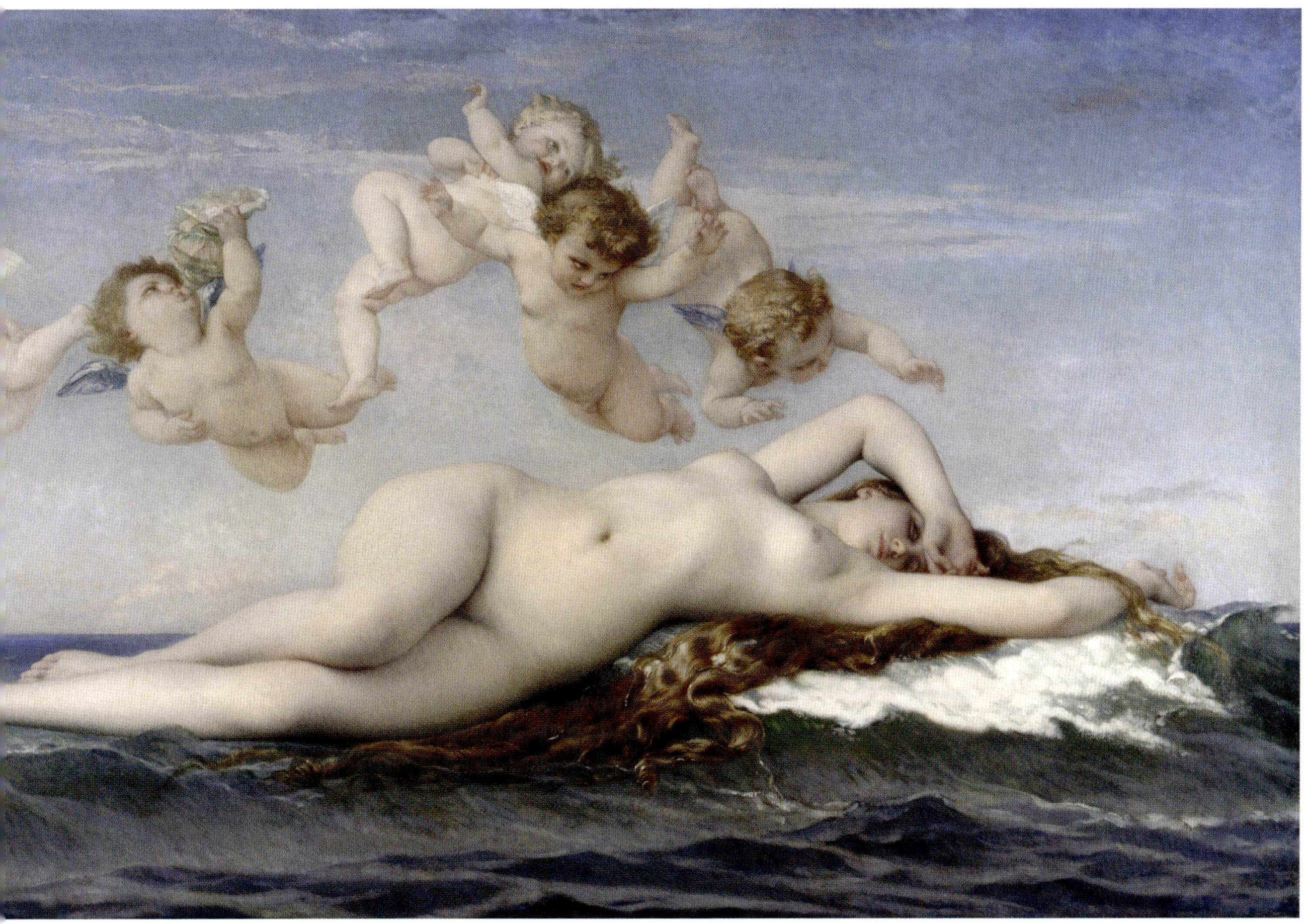

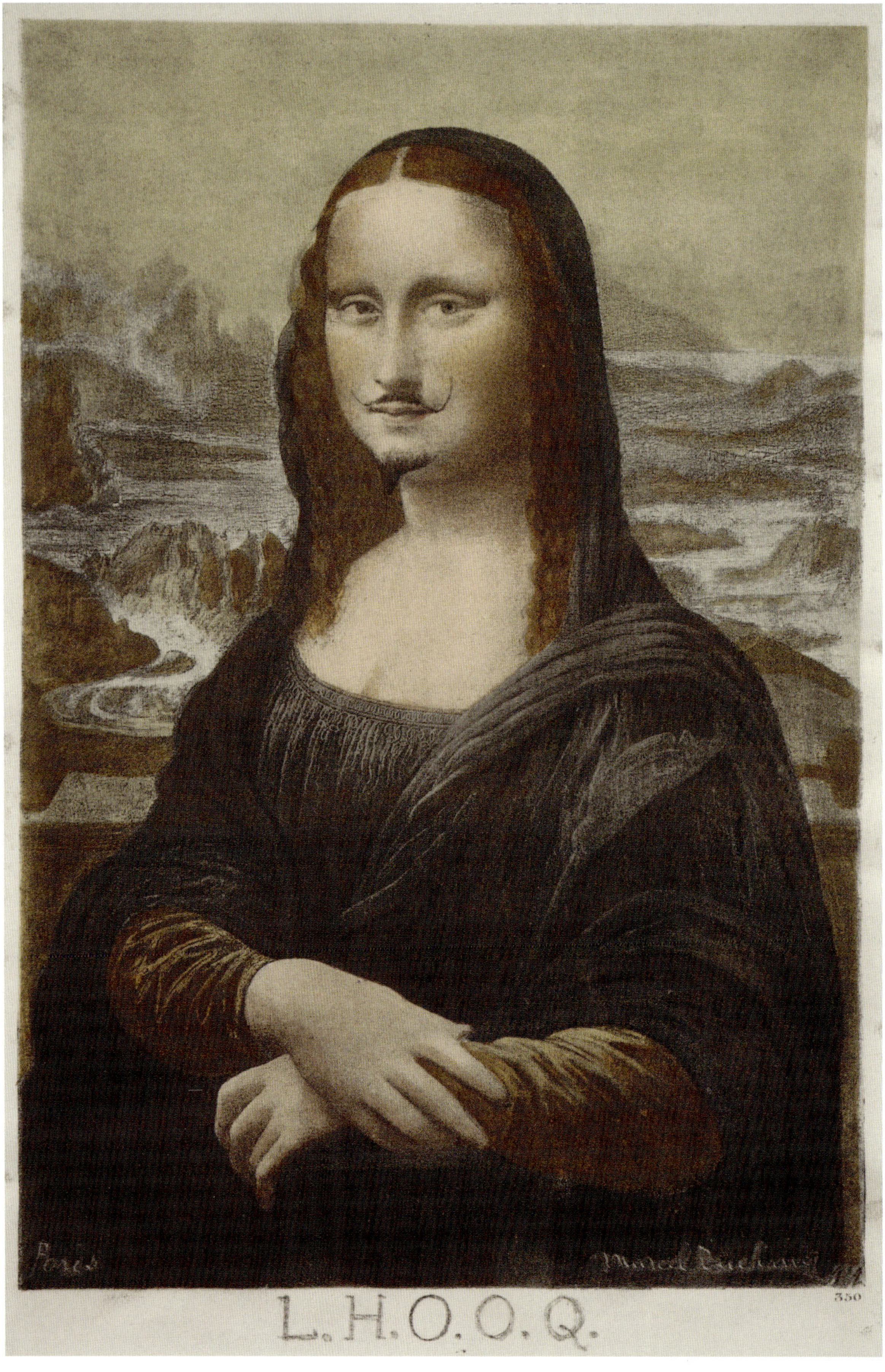
Paris
Marcel Duchamp
350
L.H.O.O.Q.

STEALING A SCHOOLBOY'S PRANK

How Duchamp made his mark on the *Mona Lisa*

With a few strokes of his pencil, Marcel Duchamp turned an iconic painting into an iconoclastic challenge to the history of art. He used a postcard purchased at a tourist stand on the Rue de Rivoli near the Musée du Louvre and a common schoolboy prank to gain notoriety as the man who drew a moustache on the *Mona Lisa*. Duchamp blocked out the photography credits, signed his own name, and on the lower border of the postcard scrawled the gramogram 'L.H.O.O.Q.' When read aloud letter by letter it sounds like the crude sexual reference *Elle a chaud au cul*.[1] Duchamp already enjoyed a reputation for audacity in exhibiting everyday objects – with little alteration – as sculpture. However, with *L.H.O.O.Q.* he took aim at a universally designated treasure of the western art tradition. Although he later claimed it was a joke, Duchamp had a clear objective to 'de-deify' the artist and call into question rules that defined art for more than four hundred years.[2] And if he could do it through defacement and wordplay, all the better.

Duchamp came to public notice with a *succès de scandale*, the painting *Nude Descending a Staircase, No. 2* (1912), a cubist interpretation of a figure in motion that abstracted the elements of the body to resemble geometric shapes. When conversative critics dismissed the work as offensive, and prominent practitioners of Cubism deemed the work too extreme, Duchamp turned to sculpture, unveiling *Bicycle Wheel* (1913), which he called a 'Readymade', to represent a new type of art based on found objects 'without an artist to make it'.[3] However, he did intervene as an artist by mounting the wheel on a stand. Other Readymades followed, including *Fountain* (1917), a urinal laid on its side and signed 'R. Mutt'. Late in his life, reflecting back on his art, Duchamp cited the Readymade as 'the only truly important idea to retain from my work'.[4] And, Duchamp was not alone at the time in pushing the boundaries of what constituted art and artistic expression. Small groups of renegade artists

◀

Marcel Duchamp (1887–1968)
L.H.O.O.Q., 1919–20, from *Rrose Sélavy (Boîte-en-valise)*
1966, rectified Readymade (reproduction of Leonardo da Vinci's *Mona Lisa* altered with pencil), 20 x 10 cm (8 x 4 in)

gathered in Zurich, Paris and New York under the meaningless name 'Dada' to respond to the chaotic circumstances throughout war-torn Europe with a spirit of anarchic absurdity. Duchamp's longtime friend, Francis Picabia, emerged as a major adherent, most notably through the illustrated journal, *391*, which he published between 1917 and 1924.

When Picabia asked to borrow *L.H.O.O.Q.* so that he could feature it on the cover of the March 1920 issue of *391*, Duchamp put it in the post. Its arrival was delayed, so Picabia made his own version of the work to send to press. Duchamp was not at all upset; he had started with a reproduction, so further copies added to the work's distance from what he believed to be the fallacy of artistic uniqueness. He regarded the circumstance with amused satisfaction: 'Picabia's "Mona Lisa" is often reproduced as mine.'[5] However, it did not escape his notice that Picabia forgot to draw the goatee, and Duchamp corrected the error, adding an explanatory inscription. He also produced replica editions of the work, including one without the graffiti, calling it the 'shaved' version. As for the 'original' version of the work, it is believed to have been lost. Over the decades Duchamp's playful desecration of a widely esteemed and beloved image inspired serious discussion about the relationship between the fine arts and mass production, as well as the role of the artist's hand in a modern, mechanized world. He also validated the use of found and commercially produced objects in defiance of conventional materials, an approach that would inform such post-war contemporary movements as Pop Art. He taunted the art world by stealing an iconic image, only to deface it, claiming the prank itself was an artistic process. ●

▶

Leonardo da Vinci (1452–1519)
Mona Lisa
c. 1503, oil on poplar, 77 x 53 cm (30 x 21 in)

Leonardo's portrait became famous even before he finished it, drawing visitors to his studio to see the work in progress. In private hands for centuries, its reputation rose through description and replication. By the time Duchamp bought the postcard, it had been on public view in the Louvre for more than 100 years and was possibly the most widely reproduced work of art in the world. When a thief wearing work clothes simply carried it out of the Louvre in 1911, visitors continued to come to the gallery to pay homage to the empty frame. The painting was recovered in Italy in 1913 and returned to the Louvre the following year.

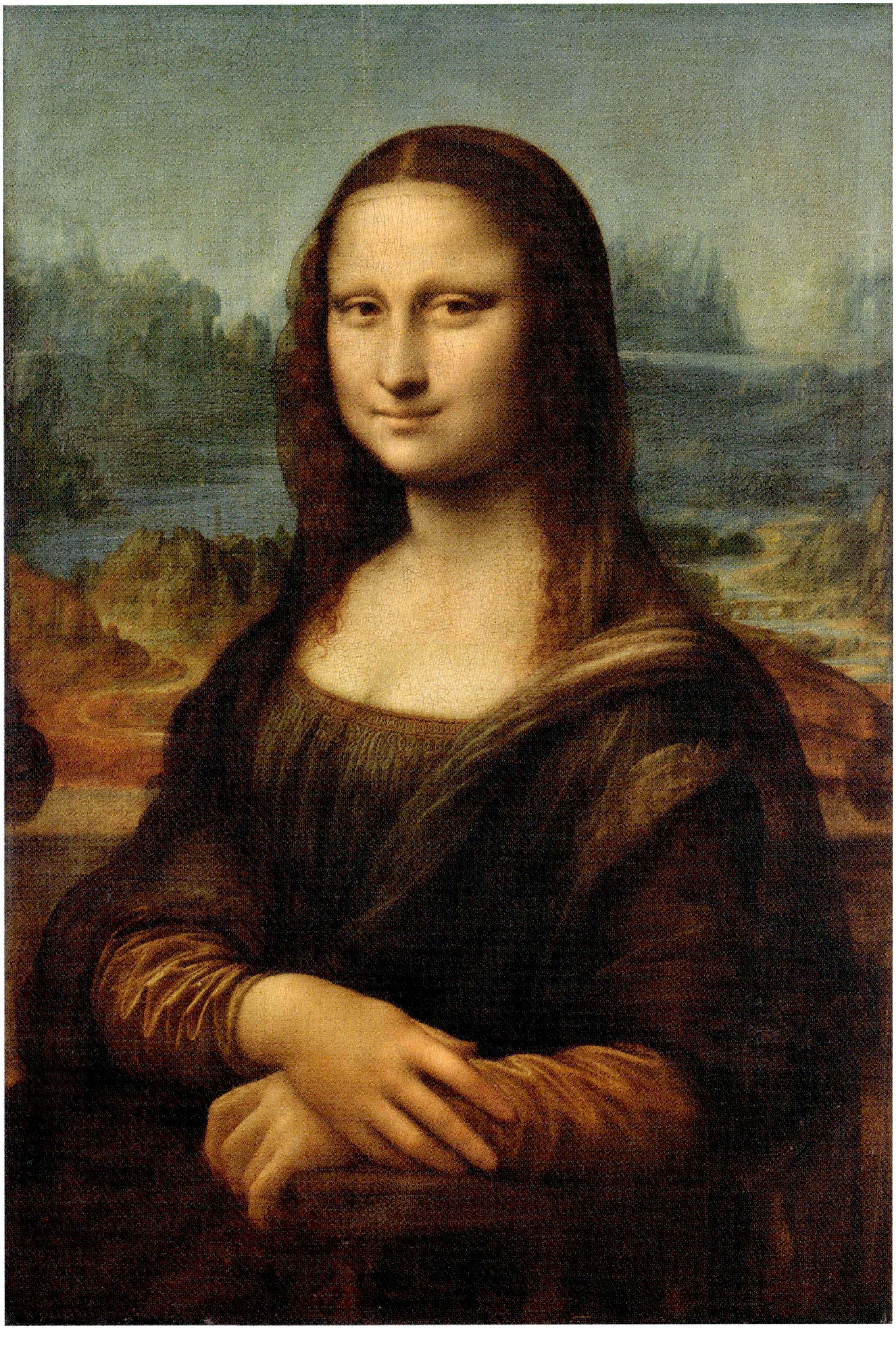

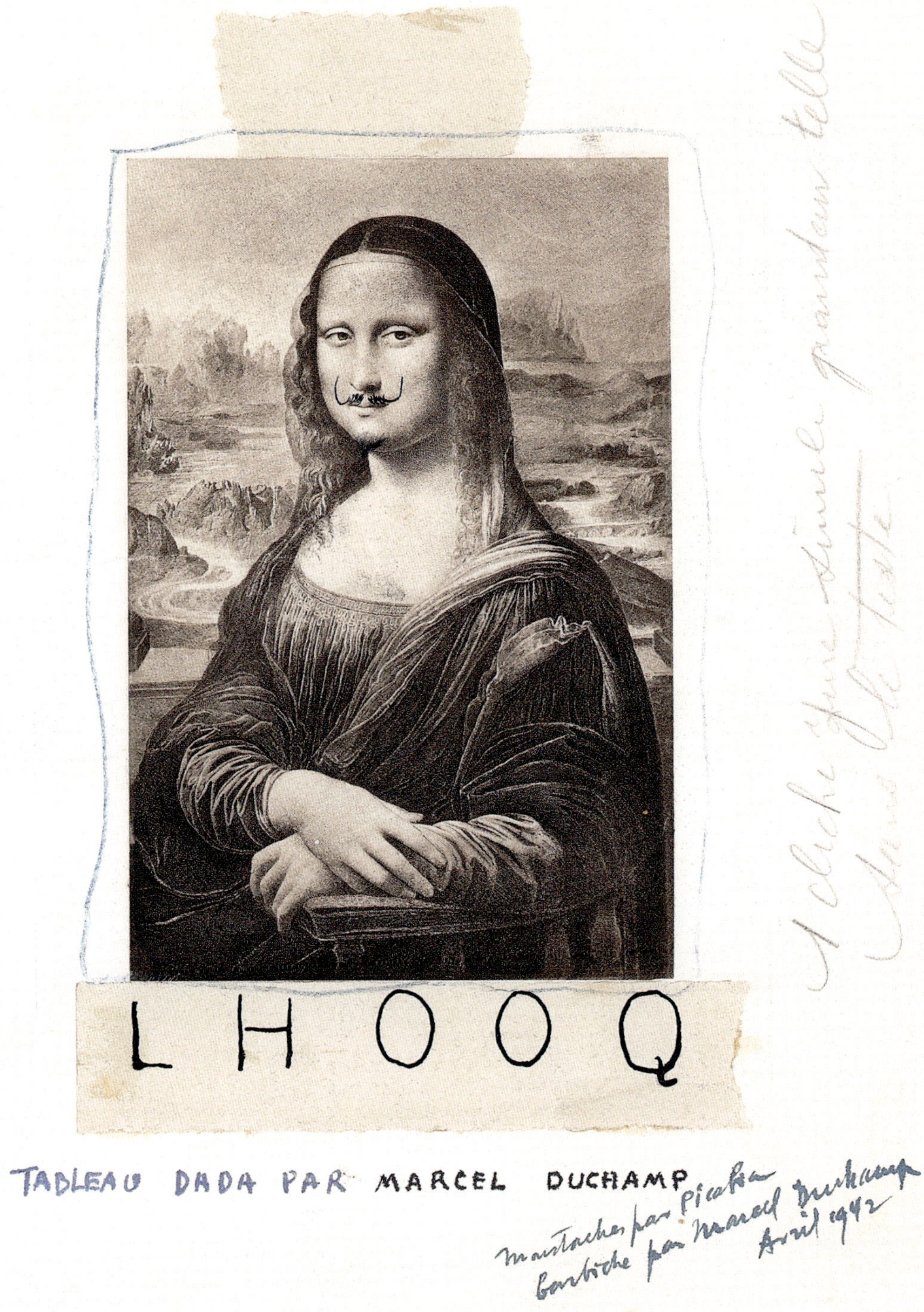
LHOOQ
TABLEAU DADA PAR MARCEL DUCHAMP
moustaches par Picabia
barbiche par Marcel Duchamp
Avril 1942

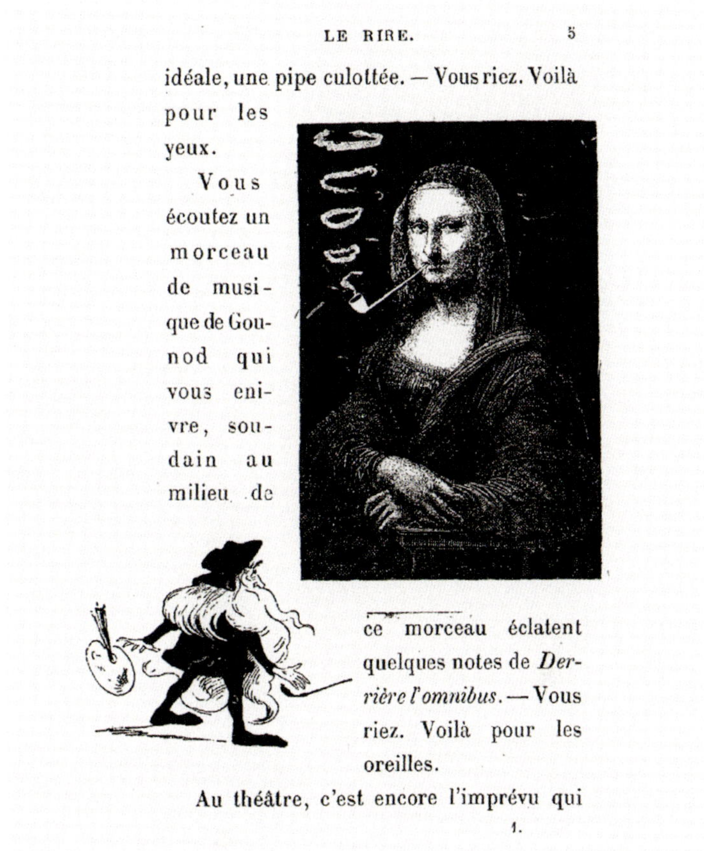

LE RIRE. 5

idéale, une pipe culottée. — Vous riez. Voilà pour les yeux.

Vous écoutez un morceau de musique de Gounod qui vous enivre, soudain au milieu de ce morceau éclatent quelques notes de *Derrière l'omnibus*. — Vous riez. Voilà pour les oreilles.

Au théâtre, c'est encore l'imprévu qui

1.

Francis Picabia (1879–1953) and Marcel Duchamp
L.H.O.O.Q. 391 (No. 12)
March 1920, paperbound periodical,
56 x 40 cm (22 x 16 in)

Duchamp posted *L.H.O.O.Q.* to Picabia shortly after finishing it to be featured on the cover of the March 1920 edition of the Dadaist journal *391*. The parcel had not arrived as the press date drew near, so Picabia simply replicated the work, using a similar postcard. This was fine with Duchamp, although he noted that Picabia had forgotten to draw the goatee, which he rectified with a few pen strokes. He later added the inscription: 'Moustache by Picabia/goatee by Marcel Duchamp, 1942.'

Eugène Bataille (Sapeck, 1854–1891)
Mona Lisa with a Pipe
1887, photo-relief illustration for *Le Rire* by Coquelin Cadet

Duchamp was hardly the first artist to reinterpret Leonardo's portrait. After Raphael visited Leonardo's studio in 1504, he drew an anonymous woman in exactly the same position and in a similar ensemble. Leonardo's assistants – and many others in subsequent centuries – replicated the painting, and some of these, including one in the nude, were passed off as being by the master's own hand. Bataille also foreshadowed Duchamp's irreverence. His illustration was published in the French humour magazine *Le Rire* (*The Laugh*) along with a little caricature of Leonardo startled to see his famous sitter smoking a pipe.

RECOVERY & RECLAMATION

How Stout summoned ancestral authority

Fetish #2 stands at 160 cm (63 in), precisely the height of the artist. Full-bodied, yet compact, the physical proportions are also those of Renée Stout; she cast the plaster figure from her own form. The face bears her likeness: wide eyes, high cheekbones, rounded jaw and chin. These similarities are deliberate. Stout has stated that she 'always regarded *Fetish #2* as a "self-portrait"'.[1] Here, the use of the word 'self-portrait', however, is nuanced. *Fetish #2* may look like her, but Stout created it to represent far more than her image. Drawing upon her memories, her fascination with the material legacy of the African diaspora, and her desire to share the healing potential she finds in art, Stout deploys her body as a vessel of convergence: past and present, cultural and contemporary, personal and universal. Born in Kansas and raised in Pittsburgh, Stout reached out of her lived experience to lay claim to a spiritual tradition embodied in a work of art she saw as a child. It took her years to comprehend the purpose and meaning of the *Nkisi Nkondi* – a West Central African power figure – but when she did, she made it her own.

The *Nkisi Nkondi* proclaims power through an aggressive stance and a ferocious expression, but its actual source of energy is not readily visible. Held in a compartment on the figure's body – typically the abdomen or back – is a piece of plant matter, a root or a relic, a pinch of earth or ash. This is the figure's *bilongo*, a healing substance chosen for its linguistic or visual connection to the desired application rather than for pharmaceutical value. These may include righting a wrong, taking an oath or even seeking revenge upon an enemy. To ignite this force, a nail is driven into the figure, arousing its anger and releasing the power within. If the request is fulfilled, the nail remains in the figure. Not only does the nail serve as a testament to the figure's efficacy, but every successful healing heightens its strength. The *Nkisi Nkondi* that Stout saw in the Carnegie Museum of Art in Pittsburgh bristled with nails. Even as a ten-year-old girl, the form intrigued her, but she did not know its meaning. Over the years, along with her art studies, Stout explored her attraction to folklore, ritual healing practices, African art, and the link between an individual's known existence and the intuitive world of the spirits.

▶

Renée Stout (b. 1958)
Fetish #2
1988, mixed media, plaster body cast, H: 160 cm (63 in)

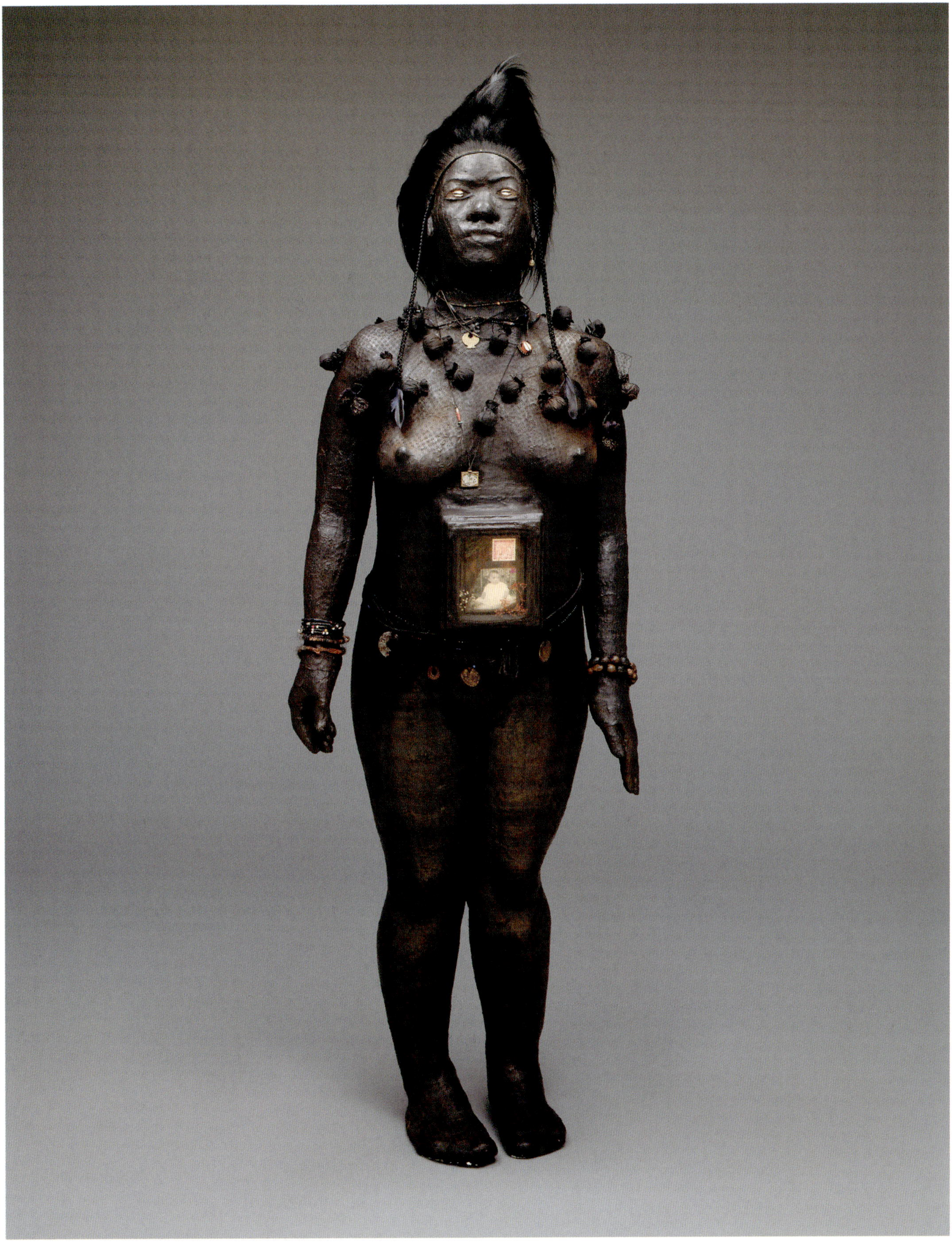

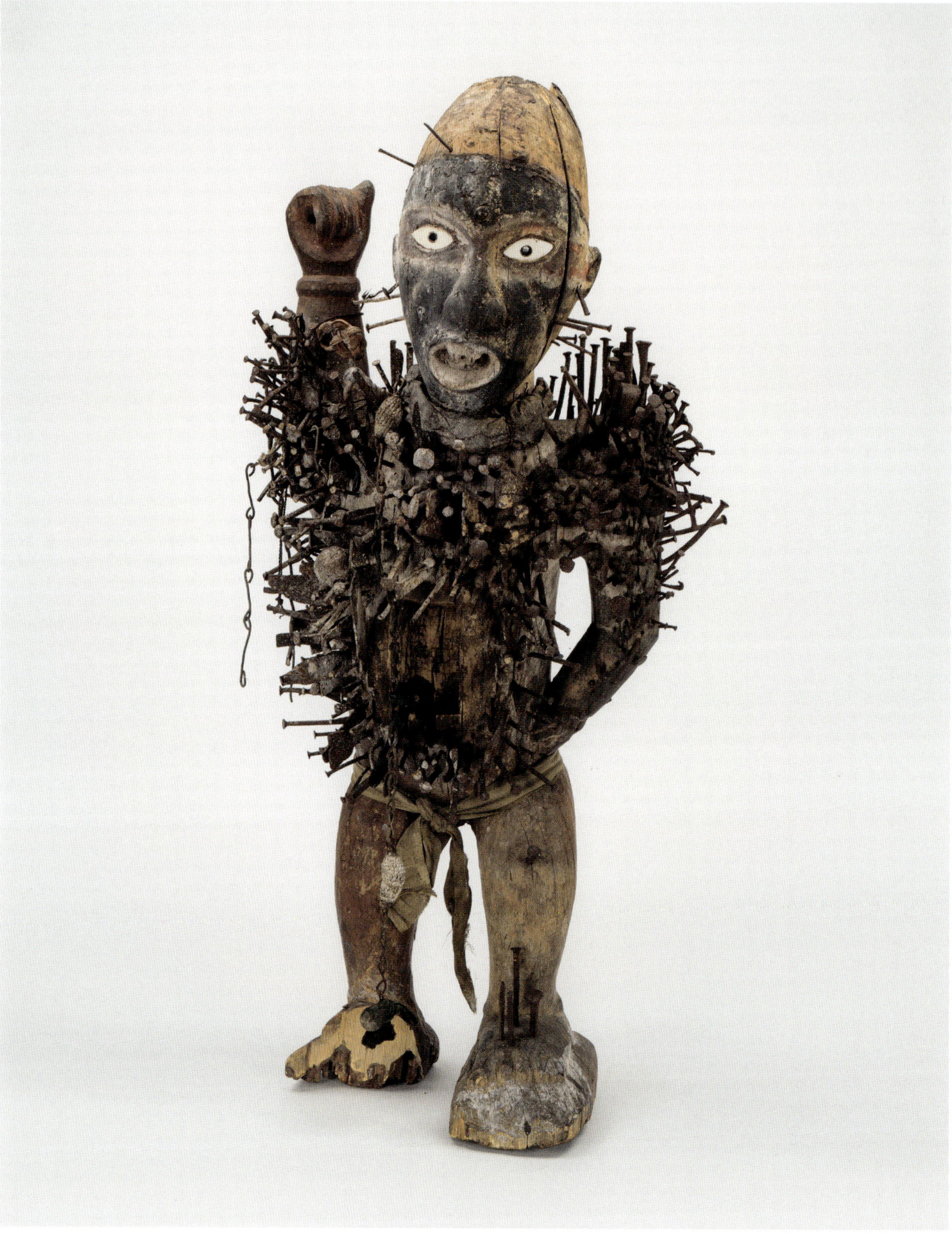

As she forged her bond with the legacy of the African diaspora, she discovered that her art could be a means to reconfigure traditional models for the contemporary world.

Stout's initial artistic engagement with the *Nkisi Nkondi* was her 1987 figure *Fetish #1*. Roughly 30 cm (12 in) high, the figure was hooded, anonymous and unspecific as to gender.[2] But *Fetish #2* could not be more specifically referential in scale and appearance. Unlike a traditional *Nkisi Nkondi*, the stance of the figure is resolutely still: feet evenly planted, shoulders squared, chin lifted. The facial expression is calm; the strength of the figure is in its composure. Although nude, the figure is adorned with a mesh collar strung with pouches, belts and necklaces carrying medallions, and a tall, monkey-fur headdress with cascading braids. These ornaments convey a sense of protection while leaving the vulnerability of nudity in clear view. A glass box is embedded in the figure's abdomen. It contains a photograph, a dried plant sprig and a postage stamp. Stout has never assigned meanings to these objects, but she purposefully used the glass to facilitate interconnectedness between the artist and the viewer. There are no nails, no oaths to declare, no need to anger or arouse *Fetish #2* for, as Stout has stated, it is activated 'every time a viewer responds to it and connects with me'.[3] More than reviving a traditional form, Stout has reclaimed it and transformed it by housing it in her body and inhabiting it with her spirit. ●

◀

Unknown
Kongo *Nkisi Nkondi* (power figure)
c. 1875, mixed media

As a ten-year-old art student at the Carnegie Museum of Art, Stout first noticed this figure when a classmate cried out, 'Look at the voodoo doll.' Their instructor offered no further explanation; it was only later that she learned of the figure's function. This particular figure strikes the characteristic dynamic stance – fist raised, striding forward – and clearly possessed great power as seen in the number of nails hammered into its body. *Nkisi Nkondi* figures were typically male, but took female and animal forms as well.

▼

Renée Stout
Detail, Medicine Box, *Fetish #2*

The container for the *bilongo* in *Fetish #2* is far more exposed than in a traditional *Nkisi Nkondi*. Stout wanted the spiritual material to be easily accessible. That is why she fronted the container with glass. But the objects within – a sprig of dry flowers, a postage stamp from Niger, a vintage photograph of a child – evoke rather than represent ideas. Stout claims she never assigned meanings to them, respecting – and trusting – the potential for power in the unknown when dealing with the spirit.

▶

Renée Stout
Wall, with List
2014, acrylic on paper, collage, 53 x 46 cm (21 x 18 in)

Stout traces her interest in folk practices to her grandmothers' little rituals, such as burning hair clippings to avoid headaches and reading warnings into the position of dropped cutlery. Over the years she became fascinated with recipes for natural healing and sought a parallel in her own work. Here, a list of medicinal substances appears as if chalked on the rough surface of an old herb shop. Some are very familiar – aloe vera, charcoal – but the lack of explanation implies secret knowledge of their potential power.

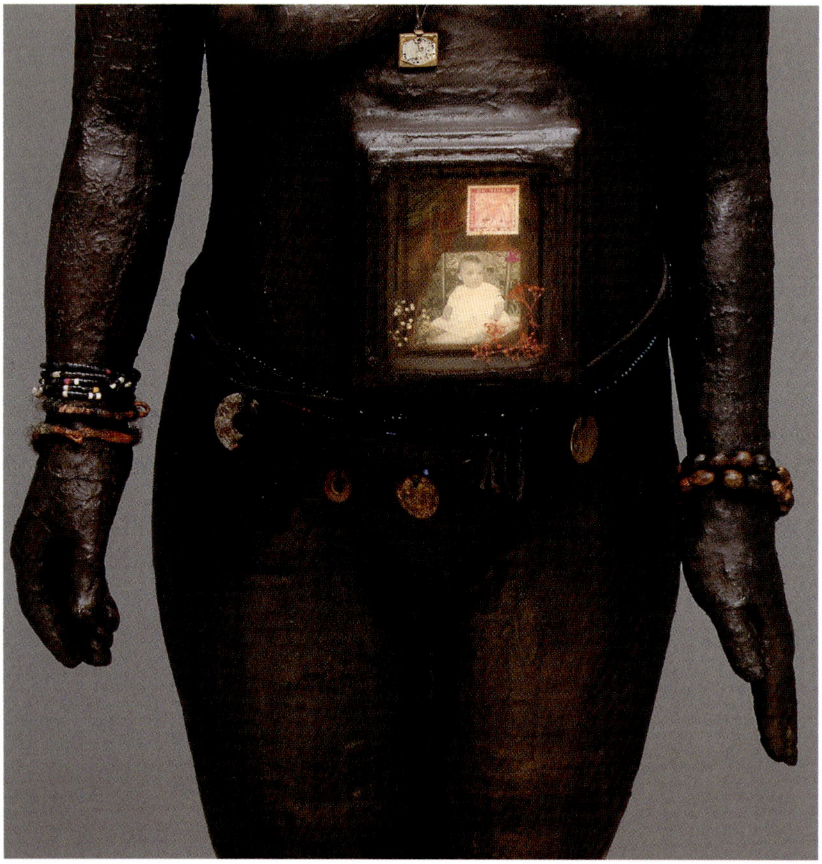

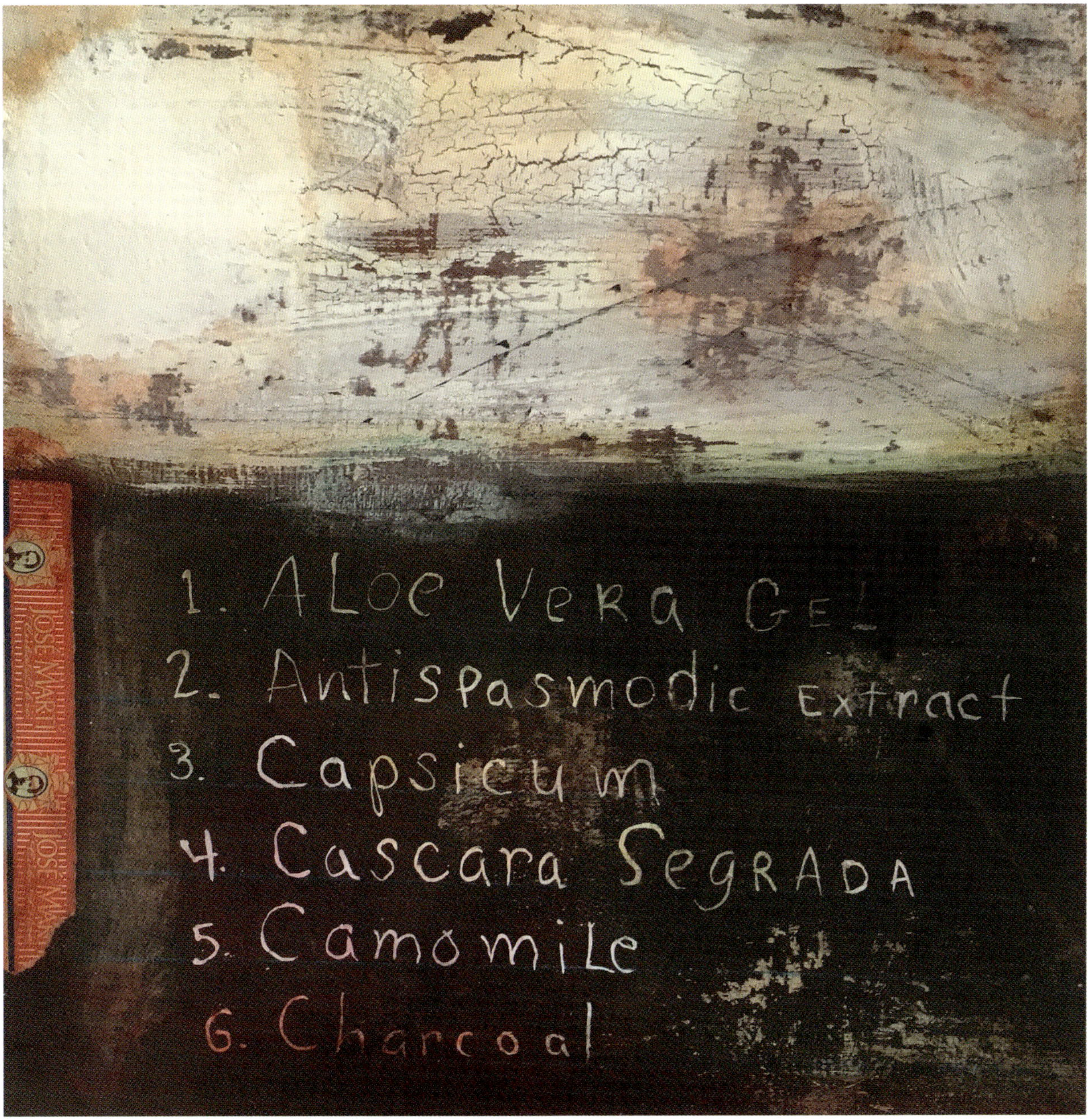
1. ALoe VeRa GeL
2. Antispasmodic Extract
3. Capsicum
4. Cascara SegRADA
5. CamomiLe
6. Charcoal

RIGHTEOUS RIDER

How Wiley modernized the equestrian monument

Few subjects in the history of art proclaim power as boldly as a bronze-cast, masterful rider. This enduring form in western culture – almost always male – derives from the ancient Roman equestrian portrait (*equus* meaning 'horse' in Latin), in which free-standing, over-life-sized statues were installed in public spaces on towering plinths to commemorate emperors, statesmen and military heroes. In 2019, drawing on this two-millennia tradition, a new equestrian portrait was installed in front of the entrance to the Virginia Museum of Fine Arts in Richmond. The proud rider displays all the features of the venerable type: strength, agility and full command over his rearing mount. The figure is anonymous, but not without identity. Dressed in contemporary streetwear and crowned with a topknot of dreadlocks, he is readily recognizable as a young, American Black man. Kehinde Wiley has dedicated his practice to bridging the disconnect he felt as a child searching for representation of his own image in the canon of art. In *Rumors of War* he takes on one of the most notorious versions of the equestrian portrait – the Confederate Monument – to force what he has described as a 'very American conversation'.[1]

Within a year of the surrender of the Confederate Army and the dissolution of the Confederacy that ended the American Civil War in 1865, a revisionist rationale gained currency in the southern states. The myth of 'The Lost Cause of the Confederacy' maintained that the South entered the conflict to protect States' Rights as put forth in 1791 in the 10th Amendment to the Constitution. Dismissing – even denying – that the preservation of slavery was the motivating issue, the Lost Cause purported that the Confederacy rose up to defend the rule of law against the incursion of an authoritarian federal government. The myth positioned the South's secession from the Union as just, moral and honourable. Over the years, as the number of surviving veterans dwindled, private southern groups began to erect public monuments to burnish their memory, drawing upon traditional forms of commemoration, including the equestrian portrait. In the first decade of the twentieth century four grand-scale statues of Confederate heroes – President Jefferson Davis, General Stonewall Jackson, Commander Matthew Fontaine Maury and General J.E.B. Stuart – were installed on the newly developed Monument Avenue in Richmond, the

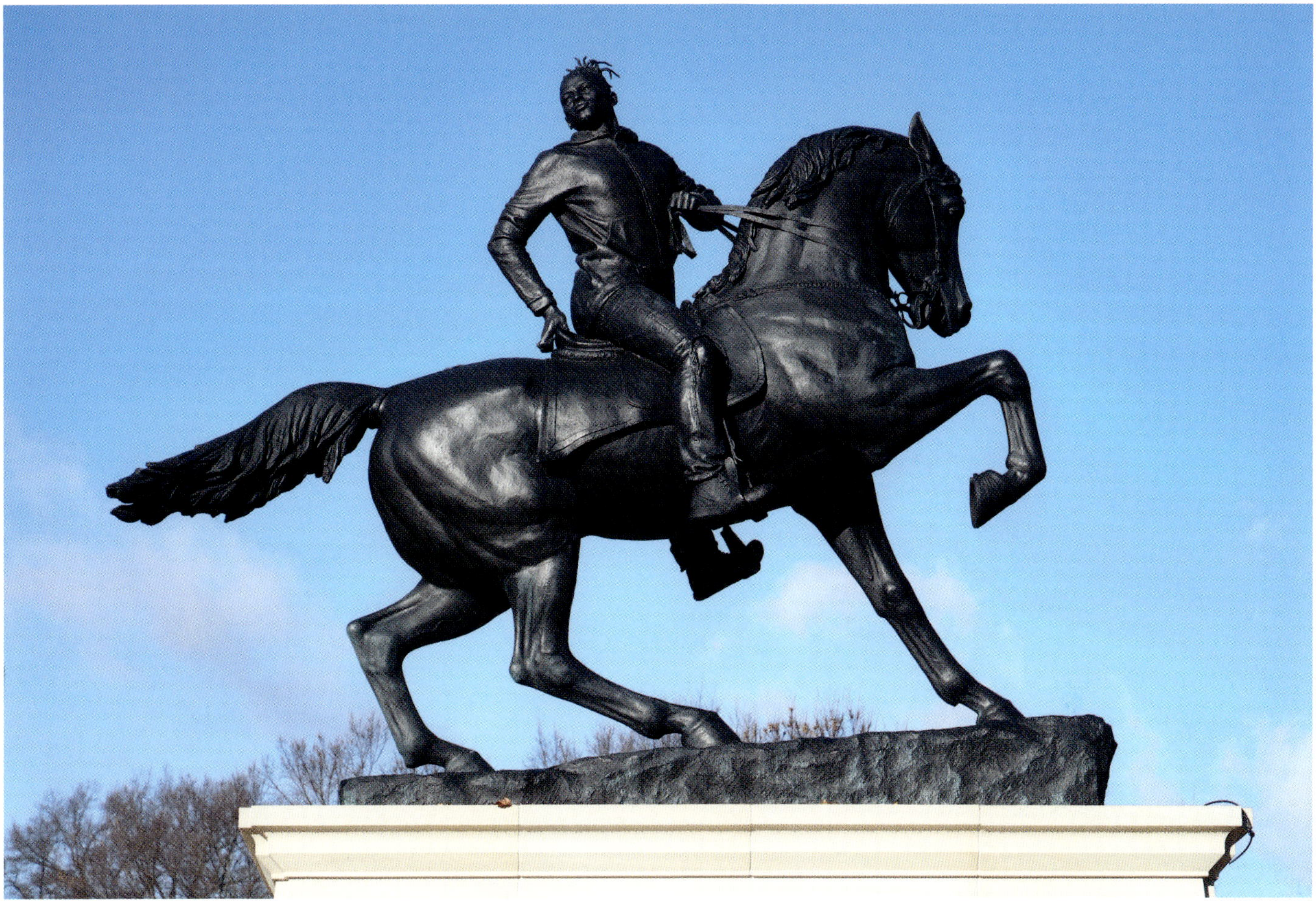

former Confederate capital. Wiley first saw these statues in 2016, when the Virginia Museum of Fine Arts hosted a retrospective of his work. Soon after, he shared an idea with museum patrons that launched a fundraising campaign to erect a new monument to respond to those that lined nearby Monument Avenue.

Wiley's rider mirrors the pose used in Frederick Moynihan's portrayal of J.E.B. Stuart. He defined his choice as deliberate, hoping to capture what he saw as an 'evocative and strangely beautiful' posture.[2] However, the figure does more than that. The lithe young man, dressed in his zipped hoodie, ripped jeans and high-top trainers, projects energetic potential. Here, the figure seems to say, is the future, in contrast to the old, disreputable past. Deliberate as well is the anonymity of the figure. Based on a composite of half a dozen faces, the 'portrait' seems familiar but not limited to a single individual. It stands for any young man you might pass on the street, someone who is part of your community, even if you never exchange more than a glance. After a brief debut in New York City's Times Square in September

▲

Kehinde Wiley (b. 1977)
Rumors of War
2019, bronze with limestone base,
836 x 777 x 480 cm (329 x 306 x 189 in)

2019, *Rumors of War* was installed in front of the museum in Richmond that December. Roughly six months later, the 'conversation' Wiley sought heated up when demonstrations erupted across the nation, supporting the Black Lives Matter movement following the murder of George Floyd. The Confederate monuments became a particular target: as a rally point, for graffiti and, ultimately, for removal. In the summer of 2020, the Monument Avenue statues were deinstalled and placed in storage.[3] While Wiley intended *Rumors of War* to counter, rather than replace, them, there is a righteous irony in that the type of American man the Lost Cause dismissed brought a new humanity and relevance to the iconic form. ●

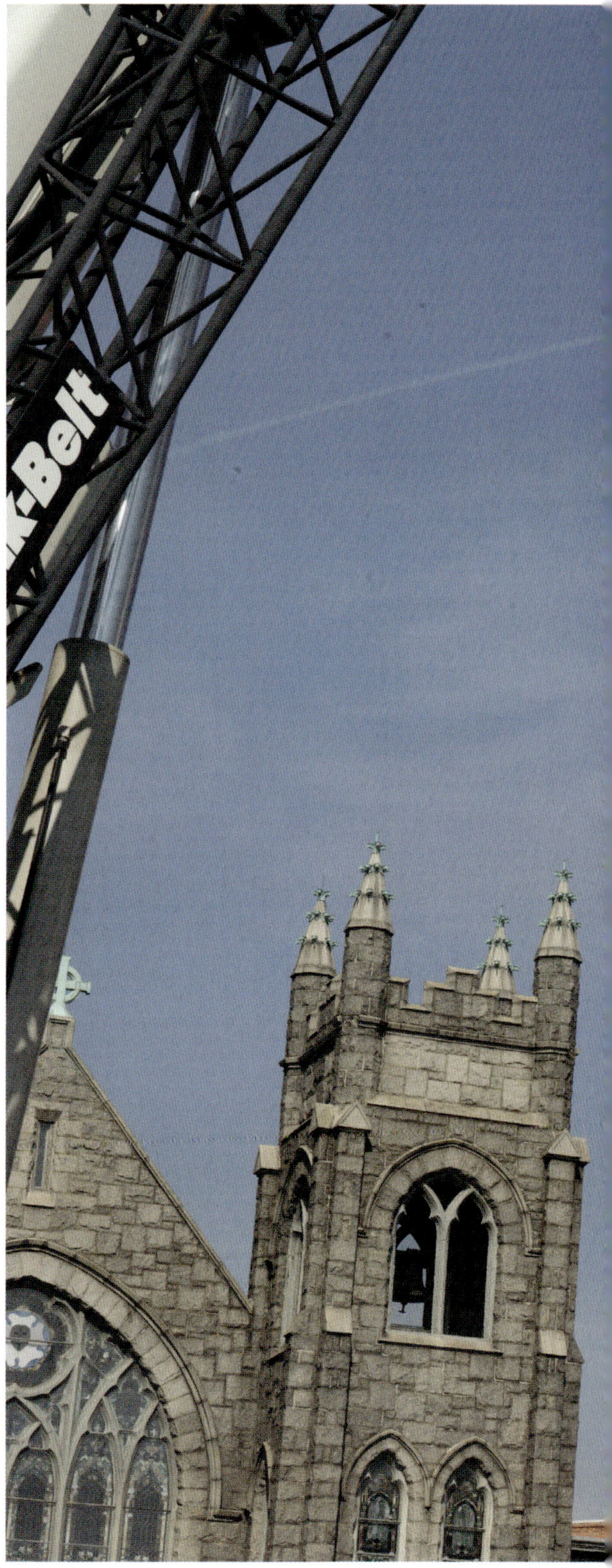

▶

Frederick Moynihan (1843–1910)
Equestrian Portrait of J.E.B. Stuart
1907, bronze, H 460 cm (181 in)

The pose that Wiley found so compelling in this monument derives from that used by Verrocchio for Colleoni's monument (see p.203), but Moynihan's version lacks the physical energy that distinguishes the other two. During the Black Lives Matter demonstrations of the summer of 2020, this work became a target; the sculpture was splashed with paint and its base was covered in graffiti. Although the reviled figure was soon removed, the base remained on Monument Avenue for two more years, a testament to the hurt and anger imposed by the myth of the Lost Cause.

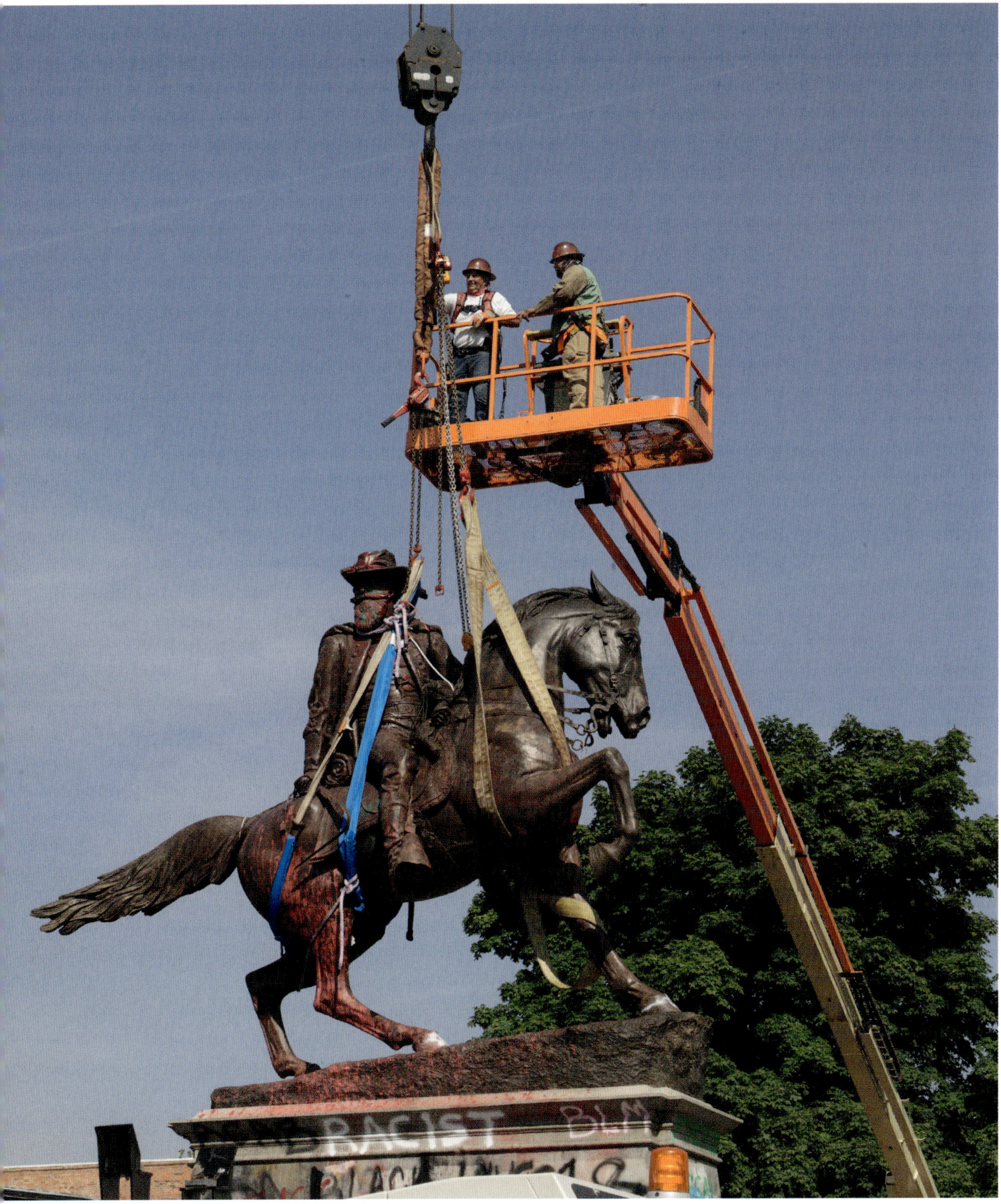
RACIST
BLM

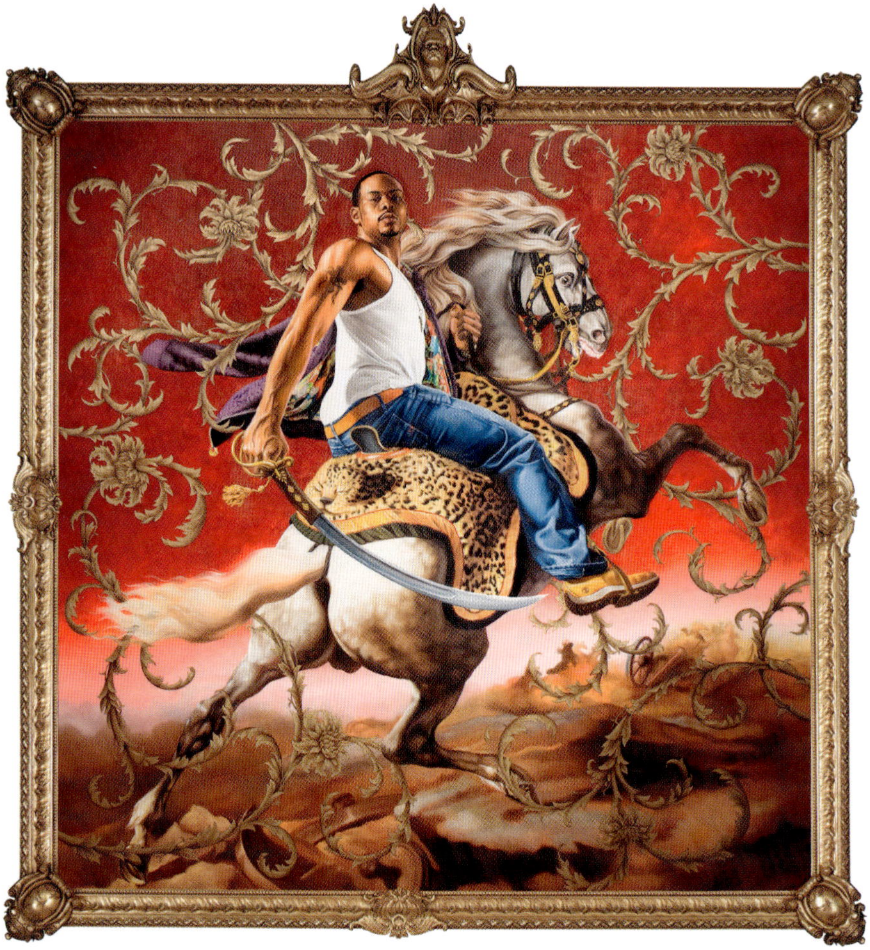

▲

Kehinde Wiley
Officer of the Hussars
2007, oil & enamel on canvas, 275 x 268 cm (108 x 106 in)

The title *Rumors of War* derives from the New Testament passage, Matthew 24:6, 'Ye shall hear of war and rumours of wars: see that ye not be troubled.' Wiley first used the title for a group of four canvases in which he replaced the rider in a famous European painting with a young Black man dressed in streetwear. Here, the painting reprises Théodore Géricault's depiction of a dashing but anonymous calvary officer on a spirited horse. The series not only offers an alternative history to the equestrian portrait tradition; it also engages traditional tropes of masculine power.

▶

Andrea del Verrocchio (*c.* 1435–88)
Equestrian Statue of Bartolomeo Colleoni
1480–88, bronze, H 395 cm (156 in)

Colleoni, a commander of a mercenary army, left a large financial legacy to the Republic of Venice to fund an equestrian portrait for public display. The Florentine master, Andrea del Verrocchio, secured the commission through a competition. He created a dynamic pair: as Colleoni rises out of the saddle to look to the side, his magnificent steed twists his head in the opposite direction. Wiley adapted this kinetic tension in *Rumors of War*, giving the figure strong vitality as well as a powerful presence.

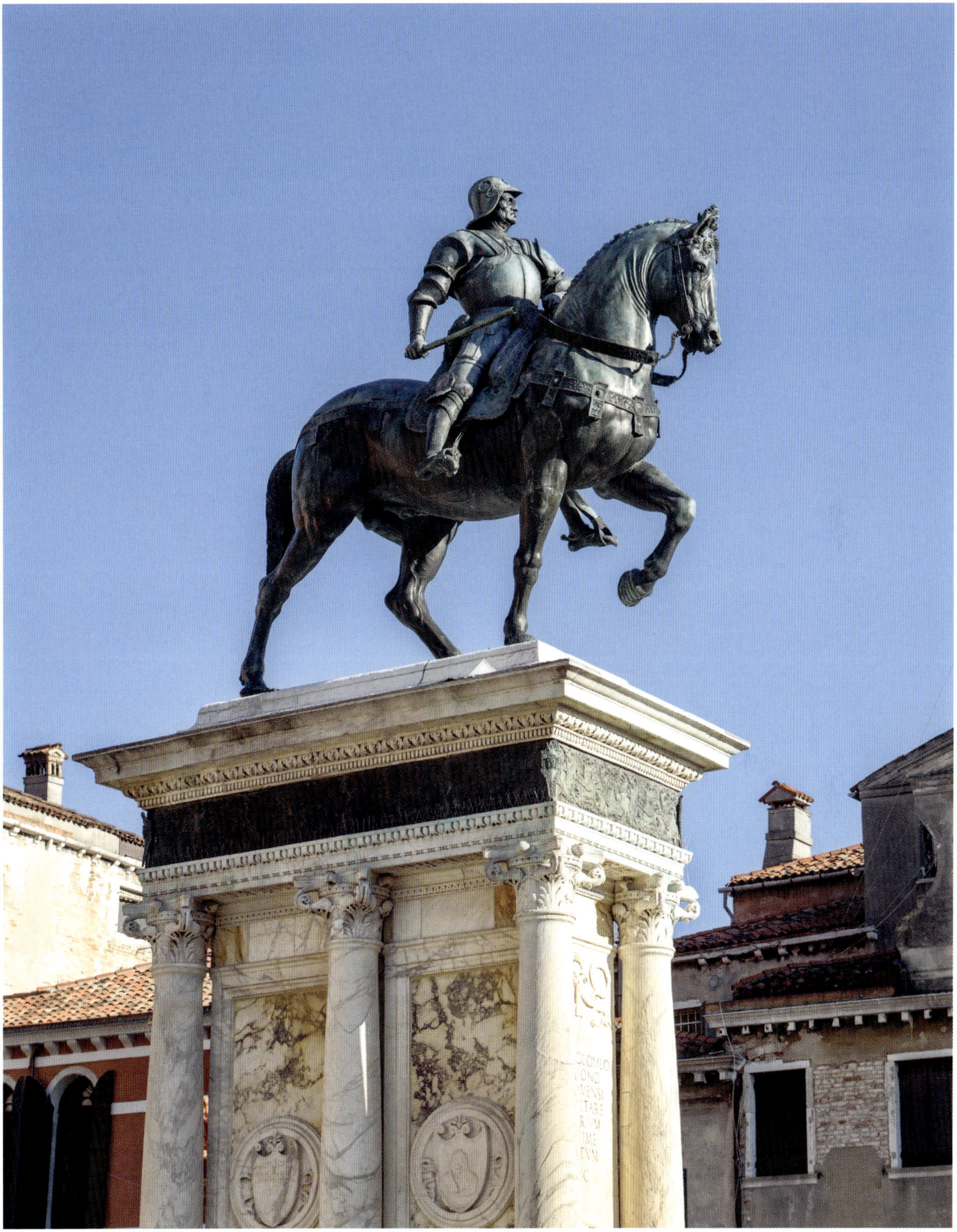

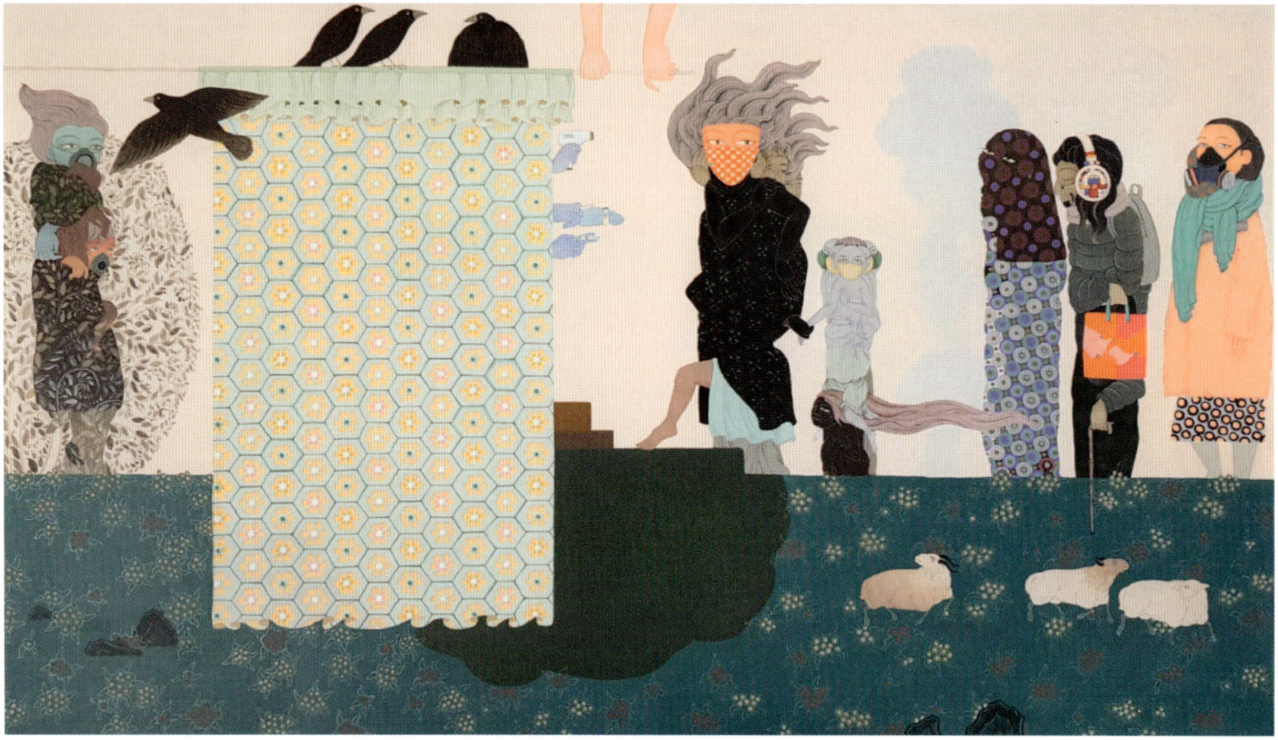

A PROCESSION FOR OUR TIME

How Dagvasambuu adapted the traditional procession motif

The clear colours, flattened forms and precise decorative patterns of Dagvasambuu's serene painting have deep roots in her homeland. The flower-spangled foreground and open-sky background evoke the lands travelled by her nomadic forebears. Some of the figures have multiple limbs, and there are disembodied hands holding objects, all of which recall the iconography of Buddhism. These elements bind Dagvasambuu's work to the traditions of her ancestry, but other details situate her subject firmly in the present. Some of the figures wear headsets; others wear

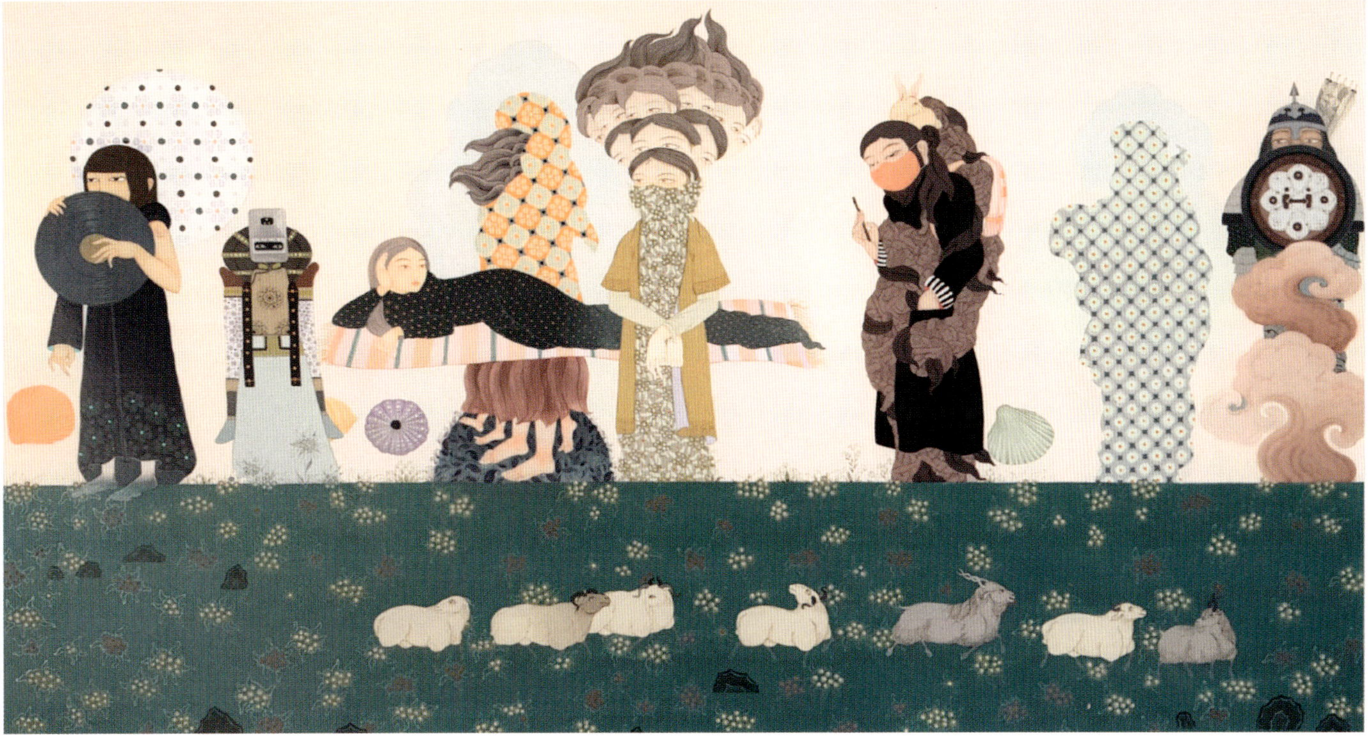

face masks. And those blue-gloved hands reaching out from behind the curtain hold thermometer guns and syringes. Dagvasambuu's distinctive approach connects her work with a style known as *Mongol Zurag*, a twentieth-century figurative approach that melds the visual conventions that emerged during the thirteenth-century Mongolian Golden Age with subjects as current and relevant as the vaccination campaign against the Covid-19 virus.

To organize her composition, Dagvasambuu turned to another traditional motif, one that has significance beyond generations, geographical borders and cultural differences. The queue of patient people takes the form of a procession; an orderly, purposeful file that moves forward to a shared, but individually important goal. From ancient times across the globe, depictions of processions commemorate acts of sacrifice, religious ceremony and other communal occasions. In European cultures, the motif gained an association with mortality after the Black Plague of the mid-fourteen century, the first recorded pandemic to decimate the continent. This was the *Danse Macabre* (or 'Dance of Death') in which animated skeletons lead figures from every social rank – mostly unwilling – to their ultimate demise. Dagvasambuu's own response to a devastating pandemic strikes a more optimistic note. Unlike earlier times, when there was no recourse from deadly disease besides prayer, isolation and resignation, her community had the benefit of a set of protective protocols and a life-saving vaccine.

▲

Uuriintuya Dagvasambuu (b. 1979)
Pandemic Diptych
2021, acrylic on canvas, 70 x 120 cm (28 x 47 in) each

In her own fresh interpretation of *Mongol Zurag*, Dagvasambuu endows venerable forms with twenty-first-century meaning through small but telling details. The gloves covering the hands ready to administer treatment recall the blue skin tone of the Hindu deity Shiva (see p.16), whose extra arms wield life-changing attributes. There are other motifs transferred from Buddhist iconography, including the vulnerable sheep and the transcendent crow. The woman in the centre of the right panel with many heads brings to mind the eleven-faced Avalokitesvara, a particularly compassionate form of bodhisattva who sacrifices their own entry into Nirvana for others. Mystical figures, such as the woman on the flying carpet, mix comfortably with modern mortals sporting shopping bags or looking at their mobile phones, and the clothing worn by those in the procession vary in ethnic origins and religious codes, as well as in contemporary and traditional fashion.

A Mongol guard in full armour stands steadfast on the outer edge of the right panel. His shield is marked with a graphic that represents the 2-m (6-ft) separation rule recommended in 2020 by the United States Center for Disease Control. However, these figures stand much closer, unifying them not only as a motif but as a community bound together by caution, tolerance and care. And all the mortal figures wear face coverings: cloth masks, KN95 masks, even the face veil of a modest headdress. By addressing the still-raw experience of the Covid-19 pandemic through the lens of imagery as old as remembered time, Dagvasambuu elevates communal memory. And, just as every great artist who 'steals', Dagvasambuu affirms her bond with the past by giving it meaning in the present, embracing a time-tested legacy in the arts which, through transformative creativity, she makes her own. ●

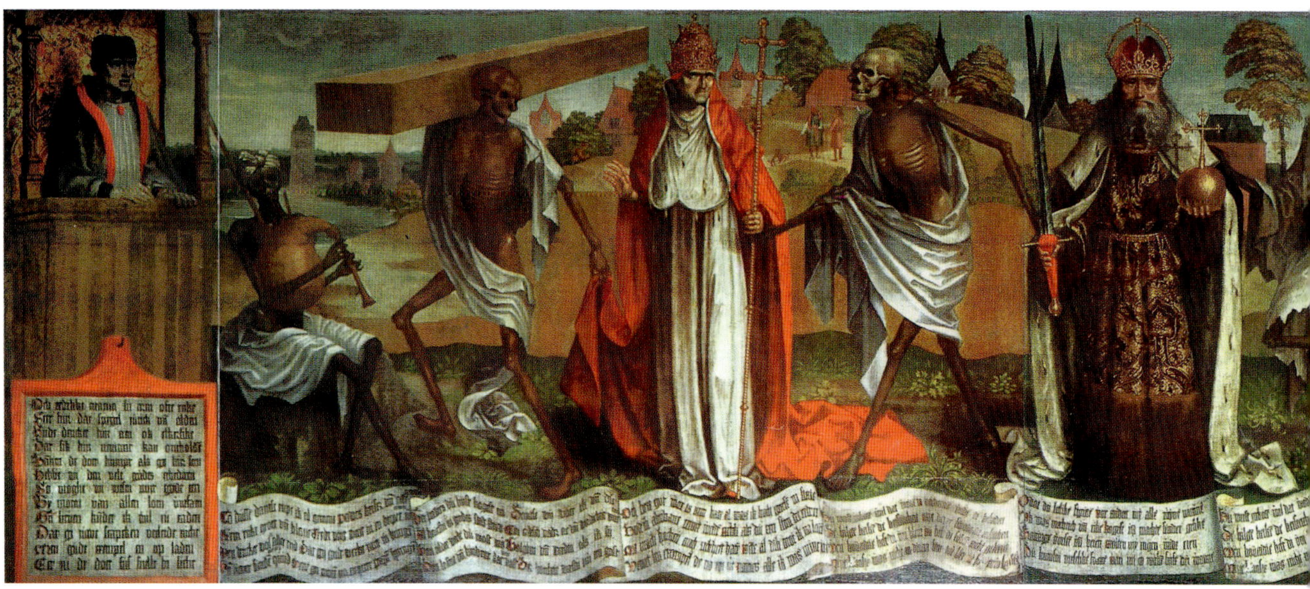

Bernt Notke (1440–1509)
Danse Macabre
1475–99, oil on canvas, 160 x 750 cm (63 x 295 in)

Pope and paupers, kings and merchants, wise men and fools – every human being – must submit to the grisly procession of the Dance of Death. With the warning *Memento Mori* ('Remember that you will die'), Death is portrayed as the great equalizer. No one can escape. In defiance of the traditional formality of processional imagery, here the skeletons shake off their shrouds and frolic as they lead their fearful companions to their inevitable fate. This iconographic scheme reached its zenith in the centuries following the Black Death (1347–51), a pandemic of bubonic plague that nearly halved the population of Europe.

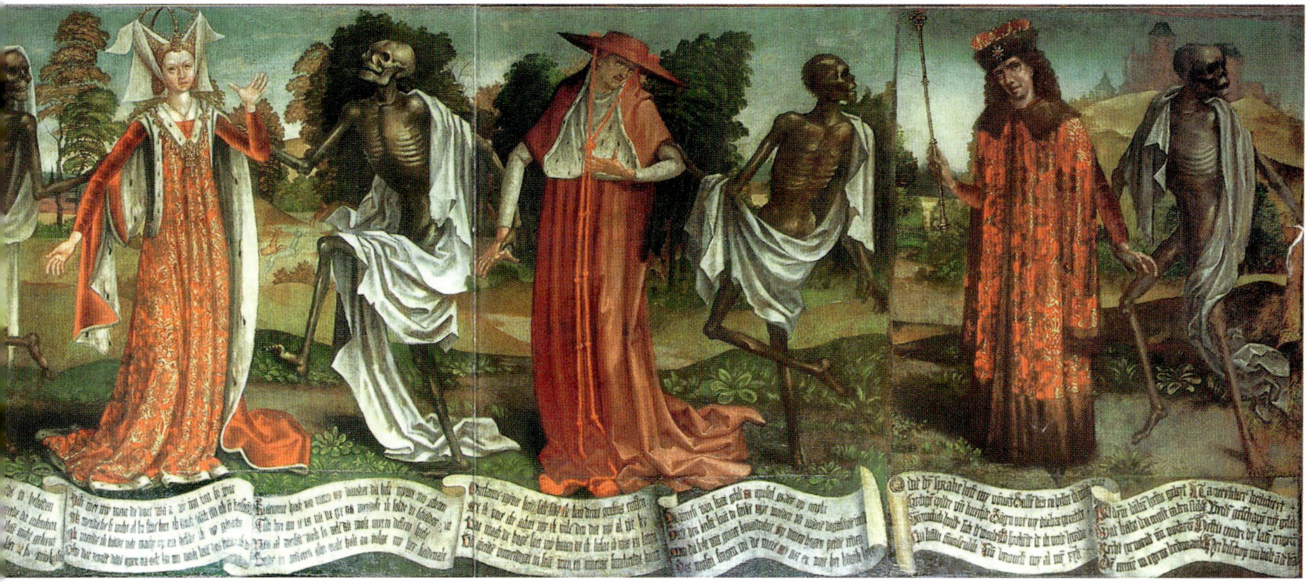

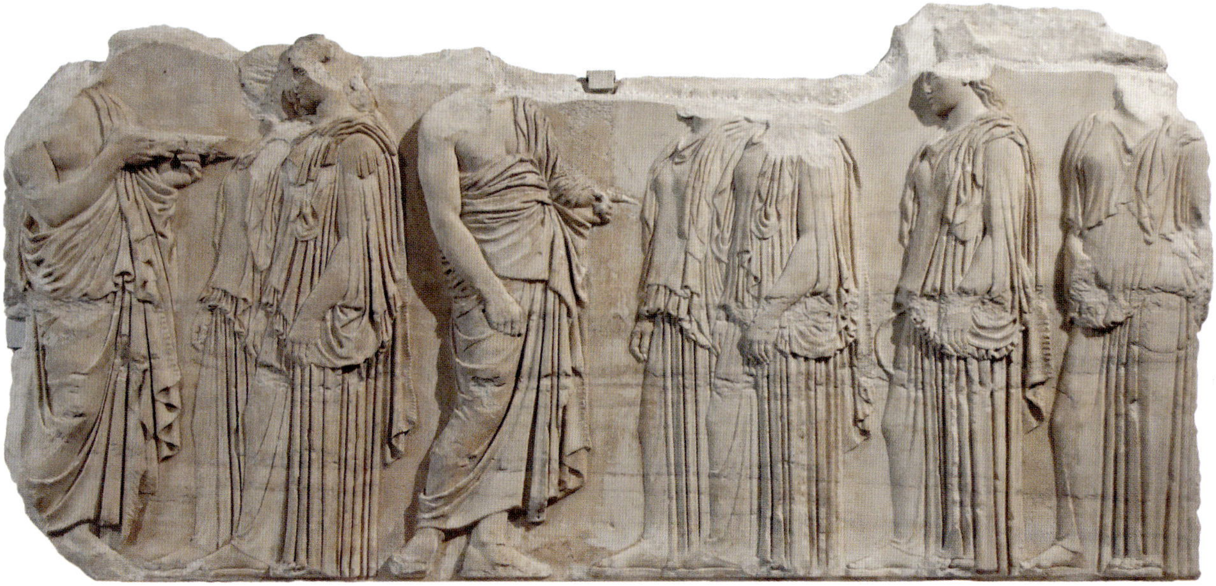

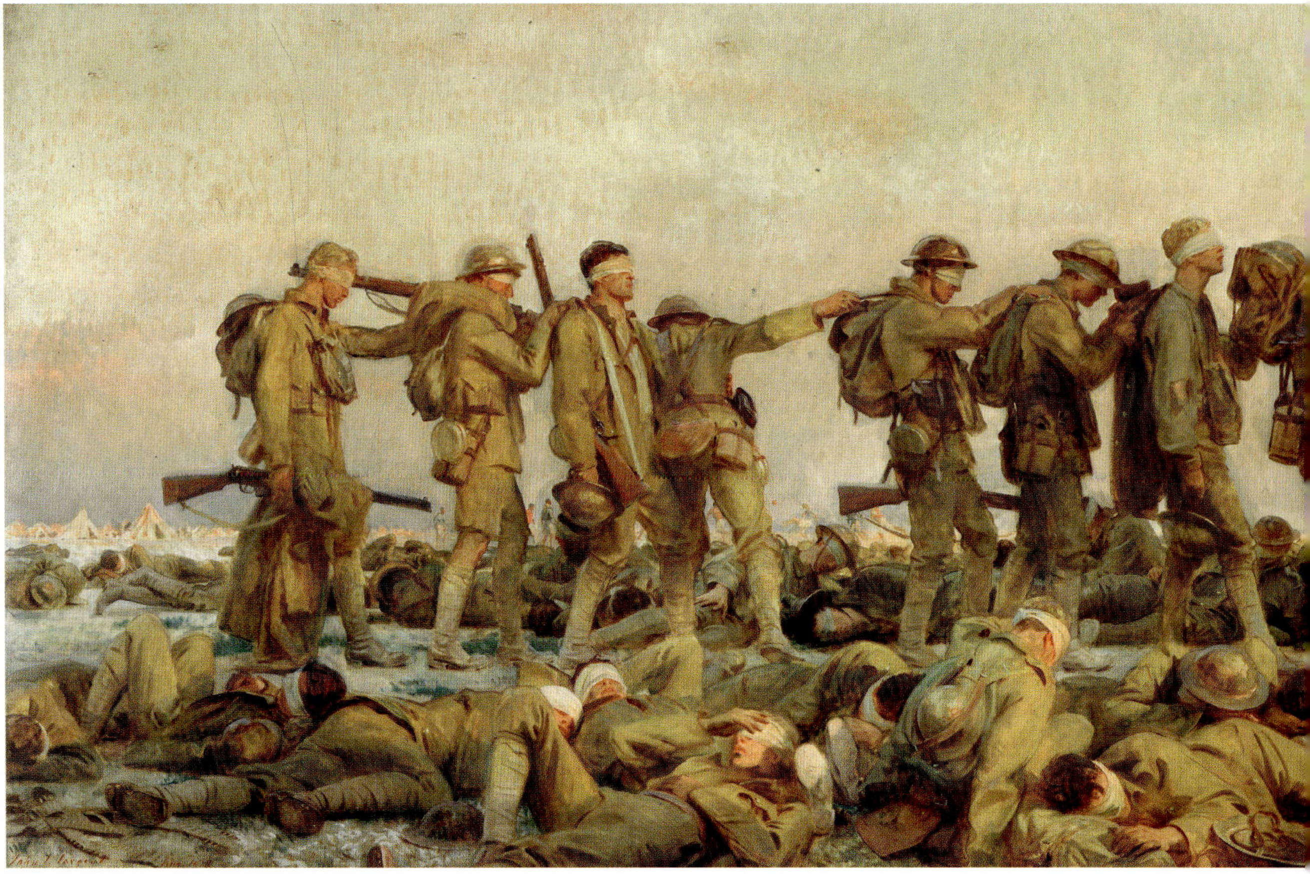

◀

Unknown, under supervision of Pheidias (d. 430 BC)
Ergastinai, east frieze of the Parthenon
c. 445–435 BC, marble, 96 x 207 cm (38 x 81 in)

Held every four years, the Panathenaic Festival honoured the goddess Athena for her protection of the ancient city-state, Athens. The central event was the presentation of a new garment to the colossal gold and ivory statue of Athena Parthenos housed in the Parthenon atop the Acropolis. The procession involved as many as one thousand people, including prominent citizens, guards, riders and young, unmarried women bearing baskets of barley and fruit. As seen in the depiction carved for the frieze of the temple, the Panathenaic procession united the community in a sedate, well-ordered tribute to their presiding patron.

▼

John Singer Sargent (1856–1925)
Gassed
1919, oil on canvas, 231 x 611 cm (91 x 241 in)

Sargent's grim presentation of blinded soldiers guided by a medical orderly was inspired by his visit to a battlefield dressing station. There he saw the victims of a mustard gas attack following one after another towards treatment. This mural, commissioned by the British government after the end of the Great War, takes the venerable motif of a procession and humanizes it by openly depicting sacrifice as an actual condition rather than a demonstration of respect. Like Dagvasambuu, Sargent instils an old motif with new relevance, but in his narrative moment it is too late for protective action.

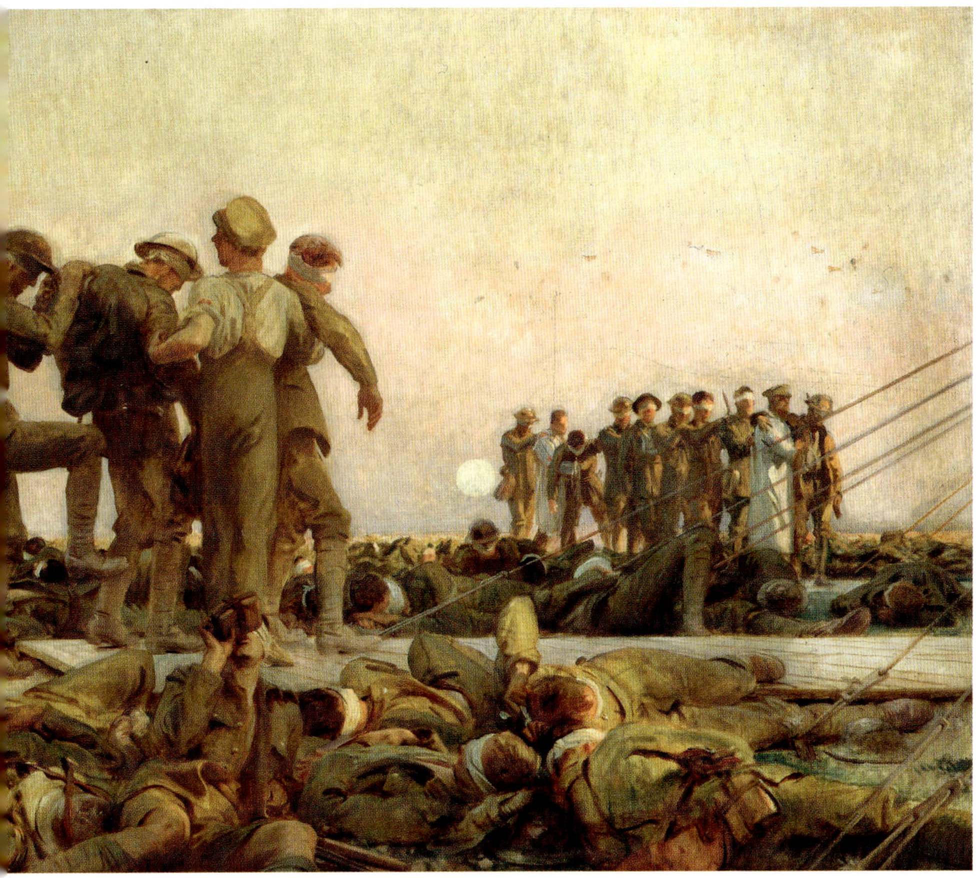

Endnotes

How artists really get their ideas

1 A.O. Scott, 'Critic's Notebook: "James," "Demon Copperhead" and the Triumph of Literary Fan Fiction,' *The New York Times*. www.nytimes.com/2024/04/22/books/review/james-percival-everett-demon-copperhead-barbara-kingsolver-dickens-twain.html (accessed 22 April 2024).

2 Rebecca Mead, 'Profiles: What Will Jonathan Anderson Transform Next?,' *The New Yorker*, 17 March 2025, p.4. www.newyorker.com/magazine/2025/03/24/jonathan-anderson-profile-fashion-designer-loewe-dior (accessed 27 November 2025). Anderson then noted that he had taken the phrase 'Steal, adapt, borrow' from filmmaker Jim Jarmusch.

3 Skye, Sherwin, 'The Last Supper Recast: Artist Tavares Strachan on Reimaging Da Vinci's dinner Guests,' The Guardian, 26 December 2023. www.theguardian.com/artanddesign/2023/dec/26/tavares-strachan (accessed 30 November 2025).

4 The figures are, left to right: Tavares Strachan, artist; Sister Rosetta Tharpe, gospel singer; Harriet Tubman, abolitionist; Shirley Chisholm, Congressional representative; Marcus Garvey, political activist; Zumbi dos Palmares, Brazilian resistance leader; Haile Selassie, Emperor of Ethiopia; Mary Seacole, nurse; Matthew Henson, polar explorer; Marsha P. Johnson, LGBTQ activist; King Tubby, dub music pioneer; Derek Walcott, poet and playwright; and Robert Henry Lawrence, Jr, astronaut.

5 Sherwin.

Shiva

1 www.britishmuseum.org/collection/object/A_2007-3005-26

Lippi

1 No more than a teenager when he took monastic vows in 1421, Lippi most likely met Bruni (roughly thirty years his junior), around 1456, when he was the chaplain of the convent of Santa Margherita in Prato. She is believed to have been a novice under his care. They had a son, Filippino, in 1457. Lippi was subsequently arrested and defrocked, but eventually received papal permission to marry.

Courbet

1 Gustave Courbet, as quoted in Petra ten-Doesschate Chu, *The Most Arrogant Man in France: Gustave Courbet and the Nineteenth-Century Media Culture*, Princeton University Press, Princeton, NJ and Oxford, 2007, pp.18; 36.

Whistler

1 Whistler's collection was sold in 1879, without a full inventory, to pay off his debts resulting from the libel suit against John Ruskin, so the exact contents are unknown.

2 'The Palace of Art (New Version)', *Punch* (7 July 1877), as quoted in Linda Merrill, *A Pot of Paint: Aesthetics on Trial In Whistler v. Ruskin*, Smithsonian Institution Press, Washington, DC and London, 1992, p.36.

3 John Ruskin, *Fors Clavigera*, 79 (July 1877), as quoted in Merrill, ibid., p.47. The trial was a public sensation, with the decision in Whistler's favour. However, he was awarded a single farthing and required to pay all court costs, which resulted in his bankruptcy.

Monir

1 Monir Shahroudy Farmanfarmaian and Zara Houshmand, *A Mirror Garden: A Memoir*, Alfred A. Knopf, New York, 2007, p.186.

2 *The Tehran Times*, 29 September 2021.

3 Hans Ulrich Obrist and Karen Mara (eds), *Monir Shahroudy Farmanfarmaian: Cosmic Geometry*, Damiani Editore, Bologna, 201, p.20.

Verrocchio

1 Born Andrea di Michele di Francesco de' Cioni, Verrocchio is believed to have taken his name, which means 'true eye', from the goldsmith who trained him.

2 Giorgio Vasari, *The Lives of the Most Excellent Painters, Sculptors, and Architects* (1550; trans. Gaston du C. de Vere), The Modern Library, New York, 2006, p.200.

3 Andrew Butterfield (ed.), *Verrocchio: Sculptor and Painter of Renaissance Florence*, Princeton University Press, Princeton, NJ, 2021, p.69.

4 Op.cit., Vasari, p.200.

Monet

1 Maurice Guillemot, 'Claude Monet', *Revue* Illustrée (15 March 1898), as quoted in, Marianne Mathieu and Dominique

Lobstein, *Monet's Impression Sunrise: the Biography of a Painting*, Musée Marmottan Monet, Paris, 2014, p.59.
2 Jules Castagnary, *Le Siècle*, (29 April 1874), as quoted in, Charles S. Moffett (ed.), *The New Painting: Impressionism 1874–1886*, Burton, San Francisco, 1986, p.61.

Van Gogh

1 Vincent van Gogh to Theo van Gogh, 7 September 1880, in *Vincent van Gogh – The Letters: The Complete Illustrated and Annotated Edition*, 2009, Letter 157. The letter written on 20 August 1880 is Letter 156. See www.vangoghletters.org.
2 Vincent van Gogh to Theo van Gogh, 21 November 1888, in *Vincent van Gogh – The Letters: The Complete Illustrated and Annotated Edition*, 2009, Letter 722. See www.vangoghletters.org.

Hoschedé-Monet

1 Ernest Hoschedé made his fortune in textile merchandising, but lost it when he expanded his interests to department stores. He arranged for his family to live with Monet, his wife and two children in the village of Vétheuil while he bolted to Belgium to avoid his creditors. Alice nursed Monet's wife when she became ill with cancer; she and her children stayed with him after her death. Hoschedé never resumed his role in the family, and Monet and Alice married in 1892, a year after Hoschedé's death.
2 Much of Blanche Hoschedé-Monet's biography is undocumented; it is not possible to place a precise date to her initial interest in the arts, which seems to have coincided with Monet's arrival in Montgeron. It is not known whether his presence sparked her talent or whether it heightened an already manifested interest. Her father was a keen collector of contemporary painting and purchased Monet's *Impression: Sunrise* (1872) after its notorious debut at the First Impressionist Exhibition, so clearly Blanche had exposure to the arts from childhood.

Raphael

1 In Raphael's time, the fresco was simply known as *Philosophy*, but by the eighteenth century the title *School of Athens* became popular and eventually replaced the original designation.
2 A drawing, attributed to Bramante, in the Uffizi Gallery's Gabinetto dei Disegni e Stampe is thought to depict his Greek cross plan. It renders only one half of the plan; scholars have assumed that the plan could be flipped to depict the whole, demonstrating symmetrical concept, but there is no documented evidence that this was the drawing Bramante intended to follow or whether it was simply an experimental example.
3 In his *Lives of the Artists,* Vasari asserts that it was Bramante who invited Raphael on the Pope's behalf. He further describes Bramante as Raphael's relative and compatriot. While Bramante hailed from the region of Urbino, this connection cannot be proven, although it is part of both artists' lore. Giorgio Vasari, *The Lives of the Most Excellent Painters, Sculptors, and Architects* (1550; trans. Gaston du C. de Vere), The Modern Library, New York, 2006, p.269.
4 The construction spanned more than a century, conceived in 1506 and consecrated in 1626. A total of twelve architects presided. It was common at the time for prominent artists in any medium to undertake architectural work, as seen in the case of Raphael (painter), Michelangelo (sculptor and painter) and Gian Lorenzo Bernini (sculptor), who all worked on St Peter's Basilica.

Caravaggio

1 Letizia Treves, *Beyond Caravaggio*, National Gallery Company Limited, London, 2016, p.16.
2 Bernd Elbert and Liesbeth M. Helmus (eds), *Utrecht, Caravaggio, and Europe*, Bayerische Staatsgemäldesammlungen, Munich, 2018, p.16.

Masanobu

1 Stephen Little, '"The Lure of the West" European Elements in the Art of the Floating World,' *Art Institute of Chicago Museum Studies*, 22:1 (1996), p.76. Little explains that *ran* derives from the abbreviated pronunciation of *Oranda* or 'Holland'.

Monet & Renoir

1 The larger version of *La Grenouillère* is known only through a photograph. It is believed that it was destroyed during the Second World War.

Cassatt

1 Mary Cassatt to Berthe Morisot, April 1890, as quoted in Nancy Mowll Mathews (ed.), *Cassatt and Her Circle: Selected Letters*, Abbeville Press, New York, 1984, p.214.

2 Camille Pissarro to Lucien Pissarro, 3 April 1891, as quoted in Adelyn Breeskin, *Mary Cassatt: A Catalogue Raisonné of Graphic Work*, Smithsonian Institution Press, Washington, DC, 1978, p.23.

Rauschenberg

1 It is worth noting that at this stage Rauschenberg did not use the term. He seemed to have coined it later in his career, most likely in the 1970s, to offer a simple designation for this phase in his work.

Michelangelo

1 Giorgio Vasari, *The Lives of the Most Excellent Painters, Sculptors, and Architects* (1550; trans. Gaston du C. de Vere), The Modern Library, New York, 2006, p.348.

Manet

1 The Salon des Refusés was a government-sponsored exhibition of the works rejected by the official 1863 Salon Jury. Although the artists lobbied for the opportunity to allow the public to judge their works on their own merits, the presentation became a notorious event, seen as a demonstration that confirmed the jury's decisions. At the same time the exhibition proved to be a foundational venue for advanced ideas, showcasing the works of such artists as Manet, James McNeill Whistler, Camille Pissarro, Paul Cézanne and Odilon Redon.

2 As quoted in Ross King, *The Judgment of Paris: The Revolutionary Decade that Gave the World Impressionism*, Walker Publishing Company, Inc., New York, 2006, p.88.

3 Louis Étienne, *Le Jury et Les Exposants* (1863), as quoted in George Heard Hamilton, *Manet and his Critics*, W.W. Norton and Company, Inc., New York, 1969, p.45.

4 As quoted in Paul Hayes Tucker (ed.), *Manet's Le Déjeuner sur l'Herbe*, Cambridge University Press, Cambridge, 1998, p.12.

Degas

1 Charles Baudelaire, 'The Painter of Modern Life' (1863), in *The Painter of Modern Life and Other Essays* (trans. Jonathan Mayne), Phaidon Press Limited, London, 1995, p.12.

2 Edgar Degas, as quoted in Elizabeth Holt (ed.), *From the Classicists to the Impressionists*, Yale University Press, New Haven, CT and London, 1986, p.401.

Steer

1 *Art Journal* (1887), p.248.

2 As quoted in Jane Munro, *Philip Wilson Steer, 1860–1947, Paintings and Watercolours*, London Arts Council of Great Britain, London, 1986, p.13.

Picasso

1 Peter Stepan, *Picasso's Collection of African and Oceanic Art*, Prestel, Munich, 2006, p.92. He referred to it simply as 'the painting' in the invitation.

2 Suzanne Preston Blier, *Picasso's Demoiselles: The Untold Origins of a Modern Masterpiece*, Duke University Press, Durham and London, 2019, p.270.

3 Ibid., p.21. The work debuted at the Salon d'Antin (also known as *L'Art moderne en France*) in October 1916. André Salmon, who organized the exhibition, supposedly gave the work its title, a reference to a red-light district in Barcelona.

4 Pablo Picasso, as quoted in Stepan, op. cit., pp.92–93. Picasso shared his account of the visit with Malraux in 1939.

Pollock

1 Henry Adams, *Thomas Hart Benton: Discoveries and Interpretations*, University of Missouri Press, Columbia, MO, 2015, p.179.

2 Jackson Pollock, 'A Questionnaire', *Arts and Architecture*, 61:2 (1944), as quoted in Anthony White (ed.), *Jackson Pollock's Blue Poles*, Thames & Hudson/ National Gallery of Australia, London, 2002, p.14.

3 Thomas Hart Benton, letter to Francis V. O'Connor (1973), as quoted in White, ibid. (2002), p.16.

Reynolds

1 Mai was known as Omai while in London and, until recently, the portrait was also given that name. Kate Fullagar anecdotally claims the misnomer resulted from an introduction in which Solander paired Mai's name with the Tahitian phrase 'it is', resulting in 'Omai'. See Kate Fullagar, *The Warrior, the Voyager, and the Artist: Three Lives in an Age of Empire*,

Yale University Press, New Haven, CT and London, 2020, p.189.
2 Frances Burney, as quoted in Martin Postle (ed.), *Joshua Reynolds: The Creation of Celebrity*, Tate Publishing, London, 2005, p.218.
3 Joshua Reynolds, 'Discourse III' (1770) in Sir Joshua Reynolds, *Discourses on Art* (ed. Robert R. Wark), Yale University Press, New Haven, CT and London 1981, p.43.
4 Winckelmann's discussion of the *Apollo Belvedere* is in his widely popular and rapidly translated *The History of Ancient Art* (1764). He defines the concept of 'noble simplicity and quiet grandeur' in the book that established his reputation, *Reflections on the Painting and Sculpture of the Greeks* (1755). See, Charles Harrison, Paul Wood and Jason Gaiger (eds), *Art in Theory 1648–1815: An Anthology of Changing Ideas*, Blackwell Publishing Ltd, Oxford, 2000, p.455 for this discussion.

Chase

1 William Merritt Chase to Dora Wheeler (1881), as quoted in Brandon Ruud and Corey Piper, *Americans in Spain: Painting and Travel, 1820–1920*, Milwaukee Art Museum, Milwaukee, WI, 2020, p.144.
2 William Merritt Chase (1903), as quoted in Erica E. Hirshler, 'Old Masters Meet New Women', in Elsa Smithgall, *William Merritt Chase: A Modern Master*, The Phillips Collection, Washington, DC; in association with Yale University Press, New Haven, CT and London, 2016, p.21.

Sleigh

1 Deborah Schwartz, 'An Interview with Sylvia Sleigh', *Arts and Sciences*, Northwestern University, Spring 1978, p.11.
2 Ibid., p.11.

Lichtenstein

1 Roy Lichtenstein to Jean-Claude Lebensztejn in 1975, as quoted in James Rondeau and Sheena Wagstaff, *Roy Lichtenstein: A Retrospective*, Art Institute of Chicago, Chicago and Tate Modern, London, 2012, p.7.
2 Dorothy Lichtenstein, as quoted in Rondeau and Wagstaff, p.36.

Sherman

1 Cindy Sherman, as quoted in Eva Respini, *Cindy Sherman*, Museum of Modern Art, New York, 2012, pp.21–22.
2 Ibid., p.18.

Shonibare

1 Deborah Sontag, 'Headless Bodies From a Bottomless Imagination', *The New York Times*, 17 June 2009, www.nytimes.com/2009/06/21/arts/design/21sont.html (accessed 14 April 2025).
2 Yinka Shonibare, as quoted in Robb Young, 'Africa's Fabric is Dutch', *The New York Times* (14 November 2012), www.nytimes.com/2012/11/15/fashion/15iht-ffabric15.html and as quoted in Samuel Reilly, 'The Wit and Wisdom of Yinka Shonibare', *Apollo Magazine* (2 May 2020), Stephen Friedman Gallery, www.stephenfriedman.com/usr/documents/press/download_url/279/sho_apollomagazine_may2020.pdf (accessed 15 April 2025).

Sargent

1 Marie-Louise Pailleron, as quoted in Erica E. Hirshler, *Fashioned by Sargent*, MFA Publications, Museum of Fine Arts, Boston, MA, 2023, p.32.
2 Coined *c.* 1917, the term 'Swagger portrait', is used to describe the performative, confident portraits of male sitters painted from the seventeenth to early twentieth centuries that convey wealth, power and social aspirations.

Duchamp

1 The literal translation is 'She has a hot ass.' In several late life interviews Duchamp used the more decorous phrase, 'She has a fire down below.'
2 Marcel Duchamp in 1963, as quoted in, Paul B. Franklin, *Marcel Duchamp and the Lure of the Copy*, Peggy Guggenheim Collection, Venice, 2023, pp.18-19.
3 Ibid., p.114.
4 Ibid., p.113.
5 Ibid., p.154.

Stout

1 Renée Stout to Lindsay J. Bosch, interview on 14 January 2008, as quoted in Debra N. Mancoff and Lindsay J. Bosch, *Icons of Beauty: Art, Culture, and the Image of Women*, 2 vols, Greenwood Press, Santa Barbara, CA, 2010, vol. 2, p.689.
2 The anthropological term 'fetish' was used as early as the sixteenth century to label objects that were non-European in origin from cultures regarded as 'primitive'. It was imposed upon objects without understanding of cultural function, belief practices or

significance. Stout explains that her title was based on 'misinformed museum labelling' and reflects that 'Most likely I would have titled the piece differently if I had the information I have now.' Stout to Bosch (2008), in Mancoff and Bosch, pp.697-98.

3 Stout to Bosch (2008), in Mancoff and Bosch, p.694.

Wiley

1 The comment is in reference to his practice in general. Kehinde Wiley, as quoted in Vinson Cunningham, 'Kehinde Wiley on Painting Masculinity and Blackness from President Obama to the People of Ferguson', *The New Yorker*, 22 October 2018.

2 As quoted in Ryan K. Smith, 'Rumors of War Arrives in the South, Changes to Richmond's Monumental Landscape', *Perspectives on History*, 18 May 2020.www.historians.org/perspectives-article/rumors-of-war-arrives-in-the-south-changes-to-richmonds-monumental-landscape-may-2020/

3 The graffiti-covered pedestal of the Stuart monument remained in place for two years after the statue was removed by the city in July 2020. In the spring of 2022, the Black History Museum and Cultural Center of Virginia took possession of both. At the time of writing, of the roughly seven hundred known Confederate Monuments, about two hundred have been removed. A countermovement, supported by the federal government, is working to restore and reinstall them.

Further Reading

TRADITIONS

Shiva

Wendy Doniger, *Hindu Myths: A Sourcebook Translated from the Sanskrit*, London/New York: Penguin, 2004.

Heinrich Zimmer, *Myths and Symbols in Indian Art and Civilization.* Princeton NJ: Princeton University Press, 1992.

Lippi

Carl Brandon Strehlke, *Fra Angelico and the Rise of the Florentine Renaissance*. London/New York: Thames & Hudson, 2019.

Barnaby Nygren, 'A Friend of the Bridegroom or a Lover of the bride? The Cuckolding Angel in Filip Lippi's Uffizi Madonna', *Notes in the History of Art,* 28:1, Fall 2008, pp.8–15.

Courbet

David Bomford, 'Rough Manners: Reflections on Courbet and Seventeenth-Century Painting', in Papers from the Symposium, *Looking at the Landscapes: Courbet and Modernism.* Los Angeles: Getty Publications, 2007.

Petra Ten-Doesschate Chu, *The Most Arrogant Man in France: Gustave Courbet and the Nineteenth-Century Media Culture*. Princeton and Oxford: Princeton University Press, 2007.

Dominique de Font-Réaulx, et. al., *Gustave Courbet*. New York: Metropolitan Museum of Art, 2008.

Whistler

Linda Merrill, *A Pot of Paint: Aesthetics on Trial In Whistler vrs. Ruskin*. Washington, D.C. and London: Smithsonian Institution Press, 1992.

Monir

Suzanne Cotter (ed.), *Monir Shahroudy Farmanfarmaian. Infinite Possibility: Mirror Works and Drawings*. Porto, Portugal; Serralves, 2014.

Monir Shahroudy Farmanfarmaian and Zara Houshmand, *A Mirror Garden: A Memoir*. New York: Alfred A. Knopf, 2007.

Ferren Gipson, *Women's Work: From feminine arts to feminist art*. London: Frances Lincoln, 2022.

Rose Issa, Ruyin Pakbaz, and Daryush Shayegan, *Iranian Contemporary Art*. London: Booth-Clibborn Editions, 2011.

Hans Ulrich Obrist and Karen Mara (eds.), *Monir Shahroudy Farman-farmaian: Cosmic Geometry*. Bologna: Damiani Editore, 2011.

LEARNING CURVE

Verrocchio

Andrew Butterfield (ed.), *Verrocchio: Sculptor and Painter of Renaissance Florence.* Princeton: Princeton University Press, 2021.

William E. Wallace, 'Verrocchio's "Giudizio dell'Occhio" ', *Notes in the History of Art*. 14:2, Winter 1995, pp.7–10.

Monet & Renoir

Marianne Mathieu and Dominique Lobstein, *Monet's Impression Sunrise: the Biography of a Painting*. Paris: Musée Marmottan Monet, 2014.

Charles S. Moffett (ed.), *The New Painting: Impressionism 1874–1886.* Geneva: Richard Burton SA, 1986.

Van Gogh

Douglas W. Druick and Peter Kort Zegers, *Van Gogh and Gauguin: The Studio of the South.* London: Thames & Hudson, 2001.

Vincent van Gogh – The Letters: The complete illustrated and annotated edition 2009. www.vangoghletters.org

Hoschedé-Monet

Janine Burke, 'Monet's "Angel": The Artistic Partnership of Claude Monet and Blanche Hoschedé-Monet', *Colloquy Text Theory Critique*. 22, 2011, pp.68–80, Monash University.

Charles Stuckey (ed.), *Monet: A Retrospective*. New York: Park Lane, 1986.

Paul Hayes Tucker, *Monet in the '90s: The Series Paintings*. New Haven and London: Yale University Press, 1989.

CREATIVE EXCHANGE

Caravaggio

Bernd Elbert and Liesbeth M. Helmus, (eds.), *Utrecht, Caravaggio, and Europe.* Munich: Bayerische Staatsgemäldesammlungen, 2018.

David Franklin and Sebastian Schütze, *Caravaggio and his Followers in Rome*. New Haven and London: Yale University Press, 2011.

Gert Jan van der Sman, *Caravaggio and the Painters of the North*. Madrid: Museo Thyssen-Bornemiszia, 2016.

Jacques Thullier, *Georges de la Tour.* Paris: Flammarion, 1993.

Letizia Treves, *Beyond Caravaggio*. London: National Gallery Company Limited, 2016.

Masanobu

Robert Vergez, *Early Ukiyo-e Master Okumura Masanobu*. Tokyo, New York, and San Francisco: Kodansha International, Ltd., 1983.

Stephen Little, 'The Lure of the West: European Elements in the Art of the Floating World', *Art Institute of Chicago Museum Studies*. 22:1, 1996, pp.74–93; 95–96.

Timon Screech, 'The Meaning of Western Perspective in Edo Popular Culture', *Archives of Asian Art*. 47, 1994, pp.58–69.

Monet

Richard Brettell, *A Day in the Country: Impressionism and the French Landscape*. New York: Harry N. Abrams, Inc., Publishers, 1985.

Robert L. Herbert, *Impressionism: Art, Leisure, and Parisian Society.* New Haven and London: Yale University Press, 1988.

Cassatt

Judith A. Barter (ed.), *Mary Cassatt: Modern Women*. New York: Harry N. Abrams, Inc. 1998.

Adelyn Breeskin, *Mary Cassatt: A Catalogue Raissoné of Graphic Work*. Washington. D.C., Smithsonian Institution Press, 1978.

Debra N. Mancoff, *Mary Cassatt: Reflections of Women's Lives*. London: Frances Lincoln, 1998.

Nancy Mowll Mathews (ed.), *Cassatt and Her Circle: Selected Letters.* New York: Abbeville Press, 1984.

Nancy Mowll Mathews and Barbara Stern Shapiro, *Mary Cassatt: The Color Prints*. New York: Harry N. Abrams, Inc., 1989.

Rauschenberg

Greg Allen, 'American Beauty: Jasper Johns, Robert Ruascheberg, and the Case of the Missing Flag', *ARTnews*, 10 May 2016.

Stephen Coppel, *The American Dream: Pop to the Present*. New York: Thames & Hudson, Inc.; London: Thames & Hudson, inc., 2017. www.artic.edu/artworks/209926/short-circuit

Laura Cumming, 'Robert Rauscheberg review-the combine master, uncut'. *The Guardian*, 4 December 2016. www.theguardian.com/artanddesign/2016/dec/04/robert-rauschenberg-review-the-combine-master-uncut-thrilling-retrospective

Robert Rauschenberg: Combines (Paul Schimmel, organizer). Los Angeles: Museum of Contemporary Art, 2005.

'Robert Rauschenberg *Combines* (1953–1964)', Paris, Centre Pompidou. mediation.centrepompidou.fr/education/ressources/ENS-Rauschenberg-EN/ENS-rauschenberg-EN.htm

INFLUENCE & INNOVATION

Michelangelo

Francis Haskell and Nicholas Penny, *Taste and the Antique: The Lure of Classical Sculpture 1500–1900*. New Haven and London: Yale University Press, 1981.

Manet

Charles Baudelaire, 'The Painter of Modern Life' (1863), *The Painter of Modern Life and Other Essays* (trans. Jonathan Mayne). London: Phaidon Press Limited, 2010.

George Heard Hamilton, *Manet and his Critics*. New York: W.W. Norton and Company, Inc., 1969.

Ross King, *The Judgment of Paris: The Revolutionary Decade that Gave the World Impressionism*. New York: Walker Publishing Company, Inc., 2006.

Paul Hayes Tucker (ed.), *Manet's Le Déjeuner sur l'Herbe*. Cambridge: Cambridge University Press, 1998.

Degas

Malcolm Daneil, *Edgar Degas, Photographer*. New York: The Metropolitan Museum of Art/ Harry N. Abrams, 1998.

Aaron Scharf, *Art and Photography*. New York: Penguin Books, 1986.

Barry Schwabsky, 'For and Against Method', *The Nation*, 31 July 2013. www.thenation.com/article/archive/and-against-method

Steer

Mark Evans, *Constable's Skies: Paintings and Sketches by John Constable*. London: Thames & Hudson/V&A, 2018.

Jane Munro, *Philip Wilson Steer, 1860–1947, Paintings and Watercolours*. London: London Arts Council of Great Britain, 1986.

Picasso

Suzanne Preston Blier, *Picasso's Demoiselles: The Untold Origins of a Modern Masterpiece*. Durham and London: Duke University Press, 2019.

Elizabeth Cowling, et. al. *Matisse Picasso*, London: Tate Publishing, 2002.

Ekow Eshun, *The Time is Always Now: Artists Reframe the Black Figure*. London: National Portrait Gallery, 2024.

Maria del Carmen Gonzáles and Susanna Harwood Rubin, *Looking at Matisse and Picasso*. New York: Museum of Modern Art, 2003.

Peter Stepan, *Picasso's Collection of African and Oceanic Art*. Munich: Prestel, 2006.

Pollock

Henry Adams, *Thomas Hart Benton: Discoveries and Interpretations*. Columbia: University of Missouri Press, 2015.

Henry Adams, *Tom and Jack: The Intertwined Lives of Thomas Hart Benton and Jackson Pollock*. New York: Bloomsbury, 2009.

Anthony White (ed.), *Jackson Pollock's Blue Poles*. London: Thames & Hudson/National Gallery of Australia, 2002.

MEANINGFUL CONNECTIONS

Reynolds

Kate Fullagar, *The Warrior, the Voyager, and the Artist: Three Lives in an Age of Empire*. New Haven and London: Yale University Press, 2020.

Martin Postle (ed.), *Joshua Reynolds: The Creation of Celebrity*. London: Tate Publishing, 2005.

Sir Joshua Reynolds, *Discourses on Art*, (ed. Robert R. Wark). New Haven and London: Yale University Press, 1981.

Goya

Michael Iarocci, *The Art of Witnessing: Francisco de Goya's 'Disasters of War.'* Toronto/Buffalo/ London: University of Toronto Press, 2023.

Hugh Thomas, *Goya: The Third of May, 1808*. New York: The Viking Press, inc., 1972.

Chase

Erica E. Hirshler, *William Merritt Chase, 1849-1916*. Boston: MFA Publications, Museum of Fine Arts, 2016.

Erica E. Hirshler, *Sargent's Daughters: the Biography of a Painting*. Boston: MFA Publications, 2009.

Brandon Ruud and Corey Piper, *Americans in Spain: Painting and Travel, 1820–1920*. Milwaukee: Milwaukee Art Museum, 2020.

Elsa Smithgall, *William Merritt Chase: A Modern Master*. Washington, D.C.: The Phillips Collection; in association with New Haven/ London: Yale University Press, 2016.

Sleigh

Russell Bowman and Dennis Adrian, *Sylvia Sleigh: Invitation to a Voyage and Other Works. Milwaukee: Milwaukee Art Museum*, 1990.

Deborah Schwartz, 'An Interview with Sylvia Sleigh', *Arts and Sciences*, Northwestern University, Spring 1978, pp.11–15.

Lichtenstein

Gunhild Bauer and Klaus Albrecht Schröder (eds.), *Roy Lichtenstein*. Vienna: Albertina; Munich: Prestel, 2024.

James Rondeau and Sheena Wagstaff, *Roy Lichtenstein: A Retrospective*. Chicago: Art Institute of Chicago; London Tate Modern, 2012.

Sherman

David Frankel (ed.), *Cindy Sherman: The Complete Untitled Film Stills*. New York: Museum of Modern Art, 2003.

Amanda Cruz, Elizabeth A.T. Smith, and Amelia Jones, *Cindy Sherman;*

Retrospective. New York: Thames & Hudson, 1997.

Eva Respini, *Cindy Sherman*. New York: Museum of Modern Art, 2012.

Shonibare

Anthony Downey and Yinka Shonibare, 'Yinka Shonibare', *Bomb* 93, Fall 2005, pp.24–31

Samuel Reilly, 'The Wit and Wisdom of Yinka Shonibare', *Apollo*, 2 May 2020. www.apollo-magazine.com/interview-yinka-shonibare/

Karen Rosenberg, 'Show and Tell: Yinka Shonibare', *New York*, 6 October 2005. nymag.com/nymetro/arts/art/14702/

Deborah Sontag, 'Headless Bodies from a Bottomless Imagination', *The New York Times*, 17 June 2009. www.nytimes.com/2009/06/21/arts/design/21sont.html

Robb Young, 'Africa's Fabric is Dutch', *New York Times*, 14 November 2012. www.nytimes.com/2012/11/15/fashion/15iht-ffabric15.html

TRANSFORMATION

Sargent

Erica E. Hirshler, *Fashioned by Sargent.* Boston: MFA Publications, Museum of Fine Arts, 2023.

Modigliani

Anette Kruszynski, *Amedeo Modigliani: Portraits and Nudes*. Munich/New York: Prestel Verlag, 1996.

Christiane Lange, Ortrud Westheimer (eds.), *Modigliani: Modern Gazes*. Munich: Prestel, 2023.

Duchamp

Paul B. Franklin, *Marcel Duchamp and the Lure of the Copy.* Venice: Peggy Guggenheim Collection, 2023.

Mary Settegast, *Mona Lisa's Moustache: Making Sense of a Dissolving World*. Grand Rapids, MI: Phanes Press, 2001.

Stout

Wyatt MacGaffrey and Michael D. Harris, *Astonishment and Power*. Washington, D.C./London: The Smithsonian Institution Press, 1994.

Debra N. Mancoff and Lindsay J. Bosch, *Icons of Beauty: Art, Culture, and the Image of Women,* 2 vols. Santa Barbara CA: Greenwood Press, 2010.

Michelle A. Owen-Workman and Stephen Bennett Phillips, *Readers, Advisors, and Storefront Churches*. Kansas City, MO: University of Missouri Kansas City Belger Center for Creative Studies, 2002.

Wiley

Atlanta History Center, 'Historical Introduction: Confederate Monuments', *Confederate Monument Interpretation Guide*. www.atlantahistorycenter.com/learning-and-research/projects-initiatives/confederate-monument-interpretation-guide/historical-introduction-confederate-monuments/

Vinson Cunningham, 'Kehinde Wiley on Painting Masculinity and Blackness from President Obama to the People of Ferguson', *The New Yorker*, 22 October 2018. www.newyorker.com/culture/culture-desk/kehinde-wiley-on-painting-president-obama-michael-jackson-and-the-people-of-ferguson

Thelma Golden, *Kehinde Wiley*. New York: Rizzoli, 2012.

Amy M. Mooney, 'Kehinde Wiley, *Officer of the Hussars, 2007*,' in 'Expressions of Political and Social Consciousness', Valerie J. Mercer, et. al., *Bulletin of the Detroit Institute of Arts* 86:¼, 2012, pp.54–55.

Eugenie Tsai (ed.), *Kehinde Wiley: A New Republic*. New York: Brooklyn Museum, 2015.

Reggi Ugwu, 'Kehinde Wiley's Times Square Monument: That's No Robert E. Lee', *The New York Times*, 28 September 2019.

Christina K. Vida, 'Monument Avenue: J.E.B Stuart Monument', The Valentine Museum, 24 June 2024. thevalentine.org

Dagvasambuu

Kealey Boyd, 'Picturing the Pandemic through the Lens of Buddhism', *Hyperallergic*, May 4 2022.
hyperallergic.com/729601/picturing-the-pandemic-through-the-lens-of-buddhism/

Annabel Keenan, 'Five New York shows explore the pandemic's effects two years after the city's first Covid-19 lockdowns', *The Art Newspaper*, 23 March 2022. www.theartnewspaper.com/2022/03/25/covid-19-pandemic-lockdown-second-anniversary-new-york-exhibitions

Botzonig Mort, 'Uuriintuya Dagvasambuu: Moods in the Metaverse', 2022. www.saparcontemporary.com/moods-in-the-meta

Index

Page numbers in *italics* refer to illustrations

Credits

Back cover:
Row 1 (l–r) Paris 16 (public domain); Papa Lima Whiskey 2 (public domain); **Row 2 (l–r)** Metropolitan Museum of Art, New York; Elsbeere (public domain); **Row 3 (l–r)** DcoetzeeBot (public domain); Livioandronico2013 (CC BY-SA 4.0); **Row 4 (both)** DcoetzeeBot (public domain).

7t Courtesy of the artist and Perrotin, collection of Glenstone Museum, Potomac, Maryland; and Marian Goodman Gallery. Photo credit: Jonty Wilde; **7b** Pixel8tor (CC BY-SA 4.0); **17** The Metropolitan Museum of Art, New York (public domain); **18** Arian Zwegers (CC BY 2.0); **19** © The Trustees of the British Museum; **20** Kate Kimber/Alamy; **22** Kate Kimber/Alamy; **23l** Godong/Alamy; **23r** DcoetzeeBot (public domain); **25** Fine Art Images/Heritage Images /Getty Images); **26** incamerastock/Alamy; **27** Album/Alamy; **28** Detroit Institute of Arts, Gift of Dexter M. Ferry, Jr., 46.309 (public domain); **31** The Metropolitan Museum of Art, New York (public domain); **32** Bridgeman Images; **33** Maltaper (public domain); **35** © Monir Shahroudy Farmanfarmaian. Photo courtesy High Museum of Art.; **36–37** Aliaksandr Mazurkevich/Alamy; **38** Jakob Fischer/Alamy; **39** © Monir Shahroudy Farmanfarmaian. Photo by Phoebe d'Heurle; **42 & 45** Livioandronico2013 (CC BY-SA 4.0); **44** Bridgeman Images; **47** Paris 16 (public domain); **48** The National Gallery, London/Universal Art Archive/Alamy; **49** Arts639 (public domain); **51** Photo12/Universal Images Group via Getty Images; **52** The Metropolitan Museum of Art, New York (public domain); **53** Album/Alamy; **54** Penta Springs Limited/Alamy; **55** DcoetzeeBot (public domain); **57** Artvee (public domain); **58–59** The Art Institute of Chicago (CC0 1.0); **60** National Gallery of Art, Washington (public domain); **61** Artepics/Alamy; **65 & 68–69** Wilfredor (CC0 1.0); **66** © The Trustees of the British Museum; **67** WideAngleEyes (public domain); **70** DcoetzeeBot (public domain); **73** SJArt/Alamy; **74** Ismoon (public domain); **75** National Gallery of Art, Washington (public domain); **77** © The Trustees of the British Museum; **78** The Walters Art Museum (CC0 1.0); **79t** The Metropolitan Museum of Art, New York (public domain); **79b** The Metropolitan Museum of Art, New York (public domain); **81** Penta Springs Limited/Alamy; **82–83** DcoetzeeBot (public domain); **84** National Gallery of Art, Washington (public domain); **85** Vidimages/Alamy; **86** Penta Springs Limited/Alamy; **89** © Boltin Picture Library/Bridgeman Images; **90** Album/Alamy; **91** The Art Institute of Chicago (CC0 1.0); **93 & 95** © 2026 Robert Rauschenberg Foundation/VAGA at ARS, NY and DACS, London. Photo: The Art Institute of Chicago/Art Resource, NY/Scala, Florence; **94** © 2026 Jasper Johns/VAGA at ARS, NY and DACS, London. Photo: Superstock/Bridgeman Images; **99** Giorgio Morara/Alamy; **100l** © Ashmolean Museum/Bridgeman Images; **100r** Heritage Image Partnership Ltd/Alamy;

101 Heritage Image Partnership Ltd/Alamy; **103** StellarHalo (public domain); **104–05** Bridgeman Images; **106** Penta Springs Limited/Alamy; **107** Heritage Image Partnership Ltd/Alamy; **109** PHAS/Universal Images Group via Getty Images; **110** VCG Wilson/Corbis via Getty Images); **111t** DcoetzeeBot (public domain); **111b** Sepia Times/Universal Images Group via Getty Images; **113** Tate Gallery, London ; **114–15** Album/Alamy; **116** Tate Gallery, London; **117** The Art Institute of Chicago (CC0 1.0); **118** © 2026 Succession Picasso/DACS, London. Photo: Peter Barritt/Alamy; **120–21** DcoetzeeBot (public domain); **122** © 2026 Jenny Saville. All rights reserved, DACS. Photo: c/o Sotheby›s; **123** © 2026 Claudette Johnson. All Rights Reserved, DACS/DACS Images. Photo: Tate Gallery, London; **124–25** © 2026 Pollock-Krasner Foundation ARS, NY and DACS, London. Image courtesy National Gallery of Australia, Canberra, Purchased 1973; **126** © 2026 T.H. and R.P. Benton Trusts/Licensed by Artists Rights Society (ARS), New York & DACS, London. Photo: © NPL - DeA Picture Library/Bridgeman Images; **127** © 2026 Pollock-Krasner Foundation ARS, NY and DACS, London. Photo: Museum of Fine Arts, Houston/Museum purchase funded by Mr. and Mrs. Frank J. Hevrdejs/Bridgeman Images; **129** © 2026 Pollock-Krasner Foundation ARS, NY and DACS, London. Photo: DeAgostini Picture Library/Scala, Florence; **132** The Artchives/Alamy; **135** VCG Wilson/Corbis via Getty Images; **136** VCG Wilson/Corbis via Getty Images; **137** RT Collection/Alamy; **139** Papa Lima Whiskey 2 (public domain); **140** The Metropolitan Museum of Art, New York (public domain); **142** Album/Alamy; **143** Crisco 1492 (public domain); **145 & 149** Artefact/Alamy; **146** Imagno/Getty Images; **147** Carlo Bollo/Alamy; **148** The Metropolitan Museum of Art, New York (public domain); **151** Photograph © 2026 courtesy of The David and Alfred Smart Museum of Art, The University of Chicago; **153** Dcoetzee (public domain); **154** classicpaintings/Alamy; **155** Fine Art Images/Heritage Images via Getty Images; **157** © 2026 Estate of Roy Lichtenstein/DACS. Digital image, The Museum of Modern Art, New York/Scala, Florence; **158** © Succession H. Matisse/Photo Scala, Florence; **159** © Succession H. Matisse/Digital image, The Museum of Modern Art, New York/Scala, Florence; **160** © Cindy Sherman. Courtesy the artist and Hauser & Wirth; **163** CSU Archives/Everett Collection/Alamy; **164** © 2026 Heirs of Josephine Hopper/Licensed by Artists Rights Society (ARS) NY/DACS, London. Photo: Artothek/Bridgeman Images; **165** © Cindy Sherman. Courtesy the artist and Hauser & Wirth; **167** © 2026 Yinka Shonibare CBE. All Rights Reserved, DACS. Photo: National Gallery of Victoria, Melbourne, Purchased with the assistance of NGV Contemporary, 2006. © Courtesy of the artist and James Cohan Gallery, New York and Stephen Friedman Gallery, London; **168** GL Archive/Alamy; **170** Philadelphia Museum of Art Library and Archives; **171** © 2026 Yinka Shonibare CBE. All Rights Reserved, DACS. Photo: Tabatha Fireman/Getty Images; **175** piemags/Alamy; **176** The Metropolitan Museum of Art, New York (public domain); **178** The Picture Art Collection/Alamy; **179** Painters/Alamy; **181** The Picture Art Collection/Alamy; **182–83** VCG Wilson/Corbis via Getty Images; **184** Darthipedist Obvious (public domain); **185** Paris 16 (public domain); **186** © 2026 Association Marcel Duchamp/ADAGP, Paris and DACS, London. Photo: Philadelphia Museum of Art/The Louise and Walter Arensberg Collection, 1950/Bridgeman Images; **189** Elsbeere (public domain); **190** © 2026 Association Marcel Duchamp/ADAGP, Paris and DACS, London. Photo: Christie›s Images/Scala, Florence; **191** Album/Alamy; **193 & 196** © Renée Stout. Photo: Metropolitan Life Foundation Purchase Grant/Bridgeman Images; **194** Carnegie Museum of Art, Pittsburgh, PA/Art Resource, NY; **197** © Renée Stout. Image courtesy Marc Straus Gallery; **199** Kehinde Wiley, *Rumors of War*, 2019. © Kehinde Wiley. Presented by Times Square Arts in partnership with the Virginia Museum of Fine Art and Sean Kelly, New York; **200–01** Andrew Lichtenstein/Corbis via Getty Images; **202** Kehinde Wiley, *Officer of the Hussars*, 2007. © Kehinde Wiley. Collection of the Detroit Institute of Arts, Michigan; **203** iStock/Getty Images Plus; **204–05** Image Courtesy of Sapar Contemporary and the Artist; **206–07** The Picture Art Collection/Alamy; **208t** Jastrow (public domain); **208b** ArteSì/Alamy.

Acknowledgements

Writing this book was an intriguing journey, one that I did not take alone. At Frances Lincoln my thanks go to John Parton for suggesting the topic and helping me shape the concept every step of the way, and to Philip Cooper for his ongoing support and encouragement. I am grateful to work so closely with my editor Laura Bulbeck whose interest, enthusiasm, insight and constant good humour smoothed the challenges and enhanced the delights. Also at Frances Lincoln, thanks go to Isabel Eeles, Rohana Yusof and Róisín Duffy. It has been a genuine pleasure to work with designer Nicki Davis, whose creative vision adds depth and visual excitement to the text. Special thanks as well to Susie Hodge. I am continually grateful to the Newberry Library for supporting my research with study space, guidance and the aid of its superb reference staff – most notably Keva Kruger, Reading Room Librarian for Public Services – who helped with sourcing books and answering queries. Thanks as well to Christian Levett and the helpful staff at the Femmes Artistes du Musée de Mougins. I thank my friends for their patience and interest throughout the project, including Paul B. Jaskot, Sarah Lea Burns, Gregory Nosan, Jeanne Steen and Patricia Wieber. To Brandon Ruud, a special thanks for his perspective on key issues, and to Michal Raz-Russo, who challenged me to think in different ways and dared me to move the project in some unexpected directions.

***Great Artists Steal* is dedicated to the memory of my friend Bob Wieber, who loved how books carry us to surprising destinations.**

Author Biography

Debra N. Mancoff is an art historian and the author of wide-ranging books on European and American art, culture and fashion. Based in Chicago, she earned her doctorate at Northwestern University and is a Scholar-in-Residence at the Newberry Library.